Materials

MITCHELL'S BUILDING CONSTRUCTION

The volumes of Mitchell's Building Construction have been completely re-written and re-illustrated by specialist authors to bring them into line with rapid technical developments in building and the consequent revision of syllabuses. All quantities are expressed in SI units and there are tables giving imperial conversions. Also included are the main CI/SfB classifications and on these are indicated the relevant volumes and chapters in Mitchell's Building Construction.

ENVIRONMENT AND SERVICES
Peter Burberry Dip. Arch. ARIBA

STRUCTURE AND FABRIC Part 1
Jack Stroud Foster FRIBA

Part 1 includes material which is introductory to both parts together with an initial consideration of various aspects of the building fabric which is extended and developed in Part 2: the two parts forming a single work on structure and fabric.

STRUCTURE AND FABRIC Part 2
Jack Stroud Foster FRIBA

COMPONENTS AND FINISHES
Harold King ARIBA
and Alan Everett ARIBA

MATERIALS
Alan Everett ARIBA

Materials deals with the properties of building materials, their manufacture in the factory and on the site. It considers the selection of materials to satisfy performance requirements; economy, deterioration and maintenance. It includes 89 tables, 50 drawings and a comprehensive index. General references to sources of more detailed information are made throughout.

The chapters are Properties generally; Timber; Boards and slabs; Stones; Ceramics; Bricks and blocks; Limes and cements; Concretes; Metals; Asbestos products; Bituminous products; Glass; Plastics and rubbers; Adhesives; Mortars for jointing; Mastics and gaskets.
(Plasters are dealt with in the *Components and Finishes* volume.)

This volume will be valuable to students preparing for the examinations of the RIBA, RICS, IQS and IOB. It provides an ideal text for the Ordinary and Higher National Certificates, and the City and Guilds of London Institute courses in building. It will also be a useful reference book for qualified architects, surveyors and engineers.

The author, Alan Everett, is Senior lecturer in Building Materials and Finishes in the BSc (Hons) course at the Polytechnic of North London School of Architecture.

MITCHELL'S BUILDING CONSTRUCTION

Materials

Alan Everett *ARIBA*

B. T. Batsford Limited

© *Text   Alan Everett 1970*
Reprinted 1972
© *Illustrations   Alan Everett and*
B. T. Batsford Limited 1970
ISBN O 7134 0516 3 (hard cover)
ISBN O 7134 0517 1 (paper back)

Made and printed in Great Britain by
William Clowes & Sons Limited
London, Beccles and Colchester
for the publishers B. T. Batsford Limited
4 Fitzhardinge Street, London W 1

Contents

CONTENTS

Acknowledgment

I am grateful to the Director General and Clerk of the Greater London Council for permission to quote from the London Building Acts 1930–39 and the Constructional Bylaws made under these Acts, and to the Controller of Her Majesty's Stationery Office for permission to quote from the Building Regulations 1972, and to the Directors of the following organizations for their kind permission for quotations to be made from their publications:

> The Building Research Establishment
> The British Standards Institution
> The Fire Research Station
> The Princes Risborough Laboratory
> The Research and Development Associations
>   of the construction industry.

I am also grateful to many firms for permission to quote from their publications.

Every effort has been made to acknowledge each quotation individually in the text, but I trust that any omission to do so will be forgiven.

Thanks are due to Sir Isaac Pitman and Sons Ltd for permission to print table 26 which is based on a table in *Properties of Concrete* by A. M. Neville MC, MSc (Eng), PhD, MICE, AMIStruct E; also to C. R. Books Ltd for permission to print figure 22 from *Concrete Practice* Vol. II by R. H. Elvery BSc (Eng), MICE, to Heinemann Ltd for the information in table 33 taken from *Stone in Building* by Hugh O'Neill, and to Butterworths Ltd for values derived from *The Metals Reference Book* by C. J. Smithells MC, DSc, FIM, an invaluable source of information.

I have endeavoured to condense information without distorting the meaning, but no matter how carefully done summaries, and quotations isolated from their context, can be misleading and the reader is referred to the original document in each case.

Sixteen chapters on diverse subjects can only be written with the help of many authorities and I have been extremely fortunate in this respect. I am particularly grateful to the undernamed experts for the time and patience they expended in reading and correcting my manuscripts, typescripts and/or proofs. The first named under each subject heading were my principal advisers who in the case of the longer chapters devoted a very considerable amount of time and energy to the task. I am very happy to have many new friends and hasten to state that they are not responsible for any errors which may have crept into the text.

Introduction and properties generally

D. E. Hull ARIBA and B. R. Currell PhD, BSc (Lond), FRIC of The Polytechnic of North London

Fire

R. W. Fisher MRSH of The Fire Protection Association and H. L. Malhotra BSc, CEng, MICE, MIFire E of the Fire Research Station

Costs

J. Nisbet FRICS

Acoustics

J. E. Moore FRIBA of The Polytechnic of North London

Timber

R. P. Wood BA For (Cantab) FIWSc, of the Timber Research and Development Association; R. L. Dawson, AIWSc; V. Serry (Metrication) of The Phoenix Timber Co Ltd and E. Joyce MSIA of Brighton College of Art

Boards and slabs

R. S. Vickerstaff and E. A. Raynham BSc, AInst P of The Fibre Building Board Development Organization Ltd (FIDOR)

Stones

R. J. H. Dix of The Stone Firms Ltd; B. L. Clarke BSc and D. B. Honeyborne BSc (Hons) of the BRS and K. W. Young FGS, MGLC of The Polytechnic of North London

Ceramics

I. L. Freeman BSc (Hons), FICeram of the BRS and J. Shore of Carters Tiles Ltd

Bricks and blocks

K. Thomas CEng, MIStruct E, ARTC and L. Bevis of the Brick Development Association (BDA) and Welwyn Hall Research Association

Limes and cements

R. A. Keen of The Cement and Concrete Association (CCA); D. E. Shirley BSc, AMIChem E, AM Inst F, AICeram of Lafarge Aluminous Cement Co Ltd and A. T. Corish BSc Eng, ACGI, MICE, AM Inst HE of The Cement Marketing Co Ltd

Concretes

B. W. Shacklock MSc, FICE, MIStruct E, MInst HE of The Cement and Concrete Association (CCA) and W. Kinniburgh FRIC (lightweight concretes) of the BRS

Metals – generally

G. M. E. Cooke BSc (Mech Eng) of the Corporate Laboratories of the British Steel Corporation (BISRA)

Corrosion of metals

K. A. Chandler BSc, ARSM, FICorr T of The Corporate Laboratories of the British Steel Corporation (BISRA)

Ferrous metals

G. M. E. Cooke BSc (Mech Eng) of The Corporate Laboratories of the British Steel Corporation (BISRA); D. T. Williams AMI Struct E, MSoc CE (France) of the British Steel Corporation; H. V. Hill MSc, AMICE, AMIStruct E of The Sheet Steel Industries Development Association (SSIDA); P. Shaw AIM of The Stainless Steel Development Association (SSDA)

Copper

E. Carr PhD, BSc of The Copper Development Association (CDA) and D. R. Harrington BSc of The Delta Metal Company Ltd

Lead and zinc

J. F. Quinn ARIBA of The Lead and Zinc Development Associations (LDA and ZDA)

Aluminium

F. C. Clarke BSc (Eng) of The Aluminium Federation

Asbestos products

P. W. Steggals of Cape Universal Building Products Ltd and D. I. Jones of Turners Asbestos Cement Co Ltd

Bituminous products

Shell International Petroleum Co Ltd

Flat glass

D. W. Armstrong BSc, ARCS, AINS of Pilkington Brothers Ltd

Decorative glass

A. R. Fisher MGP of Whitefriars Glass Works Ltd

Plastics and rubbers

W. F. Ratcliffe BSc (Eng), C Eng, API of Shell International Chemical Co Ltd; J. R. Crowder BSc, PhD of the BRS; P. Fordham AA Dip, ARIBA of Imperial Chemicals Industries Ltd; J. A. Brydson FPI and M. Kaufman PhD, FRIC of The Polytechnic of North London and E. A. Everest of the British Plastics Federation

Adhesives

E. Van der Straeten of CIBA (ARL) Ltd

Mortars

J. F. Ryder BSc of the BRS and P. Robinson of the Welwyn Hall Research Association

Mastics and gaskets

Bostik Ltd; R. G. Groeger BSc, ARPS of John Laing Research and Development Ltd; T. A. Baker of the BRS and T. A. V. Meikle AIMar E, of Expandite Ltd

ACKNOWLEDGMENT

My sincere thanks are due no less to any whom I have inadvertently omitted to mention, to whom I apologize, and to eleven experts in one organization who must remain anonymous. I am also indebted to many firms for providing information about their products.

My thanks are due also to R. E. Sowden BSc (Hons) for metrication, to G. W. Dilks for the drawings from my originals and to Ernest Joyce for figures 2, 3, 6, 7, 9, 10 and 11 concerned with timber and boards, to Margaret Bird for her skilled typewritten transcriptions from my hieroglyphics and to Mr and Mrs T. M. Doust for compiling the index.

I am extremely grateful to Thelma M. Nye for her patience, encouragement and expert editorial advice.

Infinite thanks are extended to my wife for uncomplainingly suffering the work to be done.

The author also thanks anyone who very kindly brings to his attention mistakes or who, in other ways, enables him to improve future editions of this volume.

London 1972   A.E.

SI Units

SI Units

Quantities in this volume are given in SI units which have been adopted by the construction industry in the United Kingdom. Twenty-five other countries (not including the USA or Canada) have also adopted the SI system although several of them retain the old metric system as an alternative. There are six SI basic units. Other units derived from these basic units are rationally related to them and to each other. The international adoption of the SI will remove the present necessity for conversions between national systems. The introduction of metric units gives an opportunity for the adoption of modular sizes.

Many quantities in this volume are rounded off conversions of imperial values. Where great accuracy is necessary, exact metric equivalents must be used. In the case of statutory requirements reference should be made to Building Regulations 1972 and to the equivalents contained in the Constructional Bylaws (London Building Acts 1930–39) published by the GLC.

British Standards, Codes of Practice and other documents are being progressively issued in metric units, although at the time of going to press many of those concerned with Building Construction have yet to be metricated.

Multiples and sub-multiples of SI units likely to be used in the construction industry are:

Multiplication factor	Prefix		Symbol
1 000 000	10^6	mega	M
1 000	10^3	kilo	k
100	10^2	hecto	h
10	10^1	deca	da
0·1	10^{-1}	deci	d
0·01	10^{-2}	centi	c
0·001	10^{-3}	milli	m
0·000 001	10^{-6}	micro	μ

Further information concerning metrication is contained in BS PD 6031 *A Guide for the use of the Metric System in the Construction Industry.*

Quantity	Unit	Symbol	Imperial unit × Conversion factor = SI value		
LENGTH	kilometre	km	1 mile	=	1·609 km
	metre	m	1 yard	=	0·914 m
			1 foot	=	0·305 m
	millimetre	mm	1 inch	=	25·4 mm
AREA	square kilometre	km²	1 mile²	=	2·590 km²
	hectare (1 ha = 10 000 m²)	ha	1 acre	=	0·405 ha
	square metre	m²	1 yard²	=	0·836 m²
			1 foot²	=	0·093 m²
	square millimetre	mm²	1 inch²	=	645·16 mm²
VOLUME	cubic metre	m³	1 yard³	=	0·765 m³
			1 foot³	=	0·028 m³
	cubic millimetre	mm³	1 inch³	=	1 638·7 mm³
CAPACITY	litre	1	1 UK gallon	=	4·546 litres

Quantity	Unit	Symbol	Imperial unit × Conversion factor = SI value		
MASS	kilogram gram	kg g	1 lb 1 oz 1 lb/ft (run) 1 lb/ft²	= = = =	0·454 kg 28·350 g 1·488 kg/m 4·882 kg/m²
DENSITY	kilogram per cubic metre	kg/m³	1 lb/ft³	=	16·019 kg/m³
FORCE	newton	N	1 lbf 1 tonf	= = =	4·448 N 9 964·02 N 9·964 kN
PRESSURE, STRESS	newton per square metre	N/m²	1 lbf/in²	=	6 894·8 N/m²
	meganewton per square metre or newton per square millimetre	MN/m² or N/mm²	1 tonf/ft² 1 tonf/in.² 1 lb/ft run 1 lb/ft² 1 ton/ft run	= = = = =	107·3 kN/m² 15·444 N/mm² 14·593 N/m 47·880 N/m² 32 682 kN/m
	*hectobar (10 N/mm²) *bar (0·1 N/mm²) *millibar (100 N/m²)	h bar bar m bar	1 tonf/in.²	=	1·544 h bar
VELOCITY	metre per second	m/s	1 mile/h	=	0·447 m/s
FREQUENCY	cycle per second	Hz	1 cycle/sec	=	1 Hz
ENERGY, HEAT	joule	J	1 Btu	=	1055·06 J
POWER, HEAT FLOW RATE	watt (1 watt = 1 J/s.) newtons metres per second joules per second	W Nm/s J/s	1 Btu/h 1 hp 1 ft/lbf	= = =	0·293 W 746 W 1·356 J
THERMAL CONDUCTIVITY (k)	watts per metre degree Celsius	W/m deg C	1 Btu in/ft²h	=	0·144 W/m deg C
THERMAL TRANS-MITTANCE (U)	watts per square metre degree Celsius	W/m² deg C	1 Btu/ft²h deg F	=	5·678 W/m² deg C
TEMPERATURE	degree Celsius (difference) degree Celsius (level)	deg C °C	1 deg F °F	= =	$\frac{5}{9}$ deg C $\frac{9}{5}$C + 32

* Alternative units, allied to the SI, which will be encountered in certain industries

A guide to the metric system

Introduction

The properties and costs of available materials must be related to performance and other criteria if safe, durable and economical building is to be achieved.

A knowledge of methods of preparing materials on the site and of methods of factory manufacture are required where they affect the properties and appearance of materials.

Costs

Cost decisions must take into consideration not only initial cost but running and maintenance costs, the serviceable life of each part, and where this is less than the profitable life expected of the building as a whole, the cost of replacement. Thus for example, the extra cost of superior thermal insulation may sometimes be recovered at the outset by reducing the capacity of a heating installation, and subsequently it will reduce running costs. *Cost-in-use* calculations must take into account the equivalent capital value of recurring expenditure over a period of years. For example where money is borrowed at 6 per cent interest an extra cost of £16·20 can be justified if there is a saving in maintenance costs of £1 per annum over a period of 60 years. However, in practice other factors may have to be taken into consideration such as: taxation, government and other grants as they affect capital and maintenance expenditure respectively, and inflation. The cost of disturbance during the progress of maintenance or premature replacement may be high and, clearly, if savings have to be made initially they should be obtained from finishes which can be replaced with little disturbance, rather than from basement tanking.

The 'life' of a building can be taken to be at an end when it becomes more profitable to demolish it and to erect a new building rather than to adapt it to meet changes in user requirements.

References include:

Building Economy: a synoptic approach, P. A. Stone, Pergamon Press.

Principles of modern building, Volume 1 Chapter 10, Building economics, HMSO.

In this volume *cost factors* give a guide to the relative costs of materials in 1969.

Standardization of sizes

The rationalization and standardization of product sizes reduces the multiplicity of stocks required to be held by suppliers and merchants, and reduces the labour in cutting to fit on the building site. See also *Mitchell's Building Construction: Components and Finishes* by Harold King and Alan Everett.

Research and development

The Building Research Establishment (BRE) incorporates the *Fire Research Station* (FRS) and the former Building Research Station (BRS) and *Forest Products Research Laboratory* (FPRL). Industrial organizations include: *The British Ceramic Research Association, The Brick Development Association* (BDA), *The Corporate Laboratories of the British Steel Corporation* (BISRA), *The Cement and Concrete Association* (CCA) and *The Timber Research and Development Association* (TRADA). Research and development is also undertaken by individual firms, e.g. Imperial Chemical Industries (ICI) and Pilkington Brothers Ltd, and by the Universities and Polytechnics.

Selection of products

Reputable manufacturers provide information as to the merits of their products and warn against their use in unsuitable contexts. Products should be used strictly in accordance with manufacturers' recommendations.

The *British Standards Institution* (BSI), 2 Park Street, London W1Y 4AA publishes *British Standard Specifications* (BS) and *Codes of Practice* (CP) many of which are referred to in these volumes. Broadly, British Standard Specifications deal with materials and components whereas Codes of Practice describe satisfactory methods of incorporating them in buildings. Thus, there are

Specifications (BS) for cements, aggregates and steel reinforcement, and there is a Code of Practice (CP) for reinforced concrete. They are often a means of establishing a reasonable minimum level of quality and performance and, in some cases, size and tolerances. Compliance with stipulated Specifications or Codes is in many cases 'deemed to satisfy' Building Regulations. It is necessary to be aware of the scope of a specification and where applicable to state the appropriate grade within a standard. However, British Standards do not always exist, particularly for recent developments. Formerly, long experience in use was necessary before the performance of products became known to Local Authorities and users, and before it became possible to formulate a British Standard but now the testing and certification of new products for specific uses is undertaken by The Agrément Board, Hemel Hempstead, Herts, an independent body which employs the resources of BRS and other organizations. The Agrément system encourages the development of new products and processes by examining prototypes and later by issuing certificates which are in three parts:

Part I gives an overall opinion as to suitability for the intended use and as to compliance with the standards required by the *Building Regulations* 1972 for England and Wales (except inner London) and the *Building Standards (Scotland) Regulations*.
Part II defines the product and states its purpose, including information to show how it is to be associated with other parts or materials. It also states how the product should be sorted and handled on the site and gives basic design data including maintenance requirements.
Part III summarizes the technical report.

Specification

A *conventional specification* describes materials and workmanship, a good aide mémoire being *Specification* Architectural Press Ltd, and the RIBA proposes to prepare standard specification clauses.
Performance specifications enable manufacturers to employ their specialised expertise and resources in the best way to satisfy stated functional and aesthetic requirements. However, the latter must be precisely defined, and suitable testing facilities are essential in order to compare the merits of different solutions. A reference is *Performance specification writing for building components*, HMSO.

Materials are considered in this volume under the following chapter headings:

1 Properties generally
2 Timber
3 Boards and slabs
4 Stones
5 Ceramics
6 Bricks and blocks
7 Limes and cements
8 Concretes
9 Metals
10 Asbestos products
11 Bituminous products
12 Glass
13 Plastics and rubbers
14 Adhesives
15 Mortars for jointing
16 Mastics and gaskets.

(Plasters are dealt with in *Mitchell's Building Construction: Components and Finishes*, chapter 13.)

Finishes

Finishes on stones and metals, and glass cladding are dealt with under the respective materials in this volume. Other finishes are considered under the following chapter headings in *MBC: Components and Finishes*:

12 Floorings
13 Plastering
14 Renderings
15 Wall tiling and mosaics
16 Integral finishes on concrete
17 Thin surface-finishes
18 Roof coverings.

1 Properties generally

Some properties, which relate to certain materials only, are considered in their respective chapters. Properties which relate to materials generally are:

(a) Density and specific gravity
(b) Strength
(c) Optical properties
(d) Electrical properties
(e) Colour, texture and ease of cleaning
(f) Thermal properties
(g) Acoustic properties
(h) Deformations

   1 Movements caused by applied loads
   2 Movements caused by changes in moisture content of materials
   3 Movements caused by changes in temperature
   4 Stresses due to thermal and moisture changes
   5 Common movement defects and their prevention.

(i) Deterioration — page 31

   1 Corrosion of metals. See *Metals*, chapter 9, page 177.
   2 Sunlight
   3 Biological agencies
   4 Water
   5 Crystallization of salts
   6 Frost
   7 Chemical action
   8 Loss of volatiles
   9 Abrasion and impact
   10 Vibration
   11 Fire.

(a) Density and specific gravity

BS 648 : 1964 *Schedule of weights of building materials* is a useful reference for calculation purposes. Table 1 gives densities for many materials in kg/m³, and others are given at the appropriate points in the text.

Specific gravity is a ratio of the density of a substance at a given temperature to the density of water at 4°C.

(b) Strength

Materials must be capable of safely supporting their own weight and any applied loads without distortion which would reduce the efficiency of a structure or be unsightly. Strength properties are defined and values given for a range of materials in chapter 9, pages 178–80.

When a material is said to be 'strong' it is its strength in tension which is usually referred to, but it is often necessary to know its strength properties in compression, shear and torsion. Also strength properties vary with the rate and frequency of loading and, in non-homogeneous materials, with the direction of loading. Strength properties are further influenced by the moisture content of materials such as timber and the temperature of materials such as plastics.

Materials which are subjected to a force are said to be *stressed* and the change in shape is known as *strain* (cause and effect). In *elastic* materials up to an *elastic limit* strain is proportional to the load applied and they recover their original shape and size when the load is removed.

Materials such as mild steel which suffer a relatively small amount of strain when subjected to a given load are said to be *stiff* or *rigid*, a property which must not be equated with breaking strength. Thus aluminium alloys which are as strong in tension as mild steel are far less rigid.

With increasing load, at a point which is not always clearly defined, materials cease to be *elastic* and become *plastic* and undergo permanent distortion. Materials which do this to a high degree are *ductile* as distinct from *brittle* materials. Ductility generally decreases with strength in tension.

In varying degrees, materials undergo slow plastic deformation or *creep*, under a constant stress. Steel has very small creep at normal working stresses and temperature but in concrete

Bulk density kg/m^3	Material	Thermal conductivity (k) W/m deg C	Thermal resistivity (1/k) m deg C/W
64	Expanded ebonite	0·029	34·62
16; 24	Expanded polystyrene	0·035; 0·033	28·6; 30·4
24; 40	Foamed polyurethane	0·024; 0·039	41·7; 25·6
16–48	Glass fibre quilt	0·032–0·04	31·3–25·0
48	Mineral and slag wools	0·03–0·04	33·3–25·0
120	Wool, hair and jute fibre felts	0·036	27·8
128	Corkboard (baked)	0·040	25·0
160	Balsa	0·045	22·2
80–240	Sprayed asbestos	0·043–0·058	23·25–17·3
240–350	Insulating fibre building boards	0·053–0·065	18·9–15·4
80–144	Exfoliated vermiculite (loose)	0·047–0·058	21·2–17·3
128–136	Rigid foamed glass slabs	0·050–0·052	20·0–19·2
350–800	Medium fibre building boards	0·072–0·101	13·9–9·9
320–700	Aerated concrete (low density)	0·084–0·18	11·9–5·55
365	Compressed straw slabs	0·101	9·9
450	Wood-wool slabs	0·093	10·75
400–800	Exfoliated vermiculite concrete	0·094–0·260	10·6–38·5
320–1040	Expanded clay – loose	0·12	8·83
800 and 961 (min)	Standard and tempered hardboards	0·125 and 0·180	8·0 and 5·6
513	Softwoods and plywoods	0·124	8·07
721	Diatomaceous earth brick	0·141	7·10
881 (max)	Asbestos-silica-lime insulating board (BS 3536)	0·144 (max)	6·95
449–800	Particle boards	0·101–0·158	9·92–6·34
961	Plasterboard	0·16	6·25
769	Hardwoods	0·16	6·25
641	Exfoliated vermiculite plaster	0·19	5·26
1190	Perspex (ICI)	0·21	4·8
961–1682	Foamed slag concrete	0·22–0·51	4·55–1·96
721–1522	Expanded clay and sintered PFA concretes	0·22–0·58	4·55–1·73
1620	Polyester glass fibre laminate	0·35	2·86
1522	Asbestos cement (semi-compressed (BS 690))	0·37	2·70
1041–1522	Clinker concrete	0·37–0·58	2·70–1·73
1442	Plaster (dense)	0·48	2·08
2306	Cement : sand	0·53	1·89
1142–1842	No-fines concrete	0·562–0·75	1·78–1·33
2100	Mastic asphalt	0·60	1·67
1698 (minimum)	Asbestos cement (fully compressed (BS 4036))	0·65	1·54
1602	Aerated concrete (high density)	0·65	1·54
1700	Brickwork	1·45–0·73	0·69–1·38
2520	Glass	1·04	0·98
1778	Rendering	1·15–1·21	0·87–0·83
2500	Sandstone	1·29	0·77
2260	Concrete 1 cement : 2 sand : 4 ballast	1·44	0·69
2310	Limestone	1·53	0·65
2590	Slate	1·88	0·53
2662	Granite	2·93	0·34
7850	Steel	57	0·0176
2700	Aluminium and alloys	214	0·0047
9000	Copper	400	0·0025

Values are for normal moisture contents and at normal temperatures.

Table 1   Densities, thermal conductivities and thermal resistivities of common materials

even a small load increases the deformation of a member as much as three times the initial elastic movement over a period of a year or two. *The New Science of Strong Materials* by J. E. Gordon is recommended reading.

(c) Optical properties

Some reference is made to this subject under *Glass*, chapter 12.

(d) Electrical properties

The reader is referred to *Mitchell's Building Construction: Environment and Services*, by Peter Burberry, for definitions of electrical terms.

(e) Colour, texture and ease of cleaning

See *Thin surface finishes* chapter 17, *MBC: Components and Finishes.*

(f) Thermal properties

The calculation of heat losses from buildings is dealt with in *MBC: Environment and Services.*

Heat loss occurs by air changes, eg through gaps around doors and windows and by transmittance through walls, floors and roofs.

Thermal insulation in structures is achieved by:

1 *Cavities* – preferably unventilated.
2 *Cellular materials* especially those which retain air in small and discontinuous cavities, eg cork.
3 *Reflective materials* with high reflectivity and low emissivity, eg aluminium foil.

Table 1 lists some common building materials in order of increasing thermal conductivities (k) and decreasing resistivities (1/k). Thermal conductivities are given in *The Thermal Insulation of Buildings*, C. Handisyde and D. J. Melluish, D. of E., HMSO, and in *The IHVE Guide*.

Thermal conductivity

Thermal conductivity (k) is a measure of the rate of heat transfer through a MATERIAL from FACE TO FACE (NOT from air to air). It is expressed as:

heat units transmitted in unit time	Watts (J/s)
through unit thickness	m
of unit area	m²

for unit temperature difference between the faces   deg C

ie,   W/m deg C[1]

The k values of materials vary with density, in the examples quoted from 0·029 to 3725 W/m deg C with corresponding variations in density from 64 to 9000 kg/m³. Conductivity values also vary with temperature, porosity and moisture content. With a moisture content of 20 per cent, volume by volume most building materials transmit between two and three times as much heat as they do when they are dry. Hygroscopic materials such as timber vary in moisture content with the relative humidity of the atmosphere. A common source of dampness in materials is condensation.

Thermal transmittance

Thermal transmittance (U) is the rate of heat transfer through a CONSTRUCTION from AIR TO AIR expressed as:

heat units in unit time	Watts (J/s)
over unit area	m²
with unit difference in temperature from air to air	deg C
ie	W/m² deg C

Thermal transmittance can be calculated by finding the reciprocal of all the thermal resistances offered by a construction from air to air. The thermal resistances are:

resistivities of the respective materials[2] × their thicknesses	(thickness (m)/k)
resistances of cavities (which vary with thickness, surface emissivity, direction of heat flow and ventilation if any)	R_{cav}

[1] This expression is derived from Wm/m² deg C by cancelling the metre thickness.

[2] *Thermal resistivity* (1/k) is a measure of the resistance to heat flow from FACE TO FACE of unit thickness and area of a material, ie

$$\frac{\text{thickness (m)}}{\text{thermal conductivity (W/m deg C)}} = \text{m deg C/W}$$

where m deg C/W is derived from m deg C/Wm by cancelling the metre thickness

resistances of reflective membranes
resistances of surfaces
    internally
      (resistance varies with
      direction of heat flow) R_{si}
    externally
      (resistance varies with
      surface emissivity and
      exposure) R_{so}
(resistances also vary with surface texture)

Pattern staining

Dirt in air is deposited preferentially where heat loss is greater, ie on relatively cool surfaces and shows as a pattern which mirrors the variations in thermal conduction through different parts of walls or ceilings. Typically, wide dark bands show on plaster ceilings below the voids between timber ceiling joists, and narrow dark bands show on plaster ceilings below the solid concrete beams in hollow tile floors.

Emissivity, absorptivity and reflectivity of surfaces

Any two bodies facing each other exchange heat by radiation, the rate of emission and absorption depending upon the nature of their surfaces and the temperature difference.

Figure 1 shows the mechanism of radiant heat transfer.

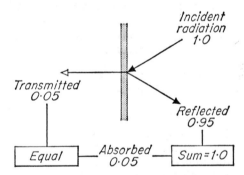

1 Mechanism of radiant heat transfer (values of typical aluminium foil at normal temperature)

Table 2 gives emissivities at normal temperatures and absorptivities of solar radiation of various surfaces.

It will be seen that highly polished aluminium is the most effective reflector of both normal temperature and solar radiation. Differences in colour are not important at normal temperatures

Surface	Emissivity at 10–38°C	Absorptivity of solar radiation
Black non-metallic surfaces	0·90–0·98	0·85–0·98
Red brick, concrete and stone, dark paints	0·85–0·95	0·65–0·80
Yellow brick and stone	0·85–0·95	0·50–0·70
White brick, tile, paint, whitewash	0·85–0·95	0·30–0·50
Window glass	0·90–0·95	transparent
Bright aluminium, gilt or bronze paints	0·40–0·60	0·30–0·50
Dull copper, aluminium and galvanized steel	0·20–0·30	0·40–0·65
Polished copper	0·02–0·05	0·30–0·50
Highly polished aluminium	0·02–0·40	0·10–0·40

From *Heating, Ventilating and Air Conditioning Guide*, published by American Society of Heating and Ventilating Engineers

Table 2   Emissivity and absorptivity of surfaces

but white is a good reflector of solar radiation and even better than aluminium which has become dulled by oxidation. Thus, the thermal resistance of an unventilated cavity 19 mm or more wide is nearly doubled if it is faced on one[1] or both sides with a surface of low emissivity such as shiny aluminium foil. Resistance is further increased if foil forms an airtight division between two cavities each at least 19 mm wide. White surfaces are particularly effective in keeping mastic asphalt and bitumen felt roofings cool in summer.

Condensation (see also *Mitchell's Building Construction: Environment and Services* by Peter Burberry)

At any given temperature air can support a limited amount of water as vapour, the quantity increasing with temperature. The amount held in air is usually expressed as *relative humidity*, ie the mass of water vapour in a unit volume of air as a percentage of the mass of water vapour in a unit volume of saturated air at the same temperature. The temperature at which air becomes saturated and vapour condenses is known as the *dew point*. Although the air in a room is usually well above

[1] Bright aluminium has high reflectivity and low emissivity so it is equally effective on either side of a cavity.

its dew point often the temperature of some surfaces is not and typically condensation shows first on the insides of window panes. The vapour pressure in such conditions being higher inside a building than outside, water vapour passes through porous constructions and where this air falls to the dew point it condenses as *interstitial condensation*. In traditional construction water vapour was able to evaporate outwards but today *interstitial condensation* often tends to form on the inner surfaces of impervious membranes on the cold side of a construction, eg flat roof coverings, metal and glass wall claddings.

Interstitial condensation can be prevented by a *vapour barrier*, provided this itself is at a temperature above the dew point of the internal atmosphere, ie it must be on the warm side of a construction, also it must be continuous. Table 3 lists some materials in order of increasing resistance to the passage of water vapour. It is important to distinguish between vapour diffusivity, resistivity and diffusance.

Vapour diffusivity is the weight of water vapour which passes through unit thickness and area of a material per second under unit water vapour pressure gradient and at a given temperature (the permeability of films to water vapour approximately doubles for every 10 deg C rise in temperature). It is expressed as $g\,m/MN\,s$.

Vapour resistivity, the reciprocal of vapour diffusivity, is expressed as $MN\,s/g\,m$. It is the time taken for unit weight vapour to flow through unit area and thickness of a material when there is a unit difference of vapour pressure between the faces.

(It will be noted that these terms ending with *ivity* relate to unit thicknesses, as *conductivity* and *resistivity* do in respect of heat transfer).

Vapour resistance The resistance of an homogeneous material is resistivity × thickness and resistance values can be added together to find the overall resistance of a compound construction which is expressed as $MN\,s/g$.

Vapour diffusance is the weight of water vapour which passes through unit area of a construction

	Vapour resistivity of materials for unit thickness MN s/g m	Vapour resistance for stated thickness	
		MN s/g	thickness mm
Foamed urea formaldehyde	20–30	0·5–0·7	25
Wood-wool slab	15–40	0·7–2·0	50
Fibre building board	15–60	0·2–0·7	13
Brickwork	25–100	2·5–10·0	100
Concretes	30–100	3·0–10·0	100
Plasterboard	45–60	0·4–0·6	9·5
Timbers	45–75	2·2–3·7	50
Compressed straw slabs	45–75	2·2–3·7	50
Plaster	60	0·75	12
Rendering	100	1·25	12
Foamed polyurethane (open or closed cell)	30–1000	0·7–25·0	25
Expanded polystyrene	100–600	2·5–15·0	25
Hardboard	450–750	2·3–3·8	6
Plywoods	1500–6000	7·0–30·0	6
Expanded ebonite	11 000–60 000	250–1500	25
Average gloss paint film	—	7·5–40	—
Polythene sheet	—	250	0·06
Aluminium foil	—	4000	—

Based on data contained in BRS Digest, 110 *Condensation*, HMSO.

Table 3   Vapour resistivities and resistances: typical values at normal temperatures

per hour under unit vapour pressure gradient and at a given temperature. It is the reciprocal of the total resistances, expressed as: $g/MN s$

The BRS consider that membranes having a vapour diffusance not exceeding 0·067 g/MN s to be effective as vapour barriers.

Specific heat is the quantity of heat required to raise unit mass of a substance through 1 deg C. Examples are:

	J/kg deg C
Granite	330
Copper	376
Mild steel	502
Glass	830
Concrete	880–1040
Aluminium	920
PVC	1040
Polystyrene	1250
Standard hardboard	1250
Insulating fibreboard	1400
Perspex (ICI)	1460
Timber	1500
Polythene	2300
Water	4187

Thermal capacity is the capacity of a body to store heat, expressed as the product of its *mass* (grammes) and its *specific heat*.

In steady temperature conditions the same U value can be provided either by a thick heavy wall or by a thin lightweight wall, but when sudden temperature changes occur the thick wall having high thermal capacity will be slow both to warm up and to cool down, and the converse is true of the second type of wall. Clearly, high thermal capacity is desirable in off-peak storage heaters, and in buildings with very high day temperatures and low night temperatures. In buildings which are heated intermittently high thermal capacity structures are not ideal, although lining interior surfaces with materials of low thermal capacity reduces the amount of heat required to warm a room. Thus, the choice between log cabin and stone castle walls, both of which may have the same U value, may depend upon the form of heating to be employed and the climate.

(g) Acoustic properties

Sound insulation is mainly achieved by mass and the avoidance of direct paths. See *MBC:*

Environment and Services. Sound absorption is considered here.

It is important to realise that sound absorbents are usually very poor sound insulators, in fact an open window which is a perfect absorbent transmits virtually all sound. However, examples of situations where sound absorbents can contribute to sound insulation are linings and baffles in ventilating ducts, in 'cut-off' lobbies, and in the reveals to double windows.

The amount of sound absorbed and the proportions absorbed at different frequencies (or pitch) vary with the nature of materials and forms of construction. Thus:

1 porous materials absorb mainly at the higher frequencies
2 resonant panels absorb mainly at the lower frequencies
3 cavity resonators absorb mainly one frequency.

In practice a wider range of absorption can be obtained by combining two or more of the methods listed. For example a perforated panel may be mounted over an air space containing porous absorbent.

Incidentally, porous treatments in particular may also provide useful thermal insulation.

Unfortunately many sound absorbent treatments introduce combustible materials which spread flame rapidly and cavities behind such materials present a fire risk. Flame retardant impregnants and paints may be of value although the latter reduce sound absorption.

We now consider the three types of absorbents:

1 Absorption of porous materials at low and middle frequencies increases with thickness. Decoration can substantially reduce sound absorption, but plastics films, provided they are not more than 0·051 mm thick and free to vibrate, allow the sound waves to pass into the absorbing material without interference. The surface of porous materials may be more or less non-porous but with holes or slots which allow sound to enter and be absorbed within the thickness of the material.

2 Resonant panels absorb mainly at their resonant frequency which becomes lower with greater weight of panel and with increased depth of the air space behind.

26

Finish	Absorption coefficient at 500 Hz	Category
Floorings		
Carpet, medium: on solid concrete floor	} 0·3	B
on boards on joists or battens		
Wood boards on joists or battens	0·1	
Linoleum and rubber		
Cork tiles	} 0·05	
Wood blocks		
Hard tiles	} 0·03	
Composition flooring		
Granolithic	0·02	
Windows		
Glass: up to 5 mm	0·1	C
6 mm or thicker in large sheets	0·04	
Walls and ceilings		
Perforated steel trays suspended below air space with: 25 mm rockwool	0·65	
51 mm rockwool	0·85	B
76 mm Wood-wool slabs, mounted solidly, unplastered	0·8	A
25 mm Glass wool or mineral wool mounted over air space on solid backing	} 0·8	B
51 mm Glass wool or mineral wool on solid backing		
25 mm Glass wool or mineral wool on solid backing	0·7	B
25 mm Hair felt covered by perforated membrane, eg muslin on solid backing	0·7	
25 mm Wood-wool slabs unplastered mounted over 19 mm air space on solid backing	0·6	B
25 mm Clinker concrete unplastered	0·6	B
Sprayed asbestos	0·55[1]	B
Curtains (medium weight): hung in folds or spaced away from wall	0·4	B
hung straight and close to wall	0·25	
25 mm Wood-wool slabs, unplastered:		B
mounted solidly	0·4	A
mounted over air space on solid backing or on joists or studs	0·3	C
ditto painted	0·15	
13 mm Insulating fibreboard on solid backing	0·15	
ditto painted	0·1	
Plywood:		
panels mounted over air space on solid backing or mounted on studs		C
panels mounted on studs with porous material in air space	0·15	C
19 mm Matchboarding over air space on solid wall	0·1	
Plaster (lime or gypsum) on lathing over air space on solid backing or on joists or studs	} 0·1	C
Plasterboards or fibrous plaster over air space on solid backing or on joists or studs		
Plywood mounted solid to wall	0·05	
Plaster (lime or gypsum) on solid backing	0·02	
Brickwork		
Concrete	} 0·02	
Tooled or polished stone including marble		
Glass bedded solid to wall		
Glazed tiles fixed direct to wall	} 0·01	
Marble fixed direct to wall		

[1] BS 3590 minimum.   Data mainly from BRS Digest 36 (first series)

Table 4   Approximate sound absorption coefficients of common finishes at 500 Hz

3 Cavity or Helmholtz resonators are usually employed in auditoria to correct a specific acoustic fault at a single frequency. The efficiency of a cavity resonator may be increased by introducing porous material into the neck.

The approximate sound absorption of surfaces at various frequencies were given in BRS Digest 36 (first series), *Sound absorbent treatments*. The absorptions of some common surfaces at the middle frequency of 500 Hz are quoted in order of decreasing effectiveness in table 4.

The more effective absorbents are broadly classified as follows:

A general wide band absorption
B preferential absorption at middle and high frequencies
C preferential absorption at low frequencies.

(h) Deformations

Quite large movements may not be important where loss of strength, watertightness or good appearance will not result but they should be foreseen and prevented, eg by keeping timber 'dry', minimized by appropriate choice of materials and structural forms, or allowed to occur in such a way that no damage results, eg by providing movement joints. See chapter 16.

Broadly, deformations may be caused by *deterioration of materials*, see page 31, eg expansion caused by sulphate attack on Portland cement, or by frost, or corrosion and fire damage. Here we consider deformations caused by:

1 applied loads, either *design loads*, or *accidental loads* arising from errors in structural design or from overloading
2 changes in moisture content of materials
3 changes in temperature of materials.

In practice, two or more causes of movement may occur together and where adjoining materials are mutually restrained the effective overall movement may be either greater or less than that of either of them.

1 *Movements caused by applied loads*

In small buildings deformations arising from applied loads are normally insignificant but in large structures they may require to be accommodated by pin joints and sliding bearings.

Most materials are elastic to some degree and many materials exhibit *plastic flow* or *creep* and are permanently distorted if a load is sustained. Steel has negligible creep at normal temperatures and stresses but concrete creeps even with small loads notably during the first month or so and then at a decreasing rate for several years, ultimate creep of gravel concrete cast in-situ being about twice the elastic strain. Creep is high in plastics, particularly in thermoplastics.

Mechanical properties are defined in chapter 9, page 174, and the properties of various materials are compared in table 68 pages 178–80.

2 *Movements caused by changes in moisture content of materials*

Most materials expand to some extent when they are wetted and contract when they dry, see table 5. These dimensional changes are known as *moisture movements*, abbreviated in timber technology to *movements* (not to be confused with the movement of moisture *through* materials). Initial movements of manufactured materials (eg shrinkage in drying of new concrete products, and expansion in absorption of water by ceramic products which begins immediately they are removed from the kiln) are partially *irreversible movements*. These tend to be greater than the *reversible movements* which accompany subsequent wetting or drying.

Clearly it is preferable to use concrete and ceramic products which have completed most if not all of their irreversible moisture movement.

3 *Movements caused by changes in temperature*

Almost all materials expand when they are heated and contract when they cool. The movement of solids is expressed as the increase in length per unit length for one degree Celsius rise in temperature. Coefficients for typical building materials are given in table 6.

Changes in temperature of materials may result from atmospheric heat, solar radiation or from heating installations.

The *Principles of Modern Building*, Vol. 1, points out that air temperatures can vary up to 22 deg C between night and day in clear summer weather, while the extreme range of temperature between a hot summer day and a cold winter night can be as much as 50 deg C. Materials with

	Movement per cent	
	Irreversible	*Reversible*
Metals, glass	—	—
Limestone – Portland		0·004
Clay brick (typical good facing)	0·10–0·20 (expansion)	0·01
Asbestos-silica-lime insulating board[1]		0·017[1]
Calcium silicate bricks	0·001–0·05	0·001–0·05
Glass fibre polyester		0·02
Semi-compressed asbestos-cement		0·25–0·30[1]
Lightweight aggregate concretes		0·03–0·35
Dense concrete and mortars	0·02–0·08 (drying shrinkage)	0·01–0·055
Aerated concrete (auto-claved)		0·06–0·07
Timber—longitudinal		0·10
Hardboards	slight	0·11–0·32
Sandstone—Darley Dale		0·15
Perspex (ICI)		0·35
Insulating fibreboard		0·20–0·37
Laminated plastics		0·10–0·50
Aerated concrete (air-cured)		0·17–0·22
Plywood		0·5
Timber: radial		3·4[2]
tangential		4·6[2]
Chipboard	appreciable	0·1–12·0

[1] From normal moisture content to saturated condition.
[2] From 27–12 per cent moisture content.

Table 5   *Moisture movements from dry to saturated condition*

	Material	Cofficient of thermal expansion $\times 10^{-6}$ per deg C
High 26–200	Polythene, HD/LD	144/198
	Acrylics	72–90
	PVC	70
	Timber—across fibres	30–60
	Phenolics	15·3–45
	Zinc	31
	Lead	29
Medium 15–25	Aluminium	24
	Polyesters	18–25
	Brass	18
	Copper	17·3
	Stainless steel	17·3
	Gypsum plaster	16·6
Low 1–14	Sandstones	7–16
	Concretes – various aggregates	10–14
	Mild steel	11–13
	Glass	6–9
	Granite	8–10
	Slates	6–10
	Marbles	1·4–11
	Limestones	2·4–9
	Aerated concretes	8
	Plywood	5–8
	Bricks and brickwork	5–7
	Asbestos-cement BS 690	12 ·
	Asbestos-silica-lime insulating board	5
	Timber—longitudinal	3–6

Table 6   *Thermal movements*

small heat capacities will respond readily to changes in air temperature, more so if they are separated from massive structures by thermal insulation.

Normally the outer parts of buildings suffer the greatest changes in temperature, in particular those parts exposed to sunshine. Those parts most exposed to solar radiation are roofs and parapets.

Table 2 shows that dark materials absorb more solar heat than light ones. Thus, in this country a black panel which is insulated at the back can rise as high as 71°C.

4 Stresses due to thermal and moisture content changes

Movements[1] can be substantial and give rise to considerable stresses and if these exceed the strength of materials, cracks or buckling occur.

Calculation of stresses is complicated by a number of factors which cannot be accurately predicted. For example:

(i) climatic conditions

[1] Movements include expansions with rise in temperature or with absorption of water by ceramic products and timber and contraction with fall in temperature and drying of cement, calcium silicate bricks and timber.

(ii) the ranges and rates of thermal and moisture content changes in materials in service

(iii) the magnitude of movements in the actual products to be used assuming them to be unrestrained. Published data for products of the same type is sufficiently accurate in this context

(iv) the degree and type of restraint afforded by connections between materials

Table 7 shows the stresses caused by a moderate rise in temperature in completely restrained walls. In Britain variation between night and day temperatures may be as much as 22 deg C. Stress is directly proportional to the elastic moduli of materials. The latter being generally higher for stronger materials the stress given for strong brickwork is quite high. It will be seen that the stresses as a fraction of failing strengths in compression are about one twelfth in the strong brickwork compared with only about one twenty-fifth in the low strength brickwork.

In practice thermal stresses may be modified by moisture movement stresses and because the larger temperature changes take place slowly the resulting stresses are reduced by one-half or more by the creep of the materials.

5 Common defects due to movement and their prevention

Some problems are now considered:

Dark coloured roof coverings on long, strong concrete slabs often cause them to expand and form horizontal cracks in top floor partitions just below the ceiling and to exert a thrust at their ends pushing the flank walls outwards. Coverings to flat roofs are always best finished with a solar heat reflecting surface and in addition roof slabs require movement joints at not more than about 30 m intervals and joints should be provided above partitions.

Copings are traditionally jointed in cement mortar which shrinks and allows the entry of water sometimes leading to sulphate attack on the mortar in clay brickwork[1] which then expands. This is a case where more than one mechanism may be at work, thus copings, particularly dark coloured copings such as slate, are liable to substantial temperature change and resulting movement. Where there are abutments at the ends they will tend to be distorted or the coping may show signs of crushing. If the ends are unrestrained the coping may extend in its length in a series of 'pushes' made possible by the settling of mortar in the joints between the slabs. A sealant topped movement joint at say 15 m intervals would usually prevent these defects.

The *Principles of modern building, Vol. I,* draws particular attention to the fact that unrestrained aluminium cladding frames 12 m long increase in length nearly 10 mm in response to a 22 deg C rise in temperature. The structure behind will remain relatively static and clearly such members must

[1] See Chapter 6 *Bricks*, page 123.

	Modulus of elasticity N/mm^2	Coefficient of thermal expansion per deg C	Failing stress in compression N/mm^2	Stress due to 15 deg C rise in temperature N/mm^2
Medium strength bricks in lime mortar	1 400	6×10^{-6}	71 000	2 800
Medium strength bricks in cement mortar	6 200	6×10^{-6}	180 000	12 000
Strong bricks in cement mortar	19 000	6×10^{-6}	400 000	33 000
Granite	48 000	10×10^{-6}	1 700 000	150 000

Table 7   Stresses caused by thermal changes

have fixings so they can move as a whole or alternatively be fixed in small units so the relative movements will not be troublesome.

Coloured glass on a sunny façade with thermal insulation behind it poses a special problem. It must be free to move with a clearance of 6 mm on a dimension of 1 m and the avoidance of any possible contact between the edge of the glass and bead screws or other metal attachments are essential precautions. Differences in temperature due to shading can also lead to cracking, especially at the edges and it is important that these should be cut cleanly and that beads should not exceed 10 mm in width.

In buildings of rectangular plan where walls are free to expand in any direction movement joints should be provided at not more than 30 m intervals. Long walls which are restrained at their ends may distort their abutments or fail at 'weak links' in their length. PMB illustrates a 90 m long steel framed building which distorted the walls of brickwork buildings at its ends. It also illustrates a garden wall 45 m long restrained by buildings at its ends in which cracks in an arch opened at midday and closed again in the early morning.

BRS Digest 65 recommends that movement joints should be provided in long brick walls sufficient to accommodate an expansion of 9·5 mm in 12 m.

(i) Deterioration

This subject is dealt with by CP 3, Code of basic design data for the design of buildings, Chapter IX : 1950 *Durability*.

All materials deteriorate and the function of the designer is to anticipate the changes which will occur in service.

Only wishful expectation of the most unlikely coincidence of good fortunes can explain the common disregard of the known causes and effects of deteriorating agencies on various materials. For example the designer who expects that two coats of varnish will preserve the new appearance of timber cladding for very long, or that a building owner will take kindly to renewing the finish at frequent intervals, has not studied *MBC: Components and Finishes*, Chapter 17, or human behaviour.

With due regard to *cost-in-use* the designer must use materials in the correct context and inform the building-owner what after care will be needed to ensure a maximum life. He must also foresee not only normal eventualities but the occasional events such as the ten year storm, attempts at burglary, and fire.

Differences in exposure have obvious effects upon durability, thus while a paint film may last a thousand years in an air-conditioned museum, on a south-facing slope in an industrial atmosphere it may fail in a year or so.

The lives of many materials which are exposed externally, or of those subject to abrasion, eg floorings (see *MBC: Components and Finishes*), are often dependent upon the removal of contaminants, the maintenance of a first line of defence in the form of protective coatings, or upon ancillary materials which have relatively short lives, such as putties and mastics.

Direct or indirect causes of deterioration include:

1 Corrosion of metals. See *Metals*, chapter 9, page 174
2 Sunlight
3 Biological agencies
4 Water
5 Crystallization of salts
6 Frost
7 Chemical action
8 Loss of volatiles
9 Abrasion and impact
10 Vibration
11 Fire.

1 *Corrosion of metals*

This important cause of deterioration is discussed in chapter 9, page 174.

2 *Sunlight*

Sunlight causes degradation of clear finishes, paints, rubber, bituminous products and some plastics and loss of colour in pigments.

3 *Biological agencies*

Insects and some animals attack organic materials, mainly timber. Importantly sulphate-reducing bacteria produce sulphides from sulphates which corrode iron, steel and lead pipes in the ground.

Plants, such as creepers and trees, sometimes cause damage but in temperate climates fungal attack upon cellulosic materials which are persistently damp or wet is the most serious hazard under this heading. See chapter 2, page 78. It is preventable by the use of inherently resistant materials or by pretreatment with fungicide and by suitably designed construction.

4 Water

Some building materials, such as gypsum plasters and magnesium oxychloride flooring, are sufficiently soluble in water to preclude their use in damp situations. Limestones may be very slowly dissolved (and thereby kept clean where they are freely washed by rain). Timber, ordinary fibreboards, wood wool slabs and similar materials lose a proportion of their strength, and many flooring materials have less resistance to abrasion when they are wet.

Water also provides conditions which favour fungal attack, certain chemical reactions including electrolytic action, and frost damage. Alternate wetting and drying causes surface crazing and cracking of timber. Water also acts as a vehicle for the migration of salts and soluble substances.

5 Crystallization of salts

Soluble salts are derived from the ground or marine atmospheres or are formed by the constituents of building materials. Moisture evaporating from surfaces brings salts forward, giving rise to *efflorescence*. Where salts crystallize on the surface the effect may be merely disfiguring, but crystallization in the pores of the surface layer may cause gradual erosion or flaking as shown in table 8. Often parts which are most sheltered suffer more severely than where rain tends to wash out the salts. Calcium sulphate may be washed from limestone on to brickwork or sandstone and cause decay. Decay of a moderate or poor brick or stone may be accelerated by the use of impervious mortar for pointing which concentrates movement of water carrying salts in solution through the less dense material.

6 Frost

Water expands when it freezes, at 4°C, and where it is contained in pores or other interstices it may cause decay. Materials with a laminar structure are more liable to deteriorate.

Class of material	How affected
Clay bricks	Good bricks rarely affected. Some underfired bricks may be badly attacked.
Clay tiles	Good tiles rarely affected. Some tiles suffer erosion at upper end.
Terra-cotta	Rarely affected unless underfired.
Sand-lime bricks	Good bricks rarely affected.
Cast stone and Portland cement concrete	Rarely affected.
Sandstones	Vary greatly in resistance. The best stones are excellent.
Limestones	Vary greatly in resistance. This is the property which is most important in distinguishing a durable stone.

Table 8 Susceptibility of materials to deterioration due to crystallization of soluble salts From Principles of Modern Building, Vol. 1, HMSO

If only part of the total pore space is filled with water the latter can expand without bursting the material. The ratio of the volume of the pore space filled by immersion in cold water to the total volume of the pore space of a specimen (as determined by prolonged immersion in boiling water followed by cooling while submerged), is called the *saturation coefficient*. This, together with other laboratory tests, including cycles of freezing and thawing, may give some indication of frost resistance, but the only reliable guide is the behaviour of a material for a number of years in conditions resembling those in which it will be used.

Table 9 gives general information about the performance of some common materials.

7 Chemical action

Chemical action may affect volume (see *Deformations*, page 28) strength as in the corrosion of metals, appearance, eg acid attack on stones, bricks and concrete and it causes deterioration of

Class of material	How affected	Class of material	How affected
Natural stone	Variable. Best stones unaffected. Some stones with pronounced cleavage along bedding planes are unsuitable for copings or cornices	Clay products	*Rarely affected,* but may retain soot
		Siliceous sandstones	*Rarely affected,* but retain soot
Clay products	Best bricks and tiles unaffected but some insufficiently fired products and those having flaws of structure originating in the machine, may deteriorate, especially bricks in copings, and tiles on flat-pitched roofs.	Slates	*Generally highly resistant,* but some suffer rapid decay. See BS 680
		Cast stone and cement products generally	*Good quality products only slightly affected.* Dense mixes desirable for high degree of pollution.
		Sand-lime bricks	*Very slightly affected.*
		Limestones	*All attacked to some extent.* The more durable stones have a long life in the worst environment. Care needed in selection
Cast stone, concrete, asbestos cement	Rarely affected if of good quality.	Calcareous sandstones	Liable to be badly attacked.

Table 9 Susceptibility of materials to deterioration as a result of frost action. From *Principles of Modern Building,* Vol. 1, HMSO

Table 10 Susceptibility of materials to attack by acid gases in polluted atmospheres. From *Principles of Modern Building,* Vol. 1, HMSO

roof coverings. Contributory factors are heat and in nearly all chemical changes water enters into the chemical change or brings together reactive substances.

Aggressive gases increase the erosive effect of rainwater, and materials in industrial plants may require special protection. See table 10.

Ground waters, industrial wastes, wet clay bricks, soil and ashes often contain *soluble sulphates* which attack cement products and metals. The effect is expansion of Portland cement and hydraulic limes and their disintegration. Incompletely burnt colliery shales swell when they are wetted and should not be used as filling below ground level concrete floor slabs.

The carbonation of Portland cement products leads to shrinkage, eg of lightweight concretes and is a cause of surface crazing of dense concretes.

8 Loss of volatiles

This is a cause of embrittlement and shrinkage of plastics, paints and mastics.

9 Abrasion and impact

In buildings these are mainly confined to floorings (see *MBC: Components and Finishes*) but where abnormal hazards can be anticipated suitably resistant surfaces should be provided, eg metal arrises in plasterwork and tiling.

10 Vibration

Vibration is most likely to be troublesome in light constructions and with brittle materials, and in such cases joints require special attention.

11 Fire

The behaviour of *materials* and *constructions* in building fires is considered here.

Fire is a chemical reaction for which fuel, heat and a critical proportion of oxygen are all needed. Most solids and liquids give off vapour when they are heated and it is this which burns as flame. Some liquids give off flammable vapours even at normal atmospheric temperatures and are readily ignited when mixed with oxygen in critical proportions, ie they have low *flash points*. The flash point of petrol, for example, is 43°C below zero and butane boils at 0°C. Solids can burn only at or near their surfaces and are relatively difficult to ignite. Open textured materials burn more rapidly having a large 'surface area' throughout their mass, while finely divided dusts of materials such as coal, wood, flour, many plastics, magnesium and aluminium become explosive when they are suspended in air.

The calorific values of materials are given in *Post-war Building Study*, No. 20, Appendix III (HMSO). The grading of building occupancies on the basis of *fire load* (expressed as kJ/m²) is dealt with in *Mitchell's Building Construction Structure and Fabric, Part* 2, J. Foster.

In fires, materials may melt, burn, lose strength, expand, or shrink and crack.

Flame and collapse of buildings cause injury and loss of life but smoke and gases are even more dangerous causing loss of sensibility, panic, loss of vision and asphyxiation, often where no flame is present.

The phenomenon of *flash over* deserves special mention. Solids can smoulder in a confined space for a long time, with only one third of the normal oxygen supply, and then suddenly and explosively burst into flame. This is explained by a gradual build-up of heat and vapour pressure causing sudden collapse, perhaps of enclosing panelling, and the entry of fresh air.

We now consider the British Standard tests and the behaviour of specific materials in fires.

British Standard tests The standard tests aim to simulate as closely as possible the conditions which arise in typical fires so that the performances of various materials and elements can be assessed and compared. It is most important that clearly defined and standard terminology is used. 'Fireproof' and 'Flame resistant' are examples of

terms which should not be employed in respect of building materials, and 'FR' often seen in trade literature is meaningless.

BS 4422: 1969 is a *Glossary of terms associated with fire.*

Advertisements for products should make it clear which tests, if any, have been carried out and the classifications achieved. This should be supported by: *Test Report FROSI No – –* being the reference allocated by the Joint Fire Research Organization, Boreham Wood, Hertfordshire. If tests have not been performed a written assessment given by the JFRO on the basis of their accumulated experience may be accepted by the Building Regulations authorities.

The main British Standard concerned with fire performance of buildings was BS 476: 1953 *Fire tests on building materials and structures.* The specification is in process of being issued in six separate parts as shown in table 11 (there will be no Part 1 or Part 2, to avoid confusion with the previous documents).

The BS tests will now be considered in turn.

External fire exposure roof tests This is the title of BS 476: Part 3: 1958. The purpose of the tests described is to provide information on the behaviour of roofs when there is a fire nearby but outside the building itself. It is important to note that the tests are neither capable of, nor intended to, predict the performance of a roof in the event of internal fire. Representative specimens of roof constructions 838 mm square are exposed to heat

New part numbers	Titles of parts	Old part numbers
—	—	Part 2: 1955[2]
3:	*External fire exposure roof tests*	Part 3: 1958
4: 1970	*Non-combustibility tests for materials*	Part 1: 1953
5: 1968	*Ignitability test for materials*	—
6: 1968	*Fire propagation test for materials*	—
7: 1971	*Surface spread of flame test for materials*	Part 1: 1953
8:[1]	*Fire resistance test for elements of building construction*	Part 1: 1953
9: 1971	*Smoke production test for materials*	—

[1] To be issued as a separate document.
[2] BS 476: Part 2: 1955 *Flammability tests for thin flexible materials* has been withdrawn, the subject being covered by BS 2782 *Methods of testing plastics*: Part 5 *Flammability.*

Table 11   BS 476 Fire tests on building materials and structures

conditions simulating a fire in a building of known size and a certain distance away. A test flame is used to simulate falling burning brands in a fire. To determine the extent of surface flaming, specimens are also subjected to a graduated intensity of radiant heat. Specimens are graded according to their resistance to the penetration of fire and the extent of surface flaming.

Each category designation consists of two letters eg AA, AC, BB:

The first letter refers to penetration of fire:

A not penetrated within 1 hour
B penetrated in not less than $\frac{1}{2}$ hour
C penetrated in less than $\frac{1}{2}$ hour
D penetrated in a preliminary flame test

The second letter refers to spread of flame:

A no spread of flame
B not more than 533 mm spread of flame
C more than 533 mm spread of flame
D those specimens which continue to burn for 5 minutes after the withdrawal of the test flame or spread more than 381 mm across the region of burning in a preliminary test

Category designations are preceded by either *EXT.F* or *EXT.S* according to whether a flat or inclined test is made.

If dripping from the underside of the specimen, any mechanical failure or development of holes takes place during the test, the suffix '*X*' is added to the designation. Thus, for example:

EXT.F.ACX
EXT.S.CCX

Combustibility The term combustibility is defined by BS 476: Part 4: 1970 *Non-combustibility tests for materials*. If small samples plunged into a furnace maintained at 750° ignite, give off flammable gases, or show appreciable self heating they are deemed to be *combustible*. Otherwise they are *non-combustible*; there is no other grading. Examples of *combustible* and *non-combustible* materials are given in table 12. The correct classification of mixtures of materials will only be known by subjecting them to the standard test. *Non-combustible* materials add nothing to the fire load, flame does not spread over them, and they are essential for purposes such as flue linings. However, non-combustibility must not be equated with *fire resistance* which is defined later.

Combustible	Non-combustible
Timber (even if impregnated with flame retardant)	Asbestos-cement products
Fibre building boards (even if impregnated with flame retardant)	Asbestos insulation board
Cork	Gypsum plaster
Wood-wool slabs	Glass
Compressed straw slabs	Glass wool (containing not more than 4–5 per cent bonding agent)
Gypsum plasterboard (rendered combustible by the paper liner)	Bricks
Bitumen felts (including asbestos fibre-based felt)	Stones
	Concretes
Glass wool or mineral wool with combustible bonding agent or covering	Metals
	Vermiculite
Bitumen protected metal sheet	Mineral wool
All plastics and rubbers	

Table 12   Combustible and non-combustible materials

Thus, *non-combustible* materials such as steel may expand and in so doing disturb adjacent structures, while loss of strength at high temperatures may cause collapse. Other *non-combustible* materials such as asbestos cement sheets may spall, shrink and allow the passage of flame through cracks.

On the other hand, although *combustible* materials such as timber cannot be made *non-combustible* by facings, coatings, or by impregnation, in certain sizes and conditions when used as building elements, they may provide a useful degree of *fire resistance*.

Ignitability BS 476: Part 5: 1968 *Ignitability test for materials* is primarily intended for materials in slab or sheet form, but not for fabrics. The test identifies easily ignitable materials of low heat contribution, the full hazard of which is not necessarily shown by the *Fire propagation test* (Part 6).

After being subjected to a standard flame for 10 seconds samples are classified as:

'*Easily ignitable*' ('*X*') if specimen flames for a further 10 seconds or if burning extends to an edge.
'*Not easily ignitable*' ('*P*') if none of three specimens is classified as easily ignitable.

Fire propagation BS 476:Part 6:1968 *Fire propagation test for materials* expresses as a numerical index the amount and rate of heat evolved by a specimen which is heated in an enclosed space.

Test results must be accompanied by a '*P*' or '*X*' classification for *ignitability* (Part 5) and it is important to state the thickness of the specimen.

Surface spread of flame Spread of flame over combustible surfaces, more particularly walls and ceilings – can assist growth of fires. In cavities it is particularly dangerous and wherever possible they should be avoided or limited by the provision of *fire stops*.

The BS 476:Part 7:1971 test for surface spread of flame is carried out by subjecting the surfaces of samples mounted perpendicular to one edge of a three foot square radiant panel to a graduated intensity of heat. The distance and rate of flame spread along the surface is measured and the material is placed into one of four classifications:

Class 1 Surfaces of *very low flame spread*
Class 2 Surfaces of *low flame spread*
Class 3 Surfaces of *medium flame spread*
Class 4 Surfaces of *rapid flame spread.*

In addition, the Building Regulations 1972 designate wholly non-combustible walls and ceilings as *Class O*. This 'highest class' for spread of flame over surfaces is also provided by a surface material which when tested in accordance with BS 476: Part 6, 1968, either by itself or where bonded throughout to a substrate provides subscribed indices of *fire propagation*.[1]

The faces of plastics surface-materials which have softening points below 120°C (102C test, BS 2782:1970) qualify as *Class O* only if they:
(a) are bonded throughout to a non-plastic substrate where the surface material and substrate tested together satisfy the stipulated criteria for fire propagation[1], or:
(b) where used as a lining to a wall, plastic surfaces with softening points below 120°C satisfy the fire propagation criteria[1] and, if the lining was not present, expose a surface, other than a plastics material with a softening point below 120°C, which satisfied the fire propagation criteria.[1]

[1] An index of performance (I) not exceeding 12 and a sub-index (I₁) not exceeding 6.   BS 476 : Part 6, 1968.

The Building Regulations 1965 control the surface spread of flame characteristics of ceilings, soffits and walls, excluding doors, windows, skirtings, trim, fitted furniture, etc, according to the purpose group of the building and the size of the room. There is relaxation of requirements in respect of stated small proportions of surfaces, provided they do not fall below *Class 3* but the requirements are generally stricter for circulation spaces, stairs, etc. Floor surfaces are not controlled. See *MBC: Components and Finishes*, chapters 9 and 10).

Table 13 gives the surface spread of flame classifications of some common building materials.

It will be seen that untreated plasterboards qualify for *Class O surface spread of flame*, the paper liner being less than 0·8 mm thick.

Classifications can be improved by impregnation with flame retardant agents or by certain surface treatments. Their effective life is not known, particularly under humid conditions. Conversely, it must be noted that the application of certain paints increases the rate of spread of flame given for untreated surfaces.

Fire resistance Fire resistance is a property of an element, eg walls, columns, floors, beams, glazing and doors, and not of individual materials. It is expressed as the period of time in hours and minutes during which an element survives the test laid down in BS 476 : Part 1 : 1953 (to be reissued as BS 476 : Part 8) while continuing to perform its normal structural or separating function. An element under test is deemed to have failed in the event of:

(a) collapse
(b) the formation of holes or orifices in a separating element through which flames can pass
(c) excessive heat transmission through a separating structure likely to lead to the ignition of combustible materials in contact with the outer face. (In the case of doors and glazing it is assumed that combustible materials will not be placed against them and this requirement is waived.)

Load bearing elements subjected to loads calculated to produce the maximum design stresses are required to resist collapse for the

	Building Regulations 1972 Class O	BS 476 Classes			
		1 Very low	2 Low	3 Medium	4 Rapid
Asbestos non-combustible boards	U/T				
Plasterboard	U/T				
Wood wool slabs		U/T			
Synthetic resin-bonded paper laminates		Including some fire-retardant additives	U/T		
Hardboards – density more than 800 kg/m³		Treated with some flame-retardant treatments Impregnated with flame-retardant salts (not tempered hardboards)	Treated with – chlorinated rubber paint some stove enamels Faced with some plastics	U/T Treated with some stove enamels emulsion paints, oil paints and enamels	Treated with some flammable paints, eg cellulose lacquers
Chipboard		Faced with exfoliated vermiculite or some flame-retardant treatments		U/T	
Timber and plywood – density more than 400 kg/m³		Treated with some flame-retardant treatments including some clear finishes		U/T	
Compressed straw slabs	Coated with 4·76 mm plaster	Faced with asbestos paper or with certain flame retardant treatments		U/T	
Acrylic sheets at least 3·17 mm thick (polymethyl methacrylate)				U/T	
Glass reinforced polyester resin laminates (GRP)		Including flame-retardant additives and containing fillers	Including flame retardant additives		U/T
Timber and plywood density less than 400 kg/m³		Treated with – some flame-retardant treatments including some clear finishes			U/T
Insulating fibre building boards density not more than 35·0 kg/m	Coated with 4·76 mm plaster	Treated with – certain flame-retardant paints, three coats non-washable distemper,[1] one coat non-washable distemper on a sized board[1] Faced with – aluminium foil asbestos paper Impregnated with flame-retardant salts	Treated with one coat flat oil paint,[1] one coat washable or non-washable distemper,[1] chlorinated rubber paint,[1] aluminium paint,[1] some emulsion paints[1]	Treated with some emulsion paints	U/T

[1] Subject to confirmatory tests being carried out by the FRS.

U/T = untreated surface

Test results indicating the performance of specific products should be obtained from manufacturers

Table 13   Spread of flame Classifications (BS 476: Part 7)

duration of the heating period while providing a margin of safety, and to withstand re-application of the test load two days after heating.

Points on the time-temperature curve operated in the furnace are:

538°C at 5 minutes
704°C at 10 minutes
843°C at 30 minutes
927°C at 1 hour
1010°C at 2 hours
1121°C at 4 hours
1204°C at 6 hours.

Elements are graded in standard periods of $\frac{1}{2}$, 1, 2, 3, 4 and 6 hours and a further grading of $1\frac{1}{2}$ hours is recognized under the Building Regulations.

The period of fire resistance required by by-laws and regulations varies according to the purpose group of the building, its height, floor area and cubic capacity and whether the element is above or below ground.

Behaviour of materials in fire This section discusses the general behaviour in fire of some common building materials used in their normal forms. See also the respective chapters.

Timber Timber is easily ignited at about 221 to 298°C. Treatment with flame retardant chemicals by impregnation or by surface coatings reduce the rate of spread of flame, but the timber still carbonizes as if untreated.

Most woods are in *class 3* ('*medium*') spread of flame. Western red cedar, obeche, poplar and willow are the only commonly used woods weighing less than 400 kg/m³ and therefore in *class 4* (*rapid spread of flame*) (BS 476).

In fires softwoods char at about 0·6 mm, and hardwoods at about 0·4 mm per minute, but the charcoal insulates the interior and, unlike steel, there is little loss of strength with a serious rise in temperature, and there is no increase in length which with steel beams often causes walls to overturn. Also the good thermal insulation of timber prevents a marked rise in the temperature of members on the side remote from the fire.

Laminated timber structures glued with synthetic resin have a fire resistance approximating to that of solid timber but the species of the timber and the adhesive have an important bearing on performance.

Fibre building boards These boards (BS 1142: 1961) are described on page 95. They are combustible, ease of ignition and spread of flame varying with density and any impregnation or surface treatment.

Insulating fibre building boards (Less than 400 kg/m³) are in *class 4* ('*rapid*') *spread of flame* (BS 476). This grading can be raised to *class 1* by: impregnation with flame retardant salts, by aluminium foil or asbestos felt surfaces or certain paint treatments. A 5 mm coat of gypsum plaster raises insulating fibreboards to *class O* of the Building Regulations 1972.

Hardboards Standard hardboard (more than 800 kg/m³) has a *class 3* ('*medium*') *spread of flame* (BS 476).

However, although it is in a superior spread of flame class than untreated insulating board, it holds surface finishes less firmly under fire conditions and is less readily improved by them.

Stones Stone blocks and slabs are generally satisfactory in fires but overhanging features and lintels are liable to fail. Free quartz, eg in granite, disrupts suddenly at 575°C and should not be included in any stone where high fire resistance is required.

Sandstones behave better than granite, but in drying they shrink and may crack, with 30 to 50 per cent loss of strength.

Limestones give off CO_2 at about 800°C with loss of strength but little change in volume. Building fires normally exceed this temperature but the chemical dissociation absorbs a great deal of heat and is normally very slow. Limestones, with the exception of those which contain quartz crystals, do not spall and for that reason behave better in fires than granites or sandstones.

(Stones used as concrete aggregates. See chapter 8.)

Plastics Although many are available in flame retardant grades all plastics are combustible, and some of them generate large quantities of toxic smoke.

The fire properties of thermoplastics vary widely

according to their composition, form and other factors. For example, PVC melts at temperatures below that at which they can be tested for spread of flame, but certain wire mesh reinforced PVC sheets are in *class 1 spread of flame* category.

Most thermosetting plastics char at temperatures above 400°C and burn at 700 to 900°C. It will be seen that while normal polyester glass-fibre reinforced laminates (GRP) are in class 3 or 4 spread of flame, modified products may be in class 1 or 2.

Clay products   Surface fusion of clay products can occur with prolonged exposure to temperatures above 1000°C and thin walled blocks have been known to fail as a result of differential temperature stresses.

Generally, however, clay products behave well, having been manufactured at temperatures in excess of those normally encountered in building fires and special refractory bricks withstand extremely high temperatures.

Calcium silicate bricks   These compare favourably with ordinary clay bricks.

Concretes   Ordinary Portland cement disintegrates at 400–500°C but the performance of concrete depends very much upon the presence of reinforcement and upon the type of aggregate.

In general, concretes made from ordinary cement and stone aggregate begin to lose strength well within the range of ordinary building fire temperatures. (High alumina cement with special refractory aggregates is used where exceptional resistance to high temperatures is required, see page 145.) In reinforced concrete, because steel and concrete have about the same coefficient of expansion, the bond between them is little affected at high temperatures and fire resistance depends largely upon the thermal insulation provided to the steel by the concrete cover. Aerated concrete and lightweight aggregate concretes are good in this respect but with dense aggregates, for periods of fire resistance above 2 hours in reinforced beams and $1\frac{1}{2}$ hours in prestressed beams, supplementary reinforcement is required in the cover.

Aggregates are placed in two classes in the Building Regulations 1972, Schedule 8; in the LCC Constructional Bylaws 1965 and in Building Regulations (Scotland) 1963, Schedule 8, Table 4. In descending order of merit:

Class 1

Lightweight aggregates

Pumice, foamed blast-furnace slag, sintered pulverized fuel ash, expanded clay and well burned clinker.

Dense aggregates

Crushed brick, blast furnace slag and crushed limestone.[1]

Class 2

Flint, gravel, granite and all crushed natural stones other than limestone. (Gravel, consisting of flint and crushed quartzites, tends to break up and spall violently and is the least reliable aggregate in common use.)

Gypsum products   Plasters have the advantage that they are continuous and free from joints through which flames can pass, although differences in expansion tend to fracture the bond between plasters and backgrounds. Heat is used in expelling the water of crystallization from gypsum plasters but they remain non-combustible, even with inclusions of organic fibre or powder up to 5 per cent by weight.

Lightweight aggregates give superior adhesion and plaster can resist fire for considerable periods if it is retained by a mechanical key such as expanded metal lathing.

Plasterboard is classed as *combustible* due to the paper liner but because the liner is thin, plasterboard has a *class O* (Building Regulations 1972) grading for spread of flame. In appropriate thicknesses and suitably fixed, plasterboard provides a substantial degree of fire resistance. See also *MBC: Components and Finishes* Chapter 13.

Metals   Those used in building are *non-combustible*, but they lose strength, and aluminium, lead and zinc melt within the range of building fire temperatures. Expansion can be troublesome and high thermal conductivity causes the temperature of surfaces remote from a source of heat to approach the temperature on the reverse and cause fires to spread.

---

[1] The freedom from spalling of limestones which is an advantage in reinforced concrete does not apply to block walls and it is likely that building regulations will be amended accordingly.

Steel The behaviour of mild steel is interesting. Up to 250°C it increases in strength; but it returns to its normal value at 400°C followed by rapid loss of strength, so that at 550°C referred to as the *critical temperature*, the yield strength is reduced to the working stress level.

Thermal expansion of 11×10^{-6}/deg C means that a 10 m member expands more than 50 mm when heated from room temperature to 550°C. Steel sheet cladding fixed in accordance with CP 143 resists the passage of fire well.

Unprotected solid steel columns more than 150 mm diameter can have half an hour *fire resistance* due to their high heat capacity, but generally, structural steelwork must be considered to have no fire resistance – light steel frameworks often collapse within twelve minutes of the commencement of a fire. Generally, structural steelwork must be protected with fire-resisting encasements, see *MBC: Structure and Fabric part 2* and the *deemed-to-satisfy* provisions contained in the *Building Regulations 1965, Part V, Schedule 8.* However, an amendment to the Regulations permits unprotected steelwork in certain multistorey car parks and it has been shown that steelwork which is outside and at least 460 mm away from external walls where windows occur, does not normally need protective encasement. Further reductions in the protection required are likely to be made as a result of investigations which are proceeding in respect of fire loadings of buildings and the performance of steel in fires.

The JFRO is able to advise as to any protection necessary in particular cases.

Wrought iron behaves similarly to steel.

Cast iron Cast iron columns often survive in building fires after steel columns have collapsed but if water jets are applied to cast iron sections brittle fracture is likely. Thermal expansion 10.8×10^{-6}/deg C is about the same as steel and it is recommended that cast iron should be similarly protected.

Aluminium Structural alloys lose strength rapidly when heated, the critical temperature being about half that for structural steel. Thermal expansion is about twice that for steel. The melting point is low and the *Building Regulations 1965* require a higher standard of protection for aluminium structures than for steel. Aluminium sheet cladding does not survive for long in fires.

Glass Although glass is non-combustible it transmits heat and may shatter at an early stage. In certain forms, however, it is fire resisting, eg wired glass, electro-copper glazing and hollow glass blocks, but not toughened glass, see page 228.

When glass is tested for fire resistance the insulation requirement is usually waived, it being assumed that combustible materials are unlikely to be stored near it. Wired glass in roofs has an '*AA*' rating (BS 476: Part 3: 1958 *External Fire Exposure Roof Tests*).

Asbestos products In its pure form asbestos is practically indestructible by fire but:

Asbestos cement products to BS 690: 1963 containing only 12 to 15 per cent by weight of asbestos fibre tend to shatter when they are heated, sometimes explosively, and make no significant contribution to fire resistance in typical structures.

Asbestos insulating boards and asbestos wallboards (BS 3536: 1962) containing at least 50 per cent by weight of asbestos fibre, retard the passage of fire and are suitable for protecting steelwork and for improving the fire resistance of structures and doors.

Asbestos sprays give very useful protection to materials such as steel, aluminium and concrete shells.

Vermiculite products Exfoliated vermiculite used as an aggregate in plasters and renderings having binders of gypsum plaster or cement/lime bond well even to smooth surfaces and adhere well in fires. Sprayed vermiculite plasters and renderings can be used to protect reinforced and prestressed concrete, asbestos cement sheets and steelwork.

Bituminous products Bitumen melts and flows readily when it is heated and is then easily ignited but as the bitumen content reduces, eg in asbestos based felts, products are less easily ignited and burn less readily. Mastic asphalt is difficult to ignite and burns only when it is melted after long exposure to heat. The external performance of bituminous felt and mastic asphalt roof coverings is improved by a finish of stone chippings, screed, tiles or slabs.

Paints Generally paint films are *combustible*

and may increase the rate of *spread of flame* over surfaces (BS 476 tests).

However, being thin, paints can make only a very small contribution to the *fire load* and on *non-combustible* substrates such as steel, most paints fall in Class I *very low* flame spread (BS 476) and being less than 0·8 mm thick they fall in *Class O* of the Building Regulations 1972, see page 36.

Performance of ordinary paints varies considerably according to the type of binder, the pigment content and on the characteristics of the background on which they are applied. On *non-combustible* substrates resistance to flame increases in the following approximate order:

Cellulose nitrate readily ignited, extremely flammable.

Polyester and Alkyd resins not difficult to ignite, usually flammable.

Oil paints flammable.

Epoxide resins difficult to ignite, burn sluggishly.

Washable distempers

Non-washable distempers

Vinyl resins

Urea and melamine formaldehydes difficult to ignite.

Phenol formaldehyde difficult to ignite, burn slowly or self extinguishing.

Chlorinated rubber used in flame retardant paints.

Chlorinated paraffin wax and antimony oxide are used in flame retardant paints

When applied to combustible substrates certain paints can reduce the spread of flame, and delay but never prevent their ultimate ignition. One form of flame retardant paint is *intumescent*, ie it expands when heated forming an insulating porous coating and others evolve smothering gases.

2 Timber

The hundreds of available timber species vary widely in their properties and appearance. In addition, within any one species there is often a wide variation between trees growing in different climatic conditions and on different soils, and between parts of trees. This variability presents problems in economic conversion and utilization, but in recent years knowledge of the properties of timber has increased and improved techniques have been developed for laminating, jointing and framing, seasoning and for protection against fungi, insects and fire. In consequence timber continues to satisfy requirements for performance and cost in a wide range of uses as a structural material, components and sometimes as a decorative finish.

Information concerning the properties of timbers is provided by the Building Research Establishment, formerly the Forest Products Research Laboratory, Princes Risborough, Buckinghamshire and the Timber Research and Development Association (TRADA), Hughenden Valley, High Wycombe, Buckinghamshire. The British Woodwork Manufacturers' Association (BWMA), Clareville House, Whitcomb Street, London WC2 is the national trade association of the joinery, timber engineering and woodworking industries.

References include:

Timber – its structure and properties, H. E. Desch, Macmillan
BS 565 : 1963 *Glossary of terms applicable to timber, plywood and joinery*

A handbook of softwoods FPRL (HMSO)
A handbook of hardwoods FPRL (HMSO)

CP 112 : 1971 *The structural use of timber*
BS 1186 : *Quality of timber and workmanship in joinery*

    Part 1 : 1971 *Quality of timber*
    Part 2 : 1971 *Quality of workmanship*

Selection of timbers

Selection of timber depends upon many factors, in particular:

    Appearance
    Strength, moisture movements and dimensional stability. Availability of species, sizes and sections. (This varies widely from place to place and time to time)
    For external uses: natural durability and ease of preservation
    Cost.

Information to aid selection of timbers is contained in table 14, which should be read in conjunction with *Strength properties* page 63; *Moisture movement* page 65; *Durability* page 80; *Preservation* page 84, and *Costs* page 87.

Hardwoods and softwoods

These are botanical terms and do not always relate to hardness. Thus, balsa is a hardwood, while yew, an extremely hard timber, is a softwood.

Hardwoods (angiosperms) are from broad-leaved trees most of which are deciduous, although holly, certain oaks and the majority of tropical trees are evergreens. Hardwoods include the densest (see figure 5), strongest (see table 16, page 63) and most durable timbers (see tables 14 and 25). Some hardwoods contain resins and/or oils which interfere with the hardening of paints and many such as teak and makoré include materials, eg silica, which make working difficult.

Cost varies considerably with the species, the cheaper hardwoods approximating in cost to the more costly softwoods. Cost also varies with dimensions. Narrow and short stock is less costly while extra long lengths, and in some species wide boards, are more costly.

Softwoods (gymnosperms) are all, for practical purposes, derived from coniferous trees which are mainly evergreens and grow chiefly in the Northern Temperate zone. Softwoods comprise about 75 per cent of the timber used in the UK although the number of genera is much smaller than the hardwoods. Examples with their Latin *genera*[2] and *species*, and BS 589 names (in bold type) include:

Pinus spp **pines**	**Redwood** / Red or yellow deal, Red pine / 'Red or 'yellow' / Norway 'fir' } imported **Scots pine** / Scots fir } home-grown	*Pinus sylvestris*
	American pitch pine / Longleaf pitch pine / Southern yellow pine	*Pinus palustris* and *Pinus elliottii*
	Yellow pine / **White pine** / Quebec pine / Weymouth pine	*Pinus strobus*
Abies spp **firs**	**Whitewood** / **Silver fir**	*Abies alba*
Picea spp **spruces**	**Whitewood**[1] / White deal / Norway spruce } imported from the Continent **European spruce** / Common spruce } home-grown	*Picea abies*
	Douglas 'fir' / British Columbian 'pine'	*Pseudotsuga taxifolia*
	Western red 'cedar'	*Thuja plicata*
	Parana 'pine'	*Araucaria angustifolia*
	Western hemlock	*Tsuga heterophylla*
	Larch, European, etc	*Larix spp*
	Cypress	*Cupressus spp*
	Yew	*Taxus baccata*
	Sequoia / Californian redwood	*Sequoia sempervirens*

[1] Often qualified by geographical origin.   [2] Colloquially *genera* are referred to as '*species*'

Nomenclature of timbers

The examples of softwoods given above show that the naming of timbers can be confusing. Douglas 'fir', also called British Columbian pine, is neither a fir nor a pine and similarly Parana 'pine', Scots 'fir' and Western red 'cedar' do not belong to the genera their names suggest. *Picea abies* and *Abies alba* are both called 'whitewood', while *Pinus sylvestris* and *Sequoia* are both sometimes called 'redwood'. There is no 'deal' as such, but *Picea abies* is called 'white deal' and *Pinus sylvestris* is called both 'red' and 'yellow deal'

British Standards 881 and 589: 1955 *Nomenclature of commercial timbers including sources of supply* give Latin, 'standard' and common names for hardwoods and softwoods respectively. Specification by British Standard names is recommended, and if it is desired to be doubly sure that the required timber is obtained, the Latin name should also be given. In addition, because the quality of timbers varies with locality of growth, and with the methods of conversion and selection employed by shippers, it is desirable to state their origin as well.

Anatomy of timber

The tree is a complex plant which uses salts from the soil and carbon dioxide from the air to manufacture food materials by the action of sunlight on chlorophyl in the leaves, and to do this the tree sometimes extends 90 m above the ground, thereby providing an excellent structural material.

The trunk (or bole) and branches grow outwards around a leading shoot by adding new rings of timber. Usually one ring is added each year, but as this is not always the case it is better to refer to the rings as *growth rings* rather than *annual rings*. The more rapid the growth, the

(continued on page 54)

Colour (1)	BS name	Latin name	Hardwood (H) or Softwood (S) / density (2)	Origin	Natural durability (3) / Resistance to impregnation with preservatives (4)	Texture
WHITE	Ash	*Fraxinus excelsior*	H/h	Europe	P/M	Coarse
	Birch	*Betula spp*	H/h	Europe	P/P	Fine
	Maple rock,	*Acer saccharum*	H/h	Canada and USA	N/R	Fine
	Obeche/ Wawa	*Triplochiton scleroxylon*	H/l	W Africa	N/R*	Medium
	Sycamore	*Acer pseudo-platanus*	H/m	Europe	P/P	Fine
	Whitewood/ European spruce	*Picea abies*	S/l	Europe	N/R	Fine
yellowish	Afara/Limba	*Terminalia superba*	H/m	W Africa	N/M	Medium
	Avodiré	*Turraeanthus africanus*	H/m	W Africa	N/Ex	Medium
	Ramin/ Melawis	*Gonystylus spp*	H/h	Sarawak and Malaya	N/P	Medium
	Western white pine	*Pinus monticola*	S/l	Canada and USA	N/M	Fine
BROWN	Abura	*Mitragyna ciliata*	H/m	W Africa	N/M*	Medium/fine
light	Afrormosia	*Pericopsis elata*	H/h	W Africa	V/Ex	Medium/fine

Table 14   Properties of some common timbers classified by colour

rking properties (5)	Uses (6)	Price range (7)	Remarks (1)
ood very good bending properties	Int J F V	Medium	Extremely tough and flexible; used for parallel bars; in short supply.
ood good bending properties	Int J F Flg V P l/P	Low	Small logs only therefore mainly used for plywood.
edium good bending properties	Int J Flg V P h/P h/I	Medium	Good resistance to abrasion; may show colour markings.
ood	P	Low	Rather too soft for joinery subject to wear; not suitable in damp conditions; sapwood sometimes highly susceptible to blue stain, pinhole borer and lyctus attack.
ood	Int J Flg V P	Medium	Some has attractive figure.
ood	Str Int J Flg (S2)	Low	Has natural lustre; liable to contain resin pockets and hard dead knots.
ood	Int J Flg V P l/P	Medium	Sapwood sometimes highly susceptible to blue stain, pinhole borers and lyctus attack.
edium	Int J F V	Medium	Quarter sawn wood often mottled.
edium	Int J F Flg n/P	Medium	Pale colour; subject to blue stain.
ood	Ext J Int J	High	Stable and suitable for good class joinery but exclusion of large knots involves high wastage; sometimes pinkish
edium/difficult	Int J F Flg l/P	Low	Variable in colour with a tendency to be pinkish
edium	Ext J Int J* F Flg V n/P	Medium/high	Similar to teak but is not oily; tends to darken on exposure and to corrode and be stained by iron.

– continued

45

Colour (1)	BS name	Latin name	Hardwood (H) or Softwood (S) / density (2)	Origin	Natural durability (3) / Resistance to impregnation with preservatives (4)	Texture
BROWN light continued	Agba	Gossweileroden-dron balsamiferum	H/m	W Africa	D/R	Medium
	Beech	Fagus spp	H/h	Europe and Japan	P/P	Fine
	Cedar – English	Cedrus spp	S/m	England	D/R‡	Fine
	Chestnut – sweet	Castanea sativa	H/m	Europe	D/Ex	Medium
	Elm	Ulmus spp	H/m	Europe, USA and Japan	N/M (Europe)	Medium
	Loliondo	Olea welwitshii	H/vh	E Africa	M/Ex	Medium/fine
	Oak	Quercus spp	H/h	Europe, America and Japan	D/Ex† (Europe/ America)	Coarse
	Olive – East African	Olea hochstetteri	H/vh	E Africa	M/–	Fine
	Tasmanian 'oak'	Eucalyptus spp	H/h	SE Australia	M/R	Coarse/mediu
	White seraya	Panashorea spp	H/m	Sabah	N/R or Ex	Medium
	Western hemlock	Tsuga heterophylla	S/m	Canada and USA	N/R	Medium/fine
	Yellow pine	Pinus strobus	S/l	E Canada	N/M†	Fine

Table 14   Properties of some common timbers classified by colour

rking properties (5)	Uses (6)	Price range (7)	Remarks (1)
ood	Ext J Int J* F Flg V P l/P	Medium	Appearance resembles light mahogany; has wide sapwood band; exudes gum and resinous odour sometimes present.
ood exceptionally good steam bending proper-ties	Int J F Flg V P h/P l/I	Medium – imported Low – home grown	Becomes pink when steamed.
ood	Int J F	Medium	Scented timber mainly used for moth-proof furniture linings; sometimes extremely knotty
ood good bending properties	Int J* F Flg V	Medium	Colour and texture resembles oak and it also corrodes and is stained by iron; but it is easier to work and has no silver grain; good grades in short supply
edium	Int J F Flg V	Low/medium	
ood/medium	F Flg h/P, l/I	Medium/high	Similar to East African olive (see below); highly resistant to abrasion
edium/difficult good bending properties	Ext J Int J F Flg V P h/P	Medium/high	Corrodes and is stained by iron; quarter sawn timber shows characteristic silver grain; sapwood sometimes highly susceptible to lyctus attack; Japanese oak is paler in colour and milder in texture
ifficult	Flg V h/I	Medium/high	Flooring equal to rock maple in resistance to heavy traffic.
edium	F Flg l/P	Medium/high	Resembles English oak, but is stronger in bending tougher and stiffer
edium	F Int J Flg l/P	Low	
ood	Str Int J* Flg (S2) l/P	Low	Widely used in UK for carcassing; moderately soft; excellent for staining or polishing but if incorrectly seasoned inclined to distort and to show grain.
ery good	patterns Int J	High	Excellent quality; sometimes pinkish; very stable, soft, even texture; suitable for carving and pattern making, but inferior grades mainly imported.

– continued

Colour (1)	BS name	Latin name	Hardwood (H) or Softwood (S) / density (2)	Origin	Natural durability (3) / Resistance to impregnation with preservatives (4)	Texture
BROWN light *continued*	Teak	*Tectona grandis*	H/h	Burma and Thailand	V/Ex	Coarse/mediu
yellowish	African 'walnut'	*Lovoa trichilioides*	H/m	W Africa	M/Ex	Medium
	Muhuhu	*Brachylaena hutchinsii*	H/vh	E Africa	V/R	Fine
reddish	Afzelia/ Doussié	*Afzelia africana and spp*	H/vh	W and E Africa	V/Ex	Coarse/mediu
	'Cedar' – Central and South American	*Cedrela spp*	H/m	Central and South America	D/Ex	Coarse/mediu
	Cherry	*Prunus avium*	H/m	Europe and Japan	M/M	Fine
	Danta	*Nesogordonia papaverifera*	H/h	W Africa	D/R	Medium
	Gedu nohor/ Edinam	*Entandrophragma angolense*	H/m	W Africa	M/Ex	Medium
	Guarea	*Guarea spp*	H/m	W Africa	D/Ex	Medium
	Apitong Gurjun/ Keruing Yang	*Dipterocarpus spp*	H/h	India, Malaya, Thailand and Philippines	M/R	Medium
	Kapur (Borneo camphor-wood)	*Dryobalanops spp*	H/h	Malaya Sabah	V/Ex	Medium
	Mahogany – African	*Khaya spp*	H/m	W Africa	M/Ex	Medium
	Mahogany – American	*Swietenia macrophylla*	H/m	Central and South America	D/Ex	Medium/fine

Table 14   Properties of some common timbers classified by colour

orking properties (5)	Uses (6)				Price range (7)	Remarks (1)
edium hard on cutting edges	Ext J	Int J* V	F P	Flg n/P	High/very high	Price varies considerably with size; contains oil; has stained masonry
edium	Ext J V	Int J	F	Flg l/P	Medium	Irregular dark tones tending to brown but colour fades.
ifficult		Flg h/I			Medium	Sapwood lighter colour; usually in short lengths
edium/difficult	Ext J	Int J*	Flg n/P		Medium	Similar performance to teak but rather heavier and harder; not easy to glue; exudes yellow dye when wet.
ood	Int J	F			Medium/high	Similar appearance and working properties to a softish Honduras mahogany; limited supplies.
edium	Int J	F	V		Medium	Chiefly used for high class work
ood		Flg h/P, l/I			Medium	Sometimes dark brown
edium	Int J	F	Flg l/P	V	Medium	Slightly inferior to sapele and utile
ood	Ext J V	Int J* P	F	Flg n/P	Medium	Of same type but less stable than mahogany; gum exudation may present difficulty in painting
edium	Ext J	Int J*	Flg h/P		Low	Exudes gum; difficult to paint.
edium	Ext J	Int J	Flg		Low	Stains in contact with iron
edium very poor bending properties	Ext J V	Int J P	F	Flg l/P	Medium	Wide differences between types in different areas; some woolly and have interlocking grain
ery good	Ext J Patterns	Int J	F	V	Very high	Becomes golden on exposure to sunlight; very stable; ideal for pattern making

–continued

Colour (1)	BS name	Latin name	Hardwood (H) or Softwood (S) / density (2)	Origin	Natural durability (3) / Resistance to impregnation with preservatives (4)	Texture
BROWN reddish *continued*	Plane	*Platanus acerifoia*	H/m	Europe	P/–	Fine
	Rhodesian 'teak'	*Baikiaea plurijuga*	H/vh	Rhodesia and Zambia	V/Ex	Fine
	Sapele	*Entandrophragma cylindricum*	H/m	W Africa	M/R	Medium/fine
	Utile	*Entandrophragma utile*	H/h	W Africa	D/Ex	Medium
pinkish	Douglas fir British Columbian pine	*Pseudotsuga taxifolia*	S/m	Canada and USA	M/R	Medium/fine
	Gaboon	*Aucoumea klaineana*	H/l	Equatorial Africa	N/M	Medium
	Niangon	*Tarrietia utilis*	H/h	W Africa	MD/R	Coarser than African mahogany
	Pitch pine	*Pinus palustris P caribaea and spp*	S/h	USA and Central America	M/M (P. caribaea) R (P. palustris)	Fine
	Scots pine/ Redwood	*Pinus sylvestris*	S/m	Europe	N/M	Fine
dark	American walnut (black walnut)	*Juglans nigra*	H/h	E USA and E Canada	D/Ex†	Rather coarse
	Ekki	*Lophira alata*	H/exh	W Africa	V/Ex	Coarse
	Iroko/ Mvule	*Chlorophora excelsa*	H/h	W Africa and E Africa	V/Ex	Medium
	Muninga	*Pterocarpus angolensis*	H/m	E Africa	V/R	Medium

Table 14   Properties of some common timbers classified by colour

rking properties (5)	Uses (6)	Price range (7)	Remarks (1)
ood	Int J V	Medium	Quarter sawn timber is known as 'lacewood'
ifficult	Flg	Medium	Sometimes marked with irregular black lines or flecks; sapwood pale in colour; Stains in contact with iron
ood	Ext J Int J F Flg V P n/P	Medium	An alternative to mahogany; has attractive stripe figure where quarter sawn
ood	Ext J Int J F Flg P n/P	Medium	Similar to sapele but straighter grained and more stable
ood	Str Ext J Int J Flg (S1) V P l/P	Medium	Clear grade; free from knots; gives excellent finish but inclined to show grain; corrodes iron; flooring should be rift sawn
edium	P	Low	Tones to light pinkish brown on exposure; low strength; fine sheen when sanded; rarely imported in the solid
edium	Str Int J F	Medium	Similar to African mahogany; sapwood is paler than heartwood; has a greasy feel
ood	Str Ext J Int J* Flg (S1)	Low/medium	Resinous; does not readily accept paint and inclined to show grain; in short supply
ood	Str Ext J Int J Flg (S2) P l/P	Low	Principal timber used in UK for joinery and cladding; knot free timber difficult to obtain
ood	F V	High	Sapwood light colour
fficult	Heavy construction Flg	Medium	Extremely heavy
edium/difficult	Ext J Int J Flg V P draining n/P boards	Medium	Initially lightish yellow; although not as strong as teak it is often used as a cheap substitute for that timber, calcareous deposits sometimes make it difficult to machine.
ood	Ext J Int J Flg V n/P	Medium	

– continued

Colour (1)	BS name	Latin name	Hardwood H (or) Softwood (S) / density (2)	Origin	Natural durability (3) / Resistance to impregnation with preservatives (4)	Texture
BROWN dark *continued*	Panga panga	*Millettia stuhlmannii*	H/vh	E Africa	V/Ex	Rather coarse
RED	Jarrah	*Eucalyptus marginata*	H/vh	S W Australia	D/Ex	Coarse/medium
	Makoré	*Tieghemella heckelii*	H/m	W Africa	V/Ex	Fine
	Meranti/Seraya	*Shorea spp*	H/m	Malaya and Sabah	M–D/R or Ex	Medium
Blood red to dark brown	Padauk	*Pterocarpus spp*	H/vh	W Africa Burma	V/Ex	Coarse/medium
			H/h	Andamans	V/M	
YELLOW	Idigbo	*Terminalia ivorensis*	H/m	W Africa	D/Ex	Medium
ORANGE	Opepe	*Nauclea diderrichii*	H/h	W Africa	V/M	Medium
VARIE-GATED COLOURS	Australian blackwood	*Acacia melanoxylon*	H/h	Australia	D/Ex	Medium
	Mansonia	*Mansonia altissima*	H/m	W Africa	V/Ex	Fine
	Rosewood	*Dalbergia* spp	H/vh	India and Honduras	V/–	Medium
	Walnut – European	*Juglans regia*	H/h	Europe	M/R	Medium

Table 14 Properties of some common timbers classified by colour

king properties (5)	Uses (6)				Price range (7)	Remarks (1)
ficult		Flg			Medium	Alternate bands of dark and light colour.
ficult	Ext J	Flg m/P	V		Medium	Pale sapwood fire resistant
edium/difficult dust sometimes irritant	Ext J V	Int J* P	F	Flg n/P	Medium	Corrodes iron
ood	Ext J	Int J l/P	Flg	P	Low/medium	Good general purpose joinery wood; apt to contain pin holes. Darker, heavier, harder, stronger and more durable material also available.
ficult	Ext J	Int J	F	V	High	
edium	Ext J V	Int J* l/P	F	Flg	Medium	Appearance resembles oak and is used in lieu, rather variable density and hardness; slight corrosive effect on metals stained by iron. Stains yellow in contact with water.
edium	Ext J	Int J n/P	Flg		Medium	Tendency to irregular grain not therefore suitable for small sections; darkens on exposure to rich orange-brown.
edium	Int J	V			High	Gold or red to dark brown with dark markings.
ood dust very irritant	Ext J	Int J l/P	Flg	V	Medium	Purple when fresh fading to light fawn on exposure.
ifficult	Int J	F	V		Very high	*Indian rosewood:* dull brown, purple, black. *American (Rio) rosewood:* handsome showy markings, bronze-black.
edium	Int J	F	V	P	High	Considerable variation in colour; greyish brown with darker markings; English walnut is the most beautiful; mainly used for veneers; solid timber therefore in short supply.

– continued

Colour (1)	BS name	Latin name	Hardwood (H) or Softwood (S) / density (2)	Origin	Natural durability (3) / Resistance to impregnation with preservatives (4)	Texture
VARIE-GATED COLOURS *continued*	Western red 'cedar'	*Thuja plicata*	S/l	Canada and USA	D/R	Coarse/mediu
	Parana 'pine'	*Araucaria angustifolia*	S/m	Brazil	N/M	Fine

(*1*) The *colours* given are approximations for newly cut heartwoods. They may vary from tree to tree and there may be wide variations within one tree. Colours change with exposure to light and all timbers become grey after exposure to the weather.

(*2*) *Densities* for seasoned timbers

	kg/m³		kg/m³
/l light	320–480	/vh very heavy	800–1040
/m medium	480–640	/exh exception-	
/h heavy	640–800	ally heavy	over 1040

(*3*) *Durabilities* relate to *heartwood* (see page 79): (sapwood of all species is non-durable or perishable)

V very durable   N non-durable
D durable   P perishable
M moderately durable

(*4*) *Resistance to impregnation with preservatives* (see page 84):

P permeable   ‡ sapwood permeable to
M moderately resistant   resistant
R resistant   † sapwood permeable
Ex extremely resistant   * often contain large
                 amounts of permeable
                 sapwood

The table is based on information provided by the Timber Research and Development Association and the British Woodwork Manufacturers' Association, BS 1186: 1971 '*Quality of timber and workman-ship in joinery* and the *Handbooks of Softwoods and Hardwoods* and Bulletin 40 *Timbers for Flooring* (Forest Products Research Laboratory, HMSO).

Table 14   Properties of some common timbers classified by colour

wider are the growth rings, and when trees of a particular species are compared, the wider the growth rings, the less dense and strong is the timber. These rings consist of minute tubular or fibrous *cells* tightly cemented together and each ring has two parts, the *early wood* or *springwood* and the *late wood* or *summerwood* which grows more slowly and is often denser, darker and narrower than the early wood (see figure 2). Timbers in which the early wood contains larger pores than the late wood are known as *ring porous* and those in which the pores are equal in size in both zones are called *diffuse porous*.

As most trees mature, for each new ring which is added forming a band of *sapwood*, reserve materials such as starch are extracted from an inner ring (or they are changed into more durable substances) and a *heartwood* core is formed. The band of sapwood varies widely in width from 25 to 152 mm, or more in some tropical hardwoods. Mechanically, there is no significant difference between sapwood and heartwood but in most species sapwood is lighter in colour and because it contains sugars, starch and water it is more attractive to fungi and certain insects. *Sap-stain* is sometimes a means of recognizing sapwood. See *Natural defects* below.

The term *grain* refers to the general direction or

rking properties (5)	Uses (6)	Price range (7)	Remarks (1)
od	Ext J Int J* cladding	Low/medium	Light pink to chocolate brown; extremely stable and resistant to decay; may be too soft for joinery; corrodes and is stained by iron; strength relatively low
od	Int J Flg P l/P	Low	Brown to bright red and dark streaks; Hard; gives smooth finish; nearly all free from knots; tends to warp if not correctly seasoned.

(5) *Working properties* include: nailing, planing, sawing and gluing.

(6) The *uses* listed are for suitable qualities of the respective species

Legend: Str   structural – CP 112 Species group in parenthesis

Ext J external joinery – sapwood must be treated with preservative or excluded; heartwood may require to be treated with preservative and/or painted, varnished etc. – (see page 84).

Int J internal joinery

Int J* internal joinery not including draining boards

F   furniture
Flg flooring –
    l/P – n/P – h/P: light/normal/ heavy-pedestrian traffic
    l/I – h/I: light/heavy-industrial traffic—see *MBC: C and F.*
V   veneers
P   plywood

(7) *Prices* are based on parcels of a normal fair average specification not less than $1 \cdot 5m^3$ 'ex yard' and should only be used as a guide. Classifications are:

'Low'	up to 1 unit
'Medium'	1 to 2 units
'high'	over 2 units

arrangement of the fibres and other wood elements (or cells) but the term is sometimes used to describe structural or ornamental features of the timber.

Natural defects

Natural defects may be described as features which develop in the tree or soon after it is felled and which may detract from the usefulness of the timber.

Other defects which occur at later stages are:
Conversion defects, see page 72
Seasoning defects, see page 68
Deterioration in use, see page 77.

For painted joinery it is often economical to remove defects such as dead knots and resin pockets and to replace them with plugs or patches. Building up members by lamination also tends to more economical use of timber which contains defects.

Brittleheart (soft-heart, spongy-heart or punky-heart)
This defect, found in the centre of many tropical trees, breaks with a brittle fracture. It can be detected by raising the grain with the point of a knife and should be avoided where strength is of importance. BS 1186 disallows soft-pith in surfaces which are to receive final decoration.

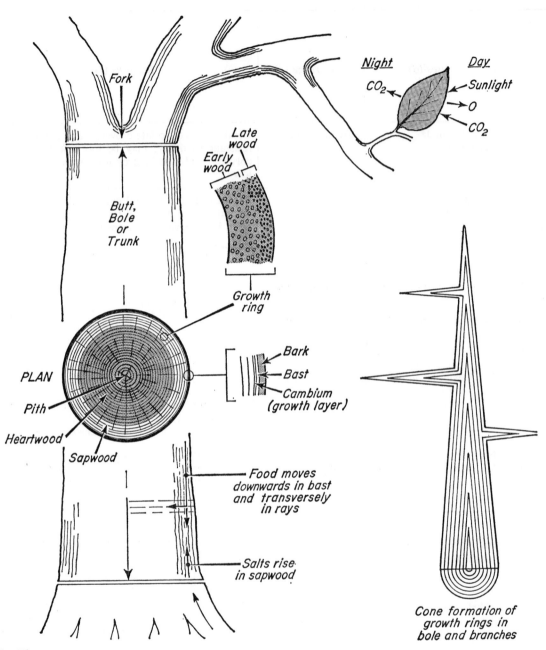

Night *Day*

CO_2 — Sunlight
— O
— CO_2

Fork

Late wood

Early wood

Butt, Bole or Trunk

Growth ring

Bark

Bast

Cambium (growth layer)

PLAN

Pith

Heartwood

Sapwood

Food moves downwards in bast and transversely in rays

Salts rise in sapwood

Cone formation of growth rings in bole and branches

2   The tree

Sapwood

Today most softwoods which are used in building come from trees which are immature and consequently have a high proportion of sapwood. Paint has proved to be an inadequate protection against fungi on sapwood in timber which is used externally and softwood must be treated with preservative. See *Preservation* page 84.

Sapwood is also more attractive to insects than heartwood and BS 1186: 1971, Part 1 *Quality of Timber in Joinery* does not allow sapwood in hardwoods other than beech and birch unless they have been treated against Lyctus beetles. See page 82.

Sapwood which is discoloured by fungi which live on the cell contents of freshly felled timber but which cannot survive in seasoned timber, see page 79 (eg *blueing* of softwood), is as strong as ordinary timber but takes up moisture more readily and thereby increases the risk of attack by destructive fungi, where timber is used in damp conditions. Internally, *sap-stain* is usually considered to spoil the appearance of unpainted joinery.

Wide growth rings

These indicate rapid growth resulting in thin-walled fibres or a smaller proportion of the denser latewood, with consequent loss of density and strength. BS 1186 : Part 1 : 1971 requires at least eight growth rings per 25 mm (as measured in the prescribed manner), and CP 112 : 1971 contains requirements in respect of the softwood grades of structural timber.

Spiral grain

CP 112 : 1971 lays down a rule for the rejection of spiral grain, which makes structural timber liable to distortion in seasoning and unsuitable for squaring.

Reaction wood

This wood, which is denser and stronger than normal timber, counteracts gravity, wind or other forces which tend to bend the trunk or branches. Reaction wood has the effect of throwing the heart off-centre, although this may be corrected by later growth. In hardwoods reaction wood usually occurs on the side which is in tension and is known as *tension wood*, while in softwoods it usually forms on the compression side and is known as *compression wood*. Unlike normal timber, movement along the grain is high and especially where it is concentrated on one side of a thin piece it often causes distortion and splitting,

particularly during seasoning. Sawn surfaces have a woolly appearance and lead to difficulties in machining and finishing.

Upsets are fibres which have been damaged by shock or crushing during growth or in *felling*.

Checks and shakes, see figure 3.

These defects are fissures extending along the grain.

Checks are small surface splits usually caused by too rapid drying.

Splits extend from face to face.

Shakes comprising ring and heart shakes, are due to stresses in the standing tree, in felling or in seasoning. Heart shakes indicate the presence of incipient decay in trees which have reached or passed maturity.

BS 1186 does not allow splits or ring shakes in any joinery timber. It also limits the size of other shakes and of checks in joinery 'ordered as selected for staining', and in 'surfaces not intended to receive final decoration' respectively.

CP 112 limits the size of fissures in structural timber. See page 62.

Resin pockets These fissures which contain resin are not permitted by BS 1186, and CP 112 does not allow 'substantial exudations of pitch or resin from the faces of laminating grades'.

Rind galls are surface wounds which become enclosed in growth.

Burrs are swellings comprising highly contorted grain resulting from many undeveloped buds which form over a wound. In trees such as oak and walnut they are often exploited as decorative veneers.

Curl is a decorative effect revealed by skilful conversion of a crotch where fibres of a branch lock with those of a trunk.

Knots

A knot is the part of a branch which became enclosed in a growing tree. See figure 4.

Where the fibres of a branch are completely continuous with those of the tree a *live knot* results and where the fibres are continuous with those of the tree to the extent of at least three-quarters of its cross sectional perimeter the knot is *intergrown*. A *dead knot* has fibres intergrown with the surrounding wood to the extent of less than a quarter of the cross sectional perimeter and if it is more or

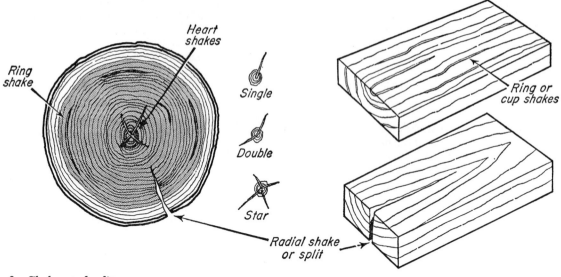

Ring shake

Heart shakes

Single

Double

Star

Ring or cup shakes

Radial shake or split

3 Shakes and splits

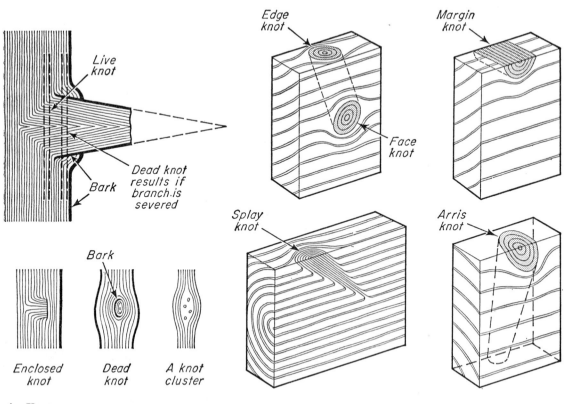

Live knot

Dead knot results if branch is severed

Bark

Edge knot

Face knot

Margin knot

Bark

Enclosed knot

Dead knot

A knot cluster

Splay knot

Arris knot

4 Knots

less surrounded with bark or resin it is an *encased knot*. Dead knots are sometimes *tight* but they are often *loose*. Knots attacked by fungus are termed *unsound* or *decayed*. An *enclosed knot* does not appear on the surface of timber. *Pin knots* are 6·7 mm or less in diameter. A *knot cluster* consists of two or more knots around which the wood fibres are deflected.

BS 1186 does not allow exposed decayed or dead knots in joinery, and because they are often considered to be unsightly, it does not allow any knots in surfaces which are ordered as 'selected for staining'. The standard allows only sound tight knots not more than 19 mm in diameter in the exposed surfaces of hardwood sills and limits the size of sound and tight knots and clusters in other surfaces.

Knots deflect grain and reduce the strength of timber, particularly in tension and particularly again, edge and arris knots. CP 112 : 1971 contains detailed rules for the maximum sizes of various types of knots in hardwood and softwood members and in laminated timber. Knots are hard, and cause uneven wear in flooring; they are difficult to work and in softwoods they often contain resin which must be sealed before the wood is painted. See *MBC: C and F*.

Fungal decay

Timber which is seriously affected must be rejected, but *dote*, an early stage of decay which shows as whitish streaks or patches (*pocket rot*), may be acceptable for timber which is to be painted or out of sight provided there is no softening of the fibres (*punk*).

Insect damage

Occasional exit holes of pinhole borers (see *Insects* page 83) are not generally regarded as defects in structural timber and they are acceptable in joinery which is to be painted or which is out of sight (BS 1186).

Chemical composition of wood

The walls of timber fibres are composed of cellulose and hemicelluloses and these are bonded together essentially by lignin.

Softwoods generally contain more lignin than hardwoods but otherwise the proportions of the constituents do not vary much from species to species.

> Average proportions in dry wood are:
> 45 to 60 per cent cellulose
> 10 to 25 per cent hemicelluloses
> 20 to 35 per cent lignin.

Minor constituents, which vary considerably in nature and amount from one species to another, are responsible for some of the characteristic features of different species. Thus, resins, tannins, alkaloids, turpentine and rosin colour timber. Starch in sapwood is attractive to fungi but tannins and other phenolic compounds in hardwoods, and oil infiltrates in Western red cedar, are toxic to insects and fungi.

Most woods are slightly acidic and produce acetic acid if stored in damp conditions. Timbers such as oak and Western red cedar contain tannic acid and thuyaplicins which corrode metals. Tannin in wood in contact with iron or iron compounds, particularly in damp conditions, causes dark stains. Gums and resins adversely affect working properties and ability to take glue and surface finishes, while silica in some hardwoods blunts tools.

Some woods contain colourless components which may become pink when acted upon by acids such as those which occur in synthetic resin glues used for adhering veneers.

Tannins and sugars in wood can inhibit the setting of Portland cement in the manufacture of wood-wool slabs (see chapter 3, page 98) or in lightweight concrete (see chapter 8, page 167) Phenolic substances in certain woods such as iroko and Brazilian rosewood have been found to prevent the hardening of polyester varnishes. Oily timbers such as teak may have to be degreased before gluing or before applying surface finishes.

PROPERTIES OF TIMBERS

Density

Table 14 classifies some timbers in respect of density, durability, resistance to impregnation and working properties.

The weight of wood tissue is about 1506 kg/m^3 for all species, but the densities of timbers vary widely. As shown in figure 5 most seasoned

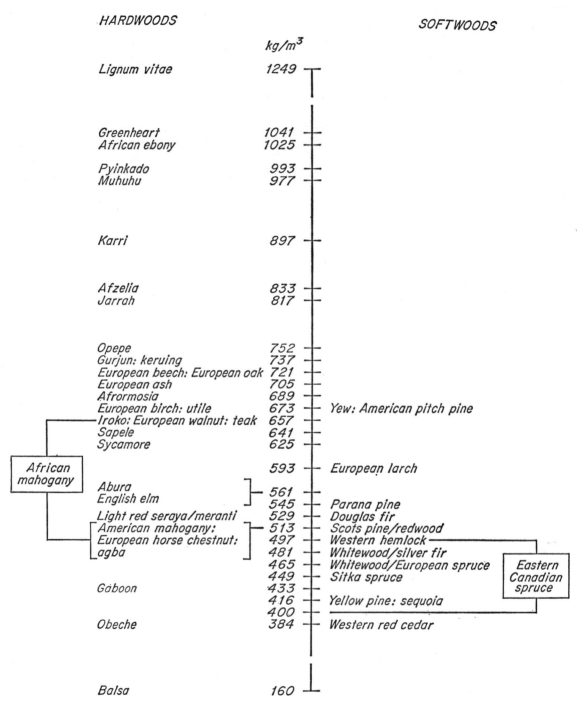

HARDWOODS
SOFTWOODS

kg/m³

Lignum vitae	1249
Greenheart	1041
African ebony	1025
Pyinkado	993
Muhuhu	977
Karri	897
Afzelia	833
Jarrah	817
Opepe	752
Gurjun: keruing	737
European beech: European oak	721
European ash	705
Afrormosia	689
European birch: utile	673	Yew: American pitch pine
Iroko: European walnut: teak	657
Sapele	641
Sycamore	625
	593	European larch
Abura	561
English elm	545	Parana pine
Light red seraya/meranti	529	Douglas fir
American mahogany:	513	Scots pine/redwood
European horse chestnut:	497	Western hemlock
agba	481	Whitewood/silver fir
	465	Whitewood/European spruce
	449	Sitka spruce
Gaboon	433
	416	Yellow pine: sequoia
	400
Obeche	384	Western red cedar
Balsa	160

African mahogany

Eastern Canadian spruce

5 *Average densities of common timbers at 15 per cent moisture content.* (Densities vary as much as 300 per cent largely due to differences in proportions of early wood and late wood)

timbers fall within the range 385–835 kg/m³ and are light in weight compared with stones (about 2082–3204 kg/m³ and common metals (2640–11 373 kg/m³).

Within the range of moisture contents 5 to 25 per cent, the weight of timbers varies approximately 0·5 per cent for every 1 per cent variation in moisture content.

Thermal insulation

Timber is a good insulator. Conductivity (k) is 0·144 W/m deg C and transmittance (U) for 102 mm thickness is about 1·19 W/m² deg C for timber weighing 481 kg/m³ with 20 per cent moisture content and for timber weighing 561 kg/m³ with 12 per cent moisture content.

Thermal movement

The coefficient is $30–60 \times 10^{-6}$ deg C across the fibres and about one tenth as much parallel to the fibres. Expansion joints are not normally required even in large structures.

Behaviour in fire

See Chapter 1, page 38.

Chemical resistance

A high cellulose and lignin content and a low hemicellulose content, low permeability, straight grain and small moisture movement contribute to good chemical resistance, criteria which are best met by softwoods such as sequoia, pitch pine, Douglas fir and southern cypress, and a few hardwoods including teak, iroko, purpleheart and greenheart.

Compared with metals, wood has good resistance to alkalis and weak acids. Sources of alkalis include casein and phenol formaldehyde glues while sources of acids include surplus hardeners in synthetic resin glues, hydrochloric acid arising from chlorine fumes in the damp conditions obtaining in swimming baths, and sulphurous acid from flue gases.

Ammonia turns oak brown, hence *fumed oak*, an effect which may be accidentally induced by the decomposition of animal glue.

Inorganic salts from soils or damp masonry, probably play a very minor role in the decomposition of wood.

Strength

Timber has a high strength : weight ratio both in tension and compression, and is elastic. It is able to sustain greater loads for a short while than it can over long periods so that in deriving working stress values from test results the rate of straining must be taken into account.

Generally, strength increases with density, particularly within a species. It reduces as moisture content rises and 1 deg C rise reduces strength about 0·3 per cent.

There is a wide variation between the strength properties of species, but also between trees of one species and between different parts of one tree. Defects, size and shape of specimens and type and distribution of loading also affect strength. Along the grain tensile strength may be two or three times the compressive strength while strength in tension along the grain may be as much as thirty times that across the grain:

CP 112 : 1971 *The Structural use of timber* contains *basic stresses*, derived from the results of tests on 'clear specimens' free from all visible defects for the unseasoned and 'dry' conditions. Stresses allowed by CP 112 are considerably higher for timber which has less than 18 per cent moisture content than for 'green' timber. See Table 16.

The Code defines grades designated *75*, *65*, *50* and *40* by the presence of visible defects and gives stresses which are appropriate in each case.

The Code also specifies three grades for laminating timbers and stresses which can be applied to Douglas fir and commercial hemlock which has been stress-graded in Canada.

For convenience in design, softwoods are placed in three groups for which the values given are necessarily based upon the weakest species in each group. The properties of hardwoods vary too widely to permit grouping.

Permissible stresses are also dependent upon the conditions of service and loading and can be found by multiplying grade stresses by *modification factors*.

Rules for visible 'defects' in each grade are given in Table 15 for the maximum sizes of various types of knots in various sizes of beams, compression and tension members respectively.

Knots disturb the normal pattern of grain and reduce most strength properties to a greater extent in tension than in compression, although they

Grade	Minimum number of growth rings per 25 mm[1]	Maximum slope of grain[1]	Maximum amount of wane expressed as a fraction of width of surface in which it occurs	Maximum size of fissures and resin pockets expressed as a fraction of the thickness of a member[2]
75	8	1 in 14	0·1	0·3
65	6	1 in 11	0·1	0·4
50	4	1 in 8	0·2	0·5
40	4	1 in 6	0·2	0·6

[1] Subject to rules for measurement.
[2] Deeper fissures are permitted outside the middle half of the depth of the end cross section and at a distance from the end equal to three times the depth of the piece for compression members.

Table 15   Rules for visible defects

may improve resistance to shear and splitting. Timber containing active infestation or showing fungal decay, brittleheart, spiral grain (as defined by the code), or other abnormal defects affecting strength is not permitted. Scattered pinholes, small occasional wormholes, and sapwood, including blue-stained sapwood, are acceptable.

In timber for laminated construction, there is no limit to the depth of fissures, but fissures having an angle of less than 45° with the wide face and those having substantial exudations of resin are not permissible.

Effects of variations in moisture content

Drying timber from the *green* to the normal seasoned condition reduces its density by 50 per cent or more with consequent shrinkage and increases in strength properties, thermal insulation, resistance to decay, and suitability for impregnation, painting and gluing.

Unless it is hermetically sealed on all sides, timber acquires a high moisture content when part of it is in contact with water or a damp material, but less obviously, being hygroscopic, it takes in or gives off moisture vapour until it reaches equilibrium with the humidity of the surrounding atmosphere. Temperature is relatively less important, at average relative humidities the moisture content of timber decreases only a few per cent between 16 and 38°C.

Equilibrium moisture contents for a typical species at various relative humidities at 16°C are shown in figure 8, and FPRL leaflet no. 47 (revised (March 1967).

The movement of timbers shows equilibrium moisture contents ranging from 9 per cent for African blackwood, to 14·5 per cent for South American cedar, where the relative humidity is 60 per cent and the temperature is 25°C.

Moisture content is expressed as the weight of water in timber as a percentage of the weight of the dry wood. Thus:

$$MC \text{ per cent} = \frac{\text{weight of specimen} - \text{dry weight of specimen}}{\text{dry weight of specimen}} \times 100$$

To determine a representative moisture content of a member, where possible a sample should be taken at least 325 mm from the end. It is carefully weighed, to obtain the 'wet' weight, and to obtain the 'dry' weight it is repeatedly dried and re-weighed until the weight remains constant. If carefully performed as described in BS 1860: Part 1 : 1959 the test is very accurate. More conveniently, but less accurately, a moisture meter can be used to measure the electrical resistance between two points in a piece of timber and its moisture content can be read off from a scale calibrated for the species being tested. Surface moisture may bear no relationship to the moisture content of the interior of a piece of timber and a

Softwood species Group	Name and origin	Density² kg/m³	Grade	Bending and tension parallel to grain N/mm²	Compression parallel to grain N/mm²	Compression perpendicular to grain N/mm²	Shear parallel to grain N/mm²	Modulus of elasticity Mean N/mm²	Modulus of elasticity Minimum N/mm²
S1	Douglas fir / Pitch pine (imported)	590 / 720	Basic	13·8 (17·20)	9·65 (13·1)	1·72 (2·48)	1·38 (1·52)	9000 (9660)	5000 (4820)
			75	10·3 (12·10)	7·23 (9·31)	1·52 (2·21)	1·03 (1·14)		
	Douglas fir / Larch (home-grown)	560 / 560	65	8·97 (10·30)	6·21 (7·58)	1·52 (2·21)	0·896 (0·965)		
			50	6·89 (7·93)	4·83 (5·52)	1·31 (1·93)	0·689 (0·758)		
			40	5·52 (6·20)	3·79 (4·49)	1·31 (1·93)	0·551 (0·620)		
S2	Western hemlock unmixed commercial (imported)	540	Basic	11·0 (13·8)	8·27 (11·00)	1·38 (2·07)	1·38 (1·52)	6900 (8270)	4100 (4490)
	Parana pine	530	75	8·27 (9·66)	6·21 (7·93)	1·17 (1·72)	1·03 (1·14)		
	Redwood	560	65	6·89 (7·93)	5·17 (6·56)	1·17 (1·72)	0·896 (0·966)		
	Whitewood¹	540	50	5·52 (6·21)	4·14 (4·83)	1·03 (1·52)	0·689 (0·758)		
	Canadian spruce	510	40	4·48 (5·17)	3·10 (3·79)	1·03 (1·52)	0·551 (0·620)		
	Scots pine (home-grown)	450 / 540							
S3	European spruce / Sitka spruce (home-grown)	380 / 400	Basic	7·58 (10·30)	5·52 (8·27)	1·03 (1·52)	0·966 (1·24)	5900 (6890)	3100 (3790)
			75	5·52 (6·56)	4·14 (5·17)	0·896 (1·31)	0·827 (0·896)		
	Western red cedar – imported	380	65	4·83 (5·52)	3·45 (4·14)	0·896 (1·31)	0·689 (0·758)		
			50	3·79 (4·49)	2·76 (3·10)	0·758 (1·10)	0·551 (0·620)		
			40	3·10 (3·45)	2·07 (2·41)	0·758 (1·10)	0·414 (0·448)		
	Greenheart (imported)	1060	Basic³	37·9 (41·4)	27·6 (30·3)	6·21 (9·30)	4·83 (5·52)	17 200 (18 600)	12 400 (13 400)
	Opepe	780		25·5 (31·0)	22·1 (24·8)	5·52 (8·27)	3·45 (4·14)	12 400 (13 800)	7 580 (9 300)
	Karri	930		22·1 (26·2)	16·5 (22·1)	4·83 (7·24)	2·48 (2·76)	13 800 (15 500)	8 270 (9 660)
	Afrormosia	720		22·1 (26·2)	15·9 (22·1)	4·14 (6·21)	2·62 (2·76)	10 300 (12 100)	6 890 (7 930)
	Teak	720		20·7 (23·4)	16·5 (22·1)	4·14 (6·21)	2·34 (2·62)	11 000 (12 100)	6 890 (7 930)
	Iroko	690		19·3 (23·4)	15·2 (19·3)	4·14 (6·21)	2·34 (2·62)	8 960 (10 300)	5 860 (6 890)
	Jarrah	910		19·3 (23·4)	15·9 (20·7)	4·14 (6·21)	2·34 (2·62)	10 300 (12 100)	6 890 (7 930)
	Sapele	690		17·2 (22·8)	15·9 (20·7)	4·14 (6·21)	2·34 (2·76)	9 660 (11 000)	6 210 (6 890)
	Gurjun/Keruing	720		13·8 (16·5)	13·8 (19·3)	3·10 (4·49)	2·34 (2·62)	12 400 (13 800)	8 270 (9 300)
	Abura	590		12·4 (15·2)	10·3 (13·8)	2·34 (3·45)	2·07 (2·41)	8 300 (9 300)	4 500 (4 830)
	African mahogany	590		12·4 (15·2)	9·66 (13·1)	2·07 (3·10)	1·72 (1·93)	7 930 (8 620)	4 140 (4 490)
	Red meranti/red seraya (home-grown)	540		12·4 (15·2)	9·66 (15·2)	1·79 (2·62)	1·52 (1·72)	7 580 (8 270)	4 140 (4 490)
	European ash	720		17·2 (22·8)	9·66 (15·2)	3·10 (4·49)	2·76 (3·10)	10 000 (11 400)	6 550 (7 240)
	European beech	720		17·2 (22·8)	9·66 (15·2)	3·10 (4·49)	2·76 (3·10)	10 000 (11 400)	6 550 (7 240)
	European oak	720		15·9 (20·7)	9·66 (15·2)	3·10 (4·49)	2·48 (3·10)	8 620 (9 660)	4 490 (5 170)

¹ Picea abies and Abies alba.   ² Densities are approximate and at a moisture content of 18 per cent.   ³ The 75, 65, 50 and 40 grades are omitted from this table.

Table 16 Stresses and moduli of elasticity for 'green' timbers having moisture content exceeding 18 per cent and for 'dry' timbers having moisture content not exceeding 18 per cent, given in parentheses (Information extracted from CP 112:1971)

meter equipped with points which penetrate to the core may be necessary.

Movements resulting from changes in moisture content

These movements referred to as *moisture movements*, (which could lead to confusion) are expressed as a percentage of original length or as movement per unit dimension.

As timber dries from the green condition, shrinkage starts when the cell walls begin to dry (*fibre saturation point*), a process which can be reversed by re-wetting the timber.

In some species radial movement is as little as half the tangential movement, while movement in the length of timber can generally be disregarded, although Parana pine containing reaction wood is an exception.

Average moisture movements of timbers for every 1 per cent variation in moisture content are:

Direction	mm per metre
Tangential	3·3
Radial	2·1
Longitudinal	0·8–1·7

Thus in typical conditions table tops in a well heated room would have a moisture content varying from about 14 per cent in the autumn to 10 per cent towards the end of winter and the seasonal movement would be:

tangentially cut $3·3 \times 4 = 13·2$ mm per metre
radially cut $2·1 \times 4 = 8·4$ mm per metre.

The FPR Laboratory uses the sums of the percentage radial and tangential movements resulting from a change in the relative humidity of air from 90 to 60 per cent, to group timbers into three broad classes:

Class 1 *Small movement* less than 3·0 per cent
Class 2 *Medium movement* between 3·0 and 4·5 per cent
Class 3 *Large movement* more than 4·5 per cent.

Table 17 shows the radial and tangential movements and the *combined movement classes* (T + R)

of some common timbers. (It will be seen that hardwoods are found in all classes but there are no softwoods in the *large movement* class.)

Stress setting

Where the movement of timber is restrained, either by compression or tension, it becomes set in sizes which are permanent for the particular combination of atmospheric humidity and temperature prevailing at the time of *stress setting*. Thus, unless the *permanent set* is relieved by steam treatment, subsequent movement of timber starts from the *stress set* size, and with any change in atmospheric humidity and temperature the final size is smaller for compression set timber, and larger for tension set timber, than it would otherwise have been. H E Desch illustrates the effect of compression setting by reference to the premature installation of seasoned timber in a 'wet' building. Thus where flooring strips, which have been dried to suit a centrally heated building are installed before the building has dried out they take up moisture; but having been cramped in position and nailed they cannot expand fully and become set in widths narrower than they would normally assume. When the building dries, the strips shrink as from the set size and their final width is less than it would have been if compression setting had not occurred.

Distortions

A small change of shape is often more objectionable than relatively large movements in all directions. Distortion can result from the application of external forces but we are concerned here with distortion which occurs because timber does not shrink equally in all directions when it dries – aggravated sometimes by defects such as knots or reaction wood.

W.C. Stevens[1] has shown that *cupping* of plain sawn boards and *diamonding* of squared timber (see figure 6) are mainly due to the excess of tangential shrinkage (in the direction of the growth rings) over radial shrinkage, and not upon the ratio of the two as has often been supposed.

Table 17 shows the difference between the tangential and radial movements in some common

[1] 'Distortion of timber' by W.C. Stevens MA, AMIMechE, *Wood* June 1946.

Movement of timber with relative humidity change from 90% down to 60% at 25°C +

Movement class	TIMBER	Tangential (T)	Radial (R)	T+R (Per cent)	T−R (Per cent)
CLASS I 'Small movement.' T+R less than 3.0%	Muninga	6	5	1·1	·1
	Western red cedar-imported SW	9	4·5	1·35	·45
	Afzelia SW	10	5	1·5	·5
	Iroko	10	5	1·5	·5
	Idigbo	10	6	1·6	·4
	Indian rosewood	10	7	1·7	·3
	Agba	13	6	1·9	·7
	Teak	12	7	1·9	·5
	Afrormosia	13	7	2·0	·6
	Obeche	12·5	8	2·05	·45
	European spruce (whitewood)	15	7	2·2	·8
	African walnut SW	13	9	2·2	·4
	Mahogany – Central American	13	10	2·3	·3
	Mahogany–African (Khaya ivorensis)]	15	9	2·4	·6
	Cedar–South American'	15	10	2·5	·5
	Balsa	20	6	2·6	1·4
	Yellow pine—home grown SW	18	9	2·7	·9
	Rhodesian 'teak'	16	10	2·6	·6
	Douglas fir SW	15	12	2·7	·3
	Western red cedar—home grown] SW	19	8	2·7	1·1
	Western hemlock SW	19	9	2·8	1·0
	Avodiré	18	10	2·8	·8
	Guarea	16	12	2·8	·4
	Makoré	16	11	2·9	·7
CLASS II 'Medium movement.' T+R 3·0– 4·5%	Utile	16	14	3·0	·2
	Ash (European)	18	13	3·1	·5
	Sapele	18	13	3·1	·5
	Mahogany–African (Khaya grandifoliola)	18	13	3·1	·5
	Scots pine (redwood) SW	22	10	3·2	1·2
	Serbian spruce SW	23	13	3·6	1·0
	Pyinkado	21	15	3·6	·6
	European walnut	20	16	3·6	·4
	English elm	24	15	3·9	·9
	Keruing	25	15	4·0	1·0
	English oak	25	15	4·0	1·0
	Caribbean pitch pine SW	26	14	4·0	1·2
	Black poplar	28	12	4·0	1·6
	Sycamore	28	14	4·2	1·4
	Parana pine SW	25	17	4·2	·8
	Dahoma	28	15	4·3	1·3
	Jarrah	26	18	4·4	·8
CLASS III 'Large movement.' T+R more than 4·5%	Ramin	31	15	4·6	1·6
	Turkey oak	33	13	4·6	2·0
	East African olive	29	17	4·6	1·2
	Black wattle	35	12	4·7	2·3
	Yellow Canadian birch	25	22	4·7	·3
	Beech	32	17	4·9	1·5
	Japanese ash	35	15	5·0	2·0
	Gurjun	33	20	5·3	1·3

★ 1 mm per m. ≡ 0·1 per cent linear movement   * The more favourable radial-tangential values are shown in heavy type

+ The atmosphere relative humidity change approximates to the conditions to which air-seasoned wood is subjected when it is 'manufactured' and used in a house

SW Softwoods   Tangential (T)   Radial (R)

Table 17   Moisture movements of common timbers

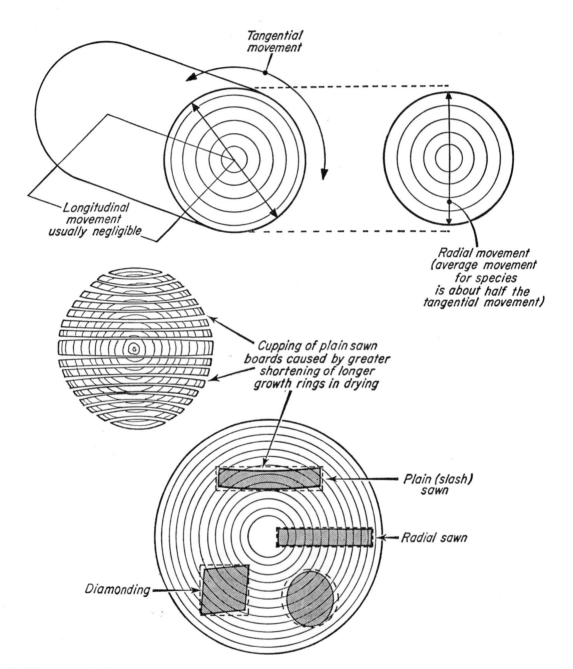

Tangential movement

Longitudinal movement usually negligible

Radial movement (average movement for species is about half the tangential movement)

Cupping of plain sawn boards caused by greater shortening of longer growth rings in drying

Plain (slash) sawn

Radial sawn

Diamonding

6   Movements in drying

timbers for a 90 to 60 per cent change in the relative humidity of the atmosphere and these figures can be taken as an index of the tendency to cupping of clear specimens. It will be seen that although the tangential and radial movements of yellow Canadian birch are large, the difference between them is small so the tendency to cupping is likely to be small with changes in moisture content.

Other distortions may be due to differential shrinkage or expansion in pieces of timber containing distorted or curved grain.

Spring and *bow* occur in the same direction as the curvature of grain in relation to the edges or faces of straight pieces and *twist* may result where spiral growth occurred in the tree. Twist may also occur in a plain sawn board which is not cut parallel to the heart of a tree. See figure 7.

UTILIZATION OF TIMBER

Minimization of changes in moisture content

Apart from obvious precautions such as the avoidance of unnecessary wetting of timber, changes in moisture content are minimized by (1) impregnation, (2) surface coatings and (3) seasoning.

1 *Impregnation* of timber with a solution of resin at present limited to small objects such as table knife handles.
2 *Surface coatings* Effectiveness in reducing the rate of intake or loss of water or water vapour varies widely as shown in table 18 but all external surfaces of general joinery should be at least primed with a 'pink' lead primer (BS 2521 : 1966). Sealing is particularly important on surfaces which will be in contact with construction before it has dried out and two full coats of aluminium based primer should be applied to all surfaces which will be in contact with external walls.
3 *Seasoning* is the controlled reduction of moisture content to a level appropriate to the end use, the advantages of which have been listed under *The effects of variations of moisture content* page 62.

Moisture contents for end uses

In traditional buildings a certain amount of shrinkage can be tolerated in carcassing timbers and

Treatment	Moisture content after 12 days in saturated atmosphere (95–100 per cent relative humidity) per cent
Untreated	28·4
2 coat surface applications:	
Nitrocellulose wood finish	23·9
Long oil phenolic/tung oil varnish	21·0
Short oil alkyd resin varnish	20·6
Chlorinated rubber modified alkyd resin medium oil varnish	16·3
Epoxy resin varnish	12·0
Hard heavy bituminous paint	8·2
Aluminium leaf wood primer	3·7
Normal 3 coat oil paintwork	8·0 approx.
Wax or other impregnants	18·2–24·9

Table 18   Moisture absorption of beech sapwood specimens after treatment with surface coatings and impregnants (Information derived from TDA Research report C/RR/2)

these are not normally fully seasoned to the moisture content they will assume in service. Movement of good class flooring, joinery and furniture, however can be serious. Ideally timber for such purposes should not be installed until the building is 'dry' and its moisture content should be the mean of the values it will have in use. If this is done movement will be limited to that occasioned by variations in the humidity of the air which surrounds it.

BRS Digest 99 (first series) *Light cladding* Part II June 1957 stated that the moisture content of timber in a well heated building is likely to be 15 per cent in the late autumn and 8 per cent in mid-winter and that an average seasonal movement of 13·3 mm per metre should be expected. Externally, moisture contents of 15 per cent in the summer (or 10 per cent in thin boards in very hot

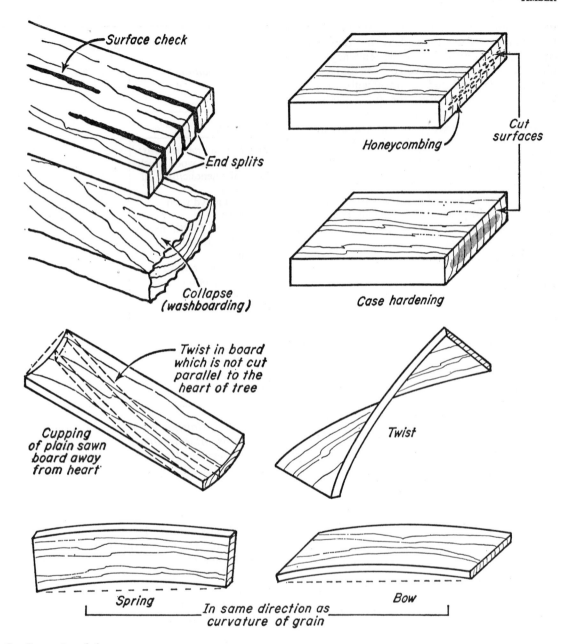

7 Seasoning defects

weather) and 22 per cent in the winter should be expected and an allowance of 17 mm per metre should be made for the large moisture content change.

Figure 8 recommends moisture contents for various uses with the approximate equivalent relative humidities of air at 16°C based on information contained in CP 112 *Structural use of timber*; FPRL leaflet no. 9 (revised 1963) *The moisture content of timber in use* and on BS

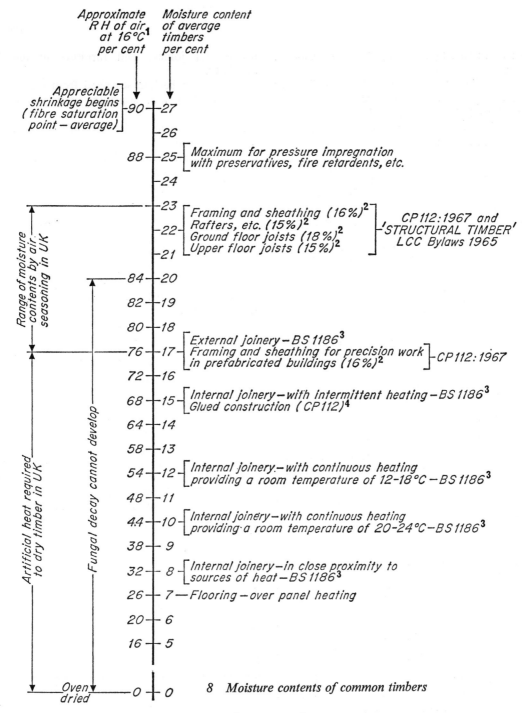

8 *Moisture contents of common timbers*

Approximate RH of air at 16°C [1] per cent / **Moisture content of average timbers per cent**

Appreciable shrinkage begins (fibre saturation point – average) — 90 — 27

— 26

88 — 25 — Maximum for pressure impregnation with preservatives, fire retardants, etc.

— 24

— 23 — Framing and sheathing (16%)[2]
— 22 — Rafters, etc. (15%)[2]
Ground floor joists (18%)[2]
— 21 — Upper floor joists (15%)[2] — CP 112:1967 and 'STRUCTURAL TIMBER' LCC Bylaws 1965

84 — 20

82 — 19

80 — 18

76 — 17 — External joinery – BS 1186[3]
Framing and sheathing for precision work in prefabricated buildings (16%)[2] — CP 112:1967

72 — 16

68 — 15 — Internal joinery – with intermittent heating – BS 1186[3]
Glued construction (CP 112)[4]

64 — 14

58 — 13

54 — 12 — Internal joinery – with continuous heating providing a room temperature of 12–18°C – BS 1186[3]

48 — 11

44 — 10 — Internal joinery – with continuous heating providing a room temperature of 20–24°C – BS 1186[3]

38 — 9

32 — 8 — Internal joinery – in close proximity to sources of heat – BS 1186[3]

26 — 7 — Flooring – over panel heating

20 — 6

16 — 5

Oven dried — 0 — 0

Range of moisture contents by air seasoning in UK

Artificial heat required to dry timber in UK

Fungal decay cannot develop

[1] The equivalent relative humidities of air are approximate for average species. See page 62.

[2] Approximate moisture contents attained in service.

[3] Values in BS 1186 : 1971 for joinery as manufactured and despatched from factory within ±2 per cent of the average equilibrium moisture content it is expected to attain in service.

[4] CP 112 *The structural use of timber* states – 'if the situation requires a moisture content lower than 15 per cent the timber should be seasoned to within 3 per cent of the average it will attain in service. Adjacent pieces in a joint must not differ by more than 6 per cent'.

1186 : 1971 : Part 1 (amended) *Quality of timber in joinery.*

The equilibrium moisture contents of different timbers vary at 60 per cent relative humidity from 9·5 to 15·0 per cent. Timbers with equilibrium moisture contents significantly lower than the average include:

Afzelia	9·5 per cent
Western red cedar (imported)	9·5 per cent
Loliondo	10 per cent
Muninga	10 per cent
Teak	10 per cent

For purposes such as interior joinery and hardwood flooring these timbers should be seasoned to slightly lower moisture contents than those generally recommended.

Methods of seasoning

If drying is too rapid the outer parts, in particular unprotected ends, shrink before the interior, surface checking and splitting results and ring and heart shakes may extend. In extreme cases the surface *case hardens* and the interior honeycombs or the timber *collapses* and becomes useless. See figure 7.

Some timber species are more difficult to season satisfactorily than others and those containing defects such as *reaction wood* are liable to distort.

Timber must be stacked, supported and sometimes restrained, so as to minimize distortion during seasoning.

Air seasoning

Timber is protected from rain and from the ground and stacked so that air can circulate freely around all surfaces and so that the risk of *degrade* and of attack by fungi and insects are minimized. In this country a moisture content of 17 to 23 per cent is usually attained with little risk of the process being too rapid except at the ends of timbers, and these can be protected. In favourable summer conditions, thin softwoods can be air-seasoned in weeks but in unfavourable conditions some hardwoods require a year or more.

Kiln seasoning

Figure 8 shows that artificial means of seasoning must be used to achieve the moisture contents needed for joinery and furniture in modern buildings.

Timber can be kiln seasoned from the 'green' condition, but kiln seasoning may follow air seasoning.

Adherence to a precise schedule of humidity and temperature enables any moisture content to be achieved without significant *degrade*. 25 mm hardwoods can be seasoned in days to months according to the species.

Water seasoning

This term is a misnomer for the process by which logs are kept under water to preserve them from attack by insects and fungi, and ring porous hardwoods are sometimes immersed in running water to wash out the sap which is attractive to Lyctus beetles.

Care of seasoned timber

It should be clearly understood that seasoning is a reversible process and its cost is wasted if timber gets wet on the site. Close piling and covering with tarpaulins delays the absorption of atmospheric moisture, particularly in the interior of a pile. If timber having 10 to 12 per cent moisture content, which is appropriate for a normally heated building, is installed before a building is dry it can well acquire a moisture content approaching 20 per cent. Hence, before delivery and installation of high class joinery, buildings should be glazed, if necessary dried by temporary heating, and tests on central heating should be completed.

Minimization of the effects of movements in service

Timber which has been seasoned will nevertheless respond to variations in atmospheric humidity. The advantages in the selection of a timber with relatively small moisture movement and to a lesser degree a small difference between radial and tangential movements, have already been considered. The juxtaposition of different species having widely varying movements is best avoided and the high cost of radially converted boards may be justified in some cases.

Generally, timber should not be restrained, and the drawing board with battens held by screws in slots, and tongued and grooved 'V' jointed boards are good examples of the application of this principle. 'Solid' timber table tops should always be fixed so that they are free to move. Tenons should be narrow so they do not loosen if they shrink, and similar traditional precautions should be adopted. Tangentially sawn members such as skirtings and cover moulds should be fixed so that they will 'cup' towards the wall or other rigid surface.

sawn boards and at right angles to the surfaces of radial sawn boards. Where the growth rings meet at an angle less than 45° on at least half of a surface, boards are known commercially as rift sawn in softwoods and quarter sawn in hardwoods.

Hardwoods are mainly converted by through and through cutting and figure 10 shows that this produces plain sawn boards (A) and others in

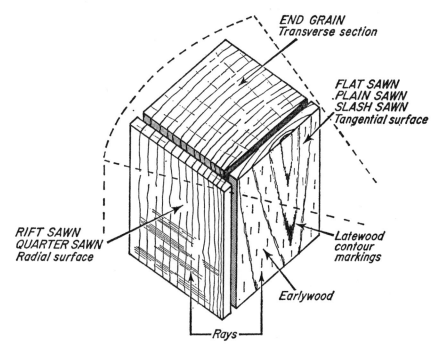

9   Surfaces of cut timber

Methods of conversion

The cutting of logs into sections before seasoning is known as *conversion*. Subsequent re-sawing and shaping is commonly called *manufacture*. Basic methods of cutting are *sawing*; *peeling* for producing plies for plywood; *slicing* of thin decorative veneers and *cleaving* or splitting, as used for palings.

Planed timber surfaces are said to be *wrought* (wrot).

Sawn timber

Figure 9 shows three ways in which the direction of the growth rings can relate to surfaces: ie, as *end grain*; more or less parallel to surfaces in *plain*

which parts remote from the heart can be said to be either commercially quarter sawn (B) or in the case of the centre board (or *crown plank*) truly quarter sawn (C).

Radially sawn boards shrink less in their width (see page 64) and are less liable to cup and twist; they are easier to season and wear more evenly than plain sawn boards. Unfortunately however, methods of cutting which produce a high proportion of quarter sawn timber are wasteful and the extra cost is justified only where the advantages are important.

Where the centre of the tree contains defects such as soft pith or heart shakes it is often cut out in one piece known as a *boxed heart*. An example is shown in figure 10.

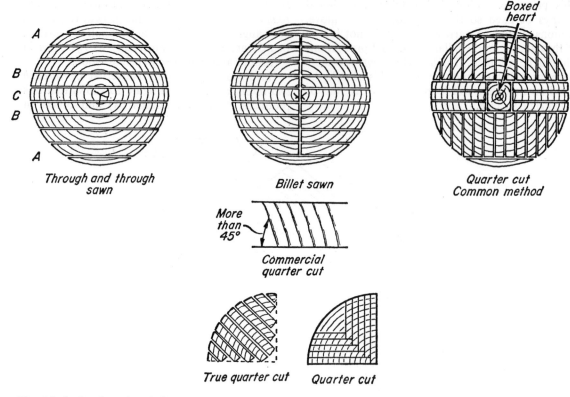

Through and through sawn

Billet sawn

Quarter cut
Common method

Boxed heart

More than 45°

Commercial quarter cut

True quarter cut   Quarter cut

10   *Methods of sawing timber*

Conversion defects

These include:

Wane which refers to the bark or rounded timber below the bark which results from over-economical conversion of softwood logs. Some wane is acceptable for structural timber (CP 112 : 1971),

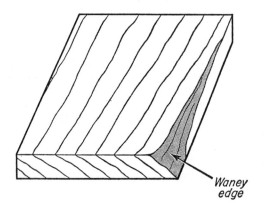

Waney edge

roof boarding and on the underside of floor boarding (BS 1297 : 1970).

Sloping grain

Because the tree is a cone-like form some slope of grain is bound to show relative to the surfaces of all converted timber and the familiar contour markings on flat sawn boards result. Pronounced slope of grain (diagram below) results from spiral growth or from conversion which is not parallel to the axis of the tree. BS 1186 limits the slope of grain with surfaces to 1 in 8 for hardwoods and 1 in 10 for softwoods. CP 112 : 1971 maxima for grades vary from 1 in 6 to 1 in 14 for hardwood and softwood and from 1 in 8 to 1 in 18 for laminated members.

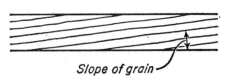

Slope of grain

Raised grain

Where plain sawn boards containing more than about 12 per cent moisture are machined the knives force the latewood bands into the early-wood bands. Later the compressed early wood recovers and raises the latewood above the surface.

Available sizes of timber

Commercially available sizes should be used wherever possible.

Sizes of softwoods

BS 4471 : 1971 *Dimensions for softwood (metric units)* specify basic ranges of metric sizes as at 20 per cent moisture content (see table 19) together with permitted reductions for manufacturing processes for various categories of products (see table 20) and for accurately dimensioned *precision timber*. Compared with the old range of imperial sizes (which continues to be imported from Canada) the metric sizes are up to about 5 per cent smaller. On the other hand the tolerances stipulated by BS 4471 are much tighter so that the modulus of section of the metric sections is not less.

Lengths Standard lengths are from 1·800 to 6·300 m in increments of 300 mm. Pieces more than about 5·100 m long are scarce and costly.

Permissible deviations on sizes as originally produced are:

	Minus mm	Plus mm	
Thicknesses and widths: not more than 100 mm more than 100 mm	1 2	3 6	on not more than 10 per cent of the pieces in any parcel.
Lengths	none	un-limited	

Re-sawing allowance Where smaller sizes are produced by resawing from larger sizes a maximum reduction of 2 mm is allowed on each piece. This reduction is not additional to the reductions allowed from basic sizes to finished sizes where two opposed faces are processed (see table 20).

Precision timber 'Precision sizes' are 1 mm less in width and thickness than basic sawn sizes produced by *regularizing*[1] on at least one face and one edge while the moisture content of the timber is between 14 and 18 per cent (18 per cent is the moisture content for *dry timber* permissible stresses in CP 112) The timber must be measured and supplied at the same moisture content.

Finished sizes Table 20 shows the maximum permitted reductions of sawn sizes by processing two opposed faces of various products where reductions are not specifically referred to in other British Standards.

Sizes of hardwoods

Where a large quantity is required, special sizes can be obtained from home grown or imported logs, but most hardwood is imported in the sawn condition in random widths and lengths as given in table 21.

Standard thicknesses are the same as those listed in BS 4471 for sawn softwoods, except that 36 and 40 mm thicknesses are omitted.

In certain species *strips* and *shorts* are cheaper than larger sizes.

Strips, in this context, are generally 25 × 75 to 140 mm wide and sometimes 25 × 51 to 140 mm wide in lengths of 1·8 m upwards. In some cases 32, 38 and 51 mm thicknesses are obtainable.

Shorts are lengths 0·9 to 1·7 m. Generally 25 × 75 mm and wider and 32, 38 and 51 mm thick are available in some species.

Grading of timber

Methods can be classified as *quality grading* and *stress grading* systems.

Quality grading

Quality grading is based on the appearance of pieces rather than upon their strength.

The traditional systems for marketing ordinary sawn timber are complicated, but basically either a *defect* or a *cutting system* is used.

---

[1] A machine process by which thicknesses and width are made uniform throughout the length of a rectangular section of timber.

Normal sources	Thickness[2]	Width[2]								
	mm	75	100	125	150	175	200	225	250	300
Europe	16	×	×	×	×					
	19	×	×	×	×					
	22	×	×	×	×					
	25	×	×	×	×	×	×	×	×	×
	32	×	×	×	×	×	×	×	×	×
	36[1]	×	×	×	×					
	38	×	×	×	×	×	×	×		
	40[1]	×	×	×	×	×	×	×		
	44	×	×	×	×	×	×	×	×	×
	50	×	×	×	×	×	×	×	×	×
	63		×	×	×	×	×	×		
	75		×	×	×	×	×	×	×	×
North and South America	100		×		×		×		×	×
	150				×		×			×
	200						×			
	250								×	
	300									×

[1] These thicknesses are unlikely to be available.

[2] The sizes given are for 20 per cent moisture content. For every 5 per cent additional moisture content up to 30 per cent sizes must be 1 per cent greater and for every 5 per cent moisture content less than 20 per cent sizes may be 1 per cent less.

Table 19 BS 4471 : 1969 Basic cross-sectional sizes of sawn softwoods at 20 per cent moisture content (Part 2 1971 describes smaller sizes)

Purpose	Sawn widths etc				
	15–22	more than 22–35	more than 35–100	more than 100–150	more than 150
Constructional timber-surfaced	2·5–3·5			4·5–5·5	
Floorings[1]				5·5–6·5	
Matchings and interlocking boards[1]	3·5–4·5				
Planed all round					
Trim	4·5–5·5		6·5–7·5		8·5–9·5
Joinery and cabinet work	6·5–7·5		8·5–9·5	10·5–11·5	12·5–13·5

[1] Reduction in width is overall the extreme size including any tongue or lap.

Table 20 Reductions of sawn softwood sizes to finished sizes by processing (planing) two opposed faces

Source	Imported condition	Species	Widths[1] mm	Lengths[2] m
West Africa	logs	various	559 min dia	3·7–9·1
	sawn		152 min min average 229	1·8 min min average 2·7
Malaya	sawn	keruing	152 min min average 178	1·8 min min average 3·7
		ramin meranti	152 min min average 229	1·8 min min average 2·7
Japan	sawn	oak elm maple	152 min	1·8 min
North America	sawn	oak	152–356	1·8–4·9
		Canadian yellow birch	152 min	2·4 min
		rock maple	102 min	1·8 min

Table 21   Sizes of hardwoods

[2] Lengths are measured to the nearest 100 mm.
[1] Widths are measured to the nearest centimetre.

Defects grading systems

Most softwoods are graded by exporters' *defects systems* which specify maximum sizes or degrees of defects for each grade in relation to the width and thickness of a board. Table 22 shows the approximate relationship between the grades of the main systems.

BS 1186:1971 *Quality of Timber in Joinery* (*Softwood and Hardwood*) defines permissible defects for *Class 1 S*—'*to be clear finished*', *Classes 1, 2* and *3* and for '*Concealed or semi-concealed surfaces*' BS 1186:1952 only that the following grades of softwood were suitable for joinery:

Redwood or whitewood	Swedish and Finnish	Better shipments of *unsorted*
	Polish	Best shipments of *unsorted*
	Russian	*Unsorted* White sea or Kara sea
Whitewood	Norwegian	Best shipments of *unsorted* planed boards
Douglas fir and		*Clear and door stock;*
Western hemlock	North American	*Select merchantable*
Sitka (silver spruce) and		*Clears* and *Select merchantable*
Western red cedar	North American	
Western white pine	North American	*1st, 2nd, 3rd;*
		Log run (*clears in, culls out*)
Parana pine	South American	*Prime* (80 per cent *first*, 20 per cent *second* export grade)

System	Grades and uses				
	I clear	*I*	*II*	*III*	*IV*
BS 3819 : 1964 *Grading rules for sawn home grown softwood*	joinery and high class structural work		general structural work and carcassing	general purposes where strength properties are not a primary requirement	
Norway, Sweden, Finland, Poland and Eastern Canada The rules are rather general and are interpreted differently by the various mills. Shipping marks indicate the quality and origin of each piece	—	*I II III IV* } sometimes marketed as unsorted (U/S)	often marketed as unsorted (U/S)	*V* the grade generally used for carcassing in this country	*VI Utskott* or *wracks*
USSR	—	*I, II, III* usually marketed as *Unsorted (U/S)*		*IV*	*V wracks*
Brazil (Parana pine)	*no. 1 no. 2*	—		—	—
British Columbia and Pacific Coast of North America (*R list*) Separate grading systems are employed for specific end products, eg door stock and flooring	*no. 1 clear* *no. 2 clear* *no. 3 clear* } usually sold as *no. 2 clear and better*	*Select merchantable*[1] *No. 1 merchantable*[1]		*No. 2 merchantable*[1] sometimes used for carcassing in this country	*No. 3 common*

[1] Sometimes sold as a grade with a percentage of the grade below.

Table 22   *Approximate equivalent Softwood Grades*

The 'cuttings' grading systems

Most hardwoods are graded by a *cuttings system* in which each grade must provide a minimum fraction of the total plank area as *acceptable cuttings* measured in rectangular units of 308 × 308 mm. Also the minimum number and size of *cuttings* is specified – depending on the size of a plank. High grades require few and large cuttings which add up to a high proportion of the total plank area.

There are three sets of hardwood grading rules applicable in the UK:

1 BS 4047 : 1966 *Grading rules for sawn home grown hardwood*

This standard describes:

Grades *1–4* under the *cutting system* and Grades *A–C* under the *defect system.*

2 The National Hardwood Lumber Association (NHLA) Rules.

These rules are widely used in North America. The main grades are: *First, Second, Select* and *nos 1 and 2 Common.* (Grades *3A* and *3B Common* and *Below grade* are not exported).

3 The Asia-Pacific Regional Grading Rules for sawn hardwoods – other than teak.

There are four basic grades: *Prime, Select, Standard* and *Serviceable,* the latter for local consumption only. Borer infested wood is graded under the defects system.

West African sawn hardwood grades are based on the higher NHLA grades and designated:

FAS (first and *second), No. 1 common* and *select)*
FAQ (fair average quality) for logs.

In practice the rules are used as a general guide only and business is transacted on the basis of mutual understanding between the vendor and purchaser.

Stress grading

Strength properties of timbers have been discussed on page 61. Because they vary considerably they have often been used 'wastefully'. Allowable stresses are allocated to individual pieces of timber on the basis of measured strengths for clear specimens of the same species and sizes, modified according to the presence of defects. Visual *stress grading* has been used to a very limited extent, but machine stress grading, which measures the modulus of elasticity of pieces and allocates appropriate allowable stresses, is very reliable and rapid and is likely to be used increasingly.

DETERIORATION OF TIMBER

In favourable conditions timber remains in good condition indefinitely but causes and effects of deterioration include the following:

Cause	Effect	
Fire	charring	
Mechanical: excessive loads	fracture	
abrasion	loss of surface	
erosion by rain, dust and sand	loss of surface	'weathering'
Water: flowing water	leaching of soluble colour erosion of surface	
wetting and drying	expansion and contraction causing mechanical failure in form of cracks	
Sunlight	fading of colour embrittlement of surface	
Chemicals: see page 61	discoloration complete disintegration	
Bacteria	superficial discoloration	'weathering'
Fungi: see page 78 (a) in moist conditions: moulds	superficial discoloration	
'dry rot' (*merulius lacrymans*)		
(b) in wet conditions microscopic rots	complete disintegration (in advanced stages)	
visible 'wet rots', eg, cellar fungus		
Marine borers, eg Teredo	tunnels	
Limnoria	tunnels (external)	
Insects: see page 81 Termites (not UK)	irregular honeycombing or wide channels	
Beetles	tunnels and exit holes	

Table 23   Causes and effects of deterioration

The causes of deterioration considered below are: weathering, fire, fungi, marine borers, insects.

Weathering

'Weathering' is an imprecise term used to describe the various effects resulting from the exposure of timber externally, the most obvious of which is loss of colour. All timbers become uniformly grey as a result of action of ultra-violet light and flowing water and are roughened by rain and wind-borne abrasives. Other effects may include colour changes caused by algae, moulds and chemical fumes, and cracks resulting from constant wetting and drying.

Fire

In fire the moisture in timber absorbs some heat but most species ignite at about 250 to 300°C and methane and other gases assist combustion. Later charcoal forms on the outside and this reduces the air supply to the timber and retards combustion. The rate of charring varies with density but for average species is about 1 mm per minute at 900 to 1200°C so that the fire endurance of a particular section can be predicted accordingly. Large solid sections and laminated timber sections survive longer in building fires than steel members of equivalent strength.

When standard steel and laminated timber roof beams were subjected to a standard time/temperature curve test the steel beam sagged within minutes and collapsed in 30 minutes while the timber beam had deformed only 57·2 mm and at mid-span 75 per cent of the original section remained undamaged.

All common timbers, with one exception, are in Class 3 *Spread of flame* when tested in accordance with BS 476 : 1971. The exception, Western red cedar, is in *Class 4*. The rate of spread of flame can be reduced by fire-retardant paints or by impregnating timber with fire-retardant chemicals which evolve an inert gas. On further heating, the chemicals melt, seal the cells of the wood and build up a more resistant form of charcoal.

Fungi

Fungi are simple plants without leaves or flowers, which consume 'ready-made' organic matter and therefore require no chlorophyll or sunlight. The spores (or seeds) are microscopically small but become visible in a mass as an extremely fine powder. They are produced in immense numbers and dispersed through air or sometimes by insects or animals. The hyphae which permeate wood are also minute and these are sometimes visible as masses of mycelium, although there are often no visible growths. Water is necessary for fungal growth but it is not true as has sometimes been stated, that repeated wetting and drying favour growth, in fact dry rot cannot live in such conditions.

Table 24 lists the four essentials for the growth

Requirements for growth	Means of denial
Suitable 'food', ie timber. In all species growth is more vigorous in sapwood than in heartwood.	Choice of heartwood only of 'durable' timber, see page 79 'Preservation of timber', see page 84
Suitable moisture content of timber At least 20 per cent moisture content is required for colonization although fungi cannot live in saturated conditions	Maintaining a low moisture content Ponding, ie submersion in water
Suitable temperature Optimum temperature is about 23°C. Growth is about twice as rapid at 21°C as at 10°C	Very high temperature (Few fungi can grow at a temperature above 38°C) Very low temperature (growth stops at about 0°C)
Oxygen	Seal timber eg, in metal. Ponding, ie submersion in water

Table 24   Requirements for growth of fungi

of fungi and means of denying them, the more generally practicable of which are underlined.

In eradicating wood-destroying fungi it must be appreciated that they can survive for long periods at very low temperatures and in dry conditions. For example dry rot can survive for about 12 months and wet rots up to seven and a half years in dry timber at 20°C.

Durability of timber

The term *durability* as applied to timber is synonymous with resistance to fungal attack.

The resistance of heartwood varies as much as 30 : 1 between the species but because the sapwood of all species has poor resistance, classifications usually relate to heartwood only. It is important to realise that by no means all *hardwoods* are *durable*, so that merely to specify *hardwood* without further qualification can result in *perishable* timbers such as birch, beech or ramin being supplied.

In order to classify timbers in respect of durability the Forest Products Research Laboratory places 50·8 × 50·8 × 609·6 mm heartwood specimens in soil leaving 228·6 mm above the ground and records their lives. See FPRL Record no. 30. Some classifications are given in table 25 and in table 14 page 44. They can be used to forecast the performance of timbers of the same species and size where they are used in contact with the ground in this country, and their relative durabilities where they are used in less severe conditions.

Types of fungi

The more important fungi can be classified as either:

(a) Non-destructive fungi or (b) Destructive fungi.

(a) Non-destructive fungi
Moulds There are many species of moulds which indicate that surfaces are damp but do not damage timber. The black or greenish powder can usually be brushed off when it is dry. A mould of the penicillium type which stains oak pale yellow, (hence *golden oak*) can grow at 43°C and may therefore present problems in seasoning.

Staining fungi These fungi feed mainly on the starch and sugar in sapwood cells but not on the cell walls, so that timber is not appreciably weakened. However, affected wood takes up moisture more readily and paint is sometimes pushed off external joinery. In softwoods *sap-stain* is usually grey-blue but other colours include blue, black, green, purple and pink, and more rarely brown.

(b) Destructive fungi or 'rots'
Each fungus has characteristic features and effects but in general, wood is often discoloured and shows softening (*brashness*) and serious loss of strength, even where the fungus is at the incipient stage of growth. Shrinkage may be apparent as waviness in painted surfaces and later as cracking. Decayed timber loses weight and may be attacked by species of insects which would not bore into sound wood. It is very absorptive and ignites more readily.

It is important to distinguish between *true dry rot* and the *wet rots. Dry Rot in Buildings. Recognition, prevention and cure* FPR Laboratory leaflet No. 6 (amended 1968) is a useful reference, (the leaflet also deals with wet rots).

Dry rot These fungi are by definition vigorous strand formers, represented in this country only by *Merulius lacrymans*. Dry rot usually spreads more extensively, causes more damage and is more difficult to eradicate than the wet rots. The optimum moisture content for the growth of both dry rot and wet rots is 30 to 40 per cent, but unlike wet rots dry rot cannot colonize very damp wood. It is generally found in timber which has been slowly moistened, often by contact with damp brickwork, and in very stable conditions, but very rarely out of doors. It is killed at 40°C sustained for 15 minutes. The maximum temperature for growth is 26°C, the optimum is 23°C and below 3°C it remains inactive.

When growing actively, in damp conditions cotton-wool-like masses develop. In drier conditions a grey skin with occasional patches of yellow or lilac forms.

Colonization of timber is by minute *hyphae* and these can spread over surfaces and through minute cracks in brickwork, plaster and other materials which provide no nourishment. The *strands* which are grey and vary from thread to pencil thickness convey nutrient materials which support the hyphae in colonizing suitably moist

Classification	Hardwoods	Softwoods
Very durable more than 25 years	Afrormosia Afzelia Guarea Greenheart Iroko Jarrah Makoré Muninga Opepe Purpleheart Pyinkado Teak	
Durable 15–25 years	Agba Chestnut, sweet Idigbo Mahogany, American Meranti, red Muhimbi Oak, European Utile	Western red cedar Yew Sequoia (Californian redwood)
Moderately durable 10–15 years	African walnut Avodiré Ayan Dahoma Gurjun, Indian Keruing, Malayan Mahogany, African Oak, Turkey Walnut, European	Douglas fir Larch, European and Japanese Pine, Caribbean pitch Pine, maritime Sequoia (home grown) Western red cedar (home grown)
Non-durable 5–10 years	Elm, Dutch Elm, English Elm, Wych Oak, American red Obeche 'Silver beech' Seraya, white Sterculia, yellow	Douglas fir (home grown) Fir, balsam Fir, grand (home grown) Fir, silver (home grown) Hemlock, western Pine, Scots (home grown)]1 Redwood (imported) Spruce, Eastern Canadian Spruce, European Spruce, Sitka (home grown) Whitewood
Perishable less than 5 years	Abura Alder, common Ash, European Balsa Beech, European Birch, European Birch, yellow Horse-chestnut, European Lime, European Plane, European Ramin Sycamore Willow, crack Willow, white	

[1] Pinus sylvestris.

Table 25   Durability classifications of heartwoods (All sapwood is either non-durable or perishable)
From Forest Products Research Record no. 30 *The Natural Durability of Timber 1959 (revised)*

timber. Occasionally the strands enable the hyphae to colonize nearby timber which would otherwise be dry but which is prevented from drying out to the atmosphere perhaps by gloss paint. Here the necessary moisture content is partly conveyed by the strands and partly synthethized by the fungus itself.

The *fruit bodies,* marked by wide shallow pores, carry minute rusty-red spores. Decay usually goes on out of sight but the *fruit body* tends to emerge into rooms in order to distribute its spores.

The presence of fungal decay may be detected by waviness in surfaces or by the softness of wood when it is prodded with a bradawl, but claims to identify dry rot by odour are of doubtful veracity.

Decayed wood is brown and divided by deep cracks both along and across the grain and the texture is dry and powdery.

Eradication of dry rot   In order of importance the operations are:

1 Eliminate all sources of moisture which are supporting the rot.
2 Dry out the timber and building thoroughly. If this is done rapidly and dry conditions continue, growth will cease but normally rapid drying cannot be obtained and it is necessary to trace and destroy all growths, which would otherwise continue to grow.
3 In addition to visibly infected wood about 300 to 500 mm of adjoining wood should be removed and burnt at once. With expert advice it may be possible to retain infected timber by boring holes at an angle to the grain and repeatedly filling them with preservative solution.
4 Non-combustible surfaces in the vicinity of the attack should be sterilized with a blowlamp, or better a brazing lamp, until they are too hot to touch. They should then be treated with a solution of 50 g sodium pentachlorophenate or sodium orthophenylphenate per litre of water. Any remaining sound timber should receive two or three coats of a preservative and new timber should be preserved, preferably by vacuum pressure methods.

Wet rots   Like dry rot, wet rots are most active in wood with a moisture content of 30 to 40 per cent and they can continue to develop in timber with a moisture content down to about 21 per cent. The most common wet rots found in buildings are:

Cellar fungus (Coniophora cerebella) Decayed wood often resembles wood attacked by dry rot but it is darker and where surface cracks occur across the grain they are usually shallower. Often, however, decay is internal without any visible growths and the fruiting body, which is a thin skin with small rounded lumps or pimples olive green in colour darkening with time to dull olive brown, is rarely found in buildings. The strands, which are never thicker than thin twine, usually darken to dark brown or almost black but they sometimes fail to darken where they occur under impervious floor coverings. *Paxillus panuoides* is similar to cellar fungus but it has paler coloured strands; yellowish or violet rather fibrous superficial growth and a small yellowish stalkless mushroom-like fruit body with gills on the underside. The wood is discoloured reddish-brown.

The rots so far described are *brown rots* which consume only the cellulose.

White rots break down both cellulose and lignin. The wood darkens at first but later becomes much lighter than normal, and 'lint-like'. When *white rot* occurs in patches it is known as *pocket rot.* Growth is usually external but *Phellinus megalaporous* (or *cryptarum*) has often caused serious damage to oak in old buildings.

Soft rot is caused by micro-fungi which grow slowly from the surfaces in wet conditions, on cooling towers, bases of oak posts and on marine structures. It is not always easy to distinguish superficial soft rot from *weathering.*

Eradication of wet rots   Defects giving rise to excess moisture must be corrected and the building must be dried. If the damp area can be dried rapidly it may only be necessary to replace seriously weakened timber and to treat lightly decayed timber with a combined fungicidal and insecticidal preparation. If rapid drying is not possible it is not necessary to sterilise brickwork or masonry but otherwise procedure should be as for dry rot.

Marine borers and insects

An excellent reference is *Insect and marine borer*

damage to timbers and woodwork, **J. D. Bletchley**, HMSO.

Marine borers

Marine borers such as *gribbles* (a crustacean) and *teredo* (a mollusc) do not live in fresh water but they are extremely destructive, particularly in warm salt waters. No timber is immune from attack but resistant species include ekki, greenheart, opepe, pyinkado, teak and totara (a softwood).

Wood-destroying insects

Termites (incorrectly called 'white ants' although like them they have a highly complex social organization) are extremely destructive in the tropics and a serious problem in many of the warmer temperate countries. Fortunately termites do not live in the UK.

In this country beetles are the chief pest, and they, together with wood wasps which sometimes emerge in buildings, are discussed below:

Beetles

In this country, unlike wood-destroying fungi, beetles rarely cause structural failure. They are not so dependent upon moisture as fungi, although dampness favours attack. Few timbers are immune but normally only sapwood is attacked.

The stages in the life of a typical wood-destroying beetle are:

1 Eggs are laid in cracks or crevices, or in the case of the *powder post beetle* in pores, not on polished or painted surfaces.
2 Eggs develop into *larvae* which are curved fleshy white grubs (*wood worms*) and enter the wood leaving holes too small to be seen with the unaided eye. They tunnel mainly in sapwood for one or more years leaving excreted *frass* behind them and are the main cause of damage to timber.
3 When fully grown the larva forms a chamber close to the surface of the wood, in which it becomes a *pupa*.
4 The pupa becomes a *beetle* and in the spring or summer 'eats' its way through the thin outer skin of timber (and sometimes emerges through paint, linoleum and even lead sheet) leaving an *exit* or *flight hole* which is usually the first indication of beetle activity.
5 The beetle may fly. Mating takes place within a few days. Beetles can be identified by:

(a) the beetle or larva – if available
(b) frass
(c) flight holes.

In this country the principal wood-destroying beetles in buildings are: (a) the common furniture beetle, (b) death watch beetle, (c) powder post beetle and (d) the house longhorn beetle.

(a) *The common furniture beetle* (*Anobium punctatum*) This beetle attacks softwoods and hardwoods and is responsible for most of the damage occasioned by beetles to structural timbers and joinery in buildings in this country. It was often found in plywood bonded with animal or vegetable glues, particularly birch and alder (modern plywood is immune), and also in wickerwork. The eggs are minute and being laid in batches of only two to four, in cracks or crevices, they cannot be detected. The larva remains in damp wood for up to three years, and longer in dry wood, leaving frass which has a sandy feel. The beetle is dusty brown to blackish brown in colour and 3 to 5 mm long. It leaves an exit hole approximately 2 mm in diameter and might be seen in the early summer flying, or crawling on surfaces.

(b) *Death watch beetle* (*Xestobium rufovillosum*) This beetle is mainly confined to large sections of hardwoods such as oak that have been softened by decay (in the south but rarely in Scotland). The larvae, which are similar to those of the furniture beetle but larger when fully grown, leave a frass containing bun-shaped pellets which are visible to the naked eye. The beetle which is brown to chocolate brown and mottled in colour about 8·5 mm long, leaves a larger hole than the furniture beetle. It attracts a mate by a rapid succession of tapping sounds, The life cycle is three years, and much longer in sound timber.

(c) *Powder post beetle* (*Lyctus brunneus*) This beetle attacks the sapwood of most hardwoods which have a high starch content and large pores in which the female can deposit her eggs. Starch content reduces with age and beech, birch and other fine-pored timbers are immune.

The bore dust is like flour to the touch. The

beetle which is reddish brown is about 4 to 5 mm long and leaves a flight hole about 1·6 mm in diameter.

(d) *House longhorn beetle* (*Hylotrupes bajulus*). The grub, which is up to 30 mm long, causes serious damage in the sapwood of seasoned softwoods, particularly in roof timbers. It is sometimes audible and bulging of timber surfaces often indicates the presence of tunnels near the surface. Frass takes the form of wood fragments and small cylinders of wood particles. The house longhorn beetle is black, 10 to 20 mm long, and leaves large oval shaped exit holes – usually far apart. The major diameter is 6·3 to 9·5 mm. The life cycle is 3 to 11 years, 6 years is a fair average. On the Continent the beetle is established as a very serious pest, but in this country it is mainly confined to the northern parts of Surrey where the Building Regulations 1972 require roof timbers to be treated with certain specified preservatives. Because the beetle could become the most serious wood-destroying pest here, any infestation should be reported to the Forest Products Research Laboratory at Princes Risborough.

Ptilinus pectinicornis This insect is less important than those so far described but is sometimes found with furniture beetles attacking hardwoods in outbuildings and in fine grained hardwood flooring such as maple. The beetle has interesting antennae, comb-like in the male and saw-like in the female, and the latter is unusual in that it bores tunnels in which to lay its eggs.

Ambrosia beetles (*pinhole and shot-hole borers*) These insects of the *Scolytidae* and *Platypodidae* families damage tropical trees soon after felling but do not persist in seasoned timber and damage is never of structural significance. The female beetle bores straight tunnels usually at right angles to the grain and in so doing introduces fungal spores. The larva does not tunnel (there is no frass), but feeds on the fungal growth which sometimes stains fair-sized areas of wood beyond the tunnels. Exit holes and tunnels are 0·5 to 3 mm in diameter. The smaller holes can usually be filled so they are not seen, even in polished timber.

Bark borers (*Ernobius mollis*) This beetle attacks the bark and the outer sapwood of softwoods. Its tunnels may be seen in waney edges of converted timber and sometimes beetles emerge through finished surfaces.

Weevils (*Pentarthrum and Euophryum spp*) Wood boring weevils are usually found attacking very damp and decayed wood. They are small, brownish and have a snout-like projection of the head. The damage resembles that of the common furniture beetle but tunnels are bored by both weevil and larva, they are smaller and the frass is darker and finer, containing pellets which are more nearly circular in shape. Flight holes are irregular and about 0·8 mm across.

Wood wasps

Female wasps of the *Sirex spp*, including the black and gold *Sirex gigas* which is up to 44·5 mm long, lay their eggs deeply in the wood beneath the bark of softwoods. They do not breed in buildings although they sometimes emerge from recently installed timber.

Eradication of wood-destroying insects

If it is not certain that an insect infestation is already extinct, treatment should be undertaken as soon as possible and if necessary it should be repeated after a few years and until no more exit holes or frass appear. Widespread infestation should be dealt with by specialists. Seriously attacked timbers should be removed and burnt and replaced with timber which has been treated to prevent attack. Timbers which are to remain in position should be liberally brushed or sprayed with a liquid insecticide and it should be fed generously into open joints, splits and shakes in order to kill eggs, newly hatched larvae and sometimes emerging beetles.

Surface applications also prevent further eggs being laid. Insecticide should be injected into exit holes to kill eggs which may have been laid there and larvae in the tunnels.

A woodworm fluid should contain one of the powerful chlorinated hydrocarbon insecticides such as dieldrin or gamma BHC in a penetrating organic solvent. Proprietary formulations also contain preservatives against fungal decay. Home made preparations are not recommended.

It is important to remember that insecticides may be injurious to humans and animals, and should not be tasted, inhaled or allowed to remain on the skin. Also, initially, they present a fire hazard.

PRESERVATION OF TIMBER

This section deals with the treatment of timber with toxic chemicals formulated to give permanent protection from attack by fungi and insects as distinct from the powerful eradicants already referred to.

Useful references are various Forest Products Research Laboratory leaflets CP 98 : 1964 *Preservative treatment of constructional timber* and BS 1282 : 1959 *Classification of wood preservatives and their methods of application.* Advice is also available from the British Wood Preserving Association, 6 Southampton Place, London WC 1.

Where timber will be damp in service, either an inherently durable timber, or a *non-durable* but preservative-treated timber must be used, and the latter often has a lower *cost-in-use.* Softwood telegraph poles which have been pressure impregnated with creosote often remain serviceable for more than sixty years, whereas untreated poles would survive for only a few years.

Table 27 recommends treatments for timbers in various conditions of service.

Under the Building Regulations 1972 the heartwood of the Western red cedar and Sequoia (Californian redwood) and of many hardwoods can be used in their natural state for external boarding but Douglas fir, Western hemlock, European and Japanese larce, Redwood (European) or Scots pine, Sitka spruce and Whitewood (or European spruce), Abura and Elm must be subject to prescribed preservative treatments additional to any protection which they may be given by paint.

FPRL Technical note 24, August 1967 states that Baltic redwood sapwood is liable to decay whenever it remains wet for an appreciable time, and windows, most of which are made in Baltic redwood, sometimes decay within 5 or 6 years. As it is generally neither practicable to use only heartwood, nor realistic to rely on good standards of building practice and of maintenance, the FPRL strongly recommend that all non-durable softwoods and hardwoods used for painted external joinery should receive preservative treatment. As the conditions here are not so severe as for timber in contact with the ground or for timber which is in the open and unpainted, 'it is believed that the lighter type of treatment such as immersion will give sufficient protection, although a higher factor of safety will be obtained from the heavier impregnation treatments'.

Protection of wood against insects is less necessary than against fungi, except where abnormal risks obtain, for example in the tropics, or in those areas of SE England in which the Building Regulations require softwood roof timbers to be protected against the house longhorn beetle.

Absorption of preservatives

Preservatives are only effective where they penetrate. They penetrate most readily into the end grain of timber and penetration is usually greater into quarter sawn than flat surfaces. Sapwood is nearly always easier to treat than heartwood. For example the sapwood of oak is *permeable* but the heartwood is extremely resistant to treatment.

Permeability of species varies widely and the Forest Products Research Laboratory places them in four classes and these are described in table 26 which includes some examples. It is impossible to force in any more liquid into wet timber so it is essential that its moisture content be reduced to 25 to 30 per cent before preservation treatment is attempted. Timber, particularly for surface treatment, must be surface dry and clean.

Treatment of plywood

Effective preservative treatment of plywood is possible if the wood is sufficiently permeable and provided the glue can withstand the temperature and moisture conditions during the process.

Methods of preservation

Processes vary from superficial treatments of limited protective value to pressure impregnation. As, however, complete penetration is rarely obtained even by pressure impregnation all work in cutting should be performed before treatment or where this is not practicable the exposed surfaces, especially end grain, should be dealt with as a separate operation.

Processes are now discussed in ascending order of effectiveness:

1 *Brush and spray*

The liquid should be flooded over surfaces so they absorb as much as possible. Externally,

	Heartwood	Sapwood
Permeable (P) may be completely pressure treated and heavily impregnated by the open tank method	beech (UK) birch (European)	Scots pine (UK) yellow pine (Canada) redwood (Russia, Finland) beech (UK) oak (European)
Moderately resistant (MR) fairly easily pressure impregnated to give 6 to 19 mm lateral penetration in approx 2 to 3 hours	Scots pine (UK) yellow pine (Canada) redwood (Russia, Finland) elm (UK)	Douglas fir (UK)
Resistant (R) difficult to pressure impregnate and require lengthy treatment. Often maximum penetration possible is 3 to 6 mm. Incising of surfaces may increase depth of treatment	Douglas fir (UK) Western red cedar (UK) spruce (UK)	Western red cedar (UK)
Extremely resistant (ER) absorb only a small amount after prolonged pressure treatment. Virtually impenetrable laterally	afrormosia (Ghana) mahogany (Uganda, Nigeria) oak (European) teak (Burma)	

Information from FPR Laboratory

Table 26   Absorption of preservatives

the treatment must be repeated every two or three years.

2 *Deluging, dipping and steeping*

Organic solvent type preservatives are usually employed but any preservative can be used. Preheating of suitable types assists penetration. Dipping should be for at least 10 seconds for very small sections; a 3-minute dip is often specified. Large sections should be dipped for 10 minutes or more. The Building Regulations 1965 require complete immersion for at least 10 minutes in certain specified preservatives as protection against house longhorn beetles in certain areas.

Deluging on a production line is usually equivalent to a short dip. Steeping of *permeable* timbers for several days may give quite deep penetration and protection sufficient even for timber which will be in contact with the ground. *Resistant* timbers however show only surface penetration even after several weeks.

3 *The hot-and-cold open tank method*

This simple method gives protection to sapwood and permeable heartwood comparable to that given by pressure impregnation but is usually confined to the treatment of fence posts. The timber is submerged in a tank of suitable preservative which is then heated to between 80 and 90°C and kept at that temperature for several hours. Absorption by the timber must then be allowed to take place as the liquid cools.

4 *Pressure impregnation*

This process provides the deepest penetration and is essential for long life of most timbers in direct contact with the ground, in sea water and

Conditions	Minimum durability classification of untreated timber	Preservative treatment for timber of any durability classification
Permanently 'dry' eg internal joinery	sapwood or heartwood of any timber	none required against fungi
Intermittent dampness: eg timber exposed to weather[1] or condensation 1 where it can redry rapidly, eg weather boarding	heartwood only of moderately durable timber[2]	brush or spray if repeated every few years dipping if subsequently brush or spray treated steeping
2 where rapid drying is not possible	heartwood only of durable or very durable timbers[2]	steeping or pressure impregnation
Permanent dampness: eg timber in contact with the ground or where dampness may arise by accident and the cost of repair would be high	heartwood only of very durable timbers[2]	pressure impregnation

[1] The only untreated timbers permitted by the Building Regulations 1965 for external wall cladding (whether painted or not) are hardwoods, Western red cedar and Californian redwood.

[2] These timbers may be difficult to obtain and more costly than timber treated with preservative.

Table 27   Practical application of durability data

in similar environments. The timber is sealed in a pressure vessel, air is removed under vacuum; preservative is forced in under strict control and a second vacuum stage removes excess liquid. More than two hundred specialized plants are available in this country. The process is described in BS 913:1954 *Pressure creosoting of timber* which requires all sapwood to be completely penetrated and the heartwood at least 6·35 mm. It states that before treatment, resistant timbers more than 76·2 mm thick, including Douglas fir, must be incised to a depth of 19·05 mm, the knife cuts to be 25·4 mm apart and in rows at 57·2 mm centres.

BS 4070:1966 *Wood preservation by means of water-borne copper/chrome/arsenic compositions* includes descriptions of composition of preservative and methods of application by vacuum/pressure or pressure impregnation.

5 *The diffusion process*

This is the only means by which certain water-borne preservatives can be introduced into green timber. After spraying or dipping in a concentrated boron salt solution the timber is close piled for several weeks during which the preservative diffuses into the timber. However the salts are water soluble and the process is unsuitable for timber which will be exposed externally.

Preservatives

In addition to penetrating well and protecting timber from attack by fungi and insects over long periods, preservatives may be required to be non-toxic to plants and animals, odourless, free from detrimental effects on adhesives, paints and polishes and generally they must not bleed or be washed out by rain. Water repellents in some preservatives reduce the movement of timber and its tendency to crack and allow water to enter leading to decay of the unprotected interior.

Care should be taken in using preservatives, eg goggles should be worn when applying them by spraying.

BS 1282:1959 *Classification of wood preserva-*

tives and their methods of application lists the following types:

TO Tar-oil types
> *TO 1*   Coal tar creosote BS 144 : 1954, for pressure impregnation
> *TO 2*   Coal tar creosote BS 3051 : 1958, for brush application.

Good creosote is a very effective and inexpensive preservative which is resistant to leaching and particularly suitable for use externally. Tar-oil types are not readily flammable and after a few months weathering they probably do not increase the fire hazard. They are not generally corrosive to metals. On the other hand they are difficult to paint over satisfactorily, and inclined to 'bleed' and to discolour adjacent porous materials. Its odour makes it unsuitable internally, especially near food, and the preservative may injure some forms of plant life.

OS   Organic solvent types
These consist of the following preservative substances in organic solvents:

> *OS 1*   chlorinated naphthalenes and other chlorinated hydrocarbons
> *OS 2*   (a) copper naphthenate (green in colour)
> (b) zinc naphthenate
> *OS 3*   pentachlorophenol and its derivatives or mixtures of organic solvent types.

Tri-butyl-tin oxide will doubtless be included in future revisions of the specification.

The organic solvents may be volatile or relatively non-volatile petroleum fractions. Specific insecticides and water repellant materials can be incorporated. Organic solvent preservatives do not corrode metals, they are suitable both internally and externally and penetration is superior to that of creosote; preserved timber can usually be painted when the volatile solvents have evaporated and the wood is then no more flammable than untreated wood. Some are colourless, although pigments may be added to indicate the extent of their penetration or for decorative purposes. Some have an odour which taints food. Although they are costly organic solvent preservatives are now being widely used for vacuum impregnation of mass produced external joinery.

WB   Water-borne types
These consist of the following preservative substances dissolved in water:

> *WB 1*   copper-chrome
> *WB 2*   copper-chrome-arsenic (the most commonly used type)
> *WB 3*   fluor-chrome-arsenate-dinitrophenol
> *WB 4*   others, eg copper sulphate, sodium fluoride, sodium pentachlorophenate, zinc chloride, organic mercurial derivatives.

Water-borne preservatives have the advantages that they can be over-painted, do not 'bleed' when they are dry, are odourless and non-combustible, but after treatment normal seasoning is necessary. Those containing two salts become insoluble in water. Apart from some of the *WB 4* class they are not corrosive. Water-borne preservatives are widely used for pressure impregnation and deep penetration is obtained in permeable timbers.

COSTS OF TIMBER

Relative cost of ranges are given in table 14. Approximate cost factors per volume of common timbers are:

		Cost factor per volume
Softwoods	carcassing	100–116 (according to lengths)
	joinery	
	Redwood	123 (average)
	Scandinavian *top grade*	135
	Parana pine	140
	Western red cedar	
	no 2 clear or better	160
	Douglas fir	
	no 2 clear or better	184
Hardwoods	25·4 mm thick	
	152 mm and up wide	
	fair average specification	
	Obeche	148
	Meranti	156
	Beech	160
	Agba	163
	Sapele	163
	West African mahogany	184
	African walnut	216
	Afrormosia	297
	Honduras mahogany	380
	Teak	575

Note: Prices vary from time to time, with quantities ordered and with delivery distances

3 Boards and slabs

Boards and slabs used in building include:

Asbestos boards, see chapter 10
Synthetic resin bonded laminates, see chapter 13
Cellular plastics boards, see chapter 13
Plasterboards, see *MBC: C and F*, chapter 13.

This chapter deals with:

1 Plywood
2 Blockboards and laminboards
3 Densified laminated wood
4 Particle boards
5 Fibre building boards
6 Wood-wool slabs
7 Compressed straw slabs.

These products vary from those with little strength which are used for wall linings and insulation, to boards and slabs which are suitable for flooring and roof decking supported on joists. It is becoming increasingly common to employ composite boards and slabs an example of which could comprise a strawslab core which provides thermal insulation, with enamelled asbestos-cement sheets bonded to each side providing ready-decorated weather-resistant surfaces. Such a stressed skin composite would have a high strength : weight ratio. Perforations in 'hard skins' can admit sound to be absorbed by a spongy core, although with some loss of sound insulation which necessitates mass as provided by lead-cored plywood, together with attention to detailing.

Table 28 gives the moduli of rupture of the common boards and slabs.

COSTS

Table 29 gives price factors for typical products as a rough guide to relative costs only.

	N/mm^2
Wood-wool slab	0·34–1·72
Fibre insulating board	1·03–3·45
Plasterboard	1·38–11·03
Chipboard	2·76–8·96
Medium fibreboard	5·55–17·24
Asbestos wallboard	10·34–20·68
Plywood	10·34–137·89
Asbestos wood	17·24–27·58
Asbestos cement sheet (BS 690)	17·24–34·47
Standard hardboard	24·13–55·16
Tempered hardboard	27·58–55·16
Decorative laminated plastics sheet (BS 3794)	103·42–206·8

Table 28   Moduli of rupture of boards and slabs (approximate ranges)

	Cost factors (approximate)
Expanded polystyrene BS 3837	
Standard grade	
12·7 mm	100
19 mm	200
25·4 mm	212
Fire resisting grade	
12·7 mm	100
19 mm	266
25·4 mm	316

Plasterboards BS 1230	Lath or baseboard	Gypsum wallboard
9·5 mm	104 (132)	138 (142)
12·7 mm	140 (168)	140 (168)
	insulating grade in brackets	

Fibre building boards BS 1142	
Homogeneous fibre wallboards	
12·7 mm	145
Insulating boards	
12·7 mm:	
natural finish	158
paint finish	199
flameproof Class 1 – BS 476	278
19 mm:	
natural finish	268
paint finish	314

	Cost factors (approximate)
Hardboards	
6.4 mm standard	274
9.5 mm medium: interior	356
exterior	390
medium exterior	534
3.2 mm flameproofed Class 2-BS 476	170
3.2 mm tempered	173
3·2 enamelled	640
Softwood boards BS 1297	
152 mm wide PT and G and PE flooring 22·2 mm	419
Flaxboard	
12·7 mm	397
Chipboard BS 2604	
12·7 mm	500
Plywood	
Finnish birch grade **BB**	
12·7 mm: internal quality	575
external quality	595
Douglas fir	
12·7 mm external quality	514–745 according to face veneers
Asbestos boards	
Fully-compressed BS 4036	
3·2 mm	308
Semi-compressed BS 690	
6·4 mm	314
9·5 mm	480
12·7 mm	805
Asbestos 'wood' BS 3536	
9·5 mm	610
12·7 mm	826
Insulating boards BS 3536	
6·4 mm	582
50·8 mm *Wood-wool slabs* BS 1105	
standard density	333
high density	389
57 mm *Cellular plasterboard panels*	422
53 mm *Compressed straw slabs*	
plain	445
class 1 (BS 476) surfaces	
1 side	545
both sides	590

	Cost factors (approximate)
'Purlboard' (ICI)	
9·5 mm plasterboard on 12·7 mm foamed polyurethane 22·2 mm	841–1080 according to quantity
'Purldek' (ICI)	
4 mm plywood (WBP grade BB finish) on 19 mm foamed polyurethane with double polythene coated kraft paper vapour barrier 23·0 mm	1100
Blockboards BS 3444	
Finnish birch	
16 mm	851
19 mm	885
Beech	
16 mm	1000
19 mm	1100
Laminboard BS 3444	
Finnish birch	
16 mm	901
19 mm	1335
Gaboon	
16 mm	992
19 mm	1470
Ceramic wall tiles BS 1281	
152 × 152 mm cushion edged	
6·4 mm	
white glazed	1050
glossy or eggshell matt	1560
Veneers on boards with balancers on reverse	
Wood veneers	
16 mm: on plywood	1200–2200
on chipboard	1800
Decorative laminated sheets	3600
19 mm: on plywood	3600
12·7 mm: on chipboard	1800
Aluminium faced plywood	
12·7 mm: single sided	2860–3040
double sided	3680–3900

Table 29   Approximate cost factors for boards and slabs

Figure 11 shows typical plywoods, blockboard, laminboard and chipboard.

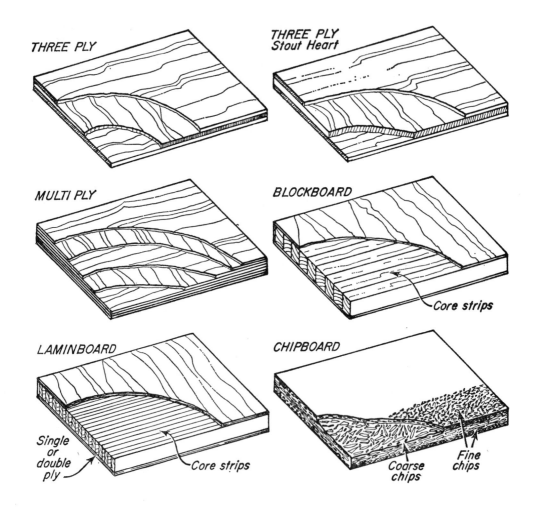

11 Typical plywood, laminboard, blockboard and chipboard

1 PLYWOOD

BS 565 : 1963[1] defines plywood as 'an assembled product made up of plies and adhesives the chief characteristic being the crossed plies which distribute the longitudinal wood strength'. BS 3493 : 1962 *Information about plywood* gives information about species, sizes, grades and bonding of plywood commonly available in the United Kingdom.

Plies are 'peeled' off a pre-boiled log by rotating it against a knife. The resulting grain pattern is perhaps less visually interesting than that of either plain sawn or quarter sawn timber.

Normally, the direction of the grain of each ply runs at right angles to that of the plies on each side so that strength properties are more uniform in the length and width of boards than in the case of 'solid' timber and moisture movement across the board is only about one tenth that in the width of plain sawn timber.

Plies are not always of equal thickness and the inner ply, or plies, can be of lower strength than those on each side, provided the strength and moisture movement properties on each side of the centre are 'balanced', from which it follows that there must always be an odd number of plies.

Plywood is stronger and stiffer than solid timber. It is difficult to split and can be nailed or screwed close to the edges and it offers high resistance to 'pull-through' of screw and nail heads.

Fire properties are essentially those of the timber which is used but plywood flooring provides rather better fire resistance than t and g boarding of the same thickness. The *spread of flame* rating under BS 476 is *Class 4* where the surface veneer is less than 400·46 kg/m^3, or is very thin. Most plywoods however achieve *Class 3* and suitable surface coatings and chemical impregnants bring plywood up to *Class 1*.

Woods commonly used in plywood are gaboon and Douglas fir of which gaboon requires filling but is the easier wood to paint. Makoré, sapele and utile are also easy to paint. Other woods include beech and birch.

Grading of face veneers

The grading of ordinary plywood refers only to

[1] BS 565 : 1963 *Glossary of terms relating to timber and woodwork*.

the quality of the face veneers and not to the type of adhesive or method of construction.

Manufacturing countries have different systems. Face and back veneers in British made plywood (BS 1455) are designated *1, 2* and *3*:

Grade 1 is normally used in its natural state. Firm smoothly cut veneer. When of more than one piece shall be well jointed and matched for colour. Slight discoloration is permitted but veneers must be free of knots, worm and beetle holes, splits, dote, glue stains or other defects. No end joints allowed.

Grade 2 is normally used where the surface is to be subsequently veneered or painted and is required to have a solid face free from open defects. When jointed, veneers need not match in colour or width. A few sound knots permitted together with occasional minor discoloration and slight glue stains, isolated pin-worm holes not along the plane of the veneer, and occasional splits not wider than 0·8 mm and of a maximum length of 1/10th panel. Neatly made, solid, level wood inlay repairs are allowed, but no end joints.

Grade 2/3 is intended for concrete formwork.

Grade 3 is normally used where it is not visible and may include wood defects excluded from Grades *1* and *2* in respect of number and size but which do not impair the serviceability of the plywood, and manufacturing defects such as rough cutting, gaps or splits, provided the use is unaffected. No end joints permitted.

Approximate equivalents are:

British	Canada and USA	Foreign
1/2	G 2S	A/B
2	G/S	B
3	Solid 2/S	BB
2/3	Solid 1/S	B/BB
3/3	C/C	—

Durability

Interior grade plywood is bonded with casein, soya, blood albumen and animal glues, or with synthetic resins extended with other substances (INT glues).

Exterior grade plywood is bonded with synthetic resin glues which, listed in ascending order of moisture resistance, include: urea, melamine, phenol and resorcinal formaldehydes (see *Adhesives*, chapter 14). For full external exposure glue should comply with BS 1203 : 1963 *Synthetic resin adhesives (phenolic and aminoplastic) for plywood* type *WBP* (water and boil proof). In addition to employing a durable glue, because durability depends upon the less durable component, where plywood will be in situations where it is liable to fungal or insect attack the wood must either be inherently *durable*, see chapter 2, page 79, or be protected with fungicides and insecticides. Thus, BS 1088 and 4079 : 1966 *Plywood for marine craft* includes: BS 1088 *Marine plywood manufactured from selected untreated tropical hardwoods* and BS 4079 *Plywood made for marine use and treated against attack by fungi or marine borers*. The latter gives a range of appropriate preservatives.

Types

In addition to the ordinary product plywoods are made in the following forms:

With 'decorative' veneers on both faces or on one face with a non-decorative balancing veneer on the other side. Decorative veneers may be single sheet, side matched, book matched or random matched. *Plywood planks* simulate natural wood planking in various ways and some have prefinished surfaces.

With etched and moulded surfaces provided by sand blasting or in some cases by a press which scorches parts of the surface.

Metal faced with galvanized steel, stainless steel, copper, aluminium and other metals. Where metal is applied to both faces and sealed at the edges plywood is protected from insects and fungi and has a very high strength : weight ratio.

Plastics faced boards are available with decorative surfaces and for concrete formwork.

Exterior grades are described in BS 1088 and 4079 : 1966 *Plywood for marine craft*. BS 1088 *Marine plywood manufactured from selected untreated tropical hardwoods* requires the wood to be at least *moderately durable*[1] with the exception of small proportions of clean, sound sapwood which is permitted. A WBP[2] adhesive must be used. BS 4079 describes *Plywood*

made for marine use and treated against attack by fungi and marine borers. BS 3842 : 1965 is entitled: *Treatment of plywood with preservatives*.

With tongued and grooved edges which provide perfect alignment at joints and dispense with the need for supporting noggings where the plywood is used for flooring, concrete formwork or wall and ceiling linings.

Lead cored for shielding against radio-active radiation or for sound insulation.

Sizes

Plywood is manufactured in many countries in a very wide range of sizes. Maximum sizes determined by the size of the press used are commonly 3048×1524 mm, occasionally 3099×1600 mm and much larger sizes are possible by scarfing joints.

Cross-grained plywood is made with the direction of the face grain across the width of the board, but in most plywood (known as *long-grain plywood*) the direction of the face grain is in the length of the board. In both cases the dimension first stated is that in the direction of the grain of the face plies. Thus dimensions are quoted as:

Long-grain boards – length × width
Cross-grain boards – width × length

Thicknesses range from 3 to 25 mm. (The thickness of USA and Canadian plywood is described in inches). Manufacturers' products vary in the number of plies in a given thickness. Because the greater the number of plies, the stronger, the more dimensionally stable and more expensive is the product, in specifying plywood both the number of plies and thickness should be stated.

2 BLOCKBOARD AND LAMINBOARD

These boards are shown in figure 11. Relevant BSs are:

BS 3444 : 1961 *Blockboard and Laminboard*
BS 3583 : 1963 *Information about blockboard and laminboard*

BLOCKBOARD varies in thickness from 12 to 43 mm and 38 to 48 mm in 'blanks for flush doors with a solid core consisting of blocks up to 25·4 mm wide, faced each side either with one thick veneer or two thinner veneers'. The grain in a

---

[1] Durability of heartwood see Chapter 2, page 80.
[2] Adhesives see Chapter 14, page 259.

single veneer runs at right angles to that of the core blocks so that a second veneer is necessary if the face grain is to run in the length of the board. They are available in sizes up to $1·651 \times 3·658$ m.

Blockboard is useful for large and rigid panels to receive veneers or paint, particularly in shop fittings and furniture.

LAMINBOARD is similar to blockboard but being freer from surface distortions and otherwise of superior quality it is an excellent base for high quality veneers or for enamel paint. The core strips are narrow (up to 7·1 mm) and unlike some blockboards they are continuously glued.

3 DENSIFIED LAMINATED WOOD

These high quality products comprise wood veneers, usually with the grain running in the same direction, hot-pressed and bonded with synthetic resin adhesives. There are two main types, *Impreg* and *Compreg*. In the case of *Impreg* the veneers are impregnated with resin before pressing. Very high temperatures and pressures are employed and the process imparts high density combined with a high strength: weight ratio; high resistance to abrasion, and to the effects of temperature and moisture, and *Impreg* is particularly suitable for engineering applications such as gear wheels and pulleys.

Hydulignum is an example of *Compreg* developed and manufactured by Hordern-Richmond Ltd which uses resorcinol formaldehyde adhesive. It has been used for stair treads, handrails, counter tops and bag rails in supermarkets.

4 PARTICLE BOARDS

Useful references are *Resin-bonded wood chipboard*, British Plastics Federation and *Particleboard in Buildings*, TRADA.

BS 1811: 1969 *Methods of test for wood chipboards and other particle boards* defines particle boards as 'boards made from particles of wood and/or other lignocellulosic material bonded with synthetic resin and/or other organic binder'. BS 2604: 1970 describes *Resin-bonded wood chipboards*, and the main non-timber particle board is made from flax shives. The usual ashesive is urea formaldehyde. Uses for particle boards include:

flooring, see *MBC: C and F* chapter 12.
roof decking
wall and ceiling linings
furniture
concrete formwork linings (boards must be sealed against absorption of water).

Sizes

Lengths: 1·8, 2·1, 2·4, 2·7, 3·0, 4·6 and 5·3 m
Widths: 0·6, 1·2, 1·5 and 1·7 m
Thicknesses: 8, 9, 10, 12, 14, 15, 18, 19, 22, 25, 31 and 40 mm
Common sizes are 2·4, 3·7 and 4·6 m $\times$ 1·2 m $\times$ 12 and 18 mm.

Types

Boards are either platen-pressed or extruded.

Platen-pressed boards

Most chipboards, and all flaxboards are pressed between heated platens, the particles being in random or criss-cross fashion, with their largest dimension parallel to the face of the board. There are three types:

1 *Single layer boards* strength properties are generally related to the density of the product.
2 *Graded density boards* have smooth high density surfaces and lower density cores. Strength is slightly lower than three layer boards.
3 *Three layer boards* are made from wood or flax with compact outer layers of flat particles usually 1 to 3 mm thick. They are reasonably strong provided the stressed skins are not cut, but they tend to delaminate.

Extruded boards

Extrusion between two parallel heated plates offers the advantages of continuous production and the ability to form thicker boards than are possible by means of platen pressing. However, the process causes most of the particles to be perpendicular to the surfaces and extruded boards are consequently much less strong in bending than platen pressed boards. The distribution of the particles also leads to much greater moisture movement, particularly in the direction of extrusion. Extruded boards are principally used as core stock for veneers.

Appearance

The surfaces of even the smoothest chipboards are pitted with minute voids which are unimportant if the board is to be veneered, but require filling if a smooth paint finish is required. Water paints swell the surface particles and accentuate their pattern.

Boards are available with sanded surfaces ready for painting and with agba, African mahogany and other wood veneers, plastics veneers, and with a flame retardant vermiculite surface.

Properties

Variations in the proportion of resin binder in wood chipboards do not cause any significant divergence from the properties of the wood particles.

Density

Wood chipboards:

high density	640–800 kg/m³ for applications where high strength is required, eg flooring
medium density	480–640 kg/m³ for panelling, furniture, shelving etc
low density	less than 480 kg/m³ for applications where strength is less important than thermal insulation or sound absorption.

(These are not BS classes.)

Flaxboards   448·5 to 512·6 kg/m³

Strength

Bending strength and rigidity of particle boards is much lower than that of most woods, blockboard and plywood. Generally, platen-pressed wood chipboards have higher bending strength but lower strength in tension than extruded boards and the strength of flaxboards is rather less than that of wood chipboards.

Strength and rigidity of typical platen-pressed wood chipboards relate to density as follows:

Density kg/m³	705	609	448
Bending strength N/mm²	14	14	5·5
Modulus of elasticity in bending N/mm²	2800	2100	825

There is progressive deformation (creep) and boards are seriously weakened in damp conditions. However, veneers increase stiffness and may well double the strength of particle boards.

Load-bearing uses of particle boards include flooring, roof decking and shelves.

Amendment 3 to BS 2604 specifies properties for flooring grades of chipboard. A minimum density of 640kg/m³ is necessary where 19 mm particle boards are used as floorings on joists at 406 mm centres. Large areas can be laid rapidly with few joints. Thickness of boards is accurate and tongued and grooved joints are available. The material is also suitable for stressed skin construction. Nailed and glued to timber joists economies can be obtained in timber sizes.

Supports for shelves must be more closely spaced than would be necessary for timber. Maximum allowable distributed loads on 18 mm, 600 kg/m³, simply supported, platen-pressed chipboard shelves are:

width mm	span mm		
	600	750	900
200	12·5	6·25	
300	18·75	9·5	5·25
500	32·35	16·0	9·25

Moisture movement

Like timber, particle boards are hygroscopic, especially at their edges, and they expand and contract with variations in moisture content. Some irreversible swelling occurs, particularly in the thickness of platen pressed boards and in the length of extruded boards. Veneers considerably reduce moisture movements but in extreme conditions the unprotected edges of extruded core boards may protrude from hardboard or plywood veneers.

Moisture movements, with 60 to 90 per cent change in relative humidity of the atmosphere, are of the following order:

	Extruded boards per cent	Platen-pressed boards per cent
length	up to 12·0	0·1–0·3
width	less than 1·0	0·1–0·3
thickness	slightly over 1·0	2·22–8·62

The moisture content of boards as manufactured is low, 8 to 12 per cent, but before fixing, boards should be conditioned for as long as possible with the heating on. Distortion is likely if:

1 boards are subjected to deforming stresses, especially when new
2 the humidity differs on the two sides, eg in the case of a door to an airing cupboard
3 the board is not 'balanced', eg is veneered on one side only.

Thermal conductivity

Thermal conductivity (k) is similar to that of wood of equal density, thus for platen-pressed wood chipboards:

kg/m^3	W/m deg C
705	0·14
609	0·12
448	0·07

Fire properties

Particle boards behave similarly to wood. They are combustible and *spread of flame* is *Class 3* (BS 476 : 1958) or with a surface of exfoliated vermiculite, *Class 1*.

Resistance to insects and fungi

Ordinary particle boards are attacked by termites, but not by insects in temperate climates. They are attacked by fungi and the Building Regulations 1972 do not permit the use of ordinary particle boards for the surfaces of external walls, even if they are painted. However, boards protected by insecticides and fungicides are available.

Machining

Working characteristics are more consistent than those of timber but cutting-tools are blunted more rapidly, particularly when used on the more dense particle boards, and *high-speed steel* cutting edges are advisable. Planing tears surfaces and if it is necessary to reduce the thickness of boards they should be sanded.

Jointing

Because there is no end grain, particle boards can be glued at any angle with tongues or dowels for location purposes. Water-based glues should not be used.

Screws hold best in the faces of single layer high density boards, but holding properties are inferior to those of solid timber and special double threaded screws should be used. Where the load is considerable wood plugs or nylon bushes should be glued in to receive screws.

Knock up and *knock down* fittings have been specially developed to form right angle joints.

5 FIBRE BUILDING BOARDS

BS 1142: 1961 and 1971 *Fibre building boards* describes these boards which are made from wood or other vegetable fibres. Information about them is obtainable from the Fibre Building Board Development Organization Ltd (FIDOR). The range extends from soft boards having good thermal insulation to boards having properties comparable with plywood.

To make *Insulating board* partially dried pulp is simply rolled to the required thickness and then reduced to the normal moisture content, bonding depends mainly upon felting of the fibres and upon their inherent adhesive properties. In the case of *Standard hardboards* the cut sheets are hydraulically hot-pressed and *Tempered hardboards* contain oils or resins.

Moisture movement

BS 1142 does not specify limits but gives typical figures for moisture movement related to environmental relative humidities as follows:

95

Type of board	Direction of measurement	Increase associated with change from 33 to 90 per cent rh RH	
		Max. per cent	Min. per cent
BS 1142: 1961 Insulating boards	crosswise lengthwise	0·37 0·37	0·22 0·20
Medium boards		0·40	—
BS 1142: 1971 Standard and Tempered hardboards	crosswise and lengthwise	0·35	

As with timber, it is important to condition fibre building board to suit the humidity of the environment in which it will be used, but here the moisture content of the factory product is low and in new and some existing buildings where humidity is high, it is necessary to increase the moisture content of the board, so that after fixing it will tighten on its fixings rather than expand and warp.

Sizes

At present standard sizes are based on imperial sizes and a module of 305 mm:

Lengths and widths	Widths	Lengths
305	1370	1830
405	1525	2135
610	1600	2440
915	1700	3050
1220		3660

Thicknesses (mm) of standard sizes and coordinated metric sizes are given in table 30.

Boards are available to special order in *coordinated metric sizes* (mm):

$$\left.\begin{array}{r}600\\900\\1200\end{array}\right\} \times \begin{array}{l}1800\\2400\\2700\\3000\end{array}$$

Described in order of increasing density the main types are: insulating fibreboards, wallboards and hardboards.

Insulating fibre building boards

Standard insulating board (softboard)

This is made from uncompressed wood, or sugar cane fibres, giving a low density (not more than 350 kg/m³) board with low thermal conductivity (k) not more than 0·06 W/m. The untreated board has a high rate of *surface spread of flame* (*Class 4 rapid*, BS 476) although this can be improved by impregnation, or by surface treatments, see table 13, page 37. Sound absorption is good but sound insulation is low, as may be expected of a low density product.

Board	2·0 2·5 3·2 4·8	6·4 9·0 9·5	10·0	12·0 12·7	13·0	16·0 19·0	25·0
Insulating boards Wallboards		√	√		√	√	√
Medium boards		√	√	√		√	
Standard and tempered hardboards	√	√	√	√			

Table 30   Common thicknesses of fibre building boards

13 mm thick boards can be bent to a radius of 1 m without special preparation. It is used as a sheet wall and ceiling lining material (the surface can be plastered), permanent shuttering to concrete and an underlay to floor coverings.

Bitumen-bonded insulating boards

These are made in multiple layers bonded together with bitumen. They have lower water vapour diffusance than standard insulating boards.

Bitumen impregnated boards

These have the same rate of water vapour diffusance as standard insulating boards, but reduced water absorption. Certain forms of insulating boards heavily impregnated with bitumen are used to fill gaps between concrete slabs and to support sealing mastic which is poured into the remaining space.

Special forms

Insulating fibreboards are also available in various special forms:

Paper faced.
Pulp faced A layer of ground wood pulp gives a light coloured and smooth textured finish.
Patterned with a coarse 'dimpled' pattern.
Decorated with a primer, a finishing coat or both.
Plastic faced.
Wood veneered.
Aluminium foil faced.
Acoustic boards These are low density boards perforated or grooved to give high sound absorption.
Flame-retardant boards Boards faced with asbestos felt, painted with flame-retardant paint or impregnated with a flame-retardant chemical have a lower rate of spread of flame, in some cases *Class 1*. See table 13, page 37.

Wallboards

Homogeneous fibre wallboard (or *building board*) is slightly denser than insulating boards (not more than 480·6 kg/m³) and thicknesses are normally 6·4 or 8·0 mm.

Production is small but uses include room linings and underlays for sheet floorings.

Medium boards and hardboards
Medium boards

Low density medium boards normally have density of 350–560 kg/m³, and high density boards, including *panelboard*, 560–800 kg/m³. Low density is suitable for 'pin-up boards'. As a wall or ceiling lining, or floor underlay, it is stronger and harder than insulating board, while providing better thermal insulation than standard hardboard. To condition medium board (and insulating board) they should be unpacked where they will be fixed, stored on edge for at least 24 hours, or preferably for 2 days, so as to allow air movement around the boards so that the moisture content of each sheet adjusts to the surrounding atmosphere.

Standard hardboard

This, generally made from wood fibres, has a minimum density of 800 kg/m³. In the ordinary product one side is smooth and the other usually has a mesh texture. Uses include wall and ceiling linings, flush door faces, floor underlays and many uses in joinery where plywood of similar thickness might otherwise be used.

Special forms of standard hardboards include:

perforated – pegboard linings for: suspending light objects, surfacing to acoustic materials and for ventilation
enamelled – various finishes, normally stoved
plastic paper laminate faced
PVC sheet faced
wood veneered
printed wood grains
moulded and embossed in the press – patterns include tiles, 'reeds', flutes, leather grain etc.
duo-faced – which is smooth on both sides
pre-primed and sealed
ivory faced – a layer of light coloured pulp is added to the surface
flame-retardant – impregnated after manufacture
bitumen impregnated.

Hardboard is despatched from the mill with a moisture content of between 5 and 8 per cent which is in equilibrium with an atmospheric relative humidity of about 65 per cent. It is recommended, particularly where boards will be used in damp surroundings, that 0·5 to 1·0 litres of water should be brushed on the back before fixing. Subsequent drying out tightens the board on its fixings.

Most hardboards can be curved without special preparation to a radius of about 300 mm. Radii of 200 mm can be obtained by cold/wet bending and 76 mm or less by hot/wet bending.

Tempered hardboard

This is generally made from wood fibres and has minimum density of 960 kg/m³. It is made by impregnating newly pressed standard hardboard with oils or resins and then applying further heat treatment. As a result it has superior resistance to water absorption and greater strength than standard hardboard. The texture is as for *standard hardboards* but the surface is harder. The colour is usually dark brown.

Uses include floor finishes, working surfaces, linings for concrete formwork and exterior uses. (*Tempered hardboard* is the only fibre building board acceptable for external wall claddings in the Building Regulations 1972.)

6 WOOD-WOOL SLABS

These are made of long wood shavings, coated with cement and compressed while leaving a high proportion of thermal insulating voids. Density is 400·5 to 480·6 kg/m³ and thermal conductivity (k) 0·093 W/m deg. C.

BS 1105 : 1963 describes *Unreinforced wood wool slabs up to 3 in. thick*. Although *combustible*, they are not readily ignited. Spread of flame is *low*, Class 1, BS 476. As roof decking the 51 mm thick slab can span joists at 610 mm centres or between the metal edges of *channel reinforced slabs*. Wood wool slabs can be used as permanent shuttering to concrete walls and soffits and they can be used for wall and ceiling linings. The open texture is a good base for plasters and renderings or the natural surface decorated by spraying with paint provides good sound absorption.

Slabs are 610 mm wide in various lengths and in thicknesses from 25·4 to 101·6 mm.

7 COMPRESSED STRAW SLABS

BS 4046 : 1972 describes *Compressed straw building slabs* which are known by the trade name *Stramit*. These consist of straw compacted only by heat and pressure, surfaced with, and bound at the edges with paper. The ordinary board has a density of 365 kg/m³, thermal conductivity (k) of 0·101 W/m deg C and *spread of flame* of *Class 3* (BS 476). Due to the method of manufacture strength is greatest across the width of boards. To support loads the largest gauge and length screw is recommended to be inserted into a pre-drilled hole into which glue is injected, or a proprietary fixing system can be used.

Compressed straw slabs for wall lining and partitions have a plaster liner paper facing to permit the direct application of *gypsum board plaster* or direct decoration. Such slabs can be butt jointed with adhesive or fixed in timber or metal sections, if required to be demountable. Slabs are available with integral service holes for electrical conduit. For lightweight thermal insulating roof decking, showerproof and pre-felted grades are available, to span over joists at 600 mm centres. Provision for ventilation of roof spaces should be made to CP 144 : Part 1 : 1968. Straw slabs lose strength and decay if they are damp in unventilated conditions.

Other products include slabs faced with:

Asbestos paper Fire retardant paint Class 1 hardboard Asbestos wall board	*Class 1 Spread of flame* (BS 476)
Asbestos wood	*Class 0 Spread of flame* (Building Regulations 1972)
PVC copolymer foil Hardboard	Vapour barrier surface

Sizes: The standard slab is 51 mm thick. Partition slabs are available 57 mm thick. The standard width is 1200 mm.

Standard lengths are:

> *Partitions*: 2200, 2300 and 2400 mm
> *Roof decking*: 1800, 2400, 2700, 3000 and 3600 mm

Slabs are easily cut but a cut to size service is available.

4 Stones

This chapter deals with the properties of the various types of stones, known to the geologist as *rocks*, and their uses in building, as blocks, slabs, flags, setts, roofing slates and damp-proof courses.

Other uses for stone mentioned in other chapters include:

1 Aggregate for concrete, terrazzo, plasters, tarmacadam, mastic asphalt, etc
2 Granules for surfacing bituminous felts, etc
3 Powders for filling paint
4 Abrasives.

Useful references are: *Stone for Building* by Hugh O'Neill, Heinemann, Limited and BS 2847: 1957 *Glossary of terms for stone used in building*.

Information is provided by the British Stone Federation, 37 Soho Square, London, W.1.

Cost

The cost of natural stone blocks and slabs is relatively high because great care must be taken not to damage stone in quarrying and because in stones such as slate there is a great deal of waste. Further, the cost of cutting, dressing and polishing is considerable, even with modern techniques, such as the flame cutting at 2760°C of granite and slate. However, the *cost in use* of slabs of economic dimensions may be considered to be reasonable if account is taken of their durability, appearance and of the fact that by cleaning, repolishing or if necessary reworking surfaces, their new appearance can usually be maintained.

Appearance

Natural stones usually retain their good appearance inside buildings. Externally if left to weather naturally, limestones usually improve in appearance and slate does sometimes, but granites and marbles seldom do.

The fact that no two blocks of stone are identical in appearance, even within one quarry, provides visual interest, but it means that even large samples can give only a general indication of colour, veining and texture.

The smoothness of materials determines the amount of light they reflect so that they darken when they are wet or polished and crystals, fossils, veins and other features become increasingly visible. For example, as quarried, Norwegian 'pearl' granites are almost indistinguishable from many featureless stones, but they become highly decorative when they are polished.

The principal descriptions of stone surfaces in increasing order of smoothness are:

Rock faced
Rough picked
Fair picked
Axed
Fine axed, dolly pointed; or flame textured (on granite and slate)
Sawn, slightly ribbed or rippled
Sanded or shot sawn
Gritted
Eggshell, honed; or fine rubbed (on slate)
Polished.

Split surfaces vary from very smooth to coarse in texture. The terms used are *riven* for slate, sandstone and quartzite and *knapped* for limestone and flints.

Great care must be taken to protect surfaces during building operations, even dense stones can be readily stained.

Properties

Some properties of natural stones are summarized in table 31. It will be seen that natural stones are strong in compression. The thermal coefficient of expansion of limestone and marble is low but allowance for thermal movement must be made with sandstone, slate and granite.

Durability

Natural stones are generally extremely durable but deterioration may result from:

Atmospheric pollution, soluble salt action, frost,

	Density kg/m³	Failing stress in compression N/mm³	Thermal movement mm/m per 90 deg C	Moisture movement mm/m for dry-wet change
Granites	2560–3200	105 335	approx. 0·93	none
Sandstones	2130 2750	27·5 195	approx. 1·0	approx. 0·7
Limestones	1950– 2400	16·5 42·5	approx. 0·25 (porous limestone) approx. 0·34 (dense limestone)	0·8 negligible
Slates	2800– 3040	42·5 216	approx. 0·93	negligible
Marbles	2880		approx. 0·34	negligible
Quartzites	2630			none

Table 31   Summary of properties of building stones

solution, wetting and drying, rusting of ferrous metals or sometimes from vegetation.

Atmospheric pollution   Sulphur compounds, mainly sulphur dioxide, formed by burning coal and oil, produce sulphurous acid when they are dissolved in rain water. This reacts with carbonates in limestones, dolomites, calcareous sandstones and mortars and where they are not freely washed by rain a hard glassy skin tends to break away and sometimes blisters form. However, there is a very considerable difference in behaviour between calcareous sandstones which usually fail relatively quickly and Portland stone, on which the skin can remain intact for centuries.

Soluble salt action   Salts, often derived from soils, exert considerable expansive force when they crystallize and are the chief cause of progressive decay. A sodium sulphate crystallization test, although not reliable with burnt clay products, is useful for assessing the salt resistance of stones.

Frost   Damage, often rapid, may occur in stones which are frozen when they are very wet or where water is retained in cracks or in shells on horizontal surfaces but it should rarely affect normal walling in this country. It is not clear to what extent frost damage results either from the expansion of water or from a mechanism analogous to *frost heave* in soils. Assessments of likely behaviour of members of a few groups of stones can be deduced from their physical properties but there is no rapid method of establishing the frost resistance of other stones.

External exposure of samples in trays which hold water provides a long term test for frost resistance. Stones which survive for three years are probably resistant and those which are unaffected after seven years are almost certainly resistant.

Solution   Limestone is slightly soluble in water and surfaces which are exposed to rain slowly dissolve away. See page 105.

Wetting and drying   Contour scaling is characteristic of certain sandstones and sometimes occurs among the less durable limestones. It is mainly attributable to rainwater penetrating to a constant depth, drying out and in so doing bringing forward soluble matter in solution. A soft layer below a relatively hard outer skin results and eventually the latter breaks away following the contours of the surface.

Corrosion of metals The rusting and consequent expansion of ferrous metals can cause serious damage and zinc salts released by galvanized steel have caused local decay.

Vegetation Lichens, mosses and virginia creeper do little harm but ivy has caused serious damage.

TYPES OF STONES

According to the manner of their geological formation all stones fall into one of three classes: igneous, sedimentary or metamorphic, each having recognisable physical characteristics.

The main stones used in building are discussed here in the following order:

Geological class	*Group*
Igneous	granites
Sedimentary	sandstones
	limestones
Metamorphic	slates
	marbles
	quartzites

Igneous stones

Examples are granites, syenites, dolerites, basalts and pumice. They are formed by the cooling of molten magma and consequently cannot contain fossils or shells.

Felspar is usually the chief ingredient in igneous stones, others are:

Quartz is an extremely hard and durable crystalline form of silica, usually transparent and colourless, but sometimes grey, pink, yellow or purple.

Mica is a silicate of aluminium with potassium (muscovite mica), which with the further inclusion of iron and magnesium (biotite mica) is soft and cleaves very easily into very thin flakes.

Hornblende. Essentially a silicate of calcium, magnesium and iron occurs as almost black six-sided prismatic crystals.

Augite is similar to hornblende but having eight-sided crystals.

Iron pyrites is a sulphide of iron occurring in small specks or cubes of brassy colour and liable to decompose rapidly.

Olivine, an iron magnesium silicate, is black, green or yellow in colour.

Asbestos is made up of various incombustible fibrous minerals related to either hornblende or olivine.

The structure of igneous stones is also dependent upon the rate at which they cooled. Thus:

Volcanic stones cooled rapidly and are very fine grained or non-crystalline and glassy. In the main volcanic stones are hard and difficult to work, unattractive in appearance and are used mainly for concrete aggregates and road metal. Basalt is such a stone. Pumice, which is porous, has been used as an aggregate for lightweight concrete.

Hypabyssal stones cooled slowly and consequently have a medium size crystalline structure. Porphyries are of this class. They take a good polish and some have been used for ornamental purposes but most are used as concrete aggregate or road metal.

Plutonic stones cooled very slowly at great depths below the earth's surface and a coarse crystalline structure results. Although the term 'granite' should strictly be limited to the acid rocks containing more than 66 per cent silica, the practice of calling similar igneous stones such as syenites granites, will be followed here.

Granites

Granites are a mosaic of crystals, sometimes several inches in length. The principal constituent is felspar, dull white to deep red in colour. Other ingredients are small grains of grey quartz and mica, which contribute 'sparkle'. Sometimes hornblende and, less frequently, augite, are present.

'Pearl' granites are highly decorative. Shap granite has unusually large red felspar crystals.

Granite has very high failing strength in compression, only a tiny fraction of which is normally employed in buildings. Because granites are extremely dense and hard, they are very costly to quarry, cut and surface, but they can be smoothed mechanically to a glass-like self polish. Being extremely resistant to knocks and abrasion, granite is eminently suitable for roadway kerbs, bridge cutwaters, jetties, spur stones, bollards and heavy-duty paving as slabs or setts.

Partly because of its high density, between 2460 to 3200 kg/m³ and its freedom from bedding planes or planes of cleavage, granite is very resistant to ordinary chemicals. Innumerable examples of the stone have retained a very high natural polish for a century or more in highly polluted industrial atmospheres which is a sure test of durability. No other stone can retain a natural polish for many years in such conditions and granite is used for external wall cladding where 'permanent' good appearance is required.

Most granites are virtually impermeable and serve as damp-proof courses provided the vertical joints between blocks are designed to prevent water movement.

On the debit side, staining of some granites which contain minute fissures has resulted from insufficient washing after acid treatment to remove iron derived from frame saws. Granite is less reliable in building fires than other stones, owing to the marked expansion of quartz and the differing expansion characteristics of the various constituents. See chapter 1, page 38.

Some granites, in common use, are listed under their predominant colours:

Colour of polished stone	Name	Country
Black	Andes	Brazil
	Bon accord	Sweden
Grey-black	Britts blue	South Africa
Grey	Rubislaw	Scotland
Light-medium grey	Creetown	Scotland
Light grey	Cornish	England
	Galloway	Ireland
Very light grey	Silver white	Norway
Green-black	Emerald pearl	Norway
Blue	Blue pearl	Norway
Red	Balmoral red	Finland
	Carnation red	Sweden
Pink	Peterhead	Scotland
	Shap	England

Sedimentary stones

Sedimentary stones are formed either from particles of older rocks which were broken down by the action of water, wind or ice, or from accumulations of organic origin. Sand and shingle are loose sediments, whereas the particles of sedimentary stones which are available as blocks and slabs have been cemented together by minerals originally carried in solution in water, and consolidated by superimposed deposits.

Sediments were carried by water and sometimes by wind, and the tendency of particles to lay horizontally often produced *natural grain*. Chan-

ges in composition from time to time produced layers of differing character, including occasional *soft beds*. Sedimentary stones are therefore often *bedded* with *bedding planes* which may be only 0·2- mm apart. Bedding planes, or grain, although rarely visible to the naked eye in recently quarried stone, sometimes lack natural cohesion and are often potentially weak. To obtain the highest strength and durability in stone masonry the *natural bed* must be respected in fixing.

Where the natural bed is parallel to an exposed face stones often delaminate, and *face bedding*, as it is called, should not be allowed, unless the stone is known to be sufficiently resistant to this form of decay.

Stones are stronger when bedding planes are at right angles to the thrust, so that in normal columns and walling they should be disposed horizontally, but cornices should be *joint bedded* with their bedding planes parallel to the vertical joints.

Some stones known as *freestones* have widely separated bedding planes and layers of homogeneous material as much as 4 m deep, and these are invaluable for blocks which are exposed to the weather on all sides.

When first quarried, some sedimentary stones, in particular Bath stones, are more or less saturated with mineral matter in solution (*quarry sap*). To avoid frost damage stones should not be exposed to the weather before their water content has been reduced to a safe level.

The main types of sedimentary stones are shown in table 32.

Sandstones

Sandstones consist of fine or coarse particles of quartz often with particles of felspar or mica, bound together by a natural cement which latter is the chief factor in deciding strength, durability and colour. Classified according to the cement, sandstones are:

Siliceous sandstones are generally extremely acid-resistant and otherwise durable, but relatively difficult to work. Silica tends to give a light grey colour. Examples are Blue Pennant and Darley Dale.

Calcareous sandstones are cemented with calcite crystals of calcium carbonate, which in their pure form are white. The stone is more easily worked than siliceous sandstone but is less durable and

Main Constituents	Sedimentary stones			Metamorphic Stones
	Unconsolidated	Bedded stones	Stones crystallized from solution	
Silica	Gravel coarse aggregate for concrete	Pudding stones (conglomerates) too coarse for building work		Quartzite (metaquartzite) wall cladding paving
	Sand fine aggregate for concrete calcium silicate bricks Silt	Sandstones wall cladding paving	Flints	
	Diatomaceous earth lightweight clay insulating bricks			
Silica and Alumina —minute particles	Clay clay bricks and other ceramic products	Shale clay bricks and other ceramic products		Slates wall cladding paving roofing d.p.c.s., etc
Calcium carbonate	Calcareous sediments	Limestones organically formed oölitic	Limestones lagoon formed cave formed	Marbles wall cladding paving, etc
Calcium sulphate			Gypsum alabaster 'onyx marble' gypsum for plaster	

Table 32 Constituents and uses of sedimentary and metamorphic stones

should be used externally only in rural areas. An example is Reigate (Surrey) stone.

Dolomitic or magnesian sandstones are bound with calcium carbonate and magnesium carbonate, both of which are white-buff. Examples are Red and White Mansfield.

Ferruginous sandstones contain oxides of iron, giving brown, red and yellow colours. As a class they weather well. Examples are Red Runcorn, Woolton, and Hollington (Coventry Cathedral).

The best sandstones are extremely durable but sandstones become dirty more readily and weather less attractively than limestones and apart from paving, steps and thresholds their use is largely confined to the quarrying areas.

The bedding planes in sandstones are very closely spaced and they are often visible. Some can be split into flagstones and a layer of mica is often seen on the riven surface. *Face-bedding* often leads to delamination. After forty years or more, some sandstones show *contour scaling* in which the lines of break are independent of the direction of bedding.

Hard and durable fine grained sandstones which

103

Colours	Texture	Name of stone	Location of quarry	Density kg/m³	Failing stress in compression N/mm²
Yellowish-white	fine	White Mansfield (Dolomitic)	Nottingham	2240	49·6
Cream	close grain	Darney	Edinburgh	2400	89·6
Buff and white	fine, close grain	Darley Dale (grit)	Derbyshire	2400	70·3
Buff to pink	medium	Birchover	Derbyshire	2560	48·2
Light brown to cream	medium/fine	Springhill Quarries	Yorkshire	2755	
Light brown	fine even grain	Silex		2560	92·4
Brown/grey	fine grain	Elland Edge Flag rock	Halifax Yorkshire	2995	89·6
Golden brown	fine even grain	Crosland Hill (millstone grit)	Huddersfield Yorkshire	2640	68·9
Brown and blue	close grain	Mouslow (gritstone)	Derbyshire	2755	193
Blue-grey	fine close grain	Blue Pennant	Pontypridd Glamorganshire	2690	172
Red/brown	even grain			2130	27·6
White and red mottled	fine/slightly coarse	Hollington	Uttoxeter Staffordshire	2210	32·4
Red	fine and even	Red St Bees	Cumberland	2145	53·1

Information from *Stone for Building* by Hugh O'Neill, William Heinemann Limited.

Table 33   Properties of some sandstones

are particularly suitable for paving are called *York stones*. An example is Silex from Halifax, Yorkshire.

Gritstones contain angular particles. An example is Darley Dale, Derbyshire.

Examples of sandstones are listed under their colours in table 33.

Limestones

Limestones consist mainly of calcium carbonate in the form of calcite. They were formed by the deposit of solids mainly in lakes or seas or by their deposit from solution:

1 *Oölitically formed stones*   Most of the lime-stones used today, including the Portland and Bath stones, are oölites or roe-stones, so called because the structure resembles fish roe. In a typical oölite small calcium carbonate oöliths are formed by the deposit of concentric layers of calcite around fragments of shell or sand and these are cemented to-

gether by calcite in which fossils and sand grains may occur.

2 *Organically formed stones*   These are accumulations of shells and other remains of animals and plants. Chalk and Hadene stone are of this type.

3 *Crystallization from solution*   This happens in pipes carrying hot water containing minerals and where dripping water forms stalactites and stalagmites, but the most important limestone of this type is Travertine which was formed by the evaporation of water around geysers. In this stone irregular voids were formed by gases.

'Pure' limestone, such as chalk, is white or off-white, but other ingredients often colour the stone cream, yellow, brown, red, grey and almost black. Coarsely crystalline calcite may impart a slight lustre.

Many limestones contain a proportion of magnesium carbonate and are called *Magnesian*

Type	Weathering	Resistance to pollution	Density kg/m^3	Porosity per cent	Absorption per cent	Failing stress in compression N/mm^2
Portland: Dorset						
Roach	Excellent	Excellent	2090	21·4	4·3	38·7
Whitbed	Excellent	Excellent	2340	12·0	3·7	42·8
Basebed	Excellent	Excellent	2210	16·9	5·7	40·9
Bath Stones:						
Box Ground	Excellent	Excellent	2070	23·2	6·8	11·7
Monk's Park	Good	Good	2240	17·5	7·76	24·3
Clipsham: Rutland	Excellent[1]	Excellent[1]	2310	14·0	4·7	31·7
Doulting: Somerset	Excellent	Good	2400	17·0	8·6	21·3
Guiting: Gloucestershire	Excellent[1]	Good[1]	1970	20·0	9·7	16·3

[1] These remarks relate to the better quality material.

Information from Stone Firms Limited

Table 34   Properties of some limestones

Limestones. Where the content of magnesium carbonate is 45·7 per cent or more by weight the stone is known as *Dolomitic Limestone.* Other common ingredients include carbonaceous matter and iron oxides.

Properties of some limestones are listed in table 34.

Limestones vary widely in hardness. Those of the Pennine Chain are extremely hard and suitable for concrete aggregates, road metal and paving slabs. Generally, however, limestones are less hard and easier to work than sandstones. Many are very suitable for carving and some are soft enough to be sawn by hand.

Limestones are soluble in water containing carbon dioxide so that they are self-cleansing where they are freely washed by rain and the more durable fossils and veins of calcite give visual character to some limestones as they weather. At the same time soot collects in protected parts giving the familiar black and white effect which is considered by some to be an attractive feature of limestone buildings.

Limestones are attacked by acids to an extent which is related to their density. Sulphurous matter in soot reacts with calcium carbonate forming a glassy skin of calcium sulphate or with magnesium carbonate forming a skin of magnesium sulphate. These skins act as a binder for further soot and dirt and cause rapid decay of the softer limestones. Sulphur gases sometimes cause blisters to form in semi-sheltered parts and cavernous decay of magnesium limestones.

Rain washings from limestones, particularly magnesium limestones, cause decay of sandstones and of the less durable clay bricks.

Limestones are now being employed in a thickness of 25·4 mm as permanent shuttering on precast concrete wallslabs. The installed cost of concrete slabs faced with limestone is often very competitive with that of concrete slabs using the same stone as aggregate.

Varieties of limestones   Limestone in this country is mainly confined to a belt from the Wash to Dorset, and most limestones used in building are obtained from the South West of England. The more important examples are:

Portland stone is creamy white. It has excellent resistance to weathering, even in polluted atmospheres. It occurs in four principal beds the first of which to be exposed is the *cap* with a crushing strength in the region of 345 N/mm^2 now being crushed and used as aggregate for concrete. Below this is the *roach* bed 455 mm to 915 mm high. It has a fairly pronounced shell formation ranging from coarse to fine texture and when worked it gives a cellular surface. It is not very suitable for working fine arrises but for ashlar it provides textural interest and weathers extremely well. It was used for facing St Paul's Cathedral Choir School and *The Economist* building in London.

Whitbed is 610 mm to 1065 mm high and is close grained, fairly even in texture and contains some shells both throughout its mass and in thin layers.

Portland stones are very strong and Whitbed is rather stronger than the other Portland stones (42·85 N/mm^2 failing stress in compression). Density is 2340 kg/m^3. Nevertheless, it is less hard than Roach, and can be worked with relative ease. Its remarkable resistance to weathering is evidenced by the loss of only 13 mm thickness from the most exposed parapets of St Paul's Cathedral, about 0·05 mm per annum. It is the bed most used for general building purposes, one modern use being the facing of the Royal Festival Hall, London.

Basebed which occurs below the Whitbed, is about 1 m high, is fine grained, even textured and has little shell. It works freely and is the best bed for carved work.

The three lower beds named polish well and are very suitable for wall linings, the shellier varieties being particularly decorative.

Bath stone is the name given to a series of free working stones found in the Bath area. The city of Bath is largely built in the stone and Apsley House in London. Bath stones include:

Monks Park which is light cream in colour, of fine grain and fairly compact. Resistance to weathering and to pollution are good, but plinths and copings would be liable to attack by frost.
St Aldhelm's Box Ground which varies in colour from light brown to cream and has a coarser grain. Resistance to weathering, pollution and frost very good.

Doulting Stone, quarried in Somerset, varies in colour from light brown, or buff to cream. It is a fine grained stone and works well.

Clipsham Stone from Rutland varies in colour from buff to cream and from oölitic to coarse shelly in texture. In the past quality has varied widely but the best stone has been excellent.

Guiting Stone is a Cotswold oölite, pale to deep ochre in colour. It has a medium grain with minute shells and works easily.

Flints are nodules of silica which are found in chalk. Formerly they were knapped to reveal a glassy brown-black interior which is extremely durable. Today they are mainly crushed for concrete aggregate, for making calcium silicate bricks, etc. They are also used, mainly in the chalk districts, as cobbles set in mortar for facing walls and for paving.

Metamorphic stones

These consist of older stones which have been subjected to immense heat and pressure causing structural change. Thus, clay becomes slate, limestone marble and sandstone quartzite, see table 32, page 103. Features such as bedding planes, large crystals and fossils are lost.

Slates, marbles and quartzite are dealt with:

Slates

Slates were formed by immense earth pressures acting upon clays and forming *planes of cleavage*, distinct from and often almost at right angles to, the original bedding planes. Slates are split along their planes of cleavage. The resulting surfaces may not be perfectly flat.

Properties Good slate, such as that complying with BS 680 : 1971 *Roofing slates*, is one of the most durable building materials. In the past, slate was used for its acid and alkali resistance as laboratory bench tops, urinal slabs and lavatory basin tops.

Poor slate however, may begin to decay in a few months, especially in damp conditions in industrial areas. Sulphide of iron in slates may form hydrated iron oxide and sulphuric acid, which latter attacks any calcium carbonate present. Similar attack may take place by the action of sulphuric acid from the atmosphere, and some Lake District slates, which contain a high proportion of calcium carbonate, may fail on that account.

Slate is strong in tension and compression when compared in equal thicknesses and otherwise equal conditions with other stones, as evidenced by its use as cantilevered stair treads. Formerly, slate was used as a good electrical insulator, eg for switchboards. It has negligible absorption and can be considered to be impervious and, therefore, suitable for d.p.c.s, provided that water is not under pressure so that it would penetrate the joints as may be the case at coping level.

Slate can be considered to have no moisture

movement and its stability is valuable for billiard tables. Thermal movement must be allowed for, however, in dark coloured slate copings which are exposed to the sun.

Appearance Slate can be had with a riven texture which varies from silky and smooth to very rough, sawn, sanded or finely rubbed surfaces. Being very hard and denser than granite it also takes a good natural polish but does not retain it as well, in fact calcareous slates lose their polish very quickly.

Colours include grey to almost black, red, blue, purple, green and brown. Striped and variegated colorations sometimes occur.

When carved, the texture of chiselled surfaces contrasts with highly polished slabs and the difference in tone is very pronounced on the darker slates. The appearance of slate can be enhanced by wax, or by varnish which is more durable but very difficult to renew satisfactorily.

Sources: North Wales This is the chief source of slate in this country. This product is typically dark and light blue, purple, blue-grey, dark and light green and dark grey – with a smooth texture. The slate can be split to almost paper thickness. The so called *bests*, which are the thinnest roofing slates, are about 5 mm thick.

Cornwall The slate is grey and grey-green and has a characteristic lustre. Naturally stained red slates (*rustics*) are occasionally available. Roofing slates are of medium thickness. They are sold mainly in the smaller standard sizes and in random widths and lengths.

Lake District The slate from Westmorland is generally green and that from North Lancashire is dark blue. The riven surfaces are pleasantly irregular. These slates contain calcium carbonate which in the case of the green slates only is attacked by sulphur gases. This weakness, however, is not so important in thick units and fortunately the Lake District roofing slates are thicker than those from other sources.

The Continent Some very good slates have been imported from France and Portugal but others from Italy have failed to meet the requirements of BS 780 for Roofing Slates.

Uses The use of slate as *blocks* for general wall masonry is mainly confined to the quarrying areas, but it is used widely for copings, window sills and surrounds.

As *slabs* it is used for flooring, external paving and wall cladding.

Slate is an excellent substrate for air-dried and stoved paint, being impervious, dimensionally stable and chemically inert.

Carved in low relief, slate is much used for memorial and other plaques. In a thinner form slate can be used for roof coverings and damp-proof courses.

Granules and chippings are used for surfacing bituminous felts (see *MBC: C and F*) and as an aggregate in concrete blocks.

Ground slate is used as a filler in mastic asphalt (see page 219), plastics (see page 238) and paints.

Tests for slates Simple tests are as follows:

(a) a good slate has no odour when wet
(b) the texture should have a somewhat rough 'feel' and should not be greasy
(c) when holed or dressed the fracture should be clean and not flakey
(d) BRS Digest 45 *The durability of roofing slates* stated that if a roofing slate decomposes to mud in a day or two when submerged in a solution of fresh battery acid poured carefully and slowly into an equal volume of water, it is unlikely to give satisfaction in use, even in country districts.

British standards for slate products are:

BS 680 : 1971   Roofing Slates

This BS contains tests which will also serve for assessing the properties of slates used for damp-proof courses and other purposes. Slates which will be subjected to only slight atmospheric pollution by sulphurous or other acid fumes are required to pass tests (1) and (2) only.

1 *Water absorption*
After storage in boiling water for 48 hours water absorption is not to exceed 0·3 per cent.

2 *Wetting and drying test*
The slate must not delaminate or split after 15 soaking and drying cycles.

3 *Sulphuric acid test*
The slate must not soften, delaminate or split when immersed in a 20 per cent sulphuric acid solution for 10 days. (Unfortunately this test eliminates North Lancashire slates which are in fact known to be durable.)

BS 3798 : 1964 Coping units contains tests which are less severe than those for roofing slates, but the acid test is nevertheless unfair to North Lancashire slates.

BS 743 : 1970   Materials for damp-proof courses

Marbles

True marbles are fully metamorphosed, but in the trade, the definition encompasses the English 'marbles', travertine and other limestones which take a good natural polish.

Pure marble is very finely crystalline and ideal for crisp carved detail. It is white, but coloured minerals often occur as a general coloration, as veins or other markings. Marbles which have a consistent pattern throughout the thickness of a block lend themselves to 'matching' of adjacent slabs.

Marble is generally very hard, dense and resistant to abrasion. Veins are sometimes weak but satisfactory repairs can be made with modern adhesives. Like granite, marble takes an excellent self-polish which greatly enhances its appearance. Unlike granite, however, marble is attacked by acids and a polished surface is not retained for very long externally in a polluted atmosphere. *Sugaring* sometimes occurs on exposure and highly coloured marbles tend to fade. Also, although marble is virtually impervious, discoloration can result in damp conditions and the backs of slabs must be sealed with shellac to protect them from 'wet' constructions.

Types A very wide range of marbles is imported, some of the varieties currently available being:

Colour of polished stone	Name	Country
Black	Belgian black	Belgium
Dark grey-black	Belgian fossil	Belgium
Grey	Dove	Italy
White	Sicilian etc	Italy
	Pentelicon	Greece
Cream	Bianco del mare	Yugoslavia
Cream-fawn	Aurisina	Italy
Cream-beige	Roman travertine	Italy
Beige	Portuguese beige	Portugal
Beige-brown	Perlato	Sicily
Brown	Napoleon	France
Golden-yellow	Golden travertine	Iran, Spain and Yugoslavia

Colour of polished stone	Name	Country
Green	Tinos	Greece (Isle of Tinos)
	Verde antico	Greece
	Serpentino	Italy
	Swedish green	Sweden
Red and pink	Norwegian rose	Norway
	Rosso levanto	Italy
	Rose aurore	Portugal

Ashburton stone from Devonshire is dark grey to black with white and red markings and Hadene stone from Derbyshire is buff and contains crinoids and other fossils.

Uses In this country marble is used mainly as slabs for wall cladding (external) and lining (internal), shop fascias and stall board risers, flooring, and external paving. Split marble slips are used for facing walls and precast concrete slabs.

Crushed marble is used as an aggregate in terrazzo and in resin-bound floorings (see *MBC: C and F*, chapter 12).

Quartzites

Quartzite was formed from standstone by intense heat and recrystallization. It comprises about 96 per cent silica, is harder even than granite and is extremely durable. Quartzites can often be split in all directions, and some of them retain traces of the original bedding planes, which permit splitting.

The riven surfaces are somewhat uneven and splintery and have a pleasant lustre. They are not very easy to keep clean but provide 'non-slip' properties for flooring.

Colours are grey, green and gold.

Sources Quartzite is imported from Norway, Sweden, South Africa and Italy.

Uses: Wall 'tiles' (or slabs), flooring and external paving, see *MBC: C and F*.

MAINTENANCE OF STONEWORK

References: BRS Digests 20 and 21 (first series) *The weathering, preservation and maintenance of natural stone masonry.*
BRS Digest 113 *Cleaning external surfaces of buildings.*

Causes of decay are dealt with on page 31. Here we are concerned with cleaning, preservation, water repellent treatments and restoration, all of which processes should be undertaken by, or with the advice of specialists.

positions limestones and sandstones may require cleaning at 5 to 10 year intervals, while in polluted atmospheres polished marble may have to be cleaned every month.

Methods of cleaning various stones are out-

Stone	Method	Remarks
Limestone Marble	Clean water spray to soften deposits followed by light brushing. Marbles can be washed with water containing mild detergent and rinsed with clean water	Relatively slow. Not suitable for heavy encrustations, in frosty weather, or where buried ferrous metals or timber might be adversely affected and the method may cause brown stains on limestones. Marble is sometimes difficult to clean COST FACTOR: 12–20
Granites	Ammonium bifluoride	Acids particularly hydrofluoric acid, are extremely dangerous in handling
All stones	Hydrofluoric acid (about 5 per cent concentration)[1]	Risk of severe damage to surrounding materials, particularly glass COST FACTOR: 13–21
	Grit-blast:[2] dry	Rapid, even with heavy encrustations No staining of stones Requires skill to avoid damage to soft stones Very dusty process, operatives must have independent breathing supply. Close screening is required but some dust escapes into atmosphere COST FACTOR: 14–30
	wet	Generally as above. Water reduces visible dust, but may give rise to the objections to the water spray process COST FACTOR: 14–30
	Mechanical: abrasive power and hand tools brushes	Rarely necessary for limestones COST FACTOR: 15–30

[1] Steam sometimes helps to remove deep seated soiling after acid cleaning.   [2] Only non-siliceous grit should be used.

Table 35   Cleaning of natural stones

Cleaning

To maintain good appearance, to minimize the likelihood of decay and to prevent defects becoming concealed by soot deposits stonework which is exposed externally should be cleaned regularly and defective joints should be raked out and repointed as necessary. The frequency of cleaning required, depends upon the degree of atmospheric pollution, the exposure and the type of stone. Thus limestone which is freely washed by rain may be 'self cleansing'; in protected

lined in table 35. Deposits on limestones can usually be softened by a fine spray of clean water, and sometimes marbles can be cleaned in this way, but rarely sandstones or granites. All stones can be cleaned by mechanical means or by hydrofluoric acid. Caustic soda and soda ash are very damaging and must never be used on any stone.

Preservation

Most stones are very durable and any decay which

does occur is usually extremely slow. It often arises from the wrong choice of stone, from defects in design or from neglect and clearly all defects should be corrected before any attempt is made to 'preserve' stone. For example, no attempt should be made to seal in salts – these should be removed by repeated wetting and sponging. Unfortunately attempts to arrest decay by the application of colourless surface treatments often do more harm than good. Some flake off and some hold soot and dirt. The BRS states that 'Nothing will be lost by awaiting with patience the outcome of trials of any new stone preservative that may be offered.' See BRS Digest 125 *Colourless treatments for masonry.*

Water repellents

These treatments which prevent capillary absorption without sealing surfaces are discussed under *Clear finishes* in *MBC: C and F.*

Impervious coatings must never be applied on pervious stones.

Restoration

Isolated repairs can be effected with carefully matched stones or by *plastic repairs* which although less costly, are liable to become disturbingly conspicuous with time. Where decay is general but superficial, the whole surface can be cut back to expose sound material. *The Department of the Environment, Ancient Monuments Branch* must be notified, and will give advice on the treatment of *Scheduled buildings.*

Vegetable growths

These are rarely destructive but are evidence of dampness. BRS Digest 139 *The control of lichens, moulds and similar growths.*

5 Ceramics

Ceramics are made from a mixture of mineral material (generally quartz sand) and a clay binder (hydrated aluminium silicate) with impurities such as chalk, dolomite and sulphates, plasticized with water. The mixture is shaped, dried to remove making and adsorbed water, and fired. During firing hydrate water, carbon dioxide and other gases are driven off, recrystallization takes place and glass is formed producing a hard, insoluble material.

Products such as hand moulded bricks and tiles which are made from raw material which may contain more than 30 per cent water have considerable drying contraction and are rarely accurate in size. However wall and floor tiles moulded from dust with only 2 to 5 per cent moisture content have little drying contraction and very much greater accuracy is possible.

Increases in temperature in firing are accompanied by more complete recrystallization and an increase in the formation of glassy material promoting greater: density, hardness, strength, resistance to chemicals and to frost, and greater dimensional stability. After firing irreversible expansion due to adsorption of water of clay products can be troublesome in bricks (see page 125) and in floor and wall tiling particularly if they are incorporated in the work during the first weeks after they are fired.

Ceramics can be glazed in any colour by coating them with a specially prepared *slip* before they are fired. The composition of a glaze must be carefully matched to the properties of the body if subsequent cracking (*crazing*) is to be avoided and products which are to be used externally must be frost resistant.

The main ceramics products used in building are listed in table 36 and they are considered below:

TERRACOTTA

Terracotta is made from yellow to brownish-red clays intermediate in uniformity and fineness between ordinary bricks and vitrified wall tiles. It was used in Victorian buildings as hollow blocks, cornices and similar details, filled with concrete during construction, where otherwise natural stone would have been used. Well burnt blocks filled with concrete containing sound aggregate have proved to be durable in many buildings such as the Natural History Museum in London. Terracotta is used now for unglazed chimney pots, air bricks and copings.

Shrinkage in firing is about one twelfth, and joints must be wide enough to accommodate variations in size and shape. Terracotta which is glazed is generally called *faience*.

FAIENCE

Faience is a glazed form of terracotta or stoneware. Much faience is first fired to the *biscuit* condition and then glazed before refiring. Alternatively, the unfired clay may be glazed and 'once fired' a process which improves resistance to crazing of the glaze while reducing the range of colours obtainable. Faience glazes tend to have an orange peel texture. They provide permanent colour and although easy to clean are by no means self-cleansing in polluted atmospheres. Crazing of inferior products collects grime and may be very unsightly. Chipped glazes are also unsightly and faience should not be used where it is likely to receive heavy knocks. Rounded corners rather than sharp arrises are to be preferred.

Ceramic glazes are inherently durable but where water is able to enter behind the glaze, crystallization of salts, and sometimes frost action, cause failure. Choice of a faience with low water absorption is some guarantee of frost resistance.

Faience is usually made in slabs up to $300 \times 400 \times 30$ mm but copings, sills, plaques and sculptural forms can be made to order.

Ceramic product	BS with date of latest revision or confirmation	Usual type of body
Bricks (including *Engineering* bricks) Roof tiles	3921 : 1969	Fired shales and clays
	402 : 1970 (plain tiles) 1424 : 1948[1] (single lap)	
Quarries	1286 : 1945/1967	
Firebacks Refractory bricks Flue linings and chimney pots Sinks and wash tubs	1251 : 1970 1758 : 1966 1181 : 1971 1229 : 1954/1957 1206 : 1954/1959[1]	Fireclay
Drain pipes and fittings Some faience products	65 : 540 : 1971	Stoneware
Floor tiles Terracotta blocks etc Copings Flue linings and chimney pots Air bricks Some faience products	1286 : 1945/1967 3798 : 1964 1181 : 1971 493 : 1965 —	Terracotta
Glazed wall tiles Some sanitary appliances	1281 : 1966 (for internal walls)	Earthenware
Sanitary appliances	3402 : 1969 1188 : 1965 (basins and pedestals) 1213 : 1945/1957[1]	Vitreous china
Special products, eg electrical insulators	—	Porcelain

[1] Dimensions and workmanship only.

Table 36   Ceramic building products

FIRECLAY

Fireclay is a simple product used for grate backs and flue liners, in which a high kaolin content in the clay binder provides high fire resistance. However, some bricks, faience and hollow clay blocks are made in fire clay where fire resistance is not the primary requirement.

STONEWARE

Stoneware is similar in composition to fireclay but because it is fired at a higher temperature it contains a higher proportion of glass, is harder and less absorbent. Stoneware is familiar in the form of *glazed ware* drainage goods which are glazed, either by introducing salt into the kiln during firing so that the sodium combines with the silica in the clay, or by conventional spraying of a glaze frit.

EARTHENWARE

Earthenware. The raw materials, blended from different sources, may contain a considerable proportion of limestone. Earthenware is a finer product than stoneware and is used as the body for glazed wall tiles, and for ordinary quality table 'china' but water absorption of the fired product may be as high as 15 per cent or even more making it less suitable for sanitary ware than vitreous china, since any small cracks in the glaze permit water to penetrate into the body.

VITREOUS CHINA

Vitreous china has a higher glass content than earthenware and its water absorption is only about 0·5 per cent, so there is negligible penetration of the body by water should the glaze crack. It is also stronger than earthenware, and vitreous china is now used for most sanitary fittings.

PORCELAIN

Porcelain is similar in most respects to vitreous china but it is often made from purer materials under more strictly controlled conditions to give properties which are required for specific uses, such as electrical insulators.

6 Bricks and blocks

BS 3921 : 1969 *Specification for bricks and blocks of fired brickearth, clay or shale; Metric units*, describes a brick as a walling unit designed to be laid in mortar and not more than 337·5 mm long, 225·0 mm wide and 112·5 mm high, as distinct from a block which is defined as a unit having one or more of these dimensions larger than those quoted. Blocks are dealt with on page 130.

Bricks

Strength and durability should be sufficient for the conditions in which the brick is to be used. Where necessary, bricks should be of good appearance or provide a good base for rendering, plastering or decoration. The size and shape of bricks should be regular to facilitate bonding. In its most common form, a brick can be held in one hand, and its length of 215·0 mm is equal to twice its width of 102·5 mm plus one 10 mm joint. The height of 65 mm allows for laying four courses of brickwork with four 10 mm joints to 300 mm. The new metric size being slightly smaller than the old imperial size permits bonding with old brickwork. Some manufacturers are likely to continue to make bricks to the old BS size and some may continue to produce the 73 mm high brick which used to be common in the North of England, the 51 mm high brick and other special sizes and shapes to order.

Figure 12 shows some typical *standard* bricks and figure 13 shows typical *standard special* types.

Most bricks have a *frog*, or depression, on one or both bed faces which serves to reduce cost in manufacture and in handling and also provides a mechanical key for mortar. Frogs are usually laid downwards but where they are laid upwards they are completely filled with mortar and this must be done where maximum strength is required. Perforations and cells also reduce weight and make for more uniform firing of clay bricks.

This chapter is concerned with bricks but it must be realized that bricks and mortars should be matched in respect of strength and weather resisting properties, and where brickwork is exposed to view the appearance and form of the mortar joints should complement the bricks.

Briefly: there is no strength advantage in using high strength mortar with low strength bricks or vice versa. Mortar must be suited to the suction properties of bricks in order to obtain good bond and consequent weather resistance. The colour and tone of brickwork is much influenced by those properties in the mortar and by the form of the joint. Crude mortar joints can ruin the appearance of brickwork. See *Mortars*, Chapter 15.

The main British Standard Codes of Practice for brickwork are:

CP 111 : 1970 *Structural recommendations for loadbearing walls*
CP 121·101 : 1951 (amendments to 1956) *Brickwork*

Bricks are made in three materials:

1 Burnt clay
2 Calcium silicate, see page 126.
3 Concrete, see page 129.

CLAY BRICKS

More than 8000 million bricks are produced annually in this country and most of these are made from clay.

Useful references include:

BRS Digests 65 and 66 *The Selection of Clay Building Bricks*
BS3921 : 1969 *Bricks and Blocks of Brickearth, Clay or Shale*
Model specification for load-bearing clay brickwork
The British Ceramic Research Association 1967.

Information is available from: The Brick Development Association Ltd, 3 Bedford Row, London, WC 1.

Sizes

BS 3921 : Part 2 : 1969 specifies only one standard format designated *225, 112·5, 75* and of the following dimensions:

	Actual dimensions (mm)	Overall measurement of 24 bricks[1] (mm)
Length	215	5160 ± 75
Width	102·5	2460 ± 45
Height	65	$1560 {+60 \atop -30}$

[1] Samples to be taken in accordance with Clauses 37 and 38 and to be tested in accordance with Clause 39.

The designation equals numerically the actual length, width and height plus a 10 mm joint in each case.

Clay bricks are also being made in modular sizes:

2M 203·2 × 101·6 × 50·8, 76·0 and 101·0 mm
(200 × 100 × 50, 75 and 100 mm[1]) } nominal

193·7 × 92·1 × 48·3 and 92·1 mm
(190 × 90 × 40 and 90 mm[1]) } actual

3M 304·8 × 101·6 × 50·8, 76·2 and 101·6 mm
(300 × 100 × 50, 75 and 100 mm[1]) } nominal

295·3 × 92·1 × 41·3, 66–7 and 92·1 mm
(290 × 90 × 40, 65 and 90 mm[1]) } actual

Larger sizes include 'V' bricks (see page 116) and *Calculon* bricks (see page 117).

Classification

All clay bricks fall into one or more of the classes under each heading, *variety*, *quality* and *type* as defined in BS 3921, see table 37. It is important to realise that the classifications are independent, eg a *solid* facing brick can also be an *engineering* brick and it could fall in any *quality* class.

[1] Proposed sizes

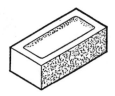

Pressed engineering brick

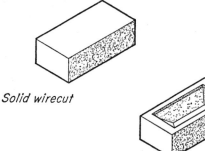

Solid wirecut

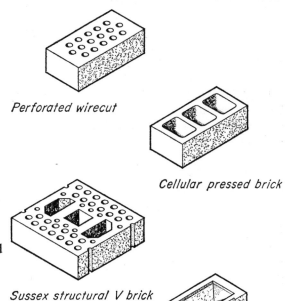

Pressed or hand moulded brick

Perforated wirecut

Cellular pressed brick

Sussex structural V brick Mark V 63 (R)

Keyed pressed brick

12   Standard bricks

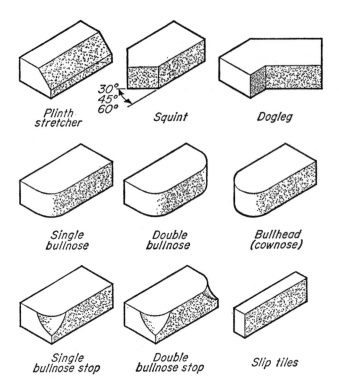

30°
45°
60°

Plinth stretcher   Squint   Dogleg

Single bullnose   Double bullnose   Bullhead (cownose)

Single bullnose stop   Double bullnose stop   Slip tiles

13 '*Standard special*' *bricks.* See BS 4729: 1971 *Shapes and dimensions of special bricks*

In addition to the BS classifications bricks can be described by the raw material, eg a *gault*; method of manufacture, eg a *wirecut*; by colour, or by texture.

Proprietary bricks

'*Phorpres*' *cellular brick*, see figure 12, has three deep depressions or cells and is 25 per cent lighter than the standard Fletton brick and brickwork is about 15 per cent lighter.

The bricks comply with the requirements for hollow units of LCC Bylaws 1965 Clause 4·12 (e). Strength is adequate for normal two storey construction when the cells are laid downwards as would be normal.

'*Phorpres*' *keyed brick* See figure 12, has dovetailed keys for plaster or renderings on one stretcher and one header face.

V Bricks The designation '*V*' is usually applied specifically to double, through bricks with vertical perforations which can be laid with one hand to provide the thermal equivalent of a conventional cavity wall but with some 30 per cent saving in labour and about 28 per cent saving in mortar. The units are laid on two strips of mortar the thickness of which can be set by a tray which also serves to prevent mortar falling into the central voids or resting on the cross webs. If laid correctly in this way there can be no capillary tracks from outside to the inside of a wall and BRS tests have indicated that rain resistance is equivalent to a 280 mm cavity wall.

'*Sussex Structural V Bricks*' These are manufactured by Redland Bricks Ltd, Horsham, Sussex; Sussex and Dorking Brick Companies Ltd, see figure 14. The standard unit is:

228·6 × 228·6 × 76·2 mm
225 × 225 × 75 mm proposed } nominal
  metric dimensions
219·1 × 219·1 × 67 mm   actual subject to
[215 × 215 × 65 mm] standard
  proposed metric size] tolerances

Perforations are about 40 per cent by volume.

Variety[2]	Quality[1,2]	Type[2]		
1 *Common* for general building work having no special claim to attractive appearance	1 *Internal* suitable only for internal use. Frost resistance is such that the bricks may require protection if exposed during one winter.	1 *Solid* may have holes less than 20 mm wide or less than 500 mm² in area passing through, or nearly through, with up to 3 hand holds each not exceeding 3250 mm	not exceeding 25 per cent of volume	
2 *Facing* specially made or selected to give an attractive appearance without surface treatment such as rendering	2 *Ordinary* suitable in face of building in normal exposures	*OR* Frogs (depressions in the bed faces)	not exceeding 20 per cent of volume	
		2 *Perforated* have small holes as above, passing through and may have up to 3 hand holds as above		'V' type Vertical perforations or hollows
3 *Engineering* having a dense vitreous body and specified strength and absorption limits – see table 40, page 124	3 *Special* durable in severe exposures where they are liable to be wet and frozen, eg retaining walls	3 *Hollow* have holes larger than above, passing through	exceeding 25 per cent of volume	'H' type Horizontal perforations or hollows
	Note: *Engineering* bricks are normally of *Special quality* and some *Common* and *Facing* bricks also qualify	4 *Cellular* have holes closed at one end	exceeding 20 per cent of volume	
		5 *Special shapes*		
		6 *Standard specials* special shapes which are in general use and may be held in stock: eg bats closers, squints, bullnoses, coping bricks – see figure 13.		

[1] See page 121.   [2] *Variety*, *quality* and *type* classifications are not related.

Table 37   Classification of bricks and blocks for walling – based on BS 3921 : 1969: Part 2

To enable traditional methods of damp-proof coursing to be maintained three *standard specials* are made, see figure 14:

ie 1 *Standard return brick*

2 *Standard perforated brick* which is marked so that it can be cut on site to give two $211 \times 105 \times 66.7$ mm half bricks to maintain a bond with standard return bricks at reveals and to enable a vertical damp-proof course to be used.

3 *Special perforated brick* $219.1 \times 89 \times 66.7$ mm. These are laid in the same way as normal cavity wall bricks where stepped horizontal damp-proof courses occur.

All standard V bricks are available sand faced on both faces in four alternative colours. Smooth face bricks can be made to order. Return bricks, standard perforated bricks and special perforated bricks are similarly faced on one side.

Average compression strength is 34·5 N/mm² (41·4 N/mm² bricks can be provided to order) Average weight of a standard brick is 3·95 kg.

'Calculon' Bricks (Redland Bricks Ltd)

Calculon bricks are designed for highly stressed internal loadbearing cross walls and spine walls. Where necessary for design purposes, they can also be used as an internal skin to cavity perimeter walls. Made in three strength grades, each type incorporates a hand hold.

117

Grade	Average compressive strength	Average weight	Perforation
	MN/m^2	kg	
A10	68·9	19·8	23 per cent
B75	51·7		
C5	34·5	3·95	'solid'

Calculon bricks

Manufacturers' tests show a 30 per cent increase in the speed of laying and a saving of approximately 40 per cent mortar when compared with 228·6 mm solid brick walling. The *C5* type is smooth all round and the *A10* and *B75* types are available either smooth all round or keyed for plaster.

Nominal dimensions are $228·6 \times 177·8 \times 76·2$ mm. Actual dimensions (subject to normal tolerances) are given in figure 15. Standard specials are quarter, half and three-quarter and bricks for returns at inter-sections between *Calculon* and 'V' brick walls and for use in 228·6 mm and 343 mm piers.

Costs

Price factors for some common bricks are given in table 38.

Manufacture

The raw material, which must be capable of being shaped, dried and burnt without undue distortion, largely determines the properties of bricks.

Brickmaking clays are composed of silica and alumina and various impurities including iron compounds, lime, magnesia, potash, soda and sulphur, most of which are combined chemically into compounds such as feldspar and mica. Clays, such as that used in the manufacture of Fletton bricks, contain natural fuel which contributes usefully to economy in firing.

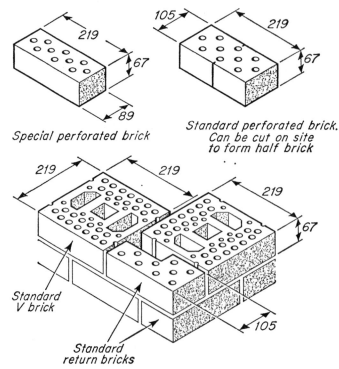

Special perforated brick

Standard perforated brick. Can be cut on site to form half brick

Standard V brick

Standard return bricks

14 *Sussex structural V bricks* (Redland Bricks Limited, Sussex and Dorking Brick Companies Ltd) Dimensions mm

		Cost factors
Flettons		
	plain	100
	keyed	101
	facings	153–170
London Stocks		
	common	183
	rough	208
	mild	236
	2nd hard	310
	1st hard	340
Calcium-silicate bricks		
	Midhurst whites	
	best facings	180
	Uxbridge flints	
	no. 2 engineering	226
	no. 1 engineering	250
	semi-engineering	188
	facings—white	204
	colours	224–300
Lingfield engineering wirecuts		
	Grade B	250
Dorking		
	pressed multi-coloured facings	268
	hand made multi-coloured facings	341
Southwater engineering		
	no. 2	300
	no. 1	372
Calculon		
	grade 5 (solid)	264
	grade 75	454
	grade 10	515

Table 38   Price factors of bricks

The main processes in the manufacture of all ceramic products involve 'winning' and preparing the raw material, forming the shape required and drying and firing it.

'Winning' and preparation

Methods of *winning* the raw material affect the economy of manufacture but not the properties of the brick. Preparation involves the removal of stones, etc. and in some cases the addition of fuel. Weathering by frost action is rare today. Grinding and in some cases the addition of water, follow.

Forming

All ceramic products must be formed to dimensions which allow for shrinkage in firing later. For hand moulding a plastic clay is essential but a relatively stiff clay can be moulded by machine and the lower moisture content reduces shrinkage in drying.

Soft mud moulding This is done exceptionally by hand in a *stock mould*, or by machine producing a relatively irregularly shaped and dimensioned brick. An interesting surface texture results from the use of sand in the moulds as a release agent.

Wire-cutting In this process a moderately stiff clay mix is forced through a die, the mouth of which has the length and width of a green brick. The continuous column formed in this way is cut by wires into lengths corresponding to green brick heights. Ordinary *wire-cuts* are recognized by the absence of frogs and by marks on the bed faces caused by solid particles in the clay having been dragged by the cutting wires.

Perforation during extrusion saves clay and simplifies drying and firing. *Perforated* and *hollow* products save weight in handling and if perforation is not excessive there is little loss of strength. No significant improvement in thermal insulation is obtained by perforating bricks, although blocks with 50 per cent voids give useful improvement.

Pressing Stiff clays can be formed into bricks by mechanical pressure, without the addition of water and this obviates the need for drying the green bricks in a separate drier.

Pressed bricks have frogs on one bed face and pressed engineering bricks often have shallow panels on both bed faces. Cellular bricks with very large frogs are also formed in this way.

Fletton bricks, first made in the village of that name, are made in Northamptonshire and Bedfordshire by the *semi-dry* process. In this method the clay is ground to a powder, pressed automatically and dried and fired in modified Hoffmann kilns.

Harder clays found in Scotland, the North of England, Staffordshire and South Wales are ground either dry or with water in edge-runner pans, mixed with water, extruded into slabs and pressed into bricks.

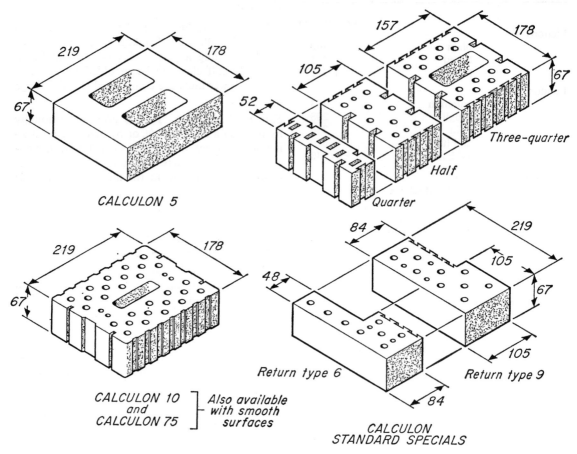

15 *'Calculon' bricks* (Redland Bricks Limited, Sussex and Dorking Brick Companies Ltd)
Dimensions mm

Drying and firing

'Green' bricks must be dried before they are fired. Natural drying in *hacks*, stacks about seven courses high, protected from rain, is rare today and most bricks are dried, either in a separate drier or in the drying zone of a continuously fired kiln.

Setting or stacking one brick upon another in a checkerwork pattern for drying and firing is a skilled operation and has not been mechanized to any large extent.

The parts of bricks which are covered by other bricks during drying and firing, the *kiss marks*, usually burn to the natural colour of the fired clay. Exposed parts are covered with 'scum' result-ing either from salts which migrate to the surface of a brick or from a reaction between the kiln gases and lime in the clay.

Firing or *burning* is still carried out to a very small extent in *clamps* in which the green bricks are set in layers alternating with coke breeze, the whole being walled and roofed over with waste bricks from previous firings. The whole mass burns and when it has cooled, the bricks are sorted. Underburnt bricks are set in a further clamp and overburnt bricks or *'burrs'*, which are highly vitrified and often badly distorted, can be used for random walling.

Today, most clay bricks are fired in permanent kilns, either intermittent or continuous-burning.

Intermittent kilns are either of open *baffle* or enclosed *muffle* types, the latter being used for special facing bricks including glazed bricks which must not be discoloured.

The great majority of bricks are fired in continuous kilns, which are economical for large scale production. They are of two types: (i) those in which the fire is moved around a circuit of interconnected chambers, eg the *Hoffmann kiln*, and (ii) the *tunnel kiln* in which the bricks are moved through a stationary fire. In both cases, the green bricks are preheated by the outgoing hot gases from the firing zone and the fired bricks are cooled by the incoming air required for combustion.

Properties of clay bricks

Although the range of clay bricks available in this country is very wide, where bricks are to be used in constantly wet conditions, where a particular appearance or very high strength are required the choice may be severely limited. Wherever possible, selection should be based on observations of the behaviour of bricks for a reasonable period, in conditions approximating as closely as possible to those in which they will be used. BRS Digests 65 and 66 *The selection of clay building bricks 1 and 2* are useful references:

The properties of clay bricks are characteristically variable even within one delivery to a site, so that tests carried out on isolated samples can be very misleading. BS 3921 recommends that manufacturers should carry out frequent tests and make the results available in the form of control charts on the lines discussed in BS 2564: 1955 *Control chart technique when manufacturing to a specification*. Such records, by showing variations in properties with time, provide more information than can be deduced from isolated tests.

In general, good clay bricks have a compact texture, are reasonably free from cracks, lime, stones and pebbles and the harder varieties give a metallic ring when struck with a trowel. Good bricks are well-burnt, ie they have achieved a good ceramic bond. This is not generally indicated by simple tests although an expert who is familiar with a particular type of brick may recognize a well-fired sample by its colour and hardness. Salt content should not be excessive.

BS 3921 *quality* requirements for bricks and blocks (see table 37, page 117) include:

1 *Internal quality* Units for *internal loadbearing walls* and for *partitions* must be reasonably free from deep or extensive cracks, damage to edges and corners and from expansive particles of lime. Cut surfaces must show a reasonably uniform texture. These units will normally be suitable for rendering but not necessarily for fair faced work. When tested as described, efflorescence must not be worse than *moderate*. There are no requirements for soluble salts content or for frost resistance.

2 *Ordinary quality* These must be as described for the above units and also 'well fired' and 'reasonably free from pebbles'.

3 *Special quality* These must be as described for the above units but 'hard fired' and 'reasonably free from cracks and damage to edges and corners'. In addition, cut surfaces must show no very coarse particles. Soluble salts content is limited as described below and manufacturers are recommended to adduce evidence of the frost resistance of their products assessed by one of the methods described below.

The following properties are now considered in greater detail:

> Appearance
> Strength
> Water absorption
> Soluble salt content
> Chemical resistance
> Frost resistance
> Moisture movements
> Thermal movement
> Fire resistance
> Sound insulation
> Weight

Appearance

Formerly bricks of good appearance were obtained by careful selection from bricks which would otherwise have been regarded as *commons*. Now *facings* are usually obtained by special processes, and care in manufacture.

Colour is either integral or superficial.

Integral colour results directly from the characteristics of the various clays from which *commons* and some *facings* are made. Natural colours of fired clay bricks include red, white, yellows, browns and blue, but not green. Many facing bricks are coloured by the addition of oxides to the clay body. Generally, colour darkens as the temperature of firing increases and where the normal colour of a clay brick would be dark, a light coloured brick (or *salmon*) suggests inadequate firing with associated lower strength and durability.

Red bricks Red, caused by iron oxide, is perhaps the typical clay brick colour, produced in most parts of the country.

White bricks are made from chalky clays including *gault* clay found in South East England. *Gaults* shaped either by wire cutting or by pressing are available almost white and also *flushed* pink.

Yellow bricks include London Stocks which are made from the brickearth and chalk found in Kent and Essex. Fuel added to the clay before firing leaves characteristic voids and burnt particles in the fired brick.

Brown bricks in various shades from light to dark.

Blue bricks result from a high content of iron compounds and firing in reducing (low oxygen) conditions as in the Staffordshire blue engineering brick.

Superficial colour results from a surface treatment such as *sand facing*, from oxide pigments applied before firing, or from control of the atmosphere in the kiln. Damage in handling, or at a later stage, exposes the body of the brick the appearance of which may be quite different from that of the thin facing.

Texture results from the method of forming, from mechanical treatment, or from sand or broken brick particles blasted onto the surfaces of the *green* bricks.

Glazes Glazed surfaces are easily kept clean, and the joints, although frequent, can be narrow, the bricks being larger in 'actual' size than standard bricks.

Salt glaze The extremely hard and impervious transparent *salt glazes* are well known as a standard finish on drainage goods. They were formerly often applied to clay bricks but the clays which are suitable limit the colours to brown and red-brown. The process is simple: sodium introduced into the kiln during firing of the bricks reacts with the silica in the clay forming sodium silicate.

Applied glazes These enamel glazes are opaque and black, white or any colour and the bricks are very much more costly than salt glazed products. The *green* brick is first partially fired to the *biscuit* condition. It is then sprayed with, or dipped in a glazing *slip* which must match the body so that it is not crazed by the expansion of the latter during subsequent refiring in a kiln which is enclosed to avoid contact with the products of combustion.

Strength

Although clay bricks may have strength up to 175 N/mm^2, considerably lower strengths are adequate for the loadings which are usual in small buildings. The Building Regulations 1972 require only 2·75 N/mm^2 for two-storey houses or two-storey buildings divided into flats, and the LCC Constructional Bylaws 1965 are satisfied with a minimum of 1·38 N/mm^2 for internal non-loadbearing walls. Nevertheless, by taking into account the properties of high strength bricks (see tables 39 and 40), and mortars in accordance with the rules laid down in CP 111, economies can be effected in the thicknesses of multistorey walls.

BRS Digest 65 emphasises that every clay brick is an individual with wide differences in strength which are not evened out when bricks are stacked on a truck. Quality control testing indicates how much uncertainty attaches to an isolated test result, and BS 3921 encourages its adoption for the benefit of users as well as manufacturers.

Water absorption

Water absorption is determined by simple boiling or vacuum tests described in the BS, and is expressed as a percentage of the dry weight of a brick. Like strength, neither water absorption nor *saturation coefficient* (the ratio of 24 hour cold absorption to maximum absorption) are reliable general indices of durability and BS 3921 lays down maximum values for water absorption only for engineering bricks and bricks for damp-proof courses, see table 40.

Type	Compressive strength (BS 3921)[1] (N/mm²)
Machine moulded	
Extreme range	3·45–172·5
Engineering variety BS 3921 : 1969	
Class A	68·9 ⎫ minimum
Class B	48·5 ⎬
Wealden engineering bricks	34·5–103·5
Carboniferous shale	34·5–103·5
Leicester red wirecuts	27·6–44·8
Flettons:	
special strength bricks	27·6 minimum
normal	20·7 minimum
cellular	6·9 minimum
Keuper marl wirecuts (Birmingham, Leicester, Nottingham, etc)	20·7–27·6
Gaults (pressed)	17·25–24·15
London stocks	3·5–17·5
Sussex structural 'V' brick	34·45 average
Calculon: A10 perforated	68·9
B75	51·7
C5 solid	34·45
Diatomaceous earth	2·76–5·62
Hand moulded	
Extreme range	6·89–58·6
Leicester sand stocks	about 27·6
Kentish stocks	6·89–17·25
Building Regulations 1972 – load-bearing walls one and two-storey houses and two-storey houses divided into flats	2·75 minimum
any other buildings: solid[2]	10·00
hollow	5·00

	Compressive strength (Schedule IV tests) N/mm²
LCC Constructional Bylaws 1965 external and internal loadbearing walls	10·35 minimum
external non-loadbearing walls	2·76
internal non-loadbearing walls	1·38

[1] Mean of tests on ten specimens with frogs filled, unless stated otherwise, see Clause 43.
[2] Aggregate volume of solid material not less than 75 per cent of total volume calculated from overall dimensions.

Table 39   Compressive strengths of clay bricks

Soluble salt content

All clay bricks contain some soluble salts varying in quantity from brick to brick even within one delivery. Soluble salts derive from the original clay or from its reaction with sulphur compounds from the coal used for firing the bricks. Salts in bricks sometimes cause staining, efflorescence, decay of certain bricks and, as sulphates, expansion and disintegration of mortars and renderings.

Staining   Ferrous sulphates often react with lime in fresh mortar and cause brown stains, and salts of vanadium and chromium sometimes cause yellow and pale green patches.

Efflorescence   Soluble salts in bricks, in particular magnesium and sodium salts, and to a less extent calcium and potassium salts, together with lime compounds in fresh cement-lime mortars, may be carried to the surface and crystallize as a white or near-white deposit. The extent to which this efflorescence appears depends upon the amount and solubility of salts present and upon wetting and drying conditions. Efflorescence is often seen, particularly in the spring, when bricks dry out after having been allowed to become wet in the stack on the site, or during laying. However, efflorescence is likely to show at any age if brickwork is saturated and subsequently dries out. Parapets and retaining walls often do this. Whether efflorescence shows mainly either on the bricks or on the mortar is largely determined by their relative permeabilities and consequent rates of evaporation from the respective surfaces.

In crystallizing, salts expand, and if this occurs below the surfaces of underfired bricks (*crypto-efflorescence*), crumbling may result. BS 3921 limits the salt content of *special quality* bricks, see table 41, and describes a test for five degrees of seriousness of efflorescence. On *ordinary* and *special* quality bricks, efflorescence must not exceed *moderate*, whereby deposits must not exceed 50 per cent of the area of a face, or cause powdering or flaking.

Sulphate attack on mortars and renderings   In persistently wet conditions sulphates react slowly with tricalcium aluminate (a constituent of Portland cement and hydraulic lime) and cause it to expand and later to soften and disintegrate. Sulphate attack is common on mortars in clay brickwork which remains wet for long periods. BRS Digest 89 states that a vertical expansion of 0·2 per

Designation	Class	Minimum average compressive strength[1] (N/mm^2)	Maximum[2] absorption after boiling or vacuum treatment (percentage by weight)
Engineering brick	*A*	69·0	4·5
	B	48·5	7·0
Load-bearing brick (for brickwork designed in accordance with CP 111)	15	103·5	No requirements specified
	10	69·0	
	7	48·5	
	5	34·5	
	4	27·5	
	3	20·5	
	2	14·0	
	1	7·0	
Bricks for damp-proof courses	'd.p.c.'	5·2 or higher strengths as required	4·5
Bricks for loadbearing brickwork 'not designed' (in accordance with CP 111)	—		No requirements specified
Bricks for non-loadbearing partitions	—	1·4	

[1] When tested in accordance with BS 3921.   [2] Average

Table 40   Strength and water absorption requirements for bricks (BS 3921 : 1969)

cent is quite common in facing brickwork where sulphation of the mortar has occurred. Sometimes renderings are attacked.

Sulphates derive from soils; gypsum plaster (which is sometimes wrongly mixed with Portland cement); from flue gases, and they are contained in clay bricks, more particularly those fired at lower temperatures. Where persistently wet conditions are unavoidable, eg in earth retaining walls, the sulphate content of clay bricks should

Soluble radicals	Maximum content[1] per cent (by weight)
Sulphate	0·30
Calcium	0·10
Magnesium	0·03
Potassium	0·03
Sodium	0·03

[1] As determined by tests on ten individual bricks

Table 41   Maximum salt content of 'Special quality' bricks (BS 3921)

not exceed the limit laid down in BS 3921 for *Special quality* bricks:

Unfortunately few works can supply clay bricks with such a low sulphate content, and wherever possible brickwork should be designed to be as dry as possible by adopting good water-shedding and damp-proofing practice. For example parapets and free-standing walls should have copings with generous overhangs and drips, and a *flexible* damp-proof course below. Where there is any likelihood of ordinary clay bricks becoming and staying wet for long periods, mortars and renderings should be rich mixes preferably based on sulphate-resisting Portland cement, supersulphated cement or, with the manufacturers' approval, high alumina cement. See chapter 7, page 142.

It is strongly recommended that expansion joints should be provided in clay facing brickwork at not more than 12 m centres.

Chemical resistance

Decay of less durable bricks results from the drainage of water from the calcium sulphate deposits which form on limestone in polluted atmospheres. Generally, however, burnt clay products have high resistance to most chemicals and in particular engineering bricks of *special* quality, with suitable mortars, are satisfactory for sewerage, industrial chimneys and pickling tanks. BS 3679 : 1963 *Acid resisting bricks and tiles* gives requirements for four types (not including floor quarries) in respect of sizes, composition and texture. Apparent porosity of red, blue and refractory bricks and tiles must not exceed 12 per cent and a percentage to be agreed for chemical stoneware bricks and tiles. Tests are described in the Standard.

Frost resistance

As with other properties, clay bricks vary widely in their resistance to frost. Also exposure hazards differ greatly and materials which may be perfectly satisfactory for walling between damp-proof course and roof, may decay rapidly if they are frozen whilst they are saturated, as may occur in earth retaining walls and brick on edge copings.

Neither high strength, low water absorption, or saturation coefficient are satisfactory indices of frost resistance. Thus some bricks which are included in the *engineering* variety are not frost resistant and some bricks approaching 48 N/mm² in crushing strength decay rapidly when they are wet and subject to frost. Flettons 20·7–34·5 N/mm² should never be used as brick-on-edge copings. On the other hand, some weaker bricks such as London stocks 3·5–17·5 N/mm² are frost resistant.

Where bricks may be frozen while they are saturated bricks of *special quality* are needed. At present the best evidence of frost resistance is provided by use in buildings for a number of years and BS 3921 requires bricks of *special quality* to have performed satisfactorily for three years under conditions of exposure at least as severe as those proposed in a building in the locality in which it is now intended to use them. If no such building exists, sample panels built in an exposed position under the supervision of an independent authority will be acceptable. Where it is not possible to obtain evidence of frost resistance by either of these methods, bricks are deemed to be frost resistant if they qualify under

the *engineering* classification in respect of strength or water absorption.

Moisture movements

The reversible moisture movement of clay products is less than that of concretes and calcium silicate bricks and is generally of no practical significance.

Material	Movements	
	Irreversible per cent	Reversible per cent
Clay bricks	0·10–0·20	negligible
Calcium silicate bricks	0·001–0·05	0·001–0·05
Lightweight concrete blocks	0·06	0·05
Concrete bricks	0·03	0·02

Table 42 *Approximate moisture movement of typical bricks and blocks*

On the other hand, irreversible expansion of clay products due to absorption of moisture from the atmosphere, varying with types of clay and temperature of firing, may amount to 0·1 or exceptionally of 0·2 per cent. See figure 16. (There is no

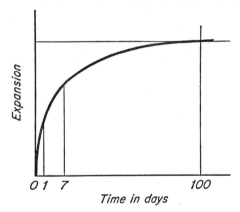

16 *Expansion of clay bricks after firing*
Graph from BRS Digest 65

test suitable for selecting clay bricks in this respect.) Because about half of the ultimate movement takes place in the first seven days after bricks begin to cool after firing BRS Digest 65 recommends that at least a week should pass before bricks are used, particularly where they are to be laid in a strong mortar which will become rigid very quickly. (The *Model specification for load-bearing clay brickwork* issued by the British Ceramic Research Association recommends that 'no bricks shall be built into the work until two days have elapsed from the time of drawing from the kiln'.)

The BRE advocates the avoidance of returns less than about 700 mm which are specially vulnerable to cracking, and in long walls it advises the inclusion of joints which can accommodate an expansion of 10 mm in 13 m.

Thermal movement

The coefficient of thermal expansion of typical clay bricks is $5-8 \times 10^{-6}$ deg C. Although small, thermal movements can be significant, for example between the inner leaf of a cavity wall and an outer leaf of dark coloured bricks exposed to solar radiation.

Diatomaceous bricks have negligible thermal expansion.

Thermal conductivity

Conductivity varies with density. Diatomaceous earth bricks which are very light, have a 'k' value of about 0·14 W/m deg C and can be used for lining flues carrying gases up to 870° C but ordinary clay bricks are poor insulators. A 'k' value of 1·15 W/m deg C is given for *common* bricks in the *IHVE Guide*. Conductivity also varies with moisture content and tests carried out by the London Brick Company showed that the measured seasonal average 'k' values in 275 mm north-facing cavity wall built in Fletton bricks in Bedfordshire were 0·995 and 0·635 W/m deg C for the outer and inner leaves respectively.

Fire resistance

Having been fired at temperatures higher than those which normally arise in building fires, clay bricks provide excellent resistance to fire, and special refractory bricks are available.

Sound insulation

Well constructed brickwork provides insulation against airborne sound in ratio to its density and thickness although this is seriously reduced by bad bricklaying which leaves small paths for sound through a wall.

Weight

Approximate average dry weights of clay bricks are:

	kg
Calculon 10 and 75	4·09
Calculon 5	3·95
V brick – 219·1 × 219·1 × 66·7 mm	3·95
Engineering	
Accrington (red) pressed	3·86
Staffordshire (blue) pressed	3·27
Fletton: pressed	2·27
cellular	1·82
London Stock	2·14–2·27
Diatomaceous earth brick	0·91
[Calcium silicate	2·84]

CALCIUM SILICATE BRICKS

Calcium silicate bricks, commonly called either sandlimes or flint-limes according to the aggregate employed, were invented in 1866 and in 1967 some 5 per cent of all bricks produced in this country were of this type.

BS 187:1969 *Calcium silicate (Sandlime and Flint-lime) bricks* describes eight classes.

MPB and W Advisory Leaflet No. 65 (1967) HMSO is entitled *Calcium silicate Bricks and how to use them*.

The Sandlime Brick Manufacturers Association Ltd, The Hall, Church Street, Welwyn, Hertfordshire provides information and advice.

The materials used, lime and silica, and the method of forming them by pressing and high pressure steaming, make for sharp arrises and remarkable uniformity in strength, size, shape, colour and texture.

In appropriate grades, the strength, hardness and durability of calcium silicate bricks is adequate for almost all purposes but they must not be exposed to acids or to strong salt solutions. Fire resistance can be taken as being equal to that of clay bricks. Values for sound and heat transmission through walls approximate to those for clay bricks of equal density. Calcium silicate bricks are free from the soluble salts, the presence of which in clay bricks sometimes gives rise to efflorescence, loss of adhesion of mortar and plaster and to sulphate attack on Portland cement. Unlike new clay bricks which tend to expand, calcium silicate bricks (and even more so concrete bricks) shrink when they dry out and this must be taken into account in the design of brickwork if cracking is to be avoided.

Manufacture

Controlled proportions of sand, crushed or uncrushed flint or combinations of such materials are mixed with hydrated lime or quicklime and water, to which stable and inert pigments may be added. Unlike clay bricks, calcium silicate bricks are not burnt. After pressing, the bricks are steamed at pressures up to 1·7 N/mm² for about eight hours in an autoclave, during which process the lime reacts with the surfaces of the silica particles forming hydrated calcium silicates and leaving practically no free lime.

When exposed to the atmosphere, the calcium silicate gradually reacts with carbon dioxide and forms calcium carbonate, the brick slowly gains in strength and hardness and finally resembles a natural calcareous sandstone.

Size

BS 187: 1970 lays down the following sizes (mm):

	lower limit	*work size*	*upper limit*
Length	212	215	217
Width	101	103	105
Height	63	65	67

Coordinating sizes are 225, 112·5 and 75.

Bricks of other sizes and of special shapes are available from some manufacturers.

The fact that dimensional tolerances are closer than those for clay bricks makes a thinner joint practicable – whether for technical or aesthetic reasons.

Properties

Strength

Table 43 indicates the requirements of BS 187 for respective classes. In addition some makers can provide calcium silicate bricks with minimum average crushing strengths up to 50 N/mm² or even higher, but the extremely high strengths of *Class A* clay *engineering* bricks cannot yet be obtained commercially. Flint-lime bricks with crushed stone aggregates show substantially higher strengths when tested with the frogs filled with mortar but sandlime bricks show no significant increase in strength where the frogs are filled and BS 187 tests are carried out with the frogs unfilled.

Requirements for uniformity of strength, which would not be practicable for other bricks, are included in the BS for calcium silicate bricks.

Hardness

Hardness (resistance to abrasion) varies with class and quality of brick, the stronger classes being suitable for lightly trafficked paving.

Moisture movement

The extent of moisture movement is intermediate between that of clay and concrete bricks. Initial irreversible drying shrinkage is equal to subsequent reversible moisture movement, ie 0·001 to 0·05 per cent linear. Table 43 shows the BS 187 limits for classes 2 to 7.

To avoid cracking where wet bricks are built into long walls or are restrained, and subsequently dry out, the following precautions should be taken:

1 Use bricks which comply with *Class 2A, 3A, 4, 5* or *7* of BS 187 : 1970 (see table 43).
2 Keep the bricks as dry as possible before and during construction and until construction is complete. If wetting is essential in very hot weather as little water as possible should be used.
3 Use a mortar which contains no more Portland cement than is required to resist possible freezing during bricklaying, to suit loading or the exposure to be expected in service. A relatively weak mortar is able to absorb the moisture movement of the bricks so that any hair cracks tend to form around individual bricks, and cracks through both joints and bricks are unlikely to occur.
4 Avoid restraint, where possible, and provide movement joints at susceptible places such as between the heads and sills of superimposed windows, at changes in thickness or height and at intervals of not more than 8 m in long walls. Movement joints are also required between calcium silicate and clay brickwork to allow

	BS 187 : 1970			Suitable uses		Recommended mortars Portland cement[3] : lime[4] : dry sand[5] – by volume	
Class	Minimum average compressive strength[1] N/mm² approx.	Maximum coefficient of variation of strength per cent	Maximum average drying shrinkage of 3 bricks percentage of wet length[2]			Normal weather during construction	Freezing weather during construction
7	48·5	16	0·025	Above and below ground level	Continuously saturated with water. Repeatedly exposed to temperature below freezing when saturated	1 : 1 : 5–6[8]	1 : ½ : 4–4½[8]
5	34·5	16	0·025				
4	27·5	} 20	0·025				
3A	20·5		0·025			1 : 1 : 5–6[9]	
3B	20·5		0·035		Boundary and parapet walls. Chimneys.		
2A	14·0	} 30	0·025	Above ground level only – unless protected from ground	Piers: Short partially restrained infill panels:	1 : 2 : 8–9[9]	1 : 1 : 5–6[9]
2B	14·0		0·035				
1	7·0		no limit stated	Internal walls and backings only. Below ground level d.p.c. only if protected	Short internal walls not restrained at both ends[7]	1 : 2 : 8–9[9,10] or 1 : 3 : 10–12 [9,10]	

[1] Of 10 bricks tested wet with frogs unfilled. [2] No limit where bricks are to be used under permanently wet conditions.
[3] A sulphate resisting cement should be used where sulphates are present in ground water.
[4] Lime refers to non-hydraulic or semi-hydraulic lime. If hydrated lime is batched 'dry' proportions may require to be increased up to 40 per cent to ensure adequate workability.
[5] If sand is damp the volume must be increased to compensate for *bulking*; where a range of sand content is given the higher quantity refers to well graded sand and the smaller quantity to coarse or uniformly fine sand.
[6] If bricks are wet the equivalent Portland cement : sand with plasticizer mortar should be used. Alternatively a plasticizer may be added to cement : lime : sand mortars to entrain 8 to 12 per cent air.
[7] The higher shrinkage of these bricks gives rise to greater risk of cracking of brickwork.
[8] For calculated load-bearing brickwork using *Classes 5 to 7* bricks the mortar should be specified by the designer to give adequate workability, strength and durability.
[9] Alternatively equivalent masonry cement : sand or Portland cement : sand with plasticizer mixes may be used.
[10] Alternatively, equivalent hydraulic lime : sand mixes may be used.

Table 43   Summary of properties of calcium silicate bricks, with suitable uses and mortars

for differential and possibly opposed movements of the different materials. Joints may be filled with a resilient material to within 13 mm of the outside face and either sealed with mastic as the work proceeds, or left open until the construction water has evaporated from the brickwork before being pointed with mortar. Rigid fixings or renderings must not be carried over such contraction joints. Shrinkage of internal walls can usually be accommodated by joints including polythene, building paper or similar separators.

Table 43 includes the minimum compressive strength and maximum drying shrinkage values for each of the eight classes described in BS 187 : 1970 *Calcium silicate bricks* (*Sandlime and Flintlime*). With the exception of *Class 1*, the bricks must be free from visible cracks, balls of clay or loam or visible particles of lime. Bricks specified for facing purposes to be of agreed colour and texture and reasonably free from damaged arrises. Suitable uses for each class and appropriate mortars, are also indicated in the table.

Durability

Calcium silicate bricks of the quality appropriate to the type of use have been found to have 'satisfactory durability' over a period of at least fifty years. Wetting and drying and repeated freezing and thawing have little significant effect on bricks of 14·0 N/mm² compressive strength and above.

Sulphur dioxide acts chemically on the calcium silicate bonding agent and in severely polluted atmospheres surface erosion and blistering have occurred, but only after twenty-five years and in bricks of relatively poor quality. Calcium silicate bricks should not be used where they would come into direct contact with sewage, or like cement products, where they would be exposed to strong acid fumes or to splashing by acids. Sea air is not damaging but they may deteriorate if they are repeatedly wetted with sea water or solutions of sodium chloride or calcium chloride, or in severe frost when they are saturated with such solutions. Sulphate salts which occur in some soils and ground waters do not harm calcium silicate bricks but the higher strength grades should be used below damp-proof courses.

Appearance

Colour The natural colour is white, off-white, cream or pale pink according to the aggregate used. By including pigments, any colour from pastel to dark tones is obtainable. Cost is increased, especially for sky blue and deep green colours. The tone darkens when the bricks are wet.

Texture Sand lime bricks are smooth and fine-textured, and flint-lime bricks are rougher and coarser. Quality control in manufacture enables bricks of uniform colour and texture to be produced in different strengths.

Fire resistance

This is good. The Building Regulations and the LCC Byelaws class calcium silicate with clay bricks. They are suitable for chimneys, but not where they would be constantly subjected to red heat.

Absorption

The water absorption of calcium silicate bricks is 7 to 21 per cent compared with less than 4·5 to 21 per cent for clay bricks. Weather resistance of brickwork is determined by the size, structure and distribution of pores, and the effectiveness of the bond between the bricks and mortar. Calcium silicate bricks provide good adhesion for mortar, rather than by the water absorption of the bricks.

Sound insulation

This is as for clay bricks of the same density.

Thermal insulation

For practical purposes all dense brickwork can be taken to provide a k value of 1·15 W/m.

Thermal expansion

Thermal expansion is $0·014 \times 10^{-3}$ deg C. As with other bricks, CP 212 recommends that allowance should be made for possible stresses in long walls.

Weight

This is similar to that of average clay bricks, ie 2·7 to 3·4 kg.

Cost

For bricks having comparable properties and appearance the cost of calcium silicate bricks is often very competitive with that of clay bricks. Moreover the accuracy and uniformity of shape and size makes them easy to lay and saves mortar and plaster.

CONCRETE BRICKS

Concrete bricks are harder, more difficult to cut and less pleasant to handle than clay or calcium silicate bricks and are less commonly used.

Drying shrinkage varies considerably, from 0·019 to 0·080 per cent of the length and is greater than that of calcium silicate bricks. As with those bricks, special care should be taken in selection,

Type of brick	Suggested uses	Average compressive strength (wet) MN/m^2 (N/mm^2)	Maximum average drying shrinkage per cent
Bricks for special purposes	in positions where they may be subject to freezing when saturated with water, eg in parapets and externally below damp-proof course	17·2	0·025
Building Class A(i)	general facing work	12·1	0·025
Building Class A(ii)	external facing work in mortars other than strong cement mortars	12·1	0·04
Building Class B	for internal work only and in mortars other than strong cement mortars	6·9	0·06

Table 44   Summary of BS requirements for concrete bricks

design and in building to avoid cracking of brick-work after construction.

BS requirements

BS 1180 : 1944 (with amendments to November 1962) describes: *Concrete Bricks and Fixing Bricks*.

Composition

These bricks are made with:

Portland cement (BS 12)
Portland blastfurnace cement (BS 146) or with High alumina cement (BS 915)

aggregate: to pass a 12·7 mm mesh BS sieve and complying with

BS 882 – for natural aggregates
BS 1165 – for well burnt surface clinker
BS 1047 – for air cooled blast-furnace slag

or granulated blast-furnace slag containing not more than 50 per cent lime.

pigment: to comply with BS 1014.

Sizes

Length × width   219·1 ± 3·2 × 104·8 ± 1·6 mm or
(222·3 ± 3·2 × 108·0 ± 1·6 mm[1])
Depth type II   66·7 ± 1·6 mm
    type III   (73·0 ± 1·6 mm[1])

Snap headers:
    Length   (104·8 ± 1·6 mm)   or   (108·0 ± 1·6 mm[1])
Closers:
    Width   (47·6 ± 1·6 mm) or (50·8 ± 1·6 mm[1])

BS 1180 requires the appearance of the interior of the brick to be similar to that of the outside, in case the latter is damaged. It describes four classes of ordinary concrete bricks and gives minimum compressive strength and maximum shrinkage and suggests suitable uses for each class. This information is summarized in table 44.

Fixing bricks are required to be 'of a consistency to permit the easy driving of, and to provide a good purchase for nails and screws'. They are often useful for coursing purposes in conjunction with lightweight concrete blocks.

Blocks

BS 3921: Part 2 : 1969 *Bricks and blocks of fired brickearth, clay or shale* defines blocks as units more than 337·5 mm long, 225·0 mm wide or 112·5 mm high intended to be laid in mortar as walling or to be used as filler blocks in reinforced concrete floors. A block as defined by BS 2028 : 1968 *Precast concrete blocks*, has a height not greater than either

[1] It is intended to delete these sizes in the revised BS.

130

its length or six times its thickness. Generally, blocks are intended to be plastered or rendered but many modern products, more particularly concrete blocks, are sufficiently regular in shape and size and otherwise of good appearance without plaster for walling.

We now consider clay blocks and concrete blocks:

CLAY BLOCKS

Clay blocks are generally extruded hollow units. After firing, ordinary clays are dense and brittle, which presents problems in cutting and fixing. Blocks made from diatomaceous earth, however, are less dense, can be easily cut and they accept nails well.

The BS 3921 : 1969 classification summarized in table 37 on page 117 applies to clay blocks as well as bricks.

Sizes

The BS *Standard formats* for wall blocks are given in table 45 and for floor blocks in table 46.

Designation			Actual dimensions (mm)		
			length	width	height
300	62·5	225	290	62·5	215
300	75	225	290	75	215
300	100	225	290	100	215
300	150	225	290	150	215

Note: In addition half blocks 140 mm long and three quarter blocks 215 mm long for bonding are given.

Table 45   Standard formats of clay wall blocks (BS 3921 *Metric units*).

Non-BS wall blocks are also available in the following (actual) dimensions:

$$238{\cdot}1 \times 238{\cdot}1 \text{ mm}$$
$$238{\cdot}1 \times 244{\cdot}5 \text{ mm}$$

$$304{\cdot}8 \times 238{\cdot}1 \text{ mm}$$
$$333{\cdot}4 \times 142{\cdot}9 \text{ mm}$$
$$304{\cdot}8 \times 141{\cdot}3 \text{ mm}$$

Figure 17 shows typical clay wall blocks and figure 18 shows a block coursing with bricks.

Figure 19 shows typical clay floor blocks with a filler tile.

Designation	Actual dimensions mm		
	length [1]	width	depth
300, 300	75 100 125 150 175 200 225 250	295	295	75 100 125 150 175 200 225 250

[1] Length is measured along the direction which is normally parallel to the concrete reinforcing in the floor.

Table 46   Part 2: Standard formats for clay floor blocks (BS 3921 : *Metric units*)

Rules are also given for dimensional tolerances and for selecting and testing blocks for squareness, bowing and twisting.

The specified minimum average compressive strengths for clay blocks tested in accordance with clause 43 of the BS are as follows:

Non-loadbearing partitions	1·38 N/mm²
Facing and common blocks *Ordinary* and *Special* qualities	
Blocks for loadbearing internal walls	2·8 N/mm²
Hollow blocks for structural floors and roofs	14 N/mm² [1]

[1] This minimum strength differs from that given for blocks for walling because the methods of testing, and expressing the results are different.

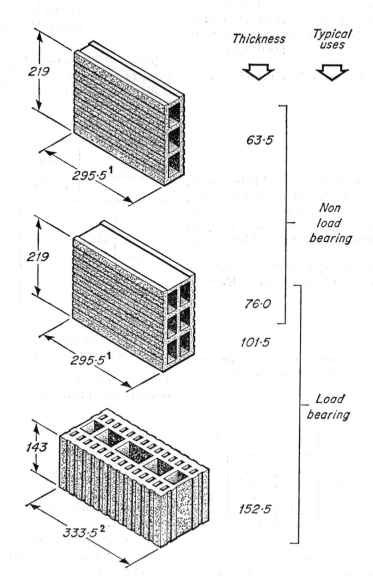

Thickness Typical uses

219

295·5[1]

63·5

Non load bearing

219

295·5[1]

76·0

101·5

Load bearing

143

333·5[2]

152·5

[1] Special bonding lengths are available.
[2] These blocks can be easily cut to length.
[3] *Phorpres* products (London Brick Company Limited).

Note: Corner, closer, fixing blocks and blocks with recesses for conduits are also available.
Dimensions mm; imperial sizes rounded to 0·5 mm

17 *Typical clay wall and partition blocks*

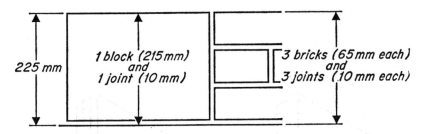

18   A block coursing with bricks

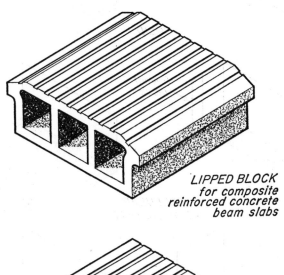

19   Typical clay floor and roof blocks and filler tiles

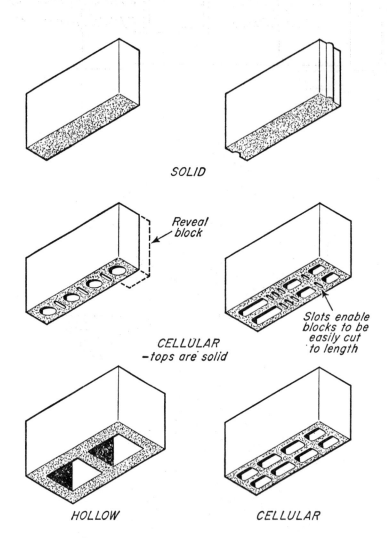

SOLID

Reveal block

CELLULAR
—tops are solid

Slots enable blocks to be easily cut to length

HOLLOW   CELLULAR

20 *Typical lightweight concrete wall and partition blocks.*
Half blocks and other standard specials including relief
and smooth faced blocks are also available

CONCRETE BLOCKS

BS 2028, 1364: 1968 amended 1970 *Specification for precast concrete blocks: Metric units* describes solid, hollow and cellular blocks

	Voids per cent of total volume
Solid	Up to 25 per cent
Hollow: large holes or cavities which pass through the block	More than 25 per cent
Cellular: large holes or cavities with one bed face closed (usually laid uppermost)	but not more than 50 per cent

The total width of cavities measured at right angles to the face of blocks as laid in a wall must not exceed 65 per cent of the block thickness.

Table 47 gives the BS dimensions. Certain other sizes will 'continue to be available while the demand lasts'. Table 48 summarizes the main requirements for properties of blocks. Any combination of materials and methods of manufacture may be used provided the resulting blocks comply with the specification.

Type A blocks are 'dense', ie not less than 1500 kg/m^3, and include the strongest blocks the use of which is permissible in all positions.

Types B and C are 'lightweight' concretes, ie less than 1500 kg/m^3, made with a lightweight aggregate or aerated cement with or without fine aggregate, high pressure steam autoclaved.

Lightweight blocks provide thermal conductivities as low as 0·14 W/m deg C. Fixing and chasing is easier than with dense clay and concrete units, although drying shrinkage is more troublesome and precautions should be taken to prevent cracking of blockwork. The manufacturer's advice should be obtained as to the best procedure for plastering and rendering lightweight concrete blocks. Blocks of good appearance include those with exposed aggregate and special facing mixes. One proprietary product has a facing of thermo-setting resin with a sand filler the edge of which projects as a lip giving an accurate and narrow joint. The sound absorption of open textured blocks is good.

Type	length	Work size[1] mm		
		height	thickness	
A B	390	90 190	75 90 100 140 190	
A	440[2]	215		
B	440[2]	190 215[3] 290[4]	75 90 100 140 190 215	
	590	190 215[3]		
C	390	190	60 75	
	440[2]	190 215[3] 290		
	590	190 215[3]		

[1] *Work sizes* are manufacturing sizes subject to specified permissible deviations, ie l and h+3 mm−5 mm. *Coordinating* sizes are 10 mm greater in each direction.
[2] 440 mm = two 215 mm brick stretchers + one 10 mm joint.
[3] 215 mm = three 65 mm brick heights + two 10 mm joints.
[4] 290 mm = four 65 mm brick heights + three 10 mm joints.

Table 47 *Work sizes of concrete blocks* from BS 2028, 1364: 1968 amended 1970.

Type B blocks are loadbearing. They may be used below ground floor damp proof course in:

(a) internal walls
(b) the inner leaf of external cavity walls
(c) external walls protected by tanking.

In other positions below ground floor dpc blocks should:

1 be solid, hollow or cellular blocks made with dense aggregates complying with BS 882 or 1047, or
2 have an average compressive strength not less than 7·0 N/mm^2, or
3 be accompanied by the manufacturer's authoritative evidence as to suitability for the intended use.

Type C blocks are non-loadbearing and not suitable for use below ground floor dpc.

135

	Type	Density of block[1]	Compressive strength		Maximum permitted drying shrinkage per cent	Wetting expansion
			Minimum average[2] N/mm²	Lowest individual block N/mm²		
Dense concretes — Load-bearing	A	Not less than 1500 kg/m³	3·5 7·0 10·5 14·0 21·0 28·0 35·0	2·8 5·6 8·4 11·2 16·8 22·4 28·0	0·05 0·05 0·06 0·06 0·06 0·06 0·06	Expansion of clinker aggregate blocks not more than 0·02% in excess of drying shrinkage value
	B	Less than 1500 kg/m³ but more than 625 kg/m³	2·8 7·0	2·25 5·6	0·07 0·08	
Light-weight concretes		625 kg/m³ and less	2·8	2·25	0·09	
— Non-load-bearing	C	Less than 1500 kg/m³ but more than 625 kg/m³	Transverse breaking load is specified (varies with size of block)		0·08	
		625 kg/m³ and less			0·09	

[1] Calculated by dividing weight of block by its overall volume including holes and cavities.
[2] Average of test sample of 10 blocks and strength of weakest individual block to be not less than 80 per cent of the average value.

Table 48   Summary of main requirements for properties of Concrete Blocks of BS 2028, 1364 : 1968

7 Limes and cements

Limes

Limes can be broadly classified as *non-hydraulic* or *hydraulic*. Non-hydraulic limes, so called because they will not harden without air being present (for example under water), comprise high calcium and magnesium limes. BS 890: 1966 *Building limes* covers hydrated lime (powder), quicklime and lime putty of non-hydraulic and semi-hydraulic limes, but not the eminently hydraulic limes.

Limes are rarely used as the sole cementitious ingredient in mortars, renderings or plasters, and never in ordinary concretes, strength development being small and slow in non-hydraulic limes and the strength of hydraulic limes being less than that of Portland cement.

HIGH CALCIUM LIMES (*pure* or *fat* limes)

These are produced by burning a fairly pure limestone, essentially calcium carbonate, so as to drive off the carbon dioxide leaving calcium oxide or *quicklime*. When water is added to quicklime considerable heat is evolved, there is considerable expansion, and the resulting product is calcium hydroxide. If the operation is carefully controlled, as it can be in a factory, so that just sufficient water is added to hydrate the quicklime, the lumps break down into a dry powder known as *dry hydrate*. Where lime is hydrated on the building site, or in a builder's yard (which is rare today), an excess of water is added and the resulting *slaked lime* should be passed through a fine sieve to remove slow slaking particles and then left to mature for at least three weeks.

Although they are unlikely to be present in hydrated lime which complies with BS 890, unslaked particles tend to slake and expand after lime has been used, causing localized *popping* and *pitting* of plaster, or expansion of brickwork.

The tendency of limes and cements to expand is expressed as *soundness*.

High calcium limes are mainly of use in building because they are *fat*, ie they make for workable mortar, rendering and plaster mixes. Fatness improves with prolonged maturing of slaked lime (no harm is done thereby) and although 'dry hydrate' can be used immediately after mixing with water, its plasticity is greatly improved by *soaking overnight*, ie for at least 12 hours.

High calcium limes also retain water even when they are applied to absorptive backgrounds. Initial stiffening depends on loss of water – by evaporation or to absorptive materials such as bricks. Hardening depends on combination with carbon dioxide from the air (*carbonation*) with reformation of the original calcium carbonate. Because hardening is necessarily from the outside, the interior of a mass hardens more slowly, even where a mix includes sand which makes access of air to the interior somewhat easier.

In addition to its use in mortars, renderings and plasters, hydrated high calcium lime is used in the manufacture of calcium silicate bricks, see page 126, and to a limited extent in lime wash, see *MBC: C and F*. (It should not be added to high alumina cement mixes lest a *flash set* should occur.)

MAGNESIUM LIMES

These non-hydraulic limes are made from limestones which contain more than 5 per cent, and usually more than 35 per cent, of magnesium oxide. They are less easily slaked than high calcium limes usually by slaking to powder under a heat-conserving thick layer of sand. After screening through a larger mesh than that used for high calcium lime to enable the sand particles to pass through, some unhydrated magnesium oxide usually remains and this carbonates and gives the mortar greater strength than high calcium limes. If the latter process is delayed, as may happen where plaster is painted at an early age, delayed hydration of this oxide may lead to expansion of the finished work.

HYDRAULIC LIMES

These limes which harden to some extent by an internal reaction are made by burning chalk or limestone which contain clay, producing compounds similar to those present in Portland cement. They are stronger but less fat or plastic than non-hydraulic limes.

Semi-hydraulic lime is derived mainly from the grey chalk of the southern counties of England, hence the term *greystone lime*.

BS 890 requires the combined content of calcium and magnesium oxides to be not less than 60 per cent for hydrated lime or 70 per cent for quicklime and lays down minimum hydraulic strengths.

Eminently hydraulic lime is not clearly distinguished from semi-hydraulic lime.

The term *blue lias* is applied to eminently hydraulic limes made from the liassic limestone found in Somerset, and elsewhere.

Table 49 shows that eminently hydraulic lime is weaker than Portland cement and as it does not improve plasticity there is no point in mixing them together.

Hydraulic limes present some difficulty in slaking. While like all limes they must be thoroughly slaked, excess water would lead to premature hardening and the exact amount of water required can only be determined by experience with the

	Crushing strength N/mm²	
	7 days	6 months
Hydraulic lime	0·69	3·44–6·89
Portland cement	17·23	27·58

Table 49 Strengths of typical Hydraulic lime and Portland cement mortars (1 : 3 mixes by volume) Information from BRS Digest 46 (First series) *Building limes* revised 1966.

particular lime concerned. Clearly, hydraulic lime cannot be soaked overnight to improve its workability.

Some eminently hydraulic lime is supplied as quicklime and this should be slaked in the manner described for magnesium lime.

POZZOLANAS

Pozzolanic materials containing silica, alumina and some iron oxide combine with slaked lime to form a hydraulic cement.

Natural pozzolanas include volcanic ashes such as that from Pozzuoli near Mount Vesuvius, trass from the Upper Rhine and santourin from Greece, while certain sands derived from igneous rocks can be substituted for ordinary sands in mortars.

Artificial pozzolanas include crushed burnt clay bricks and tiles, granulated blast furnace slag and pulverized fuel ash.

Cements

Certain adhesives (see chapter 14) and plasters (see *MBC: C and F* chapter 13) which are sometimes called 'cements' are described in other chapters.

This chapter is concerned with hydraulic cements used mainly in concretes, screeds, mortars and renderings, ie Portland cements, supersulphated cement and high alumina cement, of which Portland cements are by far the most widely used.

These cements are *hydraulic*, ie they depend upon water rather than air for strength development. When water is added to cement a chemical reaction begins immediately and continues while water is still present. Cements stiffen at first and later develop strength. Only a small quantity of water is required to hydrate cement and additional water evaporates leaving voids, which reduce the density, strength and durability of the product.

Thus, strength is related to the water:cement ratio as shown in figure 24, page 155.

Strength development ceases at about freezing point and at higher temperatures its rate is related to temperature and age, see figure 29. In the process of hydration, cements, in particular high alumina cement, evolve sufficient heat to be useful in maintaining the temperature of concrete in cold weather. In hot weather, however, exothermic heat may lead to differential stresses and resulting cracking of massive structures. In drying, cement pastes shrink and some of the movement is reversible. See figure 22, page 141.

Normally, no two Portland, supersulphated or high alumina cements must be mixed together, and all plant and tools must be carefully cleaned to prevent this happening.

Tables 50 and 51 give information comparing the properties of the more important cements.

SETTING AND HARDENING

In broad terms, *setting* means stiffening only, and *hardening* means useful strength development, which are different phases in the overall process of the hydration of a cement. Quite soon after water has been added cement pastes begin to stiffen and for convenience in use this must be neither too slow nor too rapid. A small proportion of gypsum is added in manufacture to retard setting.

The relevant British Standards describe tests by which two degrees of setting of cement pastes known as *Initial* and *Final* sets can be determined.

During setting cement pastes may expand and British Standards include a *soundness* test for assessing, and limits for, setting expansion.

The finer the cement particles, the larger the superficial area which is available for hydration by water and the more rapid are setting and early hardening of a given type of cement. Thus, in BS 12 : 1971 *Portland cement* the minimum specific surfaces are given as 2250 and 3250 cm²/g for ordinary and rapid-hardening Portland cements respectively. The setting times are controlled by the addition of suitable proportions of gypsum in manufacture.

Table 50 lists BS requirements for the setting times and strengths of six cements. Figure 21 shows the strength development of concretes made with various cements up to 12 months.

During initial drying out cement paste shrinks and if drying out occurs before sufficient strength has been developed the cement paste is bound to crack. A proportion of the initial drying shrinkage is irreversible but subsequently, with increase and decrease of water content, cements expand and contract and these reversible movements are about half as much as the initial shrinkage. See figure 22.

TYPES OF CEMENTS

The types of cement are:

Portland cements

Ordinary
Rapid-hardening
Ultra high early strength
Sulphate resisting
White
Low-heat

Cements based on Portland cement

Extra-rapid-hardening
Water repellent
Waterproof
Masonry
Coloured
Portland blast-furnace cement
Hydrophobic
Pozzolanic

Supersulphated cement

High alumina cement.

The main properties of most of these cements are given in table 51 and BS requirements for setting times and compressive strengths are given in table 50.

Portland cements

In 1824 Joseph Aspdin patented his improvement upon hydraulic lime and called the product Portland cement, because it somewhat resembled Portland stone.

Portland cements are made by calcining a slurry of clay (silica, alumina and iron oxide) with limestone (calcium carbonate), in a rotating furnace,

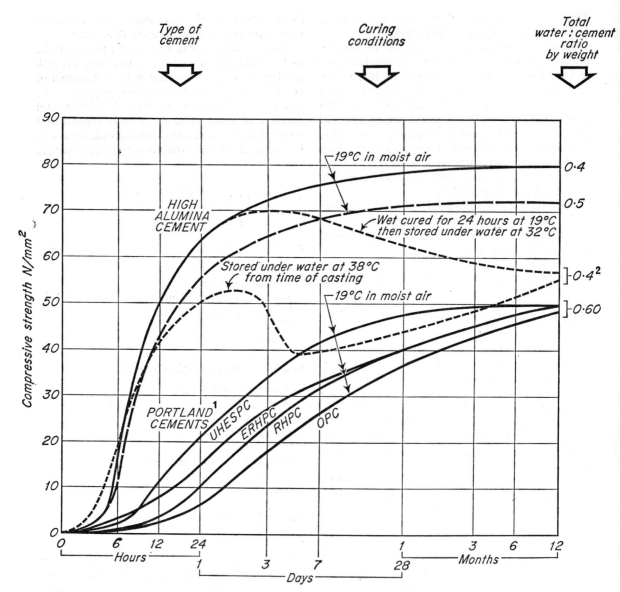

Type of
cemeut

Curing
conditions

Total
water : cement
ratio
by weight

[1] Types of Portland cements (PC)

UHESPC	ultra high early strength
ERHPC	extra rapid hardening (RHPC with calcium chloride has similar properties)
RHPC	rapid hardening
OPC	ordinary (white, coloured and sulphate resisting Portland cements have similar strength properties).

[2] 0·40 is the maximum water : cement ratio advised for high alumina cement concrete subject to high temperature and humidity. Loss of strength at high temperature and humidity is greater at higher water : cement ratios.

Note: Higher strengths in thoroughly compacted concretes are obtained at all ages with lower water : cement ratios. Strengths of 'green' concrete are difficult to measure.

21   Strength development of concretes made with various cements (approx. average cube strengths)

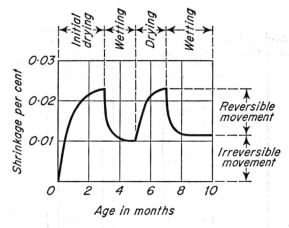

22 *Moisture movement of concrete under typical practical conditions from 'Concrete Practice' Volume II R. H. Elvery, C. R. Books Ltd.*

up to 180 m in length. The resulting clinker, with a small proportion of gypsum to retard the setting of the cement, is ground to a powder, the fineness of which influences the properties of the product. See tables 50 and 51.

Ordinary Portland cement This, the least expensive and by far the most widely used type of cement, is suitable for normal purposes. It should conform with the requirements of BS 12:1971 *Portland cement (ordinary and rapid-hardening).*

Rapid-hardening Portland cement This cement sets at the same rate as ordinary Portland cement but being more finely ground it develops strength more rapidly and is useful where early stripping of formwork and loading of structures is required. In cold weather, the high rate of heat evolution helps to prevent damage by frosts.

Rapid-hardening Portland cement is also covered by BS 12:1971.

Type of cement	BS no.	Setting times		Comparative Strengths[1] (minimum) N/mm^2			
		Initial (minimum)	Final (maximum)	24 hrs	3 days[2]	7 days[2]	28 days[2]
Ordinary Portland cement	12	45 mins	10 hours	—	15·0	23·0	—
Rapid hardening Portland cement	12	45 mins	10 hours	—	21·0	28·0	—
Portland blast furnace cement	146	45 mins	10 hours	—	15·4	23·9	35·1
Low heat Portland cement	1370	1 hour	10 hours	—	7·58	13·8	27·6
Sulphate-resisting Portland cement	4027	45 mins	10 hours	—	15·2	Greater than 3 day strength, not less than 23·4	—
High-alumina cement	915	Not less than 2 hours and not more than 6 hours	Not more than 2 hours after initial set	41·4	48·3	—	—

[1] Method tests are carried out on vibrated cubes of 1 : 3 cement/sand.   [2] Must be greater than earlier strengths.

Table 50   BS requirements for setting times and compressive strengths of cements

141

	British Standard No.	Rate of strength development	Rate of heat evolution	Drying shrinkage	Resistance to shrinkage cracking	Inherent resistance to chemical attack		
						sulphates[1]	weak acids	alkalis
Main types of Portland cement								
Ordinary	12	Medium	Medium	Medium	Medium	Low		
Rapid-hardening	12	High	High	Medium	Low	Low		
Low-heat	1370	Low	Low	Above medium	High	Medium		
Sulphate-resisting	4027	Low to medium	Low to medium	Medium	Medium	High		
Other types of Portland cement								
Extra-rapid-hardening	—	High to very high	High to very high		Medium	Low	Low	Good
Ultra-high early strength	—	Very high	Very high					
Waterproof and water-repellent	—							
Hydrophobic	—	Properties similar to those of ordinary Portland cement						
White	—							
Coloured	—							
Cements containing blastfurnace slag								
Portland blastfurnace	146	Medium	Medium	Medium	Medium	Medium	Medium	Good
Supersulphated	4248	Medium	Low	Medium	Medium	Very high	Very high	Good
High-alumina cement	915	Very high	Very high	Medium	Low	Very high	High	Low
Pozzolanic cement	—	Low	Low to medium	Above medium	High	High		Good

[1] See BRS Digest 90

Table 51 Types of cements and their properties. Based on BRS Digest 5 *Materials for concrete.*

Ultra-high early strength Portland cement Swift-crete (Cement Marketing Company Ltd.) is the subject of an Agrément Board certificate. Due to extremely fine particles (specific surface 7000 to 9000 cm²/g), concrete made with this cement achieves the 3-day strength of rapid hardening cement in 16 hours and its 7-day strength in 24 hours. There is, however, little increase in strength after 28 days. Even higher early strength can be obtained by steam curing this cement without the danger of corrosion of reinforcement which arises from the inclusion of calcium chloride in extra rapid hardening Portland cement.

The early heat of hydration is greater than that of rapid hardening cement.

Creep of concrete made with ultra high early strength cement is greater than that of other Portland cements but shrinkage is similar to that of ordinary Portland cement.

The advice of the cement manufacturer should be obtained before using admixtures.

Sulphate resisting Portland cement This cement has a reduced tricalcium aluminate content and is therefore better able to withstand chemical attack arising in wet conditions from sulphates in industrial wastes, clay bricks and flue condensates. It is suitable for use in concrete which is dense and otherwise of good quality in ground water having a concentration of sulphur trioxide up to 0·1 per cent and in subsoil containing up to 0·5 per cent. It is described by BS 4027:1966 *Sulphate-resisting Portland cement.*

White Portland cement This is manufactured from white china clay and white limestone in a special kiln and is consequently expensive. It should conform with the requirements of BS 12 : 1971.

Low-heat Portland cement This is required for thick-concrete work, where the heat generated by ordinary cements would be excessive and lead to serious cracking. BS 1370 : 1958. *Low heat Portland cement*, limits the heat of hydration, but to ensure a sufficient rate of strength development the specific surface of the cement must be at least 3200 cm²/g. It is a true Portland cement and is not diluted with inert fillers.

Cements based on Portland cement include:

Extra-rapid-hardening Portland cement This is made by adding, in manufacture, an accelerator such as calcium chloride to rapid-hardening Portland cement.

Concrete made with it stiffens in about 30 minutes and should be placed within that period. It then hardens considerably faster than rapid-hardening Portland cement. Heat evolution is also rapid and extra rapid hardening Portland cement is particularly suitable for work in cold weather but it must not be used at high ambient temperatures.

Shrinkage may be rather greater than that of ordinary Portland cement.

Water repellent cement These cements are mainly used in renderings. Mix proportions and mixing time must be carefully controlled to avoid excess air being entrained with resulting loss of strength.

Waterproof cement Although not vapourproof concrete made with this cement is rather more resistant to the penetration of liquid water and some oils than ordinary Portland cement.

Masonry cement Portland cement : sand mixes are not ideal for brick-laying and rendering. They are too strong, harden too quickly and lack the requisite plasticity and water retention. Masonry cement which contains a fine inert filler and a plasticizing agent overcomes these difficulties, while avoiding the possible expansion of lime plasticizer which is not thoroughly slaked.

Coloured Portland cements These are made by adding pigments to ordinary grey or to white cements, the latter type being more costly. The colouring matter should comply with BS 1014 : 1961.

Strength is rather lower than ordinary cement and 10 to 15 per cent additional cement should therefore be used. In other respects they should comply with the requirements of BS 12 : 1971.

Portland blast-furnace cement This is made by adding generally about 30 per cent by weight blast furnace slag to ordinary Portland cement clinker before grinding. It should comply with BS 146 : 1958 *Portland blast-furnace cement.*

The requirements for fineness, setting times, soundness and strength are as for ordinary Portland cement, but the rate of hardening in the first 28 days and the amount of heat evolved is less, so the cement is less suitable for use at low curing temperatures.

However, the strength of mature concrete is about the same as for concrete made with ordinary Portland cement. Portland blast-furnace cement has good resistance to dilute acids and sulphates and can be used for construction in sea water.

Hydrophobic cement The particles of this cement are coated with a water-repellent film and it can be stored in damp conditions for a long time without deterioration. When the cement is mixed with aggregate the film is rubbed off and hydration then takes place normally. Hydrophobic cement has better workability than ordinary Portland cement and improved waterproofing properties. It complies with the main requirements in BS 12 : 1971.

Pozzolanic cements The pozzolanic cement available in this country includes pulverized fuel ash and ordinary Portland cement. The ash reacts (see page 138) with lime which is liberated during the hydration of Portland cement.

Pozzolanic cement is a low-heat cement. Although initially slower in hardening it attains strength equal to that of ordinary Portland cement after 3, and up to 12 months.

The product has good resistance to sea water and sulphates.

Admixtures for Portland cement

Of the many products intended to modify the properties of concrete, some are of doubtful value, none of them has any useful effect upon concrete which is inherently poor in quality and some have undesirable 'side effects'.

They should be used as recommended by the manufacturers and under strict control.

The following admixtures are suitable for use with ordinary or rapid-hardening Portland cements but not generally with other types of cement.

Workability aids

These admixtures enable less water to be used.

The main types are:

1 *Water-reducing, set-retarding agents* Water-reducing admixtures, some of which entrain up to 3 per cent air, generally increase workability, cohesiveness of the mix and hence the strength of concrete, which latter they do to a greater extent than would be expected from the reduction in the amount of water added to the mix. Some water-reducing admixtures also retard setting of the cement for 2–6 hours.
2 *Fine powders* Extremely finely ground mineral powders (eg pulverized fuel ash, chalk, lime, kaolin and diatomaceous earth) act as a lubricant and improve cohesiveness by filling the pores in an ordinary concrete mix. However, if too much of these powders are added the water : cement ratio must be increased, so that strength is reduced, and there is a greater tendency to shrinkage cracking.
3 *Surface active agents* 'Wetting agents' improve workability of mixes by reducing the surface tension of water so that surfaces are wetted more easily, and, more importantly, by entraining very small air bubbles. Most such admixtures reduce strength.

Air-entraining agents

By entraining 4 to 5 per cent of minute, discontinuous and uniformly distributed air bubbles into concrete its workability, and durability, particularly in resistance to frost, are increased. Although air entrainment allows a lower water : cement ratio to be used, the reduction in density causes loss of strength of up to 15 per cent in richer mixes.

Accelerators

Accelerators increase the rate of setting and strength development of ordinary and rapid-hardening Portland cements up to about 28 days. Since accelerators increase the rate of setting of cement and may have other 'side effects' they should be used only in cold weather where the usual precautions (see page 165) are taken. In such cases the increased rate of heat evolution offsets the effects of an atmospheric temperature a few degrees below freezing point.

The most commonly used accelerator is calcium chloride ($CaCl_2$) and this is the basis of most proprietary products. It should not be added to concretes made with special purpose Portland cements or supersulphated cement without the manufacturers' approval, and never to high alumina cement concrete.

Calcium chloride should preferably be specified and batched as $1\frac{1}{2}$ per cent anhydrous calcium chloride dissolved in the mixing water, rather than using flake material (which contains about 25 per cent water of crystallization), undissolved particles of which can cause defects in the completed structure.

Calcium chloride increases resistance of concrete to abrasion, but on the other hand, the increased temperature may lead to thermal stresses causing cracking of large masses of concrete, drying shrinkage is increased by about 10 per cent and resistance to sulphates is reduced. There is also slightly increased risk of corrosion of reinforcement, more particularly in porous concretes, and calcium chloride should not be used in prestressed concrete or in the grout used in post-tensioned concrete.

Damp-proofing and permeability-reducing admixtures

Damp-proofing admixtures prevent water movement by capillary action, whereas permeability-reducing admixtures prevent its passage under pressure. No admixture, however, entirely prevents the passage of water vapour and the description 'waterproofing' admixtures is wrongly applied.

Retarders

Admixtures based on sugars, starches, zinc oxide or boric oxide retard the setting of cement without significantly affecting workability and strength. They may be used in very large masses of concrete in hot weather, exceptionally in ready-mixed concrete and as surface retarders. See *Integral finishes on concrete, MBC: C and F.*

Pigments

BS 1014:1961 describes *Pigments for cement, magnesium oxychloride and concrete*.

Except for small quantities of concrete or to obtain special colours, it is generally preferable to use cements to which pigments have been added under controlled conditions at the cement works, rather than to add them on the site.

Pozzolanic materials

Materials such as volcanic tuffs, ground blast-furnace slag and pulverized-fuel ash (PFA) the most readily available pozzolanic material in this country, combine over many months with the free lime liberated by Portland cement.

For mixes of given aggregate: cement and water: cement ratios the substitution of pulverized-fuel ash (loss on ignition not to exceed 10 per cent) for some of the Portland cement normally reduces the rate of heat evolution and, to some extent, early strength. However, provided favourable curing conditions are continued, concrete in which about 20 per cent of Portland cement is replaced by pulverized-fuel ash gives at one year about the same strength as normal concrete.

Supersulphated cement

This cement is made by grinding together 85 to 90 per cent of blast furnace slag, 10 to 15 per cent sulphate and 1 to 5 per cent of an activator such as Portland cement clinker. This cement differs in many respects from other cements and must not be mixed with them or with lime.

Calcium sulphoaluminate hydrate – the material formed when Portland cement is attacked by sulphates – is formed during hardening and it, together with a very low calcium hydroxide and tri-calcium aluminate content, accounts for the much higher resistance of supersulphated cement to sulphates.

Resistance to acids is high, the cement has been successfully used in an environment of pH3·5, and, unlike high alumina cement it is resistant to solutions of caustic alkalis (sodium and potassium hydroxides). Early strength development is slow, particularly in cold weather, but at later ages strengths are at least equal to those of comparable Portland cement mixes. Low temperature

steam curing, say at 49°C, increases the rate of early strength development but higher temperatures are not desirable. The rate of heat evolution is low, it is a *low heat* cement suitable for mass concrete and for work in hot climates. Like high alumina cement, supersulphated cement is generally used where its special properties are required, and particular attention must be paid to good concreting practice. Thus water and aggregates must be clean. Mixes should be designed for thorough compaction in proportions not leaner than 1:6 by weight for concrete or 1:2 by volume for mortar, with total water/cement ratios not exceeding 0·5. Concrete mixes should be batched by weight.

Moist curing should continue for at least three days.

High alumina cement

BS 915:1947 (with amendments to January 1962) *High Alumina Cement*.

The BS requires an alumina content at least 32 per cent by weight. Bauxite and limestone are fused continuously in reverberatory furnaces (not clinkered like Portland cement) and cast into *pigs*. These are cooled and the extremely hard product (sometimes used as an aggregate for special concrete) is broken and ground to cement.

The cement is grey-black and its properties differ from those of Portland cement. The cost of high alumina cement is about $3\frac{1}{2}$ times that of ordinary Portland cement, and the cost of a typical high alumina concrete is rather less than twice that of a concrete made with ordinary Portland cement. For this reason and because special care must be taken in its use it is generally used only where extremely high early strength (see figure 21), rapid heat evolution, superior resistance to certain chemicals, acids and sulphates and to high temperatures in service, are required.

High alumina cement is resistant to agents such as sugar, oils and fats, fertilizers, vinegar, beer and peaty waters. Also resistance to acids is superior to that of Portland cement. For example it resists solutions of sulphuric acid up to pH4, and it resists all concentrations of sulphates normally found in soils. On the other hand resistance to caustic alkalis (sodium or potassium hydroxides) is low.

High alumina cement is suitable for non-structural *refractory concrete* and with crushed firebrick aggregate it resists temperatures up to 1300°C. For temperatures up to 1800°C a purer and white cement is made. *Premixes* are available based on ordinary and the special refractory cements.

The hydrated cement comprises calcium aluminate hydrates together with aluminium hydroxide gel, in contrast to the calcium silicate hydrates and calcium hydroxide gel formed in Portland cement. This cement contains only traces of sulphur compounds and does not corrode reinforcement.

High alumina cement is not quick setting and the initial set of 2 to 6 hours (see table 50) allows adequate time for mixing and placing but when mixed with Portland cement the product sets rapidly, a *flash* set may occur, and the ultimate strength is reduced. Fresh concrete of one type may be, however, placed against hardened concrete of the other type.

About 80 per cent of the ultimate strength is developed within 24 hours of water having been added and non-supporting formwork can generally be removed for re-use once the initial set has taken place. The rapid strength development is accompanied by release of most of the heat of hydration, which like other cements is about 500 J/g. The rapid heat evolution, together with the ability of calcium aluminates to develop strength at near-freezing temperatures enables concreting to continue in cold weather where concreting with other cements would have to stop. ('Anti-freeze' additives are unnecessary, and undesirable.) Conversely, the rapid heat development of high alumina cement is sometimes troublesome in mass concrete, especially in hot weather.

Like most hydraulic cements, provided there is sufficient water present for hydration and for complete compaction of the mix, the strength of high alumina cement increases as the water: cement ratio reduces.

High alumina cement mixes are more workable than equivalent Portland cement mixes and workability aids and waterproofing agents are generally unnecessary, while those intended for use with Portland cement may be harmful. Mortars must *not* be plasticized with lime, but provided chemically aggressive conditions do not exist, an equi-valent proportion of whiting can be used. The fluidity of high alumina cement concrete with a high water: cement ratio tends to cause settling and this must not be mistaken for premature stiffening; the cement is not, in fact, quick setting.

When subjected to both heat and humidity whether during curing or at *any* time subsequently normal calcium aluminate hydrates undergo *conversion* which is a crystal change accompanied by an increase in porosity and loss of strength.

The time taken to reach full conversion appears to be almost indefinite in temperate climates and where concrete is subjected to either high temperature or humidity alone but it is more rapid in warm and humid climates.

Conversion is very rapid if a high temperature persists in concrete for much more than 24 hours while it is hardening which is rendered more likely by the rapid heat evolution of high alumina cement. The temperature of concrete must return below 26·5°C within 24 hours of having been placed. In temperate climates this means that during the first 24 hours surfaces of concrete must be kept wet and sections thicker than about 100 mm require to be cooled with running water, the effect of which can be taken to penetrate 460 mm from the surface. Concrete more than 920 mm thick must therefore be placed in lifts not more than 460 mm high and must be cooled on top as well as on each side. 560 mm thick piles, placed in-situ in moist ground have, however, been found to harden normally.

Loss of strength due to conversion is less in concrete having a low water: cement ratio and is not significant in properly cured and thoroughly

Portland cements:	Cost factors[1]
Ordinary	100
Rapid hardening	108
Sulphate resisting	125
Low heat[2]	125
Hydrophobic	127
Extra rapid hardening	133
Water repellent	133
Ultra high early strength	183
White	212
High alumina cement	310

[1] Prices delivered to Central London   [2] In bulk only

Table 52   Cost factors for cements (approximate)

compacted concrete having a total water : cement ratio below 0·5 for normal work, or below 0·4 for prestressed work, as required by CP 116. See figure 21.

Normal good concreting practice is vital if the potential advantages of high alumina cement are to be secured. Aggregates should be well graded and clean. Water should comply with BS 3148 : 1959. Salt water should *never* be used for permanent or structural work. A low water : cement ratio is desirable to obtain maximum density and resulting resistance to abrasion, frost and chemicals and in order to obtain maximum strength.

It is strongly recommended that the advice of the manufacturer should be obtained and acted upon in all but the most straightforward cases.

Costs

Some price factors for cements are given in table 52.

8 Concretes

Concrete is a mixture of cement, water and aggregate which takes the shape of its mould and when cured at a suitable temperature and humidity, forms a solid mass. Types of concretes with their main properties and uses are shown in Table 53. Those exceeding 2000 kg/m³ are classified here as *Dense concretes*. Less dense concretes, made by aerating the mix (*cellular concrete*), by using lightweight aggregates or by omitting the fine aggregate (*no-fines*) concrete, are classified as *lightweight concretes*. See page 167.

References include:

BS 2787 : 1956 *Glossary of terms for concrete and reinforced concrete*.

CP 114 : 1967 *The structural use of normal reinforced concrete in building*.

Report on concrete practice Parts 1 and 2 issued by the Institution of Structural Engineers in conjunction with the Cement and Concrete Association.

Concrete practice Vols 1 and 2, R. H. Elvery, C. R. Books Ltd.

Concrete materials and practice L. J. Murdock and G. F. Blackledge, Edward Arnold Ltd.

Concrete Technology Vols 1 and 2, D. F. Orchard, Contractors Record Ltd.

Cements and admixtures have been discussed in Chapter 7. Dense concretes are considered here, lightweight concretes on page 170 and integral finishes on concrete *in MBC: C and F* chapter 16.

DENSE CONCRETES

Concrete is one of the few materials which are often made on the building site. In practice its quality varies considerably and it is important to understand the factors which make for good and consistent quality. In short these are: suitable cement, aggregate and water, thoroughly mixed in proportions which make possible the lowest water : cement and cement : aggregate ratios consistent with thorough compaction. Drying must

be prevented and a sufficient temperature maintained until the required strength is attained.

Very broadly, for any given type of aggregate, high density in concrete is associated with high strength, hardness, durability, imperviousness and thermal conductivity.

This chapter deals with:

Properties of hardened concrete
Materials for dense concretes, page 151
Water : cement ratio, page 154
Workability, page 155
Quality control, page 155
Choice of mix proportions, page 156
Manufacture of concrete, page 158.

Properties of hardened concrete

Strength properties

Characteristic crushing strengths of the more usual structural grades of Portland cement concretes are shown in table 54.

(The direct tensile strength of concrete varies between $\frac{1}{8}$ and $\frac{1}{14}$ of its compressive strength and the tensile strength measured in bending is usually about 50 per cent greater.)

Higher early strengths are obtained by using special cements, or by steam curing Portland cement concrete and provided concrete is fully compacted strength at all ages increases as the water : cement ratio of the mix is reduced.

Table 55 gives some typical crushing strengths at various ages for dense Portland cement concretes having a water : cement ratio of 0·6.

Figure 21 shows the strength development of concretes made with other cements and up to 12 months.

CP 115 : 1969 *The structural use of prestressed concrete* gives values for moduli of elasticity '*E*' of gravel concretes of varying strengths as in table 56.

Creep, which is plastic deformation caused by a constant load, occurs more rapidly at first but slowly approaches a limit after about five years. The extent of creep is roughly in proportion to the

Type		Aggregate	Density of aggregate kg/m³	Density of concrete kg/m³	Compressive strength at 28 days N/mm²	Modulus of elasticity N/mm²	Drying shrinkage per cent	Thermal conductivity (dry) W/m deg C	Main uses
Dense Concretes		Iron shot	4005-4561	5286	up to 69			—	Radiation shielding
		Gravel	1360-1760	2240-2480	14·0-70·0	20 700-34 500	0·03-0·04	1·4-1·8	Fire resistance Class 2
					41·4-69 (special purpose)	34 500-44 800			
		Crushed limestone	1360-1600	2160-2400	24·1-34·5				Fire resistance Class 1
		Crushed brick		1680-2160	13·8-27·6				
Lightweight concretes	No-fines	Gravel	1360-1600	1600-1950			0·016-0·028	0·08-0·94[2]	Structural
		Clinker	720-1040	880-1440	2·76-6·89		0·033-0·040		
	Lightweight aggregate	Foamed slag, sintered PFA or expanded clay with some natural sand	320-1040	720-2000	2·0-62·0 (structural concrete minimum 15·0)	6 890-20 700[4]	0·030-0·070	0·24-0·93	Superior thermal insulation and fire resistance Class 1
		Various, see table 66	(64)[3] 480-1040	(400)[3] 560-1760	(0·48)[3] 1·40-27·5		0·03-0·09	0·25-0·35 0·16-0·91	
	Aerated	—	—	400-1440	1·38-10·35	1450-3120 autoclaved	0·22 air cured 0·06 autoclaved	0·08-0·26	

[1] 2·07-4·82 N/mm² concrete.
[3] These values are for exfoliated vermiculite and perlite and are not typical of the ranges.
(Information from BRS Digests 5 and 123 and other sources)

[2] For concrete 1762-1842 kg/m³.
[4] Generally $\frac{1}{3}$-$\frac{2}{3}$ of corresponding gravel concrete.

Table 53 Types of concretes

Grade	Characteristic[1] crushing strength		Comments
	7 days N/mm²	28 days N/mm²	
150	10·0	15·0	Lowest grade for rein-forced concrete with lightweight aggregate.
210[2]	—	21·0	
225[2]	15·0	22·5	Lowest grade for rein-forced concrete with natural aggregate.
255[2]	—	25·5	
300[2]	20·0	30·0	Lowest grade for pre-stressed concrete.
375	26·0	37·5	
450	32·0	45·0	
525	38·0	52·5	
600	45·0	60·0	
675	52·0	67·5	

[1] *Characteristic strength* is that below which not more than 5 per cent of the test results are allowed to fall.
[2] *Standard mixes* are specified for these grades see page 156.

Table 54   Grades of concrete

Age at test	Average crushing strength			
	Ordinary Portland cement		Rapid-hardening Portland cement	
	Storage in air 18° C 65% R H N/mm²	Storage in water N/mm²	Storage in air 18° C, 65% R H N/mm²	Storage in water N/mm²
1 day	5·5	—	6·9	—
3 days	15·1	15·2	17·2	17·2
7 days	22·0	22·7	24·1	24·8
28 days	31·0	34·5	33·1	37·2
3 months	37·2	44·1	38·6	45·5

(1 cement : 6 aggregate, by weight; 0·60 water : cement ratio.) From BRS Digest 14 (First series)

Table 55   Typical strength development of concrete

load applied and is greater with weaker and less mature concretes.

Permeability

Concrete which is made with a low water : cement ratio and is very thoroughly compacted has good

Cube strength in compression N/mm²	Modulus of elasticity N/mm²
20·7	20 700
27·6	27 600
34·5	31 000
41·3	34 500
55·1	41 300
68·9	44 800

Table 56   Moduli of elasticity of dense concretes

resistance to the absorption of water. Admixtures can sometimes contribute to impermeability, see page 144, but no concrete is completely impervious to water vapour.

Chemical resistance

The chemical resistance of cements is considered on page 142. The chemical resistance of ordinary Portland cement concretes increases with crushing strength but special cements and sometimes special aggregates are needed where conditions are severe.

Frost resistance

Concrete may be damaged by expansion of ice crystals, which are most likely to form in capillary pores or cracks resulting from mixing water which was surplus to that required to hydrate the cement. Air-entrainment admixtures, see page 144, form discontinuous pores which improve resistance to frost.

Resistance to abrasion

This depends upon the hardness of the aggregate particles and on the ability of the mortar matrix to retain them.

Resistance of concrete to fire

Up to about 120°C the strength of ordinary concrete increases but there is a serious loss of strength at higher temperatures, flexural strength being more affected than compressive strength.

Loss of strength is less with leaner mixes, with Portland blastfurnace cement and to a greater degree where high alumina cements are used. The latter cement with crushed firebrick can be classed as refractory concrete.

Loss of strength is considerably less where aggregates which do not contain free silica, eg limestone and furnace formed aggregates are used.

Low density in cellular and lightweight aggregate concretes improves fire resistance. See page 39.

Lea in *The deterioration of concrete in structures*, Journal of Civil Engineers, May 1949, shows that Portland cement concretes with ballast or siliceous aggregates perform as follows:

Temperature °C	Permanent loss of crushing strength per cent	Colour change in aggregate[1]
250	5	—
300	18	⎫ pink or grey
600	64	⎬
900	85	⎭ grey
1200		⎬ buff
above 1200		yellow

[1] Igneous rocks do not change in colour.

The survival of reinforced concrete in fire depends upon the protection afforded to the steel reinforcement by the concrete *cover*. Wire reinforcement helps to retain this but once the cover has spalled off the steel conducts heat readily and failure is rapid.

Thermal movement

The coefficient of thermal expansion of concretes varies from 5·8 to $13·7 \times 10^{-6}$ deg C according to mix proportions, type of aggregate and curing conditions. The average value is about 10×10^{-6} deg C so that a concrete member 30 m long expands about 12 mm with a 40 deg C rise in temperature. Limestones and broken brick aggregate concretes suffer about half the movement of ballast concrete.

Moisture movement

Concrete shrinks when it dries and expands when it is wetted, the greater part of the initial drying shrinkage being irreversible.

Movement increases with the richness of a mix, with water : cement ratio, and where rigid aggregate is not used, ie in lightweight aggregate and aerated concretes. On the other hand, moisture movement can be halved by high pressure (not low pressure) steam curing. See page 166.

If the stresses induced by shrinkage exceed the tensile strength of concrete, cracks tend to occur and this is particularly likely where concrete dries out before it has had time to develop much strength, or where concrete elements are fixed rigidly at their ends. Some relief is given by the ability of concrete to creep and reinforcement at close centres restrains moisture movement, so that cracks will not normally be visible in first quality reinforced concrete.

Materials for dense concrete

Cements are dealt with on page 138, water and aggregates are now considered.

Water

Water for concrete should be reasonably free from impurities such as suspended solids, organic matter and salts, which may adversely affect the setting, hardening and durability of the concrete. This requirement is usually satisfied by using water which is fit for drinking, but where the quality of water is in doubt it can be assessed by comparing the setting times of cement pastes and the compressive strengths of concretes made with it, and with distilled water, respectively. A method of test is described in BS 3148 : 1959 *Tests for water for making concrete*.

Sea water does not normally reduce the strength of Portland cement concrete and can safely be used for plain concrete. However, efflorescence may occur, and because salt promotes the corrosion of steel sea water must not be used for reinforced concrete. It must never be used with high alumina cement.

The importance of the water : cement ratio is discussed on page 154.

Aggregates

As aggregate forms the bulk of hardened concrete

and transport is costly, it is usually desirable to use local material. Aggregate must be sufficiently strong, free from constituents which can react harmfully with the cement, be well graded and have very small, or no moisture movement. Shape and texture affect the properties of concrete, and weather resistance, hardness, appearance and thermal conductivity of the aggregate are sometimes important.

Types Natural and crushed gravels, sands, and crushed stones such as granite, basalt, hard limestones and sandstones are in common use as aggregates for dense concretes. A list of rocks under their trade groups is given in Part 2 of BS 812:1967 *Methods for sampling and testing of mineral aggregates, sands and fillers.* BS 882:1967 *Aggregates from natural sources for concrete* and BS 1201:1965 *Aggregates for granolithic floor finishes* are concerned with the suitability of aggregates for concrete work. BS 812:1967 specifies methods for sampling and testing. Air-cooled blast furnace slag used as coarse aggregate is dealt with in BS 1047:1952.

Crushed clay brick, sometimes used for its fire-resisting properties or for its appearance when it is exposed, must not contain more than 1 per cent of sulphates expressed as sulphuric anhydride.

Synthetic calcium aluminate (*Alag*) used with high alumina cement, only, produces concrete with very high strength and resistance to abrasion.

Strength Normal concrete strengths are substantially lower than those of the natural aggregates which are commonly available and the strength of aggregates is rarely a limiting factor. In fact, aggregates of moderate and low strength reduce the stress in the cement paste and can increase the durability of concrete, see *lightweight structural concrete*, page 170.

Density The bulk density of natural dense aggregates varies from 1450 to 1600 kg/m³. Very heavy aggregates, such as barytes, have been used for biological shielding from radiation.

Cleanliness Aggregates should be free from significant quantities of substances which:

1 are chemically incompatible with cement, eg sulphates and organic material
2 reduce bond with aggregate, eg clay and oil coatings

3 expand, eg bituminous coal
4 decompose, eg organic matter
5 attract moisture, eg salt in excess of 2 per cent by weight of cement
6 cause staining, eg pyrites.

Gravels and sands should be washed by the suppliers to remove soluble matter and silt. BS 812:1967 describes a site test for organic impurities and a *Field settling test* which provides an approximate guide to the clay or fine silt content.

Specific surface The larger the superficial area of the aggregate particles by reason of: angularity of the aggregate, rough texture or a high proportion of small particles, the less workable the concrete will be. On the other hand, angularity and rough texture allow a greater adhesive force to develop.

Grading The proportions of the different sizes of particles is known as the *grading* of an aggregate which is usually expressed as percentages by weight passing various sieves conforming to BS 410:1969 *Test sieves.* The nominal sizes given in figure 23 from the 1962 BS are now: 75, 37·5, 20, 10, 5, 2·5 and 1·2 mm, 600, 300 and 150 μm.

Conventionally aggregate which is mainly retained on a 5 mm BS sieve (eg natural gravel and crushed gravel and stones) is called *coarse aggregate* and aggregate which mainly passes through a 5 mm sieve is called *fine aggregate*.

BS 882:1967 *Coarse and fine aggregate from natural sources* gives grading limits for the various particle sizes. Fine aggregate gradings are given in four zones of varying 'coarseness'.[1] Table 57.

In a well graded aggregate the various sizes of particles interlock, leaving the minimum volume of voids to be filled with the more costly cement. It also flows together readily, ie it is *workable*, reducing labour in placing and enabling a lower water : cement ratio to be used. Figure 23 shows typical grading limits which give satisfactory results. However, there is no ideal grading which is applicable to all aggregates and on large works, tests should be carried out to determine the grading which gives maximum workability in the

[1] It is important to note that either *coarse* or *fine* aggregates as defined above can also be described as being *coarsely* graded if they contain a high proportion of the larger particles or *finely* graded if they contain a high proportion of the smaller particles.

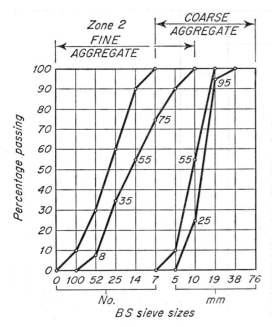

23 BS grading limits for Zone 2 fine aggregate and 19 mm down graded coarse aggregate

mix and which makes for maximum density in the concrete.

In practice aggregate is used in one of the three following combinations:

(1) normal structural concrete

- Coarse aggregate continuously graded from a specified maximum size 'down' to 5 mm
- Coarse aggregate in appropriate proportions of single-sized fractions
- Fine aggregate in one of four zones of coarseness (BS 882) graded from 5 mm 'down'

(2) high quality 'designed concrete'

- All-in aggregate includes coarse and fine components (the overall grading is rarely reliable)

(3) mass concrete only

A ratio of 1 fine aggregate : $1\frac{1}{2}$ to 3 coarse aggregate is generally satisfactory, but the most advantageous ratio depends upon the type of aggregates, the maximum size of coarse aggregate and the grading of the fine aggregate. The finer the grading of fine aggregate the smaller the proportion required to give the most satisfactory results. BS 882 : 1967 recommends the following ratios for use with coarse aggregate of 19 mm maximum size:

Grading Zone	fine		coarse
1 (the coarsest)	1	:	$1\frac{1}{2}$
2	1	:	2
3	1	:	3
4[1] (the finest)	1	:	$3\frac{3}{4}$

[1] Sand in zone 4 should not be used in reinforced concrete structures unless tests have been made to prove its suitability.

Where *all-in aggregate* is used (3), it must be remembered that the volume of a mixture of coarse and fine particles is less than the sum of the volumes of the separate parts. Approximate equivalents are:

Separate volumes		Equivalent volume of 'all-in' aggregate (approx.)
Fine aggregate	Coarse aggregate	
1	2	$2\frac{1}{2}$
$2\frac{1}{2}$	3	$3\frac{3}{4}$
2	4	5
$2\frac{1}{2}$	5	$6\frac{1}{4}$
3	6	$7\frac{3}{4}$

The procedure for determining the grading of an aggregate is given in BS 812 : 1967. So that samples for sieving truly represent the bulk of an aggregate, at least ten small samples are made into a main sample and this is reduced to a specified size by repeated *quartering*.

Size of largest particle

Generally, the largest particle of coarse aggregate should be as large as can be placed without 'bridging' between reinforcement or between reinforcement and an external face. For heavily reinforced members the largest particle should be 7 mm less

153

Coarse aggregate								BS sieve	Fine aggregate[1]			
Nominal size of graded aggregate 'continuously'			Nominal size of single-sized aggregate mm									
40 to 5	19 to 5	13 to 5	63	40	19	13	10		Grading Zone 1	Grading Zone 2	Grading Zone 3	Grading Zone 4
100	—	—	100	—	—	—	—	76 mm				
—	—	—	85–100	100	—	—	—	63 mm				
95–100	100	—	0–30	85–100	100	—	—	40 mm				
30–70	95–100	100	0–5	0–20	85–100	100	—	19 mm				
—	—	90–100	—	—	—	85–100	100	13 mm				
10–35	25–55	40–85	—	0–5	0–20	0–45	85–100	10 mm	100	100	100	100
0–5	0–10	0–10	—	—	0–5	0–10	0–20	5 mm	90–100	90–100	90–100	95–100
—	—	—	—	—	—	—	0–5	No 7	60–95	75–100	85–100	95–100
—	—	—	—	—	—	—	—	No. 14	30–70	55–90	75–100	90–400
—	—	—	—	—	—	—	—	No. 25	15–34	35–59	60–79	80–100
—	—	—	—	—	—	—	—	No. 52	5–20	8–30	12–40	15–50
—	—	—	—	—	—	—	—	No. 100	0–10[2]	0–10[2]	0–10[2]	0–15[2]

[1] The standard requires that the grading of a fine aggregate be within the limits of one of the grading zones, except that where the grading falls outside the limits of any particular grading zone on sieves other than the No. 25 sieve by a total amount not exceeding 5 per cent, it shall be regarded as falling within that grading zone. This 5 per cent can be split up; for example, it could be 1 per cent on each of three sieves and 2 per cent on another, or 4 per cent on one sieve and 1 per cent on another. No allowance is permitted for fine aggregate in any of the four grading zones on the coarser limit of Grading Zone 1, or on the finer limit of Grading Zone 4.

[2] For crushed stone sands the permissible limit is increased to 20 per cent. This does not affect the 5 per cent allowance (referred to in the following note) applying to the other sieve sizes.

Table 57   Grading limits for concrete aggregates (BS 882 : 1965), percentages by weight passing BS sieves

than the space between the main bars and it should never exceed the minimum cover to the reinforcement less 7 mm. 19 mm is usually the nominal maximum size of aggregate for ordinary reinforced concrete work. Larger sizes could sometimes be used and for mass concrete the maximum size can be 38 mm or greater, provided it does not exceed one-quarter of the minimum thickness of the member.

Aggregates are often described by their maximum size with the qualification *down*, meaning that they contain appropriate proportions of the smaller sizes.

Water : cement ratio

Concretes which are required to provide high strength, hardness, durability, imperviousness and resistance to chemicals, must be as dense as possible and this requires a low water : cement ratio expressed as:

$$\frac{\text{weight of water}}{\text{weight of cement}}$$

Any water in excess of the small quantity required to hydrate the cement – (about 4·7 litres per 50 kg for Portland cement and 9·5 litres for high-alumina cement) – causes voids, every 1 per cent of which reduces strength by about 5 per cent, see figure 28. It follows that provided there is sufficient water to hydrate the cement, and to avoid air being trapped because the mix is too stiff to compact thoroughly, the strength of concrete increases as the water : cement ratio decreases as shown in figure 24. To summarize, the densest and therefore the strongest concretes are obtained by using a *workable* aggregate with the lowest water : cement ratio which enables the

154

mix to be thoroughly compacted by mechanical means.

A low water : cement ratio also reduces the shrinkage of concrete and increases its durability. Table 58 recommends maximum values for different thicknesses of section in various conditions of exposure.

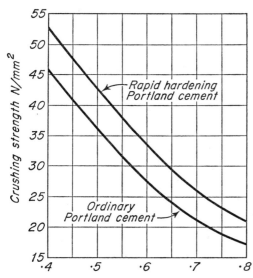

Note

A low water : cement ratio is one factor which reduces the workability of concrete and mechanical compaction is required to obtain the higher strengths.

24 Relation between crushing strengh and water : cement ratio of fully compacted Portland cement concrete cubes at 28 days

Condition of exposure	Water : cement ratio by weight	
	Thin sections	*Mass concrete*
Regular wetting and drying	0·45	0·55
Normal outside exposure:		
severe climate	0·50	0·60
temperate climate	0·55	0·65
Continuously under water	0·55	0·65

Table 58 Maximum water : cement ratios for various exposures

Loss of strength due to the conversion of high alumina cement is much more pronounced at higher water : cement ratios and CP 116 requires values not exceeding 0·5 for reinforced concrete and 0·4 for prestressed concrete made with this cement.

Workability

The term *workability* is used to describe the ease with which concrete mixes can be compacted and the highest possible workability must be aimed at so that concrete will be as completely compacted as possible while using the lowest possible water : cement ratio.

Workability should be obtained by the use of a well graded aggregate and one which has the largest maximum particle size which will pass readily between and around the reinforcement, see page 153, rather than by increasing the cement : aggregate ratio which increases the shrinkage, and cost of concrete.

The use of smooth and rounded, rather than irregularly shaped aggregate also increases workability but in high strength concretes there may be no overall increase in strength, because with equal water : cement ratios irregularly shaped aggregate produces the stronger concrete.

Air-entraining admixtures improve the workability of mixes (and improve the frost resistance of hardened concrete) but the reduction in density of the concrete is accompanied by a loss of strength up to about 15 per cent.

On most building sites a rough indication of workability is obtained by the *slump test*. See page 162. This, and the more accurate *compacting factor test*, are both fully described in BS 1881 : 1970 *Methods of testing concrete*.

Quality control

Owing to the inevitable variation in the quality of concrete which is made from time to time, in order to ensure that very few samples fall below a stated strength, most of the concrete which is produced must be stronger and therefore more costly than it is required to be.

Figure 25 shows how a *mean strength* is derived from a *characteristic strength* (below which not more than 5 per cent samples may fall – as proposed by the draft unified British Standard Code of Practice) and the variation in quality. It is

155

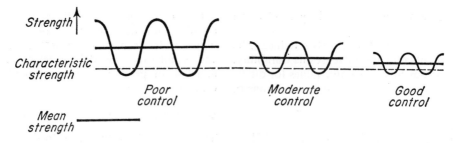

25   *Variations in strengths of samples*

evident that the less efficient the *control* in the measurement of ingredients and in the processes of manufacture, the higher the mean strength must be to maintain the specified *characteristic strength*.

BRS Digest 13 states that for concretes having $21 \cdot 0$ N/mm² crushing strength, almost twice as much cement was needed in volume-batched concrete with poor control, as in weight-batched concrete with constant supervision. Apart from saving cement, good control reduces honeycombing, laitence and permeability – factors which adversely affect durability and appearance.

For design purposes the mean crushing strength required is obtained by multiplying the characteristic strength by the following *control factors*:

Control	Control factor
Good Cement and aggregates weight-batched Regular checking of water content of aggregates Competent supervision	$1 \cdot 33$
Moderate Cement and aggregates weight-batched Water content of aggregate checked Average supervision	$1 \cdot 66$
Poor Aggregate batched by volume Inexperienced supervision	$2 \cdot 00$

Table 59   Control factors

Choice of mix proportions

Nominal mixes, ie mixes specified by volume,

should be used only for work of a 'do-it-yourself' type. Mixes of cement, aggregate fractions and water by weight can be specified as *Standard mixes*,[1] or for important work they will be calculated.

Standard mixes: based on dry weights of BS 12 or 146 cements and BS 882 or 1047 aggregates are given in CP 114.

Calculation of mix proportions If the larger contractors are given a performance specification including a minimum strength (usually at 28 days), maximum water:cement ratio, and maximum cement:aggregate ratio and type of finish, they can design a mix to satisfy the specification in the most economical way. Contractors which are not equipped to design mixes must be provided with a specification by a consulting engineer, supplier of ready-mixed concrete, or by one of the larger suppliers of aggregate.

The processes in design of high strength concrete are complex, but those for ordinary concrete are outlined in figure 26 as follows:

1 state the functional requirements (minimum strength,[2] durability, etc) for the hardened concrete
2 note the characteristics of available materials
3 decide the degree of quality control to be employed, see table 59
4 decide the mean crushing strength. The ratio

---

[1] Standard mixes are not intended for use where special properties such as low heat evolution, high strength or density, or workability suitable for pumping are required, for air-entrained concrete or with: 1 cement not complying with BS 12 or BS 146; 2 aggregates not complying with BS 882 or BS 1047, eg lightweight aggregates; 3 sand which does not fall in Zone 1, 2 or 3 of BS 882.
[2] The minimum strength is sometimes taken as the strength to be attained by 99 per cent of all test results.

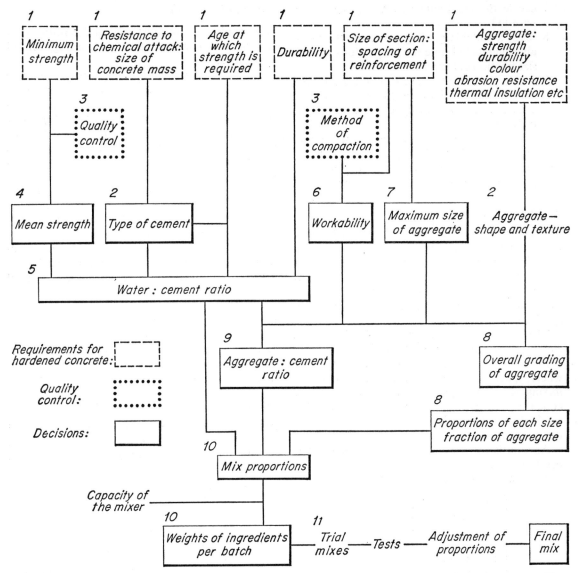

26 *Factors and steps in mix design*—based on diagram in *Properties of Concrete* by A. M. Neville, I. Pitman & Sons Ltd

between minimum and mean strength is given by a control factor, see table 59

(The greater the degree of quality control the less is the difference between the minimum strength and the mean strength, and the less cement is required to achieve the mean strength)

5 decide the water : cement ratio which will give the required mean crushing strength, see table or graph[1] and the required durability see table 58

6 decide the workability (compaction factor) required for the conditions of placing, see table 64

[1] eg from Road Note no. 4, HMSO.

157

7 decide the maximum size of aggregate, see page 153

8 select a suitable grading curve for the available aggregate,[1] note the proportions of each size fraction of aggregate

9 decide the aggregate : cement ratio required to give the workability (6) at the water : cement ratio (5) already decided upon, see table 60

10 calculate the proportions and the weights of ingredients to suit the capacity of the mixer

11 make and test trial mixes and adjust the proportions of ingredients as necessary.

Manufacture of concrete

Concrete can either be made wholly on the site, or the advantages of factory production can be partially secured by the use of ready-mixed concrete, or wholly secured by the use of pre-cast products. Table 61 suggests production methods for varying qualities of concrete on small, medium-sized and large sites.

The delivery to building sites of BS 1926:1962 *Ready-mixed concrete* is particularly useful where continuous site production is not possible or where space for storage of materials and for mixing is restricted, and it makes high quality concrete and special mixes available on the smallest sites. Normal site tests should be carried out on the mixed concrete.

Apparatus for the manufacture of concrete is described in *MBC: Structure and Fabric Part 2*.

The processes of manufacture are:

Site production
- Storage of materials ⎫
- Batching ⎬ Ready-mixed concrete
- Mixing ⎪
- Tests on mixed concrete ⎭
- Formwork and reinforcement ⎫ Precast products
- Transport to formwork and placing
- Compaction
- Curing
- Removal of formwork
- Protection
- Construction joints ⎭

[1] eg from Road Note no. 4, HMSO.

Storage of materials

Storage of materials must prevent deterioration of cement and contamination and segregation of aggregates.

Cement must be kept dry. Paper bags cannot be relied upon to prevent *air-setting* and resulting lumpiness. Exceptionally, where it is not certain that cement can be stored in dry conditions or that it can be used soon after delivery it may be advantageous to use hydrophobic Portland cement, see page 143. Particular care should be taken in storing extra rapid hardening and ultra high early strength Portland cements, and super-sulphated cement, see page 145. High alumina cement, see page 145, should preferably be kept in a store separate from Portland cement.

Paper bags should not be stacked more than four or five feet high to avoid *warehouse set* caused by compaction. Cement should be used in the order in which it was received.

Aggregates should be kept on clean hard surfaces and not directly on the ground. The various sizes of aggregates should be kept separately and where possible stock piles should be duplicated so that deliveries can drain for at least twelve hours before use.

Batching

Accurate batching of cement, aggregates and water make for savings in cost of designed mixes by enabling a lower control factor to be employed. It used to be customary to specify and to batch cement and aggregates in proportions by volume, as so called *nominal mixes* but, volume batching tends to be inaccurate because both cement and sand are subject to *bulking* and coarse aggregate is difficult to measure accurately by volume. Today, except for very small sites, cement is batched by weight and normally, and preferably, the aggregates also. Thus:

Cement Cement varies in bulk density from about 1120–1600 kg/m³ according to the way in which the container is filled. Where a weighing device is not available, the bag can be used as a unit. Only exceptionally should a bag be split.

Sand Dry and wet sands have the same volume, but damp sand has a greater volume and if sand is measured by volume and allowance is not made for *bulking* concrete mixes may be seriously under-

Workability	Water : cement ratio	Gravel aggregate			Crushed rock aggregate		
		10 mm	19 mm	40 mm	10 mm	19 mm	40 mm
Very low	0·4	3·5	4·5	5	3	4	4·5
	0·5	5·5	6·5	7·5	4·5	5·5	6·5
	0·6	7·5	—	—	6	7	—
	0·7	—	—	—	—	—	—
Low	0·4	3	4	4·5	—	3·7	4
	0·5	4·5	5·5	6·5	4	5	5·5
	0·6	6	7	7·5	5	6	7
	0·7	7	8	—	6	7	8
Medium	0·4	—	3·5	4	—	3	3·5
	0·5	4	5	5·5	3·5	4	5
	0·6	5	6	7	4·5	5	6
	0·7	6	7	8	5·5	6	7
High	0·4	—	3	3·5	—	3	3
	0·5	3·5	4	5	3	4	4·5
	0·6	4·5	5	6·5	4	4·5	5·5
	0·7	5·5	6	7·5	5	5·5	6·5

Table 60   Total aggregate : cement ratio (by weight) to give various degrees of workability with given water : cement ratios

Size of site	Ordinary concrete	High quality concrete (designed)
Small	Production of good quality site-mixed concrete may be difficult to achieve on very small sites	Requisite standard of batching, mixing, placing, compacting and curing not practicable on small sites
	Good quality concrete can be achieved by employing ready-mixed concrete	Ready mixed concrete; can be of high quality but requisite standard of placing, compacting and curing unlikely to be economical
Medium	Production of good quality site-mixed concrete is practicable	Requisite standard of batching, mixing, placing, compacting and curing may not be economical
	Ready-mixed concrete may be economical	Ready-mixed concrete; placing, compacting and curing requires special care
Large	Production of ordinary concrete economical only for small quantities	Production on site is economical
	Ready-mixed concrete may be economical particularly for small quantities	

Note: Factory pre-cast concrete of ordinary or high quality can be used on all sites

Table 61   Production methods for sizes of sites and qualities of concrete

sanded. Figure 27 shows the *bulking* of a typical sand. It is greater for the finer sands and may be as much as 40 per cent. In volume batching of damp sand a rule of thumb addition of 25 per cent by volume is often made but an accurate assessment can easily be made by inundating a sample of the sand and noting the reduction in volume which results. In either case checking by eye is always useful to avoid either 'hungry looking' or unduly 'fatty' mixes.

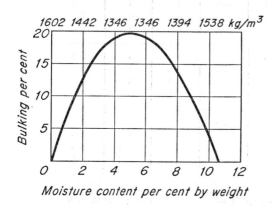

27   Bulking of a typical sand

In weight batching the water content of sand must be determined from time to time and the weight of batches adjusted accordingly.

For example, in a batch of concrete containing 400 kg of sand having an average moisture content of 5 per cent the corrected batch weight is

$$400 \times \frac{105}{100} = 420 \text{ kg sand}$$

Coarse aggregate Deep and narrow gauging boxes reduce error in volume batching but the method is laborious. Properly maintained weight-batching machines are very accurate and easy to use.

Conversion from volume to weight proportions It is usually assumed that 50 kg of cement occupies 0·04 m³. The equivalent proportions for a nominal 1 : 2 : 4 mix, therefore, are 50 kg cement : 2 × 0·04 m³ fine aggregate : 4 × 0·04 m³ coarse aggregate, ie 50 kg cement : 0·08 m³ fine aggregate : 0·16 m³ coarse aggregate. Similarly a nominal 1 : 5 all-in mix becomes 50 kg cement : 0·20 m³ all-in aggregate.

Table 62 shows how a 1 : 2 : 4 nominal mix can be converted into a mix by weight when the usual assumptions are made for the bulk densities of cement, sand and gravel.

	Typical loose dry densities kg/m³	Pro-portions by volume	Weight per volume of cement kg/m³	Pro-portions by weight
Cement	1440	1	1440	1
Sand	1600	2	3200	2·2
Gravel	1360	4	5440	3·8

Table 62   Conversion from volume to weight proportions

For important work the weights of batches must be adjusted to allow for the water contained in coarse aggregate. For example the corrected batch weight for 1000 kg of coarse aggregate with an average moisture content of 2 per cent would be:

$$1000 \times \frac{102}{100} = 1020 \text{ kg coarse aggregate}$$

Water As the water : cement ratio determines the strength and durability of concrete, see page 154, the amount of water contained in each batch is critical. The gross weight of water (kg) per batch is water : cement ratio × weight of cement (kg).

The tanks fitted to the larger mixers have gauges which enable a measured quantity of water to be added to each batch. This must be adjusted from time to time to allow for the water contained in the aggregate.

The following approximations may suffice:

Condition of aggregate	Fine aggregate l/m³	Coarse aggregate l/m³
Very wet	120	60
Moderately wet	80	40
Moist	40	20

Table 63   Approximate moisture content of aggregates

For more important work the water contained in the aggregate can be determined either: by weighing a sample, drying it and noting the loss in weight, or by one of the displacement methods.

During the progress of work if changes in the moisture contents of aggregates are small provided the quantities of cement and aggregates and the type of aggregates remain the same, the quantity of added water can be adjusted so as to maintain the workability indicated by a slump test on the first batch.

Mixing

Concrete may be mixed on the site, or 'at works' for pre-cast concrete or for delivery to the site as ready-mixed concrete.

Mixing on the site The most commonly used mixers are batch mixers of the single-compartment drum type. BS 1305: 1967 describes them as:

Tilting (T) – having a drum with one opening which rotates on an inclinable axis; and
Non-tilting (NT) – having a drum with two openings which rotates on a horizontal axis.

Mixed-batch capacity in cu. ft is indicated by a numeral. Standard sizes are:

$3\frac{1}{2}T$, *5T* and *7T*
5NT, 7NT, 10NT, 14NT, 28NT and *56NT*.

Some mixers incorporate weight batching equipment and attachments for hand scrapers to assist in loading the hoppers.

So that water is evenly distributed, it should enter the mixer before or at the same time as the other materials. The proportion of coarse aggregate should be reduced for the first batch or two each day to compensate for the loss of mortar which sticks to the blades and inside the drum.

The time required for thorough mixing varies according to the characteristics of the mix and of the mixer. With batch type mixers it has been customary to require mixing for at least two minutes although some machines mix thoroughly in shorter periods. In all cases the product should be uniform in colour and consistency.

When the concrete has been mixed the complete contents of the drum should be discharged in one operation to avoid segregation of the larger stones.

Mixers should be thoroughly washed out and cleaned daily, and even after short stoppages, to prevent 'caking' with hardened concrete which reduces the machine's efficiency and they should be cleaned out when the type of cement is changed.

Tests on mixed concrete

Site tests and the apparatus required for these are described in BS 1881: 1970 *Methods of testing concrete.*

Consistency of manufacture Variations in *slump* indicate changes in the shape or grading of aggregate or in the proportion of water being used. See page 162.

Workability The slump test is easy to carry out, gives an approximate indication of the workability of Portland cement mixes which are neither too stiff nor too plastic, but it is not always applicable to high alumina cement concrete. The compaction factor test is more accurate but neither test is suitable where the maximum size of aggregate exceeds 38 mm.

Compression tests Cubes made before and during the placing of concrete on the site are tested in crushing machines to give some indication of the strength which would be acquired by the actual work.

Preliminary cube tests Preliminary compression tests require very accurate control of materials and test conditions. The materials intended to be used are mixed in the laboratory in the proportions to be used in the work.

Works cube tests Samples of the concrete which is being placed in each part of the work should be made into cubes in accordance with BS 1881: 1970. Specimens to be tested should be kept free from vibration and under damp sacks for 24 hours $\pm\frac{1}{2}$ hour before removing them from the moulds. They should be marked and stored in water at a temperature between 10 and 21 °C. They should be covered with damp material to be taken to a laboratory where they must be stored in water again for 24 hours before being tested.

A typical specification requires that if a cube fails at 7 days to attain the strength specified for that age, another cube made from the same concrete may be tested at 28 days. If the second cube fails to attain the strength specified for 28 days, the specification may give the contractor the opportunity of testing cores cut from the placed concrete to prove that the concrete which was placed provides the strength required.

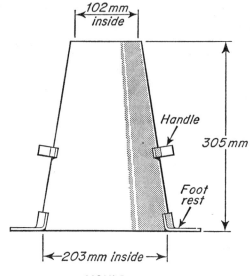

TAMPING ROD 610mm long x 16mm dia.

1 Take representative sample
   of concrete, and within
   2 minutes fill mould
   in 4 equal layers

2 Tamp each layer 25
   times with steel rod

3 Strike off top level and
   clean off any leakage
   around base of mould,
   and without delay:

4 Raise mould carefully
   in vertical direction

5 Measure slump to nearest
   6mm. If shear or collapse
   slumps occur, repeat test
   with another sample

6 Record results

7 Clean and dry mould.
   Do not oil

102 mm inside

Handle

305 mm

Foot rest

203mm inside

MOULD

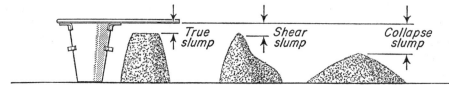

True slump   Shear slump   Collapse slump

SLUMP TEST

Formwork

Formwork provides the shape and surface texture of concrete members and supports them during setting and hardening. It must be grout-tight, true in line, level, face and profile, and strong enough to accept all constructional loads including those resulting from mechanical compaction. Formwork is best constructed in units for easy erection, striking without damaging the concrete, and so that it can be re-used. It should allow easy removal of sides without disturbing soffits and removal of soffits without disturbing props.

The faces of formwork should be treated with mould oil to give a clean release but avoiding excess oil which stains concrete and which may interfere with the bond for plaster.

Reinforcement

Reinforcement should comply with the following standards:

Hot rolled steel bars,	BS 4449 : 1969
Hard drawn mild steel wire,	BS 4482 : 1969
Cold worked steel bars,	BS 4461 : 1969
Steel fabric,	BS 4483 : 1969
Steel wire for prestressed concrete,	
	BS 2691 : 1969.

Reinforcement should be free from loose mill scale, loose rust, oil or grease.

Steel is protected from corrosion where it is embedded in dense Portland cement concrete but a zinc coating of 200 to 700 g/m² (0·03 to 0·10 mm) provides a hedge against poor workmanship and

Type of concrete	Means of compaction pressure	Compaction factor	Slump mm
Very high strength prestressed	Pressure	less than 0·70 approx.	0
	Heavy vibration	0·70–0·80	
High strength prestressed, reinforced paving and mass concrete	Vibration	0·78–0·85	0–25
Normally reinforced	Vibration	0·85–0·92	25–50
Mass concrete	Hand		
Heavily reinforced	Vibration	0·92–0·95	50–100
Normally reinforced	Hand		
Heavily reinforced Complex shapes	Hand	0·95	100–150

Table 64   Guide to workabilities for various purposes

diminishes the adverse effects of any variations in the physical properties of the concrete cover. Zinc coatings allow the depth of concrete cover to be reduced without increasing the risk of corrosion. Alternatively, the depths of cover now recommended for dense aggregate concretes can be used with lightweight aggregates.[1]

Reinforcement should be placed in the exact positions shown on the drawings and the specified cover ensured, eg by spacers fixed to the reinforcement. Great care should be taken to avoid damage or disturbance to formwork when positioning reinforcement. Prefabrication of reinforcement helps in this respect.

Wire ties, usually 1·6 mm soft iron, used to secure intersections in the reinforcement, must be kept away from form faces, particularly those which will be exposed to the weather.

Transport to formwork and placing
Whether concrete is moved from the mixer by lorries, barrows, dumpers, mechanical skips or pipe-line it is important that the composition of the mix is not altered and that segregation does not take place.

All plant, chutes etc, should be thoroughly cleaned after use without allowing the waste water to enter formwork.

[1] See BRS Digest 109 HMSO and *Corrosion* Chapter 9.

'Wet' mixes are particularly likely to segregate and, where possible, these should not be dropped into position. Chutes should be arranged so that a continuous flow is discharged at the lower end. Like mixers, chutes accumulate mortar and where they are used the first mixes should contain less coarse aggregate. Where concrete is discharged from long chutes it can first enter a hopper or bunker in which it is partially remixed before being placed in the forms.

A continuous supply of suitable mixes can be transported through pipe-lines 100–200 mm in diameter, by force pump or by pneumatic pressure. Force pumps can move concrete up to about 30 m vertically, or 300 m horizontally.

The mix should be of uniform consistency, not leaner than 1 : 6 by weight with a compacting factor in the range 0·92–0·95 and 50–100 mm slump. The pipe-line must be lubricated with mortar before pumping of concrete starts, and when pumping stops it must be cleaned out, usually with compressed air and water aided by a dolly. See BRS Digest 133.

Immediately before concrete is placed, formwork should be thoroughly cleaned out and formwork and reinforcement should be re-checked.

'Flowing' in the formwork should be prevented by placing the concrete in layers of uniform thickness. When placing high alumina cement concrete it is sometimes necessary to limit the depth of 'lift' (see page 146).

Compaction

Air which is trapped in concrete when it is placed must be released if the maximum density with associated resistance to chemicals, water vapour, frost and abrasion is to be obtained. Figure 28 shows that 1 per cent of entrapped air causes a loss of about 5 per cent strength. Thorough compaction is also very important wherever concrete faces are to be exposed to view. Air is very liable to be trapped against form faces and at joints between hardened and newly placed concrete. Compaction should commence as soon as possible once water

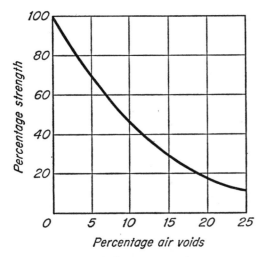

28 *Loss of strength due to air voids*

has been added to concrete although so long as it remains possible to fully compact concrete by the means available, delay in doing so may not be serious up to perhaps two hours in cool weather.

Minimum degrees of workability, expressed as slumps and compacting factors, which permit full compaction by hand or by machine of various Portland cement concretes are given in Table 64.

Hand compaction Concrete which is sufficiently workable can be worked into place with spades. Air must be released from the surfaces by *slicing tools* to obtain a good finish.

By machine The stiffer mixes can only be thoroughly compacted by vibrators, rollers, or presses.

Vibrators CP 114 : 1957 Structural use of Reinforced concrete in buildings strongly recommends the use of vibrators provided that reduced water : cement ratios are adopted. Over-vibration leads to segregation. Vibration should stop when air bubbles no longer come to the surface. Vibrators are of the following types:

Immersion vibrators – or *poker* vibrators These should be operated by experienced men. They should be inserted vertically at points not more than 450 mm apart. They should not be brought too close to the formwork or reinforcement and never drawn along horizontally. Vibrators should be withdrawn very slowly so that a hole is not left in the concrete.

External vibrators These are necessary where the reinforcement does not allow space for poke vibrators. They must be firmly fixed to the formwork or hand-held mechanical hammers can be used. Formwork must be sufficiently rigid to transmit the vibration without being damaged.

Beam vibrators Tamping beams with vibrators fixed to them are suitable for compacting the upper surfaces of horizontal slabs.

Table vibrators These are suitable for vibrating pre-cast goods. The moulds in which they are cast must be rigidly clamped to the vibrating table top.

Pan vibrators These consist of a steel-bottomed pan about 0.75^2 m in area with a vibrator fixed to the upper surface. They are suitable for awkwardly shaped horizontal surfaces but do not leave a truly flat surface.

Presses Hydraulically actuated presses are used for compressing paving flags and tiles in factory production.

Curing

In order to obtain the desired strength, compacted concrete must be free from physical disturbance, (a) water must be retained in the concrete and (b) temperature must be controlled.

(a) *Retention of water in the mix* Water is essential for hydration of cement and concrete ceases to develop strength if it dries. (There is no conflict here with the statement that a low water : cement ratio makes for high strength in thoroughly compacted concrete.) If concrete dries before it has developed sufficient strength, cracking (due to shrinkage) results, see page 151. Loss of water can be prevented in the laboratory or factory by covering concrete with damp sacks at first and later by immersing it in water. Steam curing guarantees that no water will be lost from the concrete.

In situ concrete can be protected from sun and drying winds by sheets of waterproof paper or plastics. Clean sand can be laid on horizontal surfaces and kept wet for at least seven days. Alternatively, surfaces can be sprayed with an impervious composition which reduces evaporation.

Drying out should be prevented for the following periods:

Type of cement	Ordinary concrete (days)	Concrete subject to abrasion (days)
Ordinary Portland cement	4	7
Rapid hardening Portland cement	3	4
Extra rapid hardening Portland cement	2	—
High alumina cement	1	—
Supersulphated cement	4	—

(b) *Control of temperature* At about freezing point cements cease to develop strength, and if the water is frozen concrete is permanently damaged. At temperatures up to about 40°C strength development is a function of temperature and time (or *maturity*). Figure 29 shows the 28 day compressive strength of a concrete cured at 3°C to be 85 per cent of the same mix cured at 17°C.

Thus, temperature during curing may require to be artificially raised to prevent freezing and to ensure a sufficient rate of strength development. On the other hand excessive rise in temperature naturally or artificially induced can lead to a flash set of cement and to cracking of concrete due to differential thermal stresses. Specific problems arise in cold and hot weather:

Cold weather The temperature of concrete should never fall below 5°C before and during placing, or below 4°C until it has hardened.

When the atmospheric temperature falls below about 4°C special steps such as the following are normally essential to prevent freezing:

1 Increase heat evolved by cement:

(a) Use special cement, eg rapid-hardening

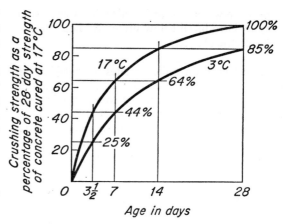

29 *Effect of temperature upon the rate of hardening of a typical ordinary Portland cement concrete. Based on graph from Report on 'Concrete Practice' Volume I (ISE and CCA)*

Portland cement, extra rapid-hardening Portland cement or high alumina cement;

(b) Add an accelerator, eg a solution of 1½ per cent anhydrous calcium chloride in the mixing water with ordinary or rapid-hardening Portland cements (but not to supersulphated or high alumina cements). Accelerators must not be used without adequate heating and heat conservation.

2 Heat ingredients:

(a) Water-temperature should not exceed about 82°C

(b) Frozen aggregate must *never* be used. Heating can be by steam pipes carried through stock piles.

To avoid a *flash set* of the cement, the aggregates and mixing water should be mixed before the cement is added so that their temperature is unlikely to exceed about 32°C.

3 Conserve heat:
Surfaces of concrete can be covered with straw-boards or other insulating materials, and screens keep off cold wind. Thick timber formwork provides useful insulation.

4 Heat the building. Hot air blowers are available. Great care, however, must be taken to avoid drying fresh concrete.

5 Heat the formwork. Concrete must never be placed in frost covered formwork or against frozen ground. Formwork can be heated by low

165

pressure wet steam or hot air with a fine water spray introduced below protective housings, or by electric blankets.

Circumstances on building sites vary widely so that it is not possible to recommend specific measures. However, in frosty weather, when the day temperatures rise above 0°C it may be sufficient to add an accelerator to ordinary Portland cement or to use rapid-hardening or extra-rapid-hardening Portland cement, to heat the mixing water and to insulate the formwork.

Steam curing High temperature during the setting of cements reduces their ultimate strength and all concrete should be cured for several hours at room temperature. Subsequently however, steam curing, which combines high temperature with conditions which prevent loss of water, enables very high early strengths to be obtained in Portland cement concretes (including most Portland cement concretes which include calcium chloride). Final strength, however, is not improved. Low pressure steam curing can be carried out inexpensively, even on a building site. High pressure steam curing, usually at about 1·0 N/mm², requires an autoclave but has several advantages. Thus the 28 day strength of air-cured concrete can be attained in 24 hours, drying shrinkage, moisture movement and efflorescence are reduced and resistance to sulphate attack is improved.

High alumina cement would undergo rapid conversion, see page 146.

Hot weather In particular, slabs must be protected from sunlight and drying winds by covering with damp sand, impervious sheets or water. Special measures, eg the use of low heat Portland cement, see page 143, may be necessary to avoid excessive temperature gain in large masses of Portland cement concrete and to prevent cracking which can result from differential thermal stresses. Cooling of high alumina cement concrete is discussed on page 146.

Removal of formwork

Formwork must be left in position, and the supports maintained, until concrete is sufficiently strong to safely support its own weight and any loads which may be put on it. Concrete should have a cube strength at least twice the stress to which the concrete is likely to be subjected at the time of striking.

The times which should elapse before formwork is removed vary considerably according to the cement used, temperature of the concrete during curing and other factors. Minimum times are recommended in table 65.

Times for intermediate temperatures may be interpolated pro rata and for Portland cements one day should be added for each day the temperature is at, or below, freezing point. Times

	Type of cement						
	Ordinary and sulphate-resisting Portland cements		Rapid-hardening Portland cement		Extra-rapid hardening Portland cement		High alumina cement
	3°C	16°C	3°C	16°C	3°C	16°C	3°C
Walls and sides of beams and columns	5	1	3	1	2	1	$\frac{1}{4}$ (6 hours)
Slabs:							
props left under	7	3½	4	2	3	1½	
props to slabs	14	7	8	4	6	3	1
Beam soffits:							
props left under	14	7	8	4	6	3	
props to soffits	28	14	16	8	12	6	

Table 65 Minimum number of days before removing formwork from concrete carrying its own weight only

must be increased if loads such as building materials are being carried by new structures.

Supports should be eased away uniformly and very slowly, so that the load is not suddenly imposed on partly hardened concrete. Formwork must be stripped carefully to avoid damage to arrises and projections, especially where vertical surfaces are exposed within twelve hours of casting.

Protection

After stripping formwork it may be necessary to protect concrete from damage by knocks, shock and vibration; from drying in hot weather (see page 166) and from loss of heat in cold weather (see page 165).

Construction joints

Whenever concreting is interrupted the construction joints which are inevitably formed are potentially weak, they may allow water to enter and they are always visible, particularly after a period of weathering. The positions and design of construction joints should, therefore, be decided at an early stage.

Joints should be straight, either vertical or horizontal, and in walls in positions related to window openings and other features. Generally, in columns construction joints are made as near as possible to the beam haunching and in beams and slabs within the middle third of the span. Vertical joints should be formed against temporary but rigid stop boards which must be designed to allow reinforcement to pass through.

To ensure the best possible bond between new and 'old' concrete lifts *laitance* (a scum of cement and very fine material) must not be allowed to form on horizontal surfaces, the use of a drier mix at the end of each day helps in this respect. Preferably, within an hour or so after placing the lower lift its surface should be sprayed with water and brushed to expose the coarse aggregate. If these measures are delayed it may be necessary to use a stiff brush to roughen the surface, or if it has hardened, to hack the surface but without damaging the aggregate. Then, although difficulties of access often make such operations difficult, the roughened surface should always be thoroughly cleaned and loose matter removed, preferably without re-wetting.

New concrete is satisfactorily placed directly against freshly cleaned and relatively dry concrete only if the newly placed concrete is very thoroughly compacted so that some of the water and fine material is absorbed into the surface pores of the hardened concrete. Alternatively:

(a) The clean surface is wetted sufficiently only to reduce the absorption of the hardened concrete.
(b) A thin grout of cement is brushed over the surface.
(c) Mortar about 3 to 7 mm thick, of the same materials and not weaker than the cement and sand in the new concrete, is laid immediately.
(d) The new concrete must be placed within 30 minutes. If the mortar is allowed to dry a weak joint will result.

Avoidance of segregation and thorough compaction of newly placed concrete are particularly important along the joint plane.

LIGHTWEIGHT CONCRETES

Lightweight concretes, ie *aerated concretes, lightweight aggregate concretes* and '*no-fines*' *concretes*, are defined as those weighing less than 1920 kg/m³ and are made in densities down to about 160 kg/m³. The subject is dealt with very thoroughly in *Lightweight concrete* by A. Short M.Sc, AMICE, MI Struct E and W. Kinniburgh FRIC (Maclaren and Son Ltd) and in the BRS Digests referred to later.

The 44 m diameter dome of the Pantheon Rome was largely constructed of pumice lightweight concrete in the second century AD. Today, advantages in the use of lightweight rather than dense concrete include: savings in the costs of handling materials and of supporting structures, superior thermal insulation and fire resistance; superior sound absorption of unplastered surfaces, some of which offer a better key for plaster. Lightweight concretes are usually easier to cut, chase and nail into. On the other hand: compressive strength and the modulus of elasticity are reduced (although the latter reduction may improve resistance to mechanical damage). The moisture movement of aerated and lightweight aggregate concretes is high. Protection of reinforcement against corrosion may reduce, and sound insulation reduces as density of the concrete decreases. Lightweight concretes are made in three main ways:

1 *Aerated or cellular concrete* Minute and non-communicating cells are formed by introducing air or gas into a matrix of cement (or in the case of autoclaved concretes, sometimes lime) with, in all but the lightest non-structural concretes, ground sand, pulverized-fuel ash or other fine siliceous material as fine aggregate.
2 *Lightweight aggregate concrete* Made by incorporating a cellular coarse aggregate
3 *No-fines concrete* Made by omitting the fine aggregate and the smaller particles of coarse aggregate so as to leave voids.

Some properties of lightweight aggregate and aerated concretes are compared with those of dense concrete in table 66.

Aerated concretes

Concretes of this type have the lowest densities, thermal conductivities and strengths. Like timber they can be sawn, screwed and nailed, but they are non-combustible.

References are BRS Digest 16 and 17 *Aerated concrete 1 – Manufacture and properties* and *Aerated concrete 2 – Uses*, respectively.

For work in situ the usual methods of aeration are by mixing in a stabilized foam or by whipping air in with the aid of an air entraining agent. In this country precast products are usually made by the addition of about 0·2 per cent aluminium powder to the mix which reacts with alkaline substances in the binder forming hydrogen bubbles. Air-cured aerated concrete is used where little strength is required, eg for roof screeds and pipe lagging, in densities as low as 160 kg/m³. Full strength development depends upon the reaction of lime with the siliceous aggregate, and for equal densities the strength of high pressure steam-cured concrete is about twice that of air-cured concrete, and shrinkage is only one third, or less. No further curing is required after autoclaving. Blocks are usually cut at works to the required size from larger units.

Strength

Strengths sufficient for structural work are obtainable but the modulus of elasticity of aerated

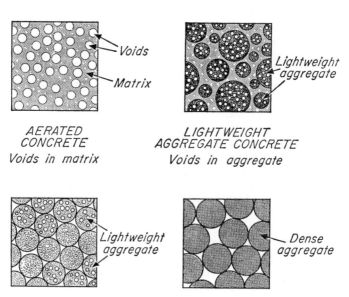

AERATED
CONCRETE
Voids in matrix

LIGHTWEIGHT
AGGREGATE CONCRETE
Voids in aggregate

NO-FINES CONCRETE
Voids between aggregate

30 Types of lightweight concretes

Table 66 Properties of lightweight aggregate and aerated concretes (Information from BRS Digests and other sources)

Aggregate	Density of aggregate kg/m³	Dry density of concrete kg/m³	Compressive strength N/mm²	Modulus of elasticity N/mm²	Drying shrinkage per cent	Thermal conductivity W/m deg C	Main uses
Dense concrete							
Gravel aggregate	1360–1760	2240–2480	14·0–70·0	20 700 – 34 500 –	0·03–0·04	1·4–1·8	Structural uses, anti-corrosion and fire protection (Class 2)
Lightweight aggregate concretes							
Clinker	720–1040	1040–1520	2·0–7·0	6890 – 20 700 short duration loads	0·04–0·08	0·35–0·67	Structural reinforced concrete⁴ / Wall blocks² — Structural, Fire protection (Class 1)
Foamed blast furnace slag	320–880	960–2000	2·0–24·0		0·03–0·07	0·24–0·93 (960–1610)[1]	
Expanded clay	320–1040	720–1760	2·0–62·0		0·04–0·07	0·24–0·91 (720–1520)[1]	
Sintered pulverized-fuel ash	640–960	960–1760	2·8–55·0		0·04–0·07	0·32–0·91 (960–1520)[1]	
Expanded slate	320–960	560–1760	1·4–27·5		0·03–0·09	0·19–0·91 (560–1520)[1]	
Pumice	500–880	640–1440	2·0–14·0		0·04–0·08	0·21–0·60	
Exfoliated vermiculite	65–200	400–800	0·7–3·5		0·25–0·35	0·16–0·26	Thermal insulation
Expanded perlite	80–240	400–1120	0·5–7·0		0·20–0·30	0·16–0·39	
Aerated concretes (air-cured)	— / 3	352–833 / 721–1217	0·48–3·45 / 2·60–5·15		0·33–0·44 / 0·18–0·36	0·86–1·89 / 2·02–4·03	Thermal insulation / Wall² blocks — Fire protection (Class 1)
(autoclaved)	—	960			0·06	0·26	
	—	800	4·83	3100	–	0·20	
	—	640	3·45	2270	0·07	0·14	
	—	480	2·07	1445		0·11	
	—	320		—		0·08	

1 Density ranges corresponding with thermal conductivity ranges.
2 See chapter 6 page 135 for minimum strengths of loadbearing and non-loadbearing blocks.
3 1 cement: 1–3 pfa and ground sand.
4 See page 170 and BRS Digest 111.

No-fines concrete see page 172

concrete is about one tenth that of dense concrete. Creep at working loads is not thought to be greater.

Moisture movement

The moisture movement of cement not being restrained by rigid aggregate, air-cured aerated concrete has very high drying shrinkage and without frequent shrinkage joints concrete which is placed in situ would crack.

Precast products which are steam cured shrink only $\frac{1}{4}$ to $\frac{1}{3}$ as much as air-cured concrete, but even where this movement takes place before precast units are incorporated in buildings the following precautions may be necessary:
(a) Specify BS 2028 : 1364 : 1968 *Precast concrete blocks* which stipulates maximum drying shrinkages of 0·05 to 0·09 per cent according to use, compressive strength and block density
(b) Keep units as dry as possible
(c) Use weak mortar, see chapter 15
(d) Provide shrinkage joints
(e) Before plastering or rendering allow concrete to dry fully and limit the areas. See *MBC: C and F* chapters 13 and 14.

Weather resistance

Experience indicates that unprotected single leaf aerated concrete block walls have good resistance to rain penetration and to frost. However, for densities of 825 and 497 kg/m³ water absorptions are about four times and eight times greater than that of dense concrete and external rendering is desirable wherever reinforcement is present.

Thermal insulation

Thermal conductivities of 0·084 W/m deg C and less are obtainable in dry concrete. External surfaces should be rendered or otherwise protected to avoid serious loss of thermal insulation due to absorption of water.

Fire resistance

Fire resistance as defined by BS 476 : 1953 tests is good, for example for walls without finishes:

102 mm loadbearing wall	2 hours
102 mm non-loadbearing wall	4 hours
142 mm non-loadbearing wall	6 hours

Hardness

Aerated concrete is much softer than dense concretes and requires protection from abrasion in the lower parts of walls and in similar positions. It can be easily sawn, worked with simple tools and nailed into. Retention of nails is better with cut nails than wire nails, and with the denser concretes.

Lightweight aggregate concretes

These concretes are dealt with in BRS Digests 123 *Lightweight aggregate concretes* and 111 *Lightweight aggregate concretes: Structural applications.*

Typical values for density, strength, thermal conductivity and drying shrinkage are given in table 66.

The least dense lightweight aggregate concretes, ie exfoliated vermiculite and expanded perlite concretes have strengths and thermal conductivities comparable to aerated concretes of the same density and are used for lagging pipes and for thermal insulating screeds. Intermediate densities are suitable for building blocks. See page 135.

Strength

Foamed slag, expanded clay, expanded slate and sintered pulverized-fuel ash concretes are suitable for reinforced concrete structures with strengths in compression up to 62 N/mm², and with densities 30–40 per cent, and thermal conductivities 50 per cent or more, less than those of gravel concretes.

As with dense aggregate concretes, the strength properties of *lightweight aggregate concretes* depend upon:
(i) type of aggregate
(ii) grading of aggregate
(iii) cement : aggregate ratio
(iv) water : cement ratio
(v) the degree of compaction.

Compared with ordinary dense concretes the following assumptions can be made:

Creep: 100 per cent greater

Permissible shear strength: 20 to 25 per cent less

Bond strength: 50 per cent less (except for vertically cast members)

Span : depth ratio: at least 10 per cent less

Elastic modulus: generally $\frac{1}{3}$ to $\frac{2}{3}$ of values for corresponding dense aggregate mixes increasing with compressive strength and density.

The GLC requires mixes to be not leaner than 1 cement : 6 aggregate by volume. Because lightweight concrete is more porous and more likely to crack than dense concrete, discounting clinker which should not be used in reinforced concrete, protection of reinforcement against corrosion depends much more upon the quality of the concrete than on the type of aggregate used. Complete compaction is particularly important. The BRS recommend: 'where reinforced lightweight concrete is exposed to the weather, the concrete cover over the reinforcement should be not less than 51 mm and the maximum aggregate size should not exceed 13 mm'.

Moisture movement

Drying shrinkage is generally about twice that of dense concretes. The poor workability of some lightweight aggregates should be compensated for by the addition of sand or an air entraining agent rather than by using a richer mix which would increase drying shrinkage. Although the proneness of lightweight concrete to shrink and crack may be largely offset by its lower modulus of elasticity, the precautions advised for aerated concrete should be taken.

Fire resistance

In concretes the fire resistance of elements of structure (see chapter 1, page 36) depends largely upon the properties of the aggregate. Because furnace-formed lightweight aggregates are in *Class 1* (see page 39) reinforced concrete elements can be thinner than would be required if they were constructed with Class 2 aggregates.

Lightweight aggregates

Table 66 lists the aggregates in common use with their densities and some properties of typical concretes made with them. BS 3797 : 1964 *Lightweight aggregates for concrete* includes requirements for exfoliated vermiculite, expanded perlite, expanded clay, expanded shale, sintered PFA and pumice. Some notes follow:

Clinker (not to be confused with *breeze* (small coke) which is no longer used as aggregate) consists of furnace residues sintered into lumps. It must be thoroughly burnt to avoid serious expansion later. BS 1165 : 1966 *Clinker aggregate*

for concrete limits combustible constituents to 10 per cent for general purposes and to 25 per cent for work which will not be in damp conditions. Some clinkers contain particles of iron which can cause stains and others may contain materials, particularly hard burnt lime, which expand when they are wet. The ill effects of the latter can be avoided by weathering the clinker before it is used. Tests for soundness and limits for sulphates are contained in the BS.

Foamed slag (BS 877 : 1967) In this country foamed slag is, after clinker, the most widely used lightweight aggregate. It is produced by directing jets of steam and compressed air onto molten blast furnace slag and then crushing and grinding the product.

Foamed slag concrete provides better thermal insulation than clinker concrete. It is used mainly for wall blocks and for insulating roof screeds but unlike clinker concrete it is suitable for reinforced concrete.

Expanded clay Certain clays which evolve gas and bloat when they are heated are formed as rounded pellets in a rotary kiln or into particles by crushing the porous cake from a sinter strand. Expanded clay provides the highest strength lightweight aggregate structural concrete and is used for the same purposes as foamed slag concrete. *Aglite* and *Leca* are proprietary products.

Sintered pulverized-fuel ash (BS 3892 : 1965). Ash from powdered coal which has been burnt in electric power stations (PFA or *fly ash*) is moistened and formed into pellets which are fired at about 1200°C. The resulting spherical particles are graded into large and medium sizes or crushed to form fine aggregate. Concrete made with sintered PFA has drying shrinkage and moisture movement similar to those of expanded clay concrete. Uses are wall blocks, screeds and high strength structural reinforced concrete. *Lytag* is a proprietary product.

Exfoliated vermiculite Vermiculite is a mineral resembling mica which exfoliates when it is heated rapidly, producing the lightest aggregate apart from expanded polystyrene beads. Exfoliated vermiculite concrete has low thermal conductivity, but also low strength and its moisture movement is high. Its main use is for insulating screeds on flat roofs.

Expanded perlite This very light cellular aggregate is made by rapidly heating a glassy volcanic rock. Expanded perlite concrete is capable of higher crushing strengths but in other respects it is similar to exfoliated vermiculite concrete. Its use in this country is small but increasing.

Other lightweight aggregates These include expanded slate (*Solite*) which is now being made in this country, imported pumice, and sawdust chemically treated to prevent adverse reactions with cement. The moisture movement of sawdust concrete tends to be high. At present synthetic materials such as foamed polystyrene beads are used only where superior thermal insulation justifies their higher cost.

No-fines concretes

This description is commonly applied to concretes which contain only a single-size 19·0 to 9·5 mm coarse aggregate (either a dense aggregate or a lightweight aggregate such as sintered PFA) with sufficient cement to join the particles while leaving voids between them. The density is about two thirds to three quarters that of dense concretes made with the same aggregates.

No-fines concrete is almost always cast in situ mainly as loadbearing and non-loadbearing walls including in-filling walls in framed structures, but sometimes as filling below solid ground floors, and for roof screeds.

Walls

The surfaces of no-fines concrete provide an excellent key for external rendering and internal plaster finishes, which are essential to prevent air movement through walls with loss of thermal and sound insulation. Any rain which penetrates external renderings will travel inwards only 20 to 50 mm or so, but damp courses and construction joints should be designed to throw such water outwards.

In Germany no-fines dense aggregate concrete has been used in loadbearing walls up to twenty storeys. In this country walls 305 mm thick have been built up to ten storeys using a 1 cement : 6 gravel aggregate mix at the lowest level reducing in richness to 1 : 10 at the top floor. Lightweight aggregates such as foamed blast furnace slag, clinker, sintered pulverized-fuel ash and expanded clay provide concretes which are less strong than

those made with dense aggregates, but thermal insulation is superior and fixing and chasing are easier.

CP 111 : 1964 *Structural recommendations for load-bearing walls* requires a minimum crushing strength at 28 days of 2·76 N/mm². Short and Kinniburgh give average results of tests on 152·4 mm cubes made with 1 : 8 (the most commonly used proportions) with a water : cement ratio of 0·40 as follows:

Aggregate	Compressive strength at 28 days N/mm²
Rounded quartzite gravel	8·62
Irregular flint gravel	4·83
Crushed limestone	6·89
Crushed granite	7·58

The CP gives permissible stresses related to mix proportions and the crushing strengths of no-fines cubes.

Drying shrinkage

Aerated and lightweight aggregate concretes have high drying shrinkage but that of no-fines concrete is usually less even than that of a dense concrete made with the same aggregate. Also because no-fines concrete shrinks more rapidly than dense concrete, plasters and renderings are less likely to crack.

Thermal insulation

The thermal conductivity (k) of no-fines gravel aggregate concrete is comparable to that of typical brickwork. Thermal transmittances for walls are as follows:

279 mm brick cavity wall,
  plastered inside
305 mm no-fines dense
  aggregate concrete,
  rendered and plastered   } U = 1·7 W/m² deg C
203 mm no-fines clinker
  aggregate concrete,
  rendered and plastered
305 mm no-fines clinker
  aggregate concrete,   } U = 1·3 W/m² deg C
  rendered and plastered

Sound insulation

The sound insulation of plastered no-fines concrete walls is slightly inferior to that of solid brick walls of comparable thickness.

Mixing

Aggregate should be damped before being placed in the mixer, cement and then sufficient water should be added so that particles of aggregate are coated with cement without it bridging between them.

Formwork

Because no-fines concrete exerts only about one third of the pressure exerted by ordinary concrete, formwork can be of light construction. It does not require to be grout tight and if expanded metal is used the mix can be seen as it is placed.

Reinforcement

Light reinforcement is advisable across the angles at openings. A coating of cement grout reduces the likelihood of corrosion.

Placing

Mixes should pour freely. Some gentle rodding may be needed but vibration should never be resorted to.

The concrete should be placed evenly in horizontal layers. As no-fines concrete does not segregate horizontal joints can be at three storey intervals. Cement slurry should be brushed on immediately before placing new concrete.

Fixings

Lightweight aggregate concretes may accept nails but lugs should be built into walls made with dense aggregates.

9 Metals

References include:

Metals in the service of man, W. Alexander and A. Street, Pelican Ltd.

BS Codes of Practice and British Standards as listed later.

Metals can be defined as being elements which readily form positive ions and which are characterized by their opacity and high thermal and electrical conductivities. The lightest metal in common use, aluminium, has about the same density as granite, about 2640 kg/m³, the densest, lead, weighs about 11 400 kg/m³

In the pure form metals are often very soft, eg lead, aluminium and iron, so that most metals used in building are alloys containing controlled proportions of different metals. Generally the melting point of alloys is lower, and in other respects their properties are not directly related to those of the parent metals.

Metals must be selected to provide the required properties, including high strength, toughness at low temperatures, corrosion resistance, heat resistance and properties such as ductility to suit the intended method of forming and joining. Appearance may be important, while both the *initial cost* of products and their *cost in-use* must be considered.

Metals are described as either *ferrous*, containing a substantial proportion of iron (Fe) or as *non-ferrous*. Figures 31 and 32 show in broad outline the principal metals and alloys used in building.

Definitions

Stress is the force carried by unit area, expressed as N/mm².

Tenacity is strength in tension, usually expressed as: *tensile stress* at failure ie

$$\frac{\text{maximum load}}{\text{original cross-sectional area}}$$

Strain is the deformation caused by a force.

Tensile and compressive strains are expressed as ratios:

$$\frac{\text{increase (or decrease) in length}}{\text{original length}}$$

Strains also result from shear and torsional stresses.

Modulus of elasticity (E) or Young's modulus. Within the elastic range stress is proportional to strain so that $E = \text{stress/strain}$, see figure 33. Of the metals commonly used in buildings, steel has the highest E value, approximately 3 times greater than that of aluminium alloys, hence steel is far *stiffer* or more *rigid*, see figure 34.

The elastic limit is the point at which deformation of a stressed material ceases to be elastic and becomes plastic.

Yield is an increase of strain without any increase of stress. The *upper yield stress* is where yield begins and the *lower yield stress* is the lowest stress at which it proceeds. See figure 33.

Proof stress Non-ferrous metals and ultra-high strength steels have no clearly defined yield point and it is necessary to use a *proof stress* for specification and design purposes. Proof stress is the stress required to produce a specified amount, usually taken as either 0·1 or 0·2 per cent of non-proportional permanent strain. See figure 35.

Design stress often termed the *permissible* or *allowable* stress ensures structural safety in all conditions allowing for the possibility of defects in materials, bad workmanship, errors in design and for overloading in service. For example, the design stress in bending for mild steel beams is commonly taken as 165 N/mm² which is about two thirds of the yield point stress of 247 N/mm².

Ductility is the ability of a material to undergo plastic deformation before tensile failure. In uniaxial stress, eg in the stretching of a wire, ductility can be expressed as the percentage elongation or reduction in cross sectional area. For triaxial stress conditions, eg in thick material subjected to flexure, ductility is determined mainly by the *Charpy V-notch test* and expressed as

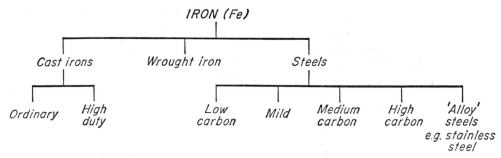

31 Ferrous metals

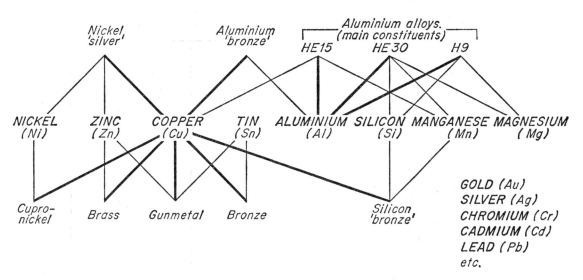

Elements are in bold type.
The thick lines indicate the
predominant ingredients in alloys

32 Non-ferrous metals and alloys

joules of energy required to cause failure. In the test a notched specimen supported at its ends is struck in the middle.

Brittleness is the opposite of ductility, fracture occurs with no plastic deformation. It is not related to tensile strength, thus high tensile steel is more brittle (less ductile) than mild steel. With steels lowering of temperature to the *transition temperature* suddenly changes the mode of failure from a ductile and fibrous to a brittle crystalline fracture. Compliance with BS 449 safeguards against brittle fracture which could only occur where there is a severe notch or crack in a structure.

Metals such as ordinary cast iron which are brittle at normal temperatures are called *cold short*, and those such as alpha brass which are brittle at elevated temperatures are called *hot short*.

Toughness is a combination of strength and ductility which enables a material to withstand shock loadings.

Hardness, ie resistance to abrasion and penetration, is determined for metals by the Brinell, Rockwell and Vickers tests. The higher the number the greater the hardness. Hard metals include tungsten and cast irons. The expression *temper*

175

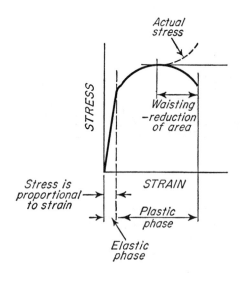

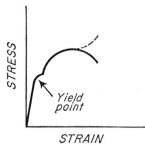

33 *Stress-strain curves for steel*

is often used to describe hardness, a soft and ductile metal being said to be of 'low temper'.

Fatigue is a term used to describe the loss of strength resulting from repeated applications of a force which is less than would cause failure with a single application.

Creep is slow plastic deformation under a constant stress, normally critical only at high temperatures.

Work hardening is an increase in strength and hardness of metals when rolled, forged or otherwise manipulated at normal temperature. Unlike hot working in which the grain structure during manipulation is constantly refined, cold working distorts the grain structure thus increasing strength and hardness. Work hardening can be either an advantage, eg steel sheet is strengthened by cold rolling while retaining sufficient ductility for subsequent manipulation, or, a disadvantage, eg when ductility has been reduced to a level

which will not allow further manipulation without heat treatment.

Heat treatments are highly specialized processes for softening, stress relieving, and hardening. They involve heating the metal to a critical temperature well below its melting point and controlling the rate of cooling. Heat treatments for steel are given on page 196 and for aluminium on page 209.

Ageing is an increase in strength and hardness which occurs in certain aluminium alloys after heat treatment and in steels as a continuation of work hardening.

Former standard wire gauge SWG	Metals other than lead mm	Lead no. formerly lb/ft²	Former English zinc gauge ZG
40	0·12		
33	0·25		
30	0·31		
27	0·42		
26	0·46		
25	0·51		10
24	0·56		
23	0·61		
	0·63		12
22	0·71		13
	0·79		14
21	0·81		
20	0·91		15
19	1·02		
	1·04		16
18	1·22		
	1·25	3	
17	1·42		
16	1·63		
	1·80	4	
15	1·83		
14	2·03		
	2·24	5	
13	2·34		
	2·50	6	
12	2·64		
11	2·95		
	3·15	7	
10	3·25		
	3·55	8	

Table 67   *Equivalent thicknesses of sheet metals*

176

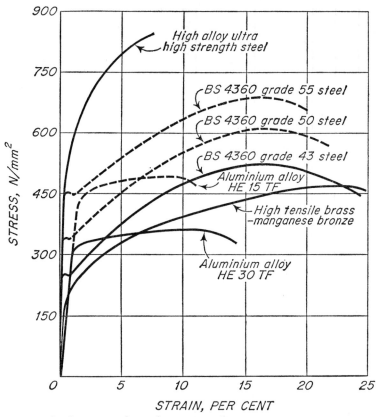

34   *Stress-strain curves for ferrous and non-ferrous metals*

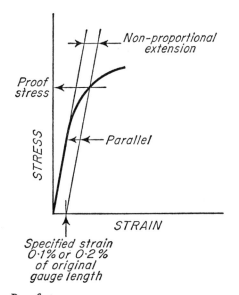

35   *Proof stress*

Equivalent thicknesses of sheet metals

Table 67 shows the thicknesses of the gauges formerly used for sheet metals which will now be made in millimetre thicknesses.

Properties of common metals

As a class of materials metals are dense, strong and often elastic at room temperatures, and have high electrical and thermal conductivity.

Table 68 compares these properties in some metals with those in typical timbers and plastics.

Corrosion

Metals tend to revert to stable compounds, the nature and the rate of the process depending on the characteristics of the particular metal, the environment and temperature; corrosion is more rapid at higher temperatures.

Generally, in reasonably clean atmospheres a

177

Material	Density kg/m³	Proof stress 0·1 per cent N/mm²	Tensile strength[1] N/mm²	Elongation on 50 mm per cent	Modulus of elasticity E N/mm²	Hardness Brinell no.	Thermal conductivity W/m deg C	Linear thermal expansion mm/mm ×10⁻⁶ per deg C	Electrical conductivity at 20° C per cent of tough high conductivity copper	Melting point °C
Gold (Au)	19 300								67	1063
Silver (Ag)	10 500								105	960
Lead (Pb) 99·99% pure	11 340		15 (rolled) 18 (extruded)	50 (on 153 mm)	13 800	4	35	29·5	8	327
Copper (Cu) 99·2–99·9% pure	8940	46–371	216–355	8–65	96 600–132 000	42–96	400	17	101·5[2] 102[3] 54–90[4] 45[5]	1083
Cupro-nickels 70–93% Cu : Ni	8900	114–525	386–509	7–46	119 000–152 000	69–162	21–69	16	4–8	1120–1240
Nickel (Ni) 99·99% pure	8880		316	28	200 000	85	62	13	16	1453
Phosphor bronzes 99·99% Cu : Sn : P	8887–8929	108–679	323–739	6–70	100 000	69–234	47–120	18–19	10–27	1032–1065
Monel Cu : Ni : Fe : Mn	8830		535–752	5–40	172 000–221 000	125–240	27	14	4	1350
'Nickel silvers' Cu : 10–30% Ni : Zn	8750–8872	100–618	339–695	4–75	120 000–127 000	66–166	20–27	16–17	5–7	1100
Brass 60 Cu : 40% Zn	8380	108[6] 386[7] 124[8]	371[6] 541[7] 386[8]	40[6] 57[7] 45[8]	103 000	75[6] 150[7] 75[8]	129	21	29	904
High tensile brass ('Manganese bronze') Cu : Zn : Mn etc	8300–8400	247–463	530–725	13–35	103 000	140–200	90–112	21	20–25	990
'Aluminium bronze' 5–10% Cu : Al etc	7570–8150	93–556	417–687	13–69	120 000	66–175	64–85	17–18	13–18	1041–1063

Table 68a Properties of metals (approximate values) listed in order of decreasing density

	Density									Melting point
Stainless steels Fe : Cr : Ni : (Mo)	7850	210	510[9] 540[10]	50	—	170	15	17	2·5	1440[9] 1430[10]
High strength steel		350–430	495–617	19	207 000	150–180	52–63	12	12	1900
Mild (structural) steel			423–510	22		130		12		
Wrought iron			355	25–40		100		12		
Grey cast irons[11]	7150[12]	100–200	155–310	0·5–1·0	120 000[12]	140–250	45–50	11	2·0	1150–1350
Nodular and malleable cast irons[11]	7225[12]	193–440	310–800	20–2·0	172 000[12]	120–300	31–47	11	2·0	1150–1350
Zinc (Zn) 99·99% pure	7140		139[13] 216[14]	25[13] 10[14]	96 500	45–50	113	23[13] 40[14]	28	419
Aluminium alloy HE 30 TF	2700	270[15]	310[15]	18	69 950	60–100[16]	184–206[16]	23	32–52[16]	570–660
Aluminium (Al) 99·0% pure	2650	—	70–140	2–20	68 300– 72 400	23 (extrusions) 22–42 (sheet)	214	24	60·5	660
99·99% pure		—	80–100	3–45		15 (extrusions) 15–30 (sheet)	244	24	60·5	660

1 The ranges given relate to methods of forming and condition. Strength increases in the following orders: Cast, rolled, extruded, drawn. Annealed, half-hard, hard with corresponding reductions in elongation.

2 Oxygen-free high conductivity copper.

3 Tough pitch high conductivity copper.

4 Deoxidized non-arsenical copper.

5 Deoxidized and tough pitch arsenical coppers

6 Hot-rolled.

7 Cold-rolled.

8 Cold-rolled and annealed

9 18 Cr : 10 Ni

10 17 Cr : 11 Ni : 2·5 Mo.

11 Ranges; except for melting point, are for low–high strength irons.

12 Average values.

13 Parallel to direction of rolling.

14 Perpendicular to direction of rolling.

15 BS 1474 minima for bars and sections.

16 Various alloys.

The principal sources of information are The Corporate Laboratories of the British Steel Corporation (BISRA); The British Cast Iron Research Association; The Development Associations for Copper, Zinc and Lead; The Aluminium Federation; Metals Reference Book, Vol. II, C. J. Smithells, Butterworths Ltd

Material	Density kg/m³	Proof stress 0·1 per cent N/mm²	Tensile strength N/mm²	Elongation on 50 mm per cent	Modulus of elasticity E N/mm²	Hardness Brinell no.	Thermal conductivity W/m deg C	Linear thermal expansion mm/mm ×10⁻⁶ per deg C	Electrical conductivity at 20° C per cent of tough high pitch conductivity copper	Melting point °C
Glass	2520		34–172		68 900		1·04	8·9		1500
Concrete:[17] dense aggregate	2240– 2400		4[18]		28 600[18]		1·0–1·4	10–14		—
lightweight aggregate	320– 2000		3[19]		8 000[19]		0·5[19]	6·5–8·1[9]		
Plastics	900– 2300 3·2–128[22] 1900[24]		7[20]–90[21] 0·14–0·55[22] 68–310[24]	5–800[20] nil[21]	172[20]– 10 300[21] 20 600[24]		0·2	7–210		80–295 (softening point)
Timbers[23]	380– 900		20–110		5 860– 18 600		0·14	4·5		

17 Properties vary with density of concrete and type of aggregate.
18 Approximate values for concrete having crushing strength of 28 N/mm².
19 Approximate values for expanded clay aggregate concrete having crushing strength of 14 N/mm².

20 Thermoplastics.
21 Thermosetting plastics.
22 Cellular plastics.
23 The properties of timbers vary with species, density, moisture content and direction of loading. See chapter 2.
24 Maximum for grp.

Table 68b Properties of some non-metals

coating of corrosion products forms quickly, and in the case of non-ferrous metals and some ferrous metals it is often firmly adherent and stifles further corrosion.

Destructive corrosion usually occurs in moist conditions where different metals are in electrical contact, and in the presence of atmospheric pollution or flue gases.

Clearly, wherever practicable, metal structures and components should be designed so as to discourage condensation and to allow water to drain away rapidly. Where corrosive conditions are unavoidable dissimilar metals should be separated and the more corrosion-resistant metals, or possibly non-metallic materials, may show a favourable 'cost-in-use'. Discussions of typical environments and of corrosion mechanisms follow:

Environments

Water BRS Digest 98 *Durability of metals in natural waters* is a valuable reference.

Natural waters contain mineral impurities, dissolved oxygen and carbon dioxide, the latter derived from rainfall. Water containing the equivalent of 50 parts per million of calcium carbonate, derived from chalk, may be classed as soft and over 350 ppm as very hard. Fortunately deposits of calcium carbonate combined with corrosion products can form a protective layer, thin eggshell scales being far more effective than thick nodular scales.

Iron filings or rubbish often impede the formation of a protective scale of carbonate deposits on the surfaces of galvanized steel hot water tanks and acidic or alkaline waters of high chloride content cause dezincification of hot-pressed alpha-beta brasses. See page 201.

Excessive amounts of detergents, bleaches and cleansers corrode copper and lead waste pipes, and zinc alloy waste traps.

Acids are present in rain, in some soils, water supplies, plasters and woods particularly Western red cedar, Douglas fir, oak and sweet chestnut, and they are produced by algae and mosses. Even copper and lead, which are otherwise very durable metals, may be perforated by washings from Western red cedar shingles or from mosses growing on roof tiles.

Salts Fortunately, most potable waters form a protective layer which inhibits corrosion. However, moorland waters which contain organic acids or inorganic salts may be plumbosolvent or cuprosolvent and lead pipes can give rise to a health risk, and copper pipes may stain ceramic fittings.

Sulphates in soils and in clay products, and calcium chloride can intensify corrosion. Calcium chloride additions to Portland cement must not exceed 2 per cent by weight as a solution (not flake) see chapter 7 page 144, if corrosion of steel reinforcement, or of aluminium, is to be avoided. Magnesium oxychloride which is used in flooring, is highly corrosive to all metals.

Alkalis Sodium and potassium hydroxides released by Portland cement are very harmful to zinc and aluminium and to lead in continuously damp conditions. Copper is not affected, and the protection afforded to ferrous metals is useful where steel is embedded in concrete, particularly in cement-rich mixes. However, the pH value increases as concrete carbonates and corrosion can result from variations in the rate of carbonation on the two sides of an embedded steel member.

Soil type	Effect
Light, sandy soils Chalk	not generally aggressive, non-saline sand, or chalk can be used to protect pipes in aggressive soils (provided care is taken to prevent the backfill becoming a land drain)
Cinders Builders' rubble	very corrosive to steel, copper and aluminium
Heavy anaerobic clays	corrosive to ferrous metals
Saline soils	cause severe corrosion of aluminium and galvanized steel, and of lead if it is connected to copper
Sulphate bearing soils	in anaerobic conditions sulphate-reducing bacteria convert cast iron into ferrous sulphide leaving soft spongy graphite

Table 69   Soils

Concrete should be dense and the depth of cover must be adequate.

High calcium lime may corrode aluminium and is slightly corrosive to lead and zinc. It has no effect on copper and so long as it remains uncarbonated it protects ferrous metals.

Ammonia, eg from ammonia-stabilized latex adhesives for floorings, can contribute to *stress corrosion*. See page 184, of copper embedded in screeds.

Mechanisms of corrosion

Corrosion usually results from a complex electrochemical action. (Direct chemical action by dry gases at high temperatures rarely occurs in buildings.)

Where dissimilar metals which are electrically connected are immersed in a conducting liquid (an *electrolyte*), a short circuited galvanic cell is formed. Metal in the form of positively charged *ions* is removed at the *anode* but the *cathode* does not corrode. Thus, zinc protects steel *sacrificially* because it develops a lower potential and becomes the anode in a cell. Sometimes the anodic metal protects the cathode by *plating out*, eg silver plating on nickel (*EPNS*).

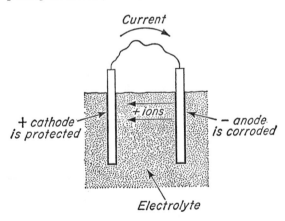

Current

+ *cathode is protected*   + *ions*   − *anode is corroded*

Electrolyte

The rate at which electrolytic corrosion proceeds depends upon:

(i) the potential difference between metals in a particular environment. The scale in the next column is for normal conditions; it may vary due to many factors. Metals above corrode in preference to those below and the more remote two metals are in the scale the greater is the reaction.

ANODIC END	magnesium
negative	zinc including
'base metals'	galvanized
	coatings
	aluminium
	cadmium
	aluminium-magnesium
	-silicon alloys
	copper-aluminium
	alloys
	iron and mild steel
	chromium
	lead
	tin
	nickel
	brasses
	bronzes
positive	copper
'noble metals'	stainless steel (austenitic)
CATHODIC END	silver

In particular, in practice the following pairs of metals should not be used in contact in the presence of moisture:

Metal attacked

copper and copper alloys
{ cast iron
mild steel
cadmium plated steel
galvanized steel
zinc
aluminium

copper
phosphor bronze
gunmetal
aluminium bronze
silicon bronze
} high tensile brass (manganese bronze)

nickel
mild steel
} aluminium
zinc, galvanized steel

(ii) the relative areas of metals. Corrosion is particularly serious where the area of the anode is small compared with that of the cathode.

(iii) characteristics of the electrolyte. Corrosion is more rapid where strong mineral acids or their salts, eg chlorides or sulphates, are present.

(iv) temperature. Often the rate of corrosion increases with temperature. In the case of combinations of zinc and steel a reversal of polarity occurs at about 70°C, so that if the temperature of water in galvanized steel systems exceeds this value, unless a protective scale has been allowed to develop, the normally protective zinc coating will tend to corrode the steel.

Electrolytic cells are formed in five ways:
(1) By different metals (*bimetallic corrosion*): examples are:

This form of corrosion occurs where hot water which passes through copper pipes picks up as little as 0·1 ppm of copper and flows into galvanized and aluminium vessels. (In well designed indirect hot water systems the free oxygen con-

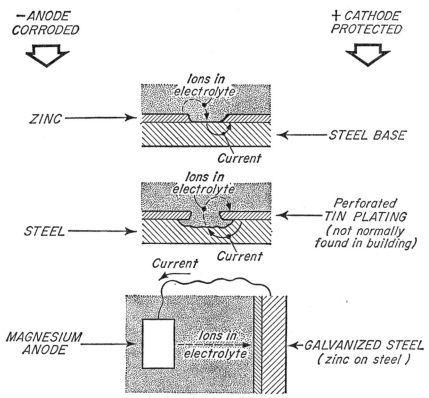

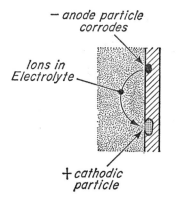

An immersed magnesium anode connected electrically to a galvanized steel cylinder or cistern protects the zinc coating while the protective scale is forming. This use of a *sacrificial anode* is particularly effective in soft waters and in many cases it is not necessary to replace them when they have all been deposited as scale.
(2) By *particles deposited from solution:*

tent of the water quickly diminishes and attack usually ceases.)

The action is more pronounced at higher temperatures but rainwater which has passed over copper-clad roofs should never be taken into unprotected aluminium or cast iron gutters and pipes. (3) Less commonly by *different constituents in a metal:*

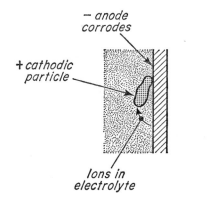

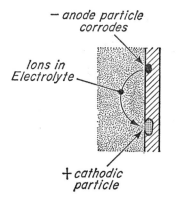

183

In certain waters selective dissolution of one constituent happens in certain high strength aluminium copper alloys and some brass pressings containing about 40 per cent zinc, may undergo *dezincification* in this way. See page 201.

(4) *Differential aeration.* Corrosion takes place, even in pure metals, where there is a difference in oxygen concentration in an electrolyte: the parts in contact with an aerated electrolyte become cathodic and are protected, while the parts in contact with the non-aerated electrolyte become anodic, and corrode. For example, the open surface of a film of water which is held between two sheets of metal is more highly oxygenated than the enclosed water and the metal in contact with the latter corrodes.

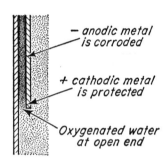

— anodic metal is corroded

+ cathodic metal is protected

Oxygenated water at open end

Similarly, under scale deposits and in depressions, the parts of metal having greater access to oxygen become cathodic relative to those where the electrolyte is confined, and the latter corrode preferentially. *Pitting corrosion* is further assisted by the fact that the cathodic area is much larger than the anodic area and because accumulations of corrosion products at the mouth of the pit prevent aeration of the trapped liquid. Thus:

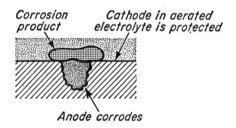

Corrosion product

Cathode in aerated electrolyte is protected

Anode corrodes

Corrosion also occurs where parts of metal components are in *different environments*, for example where a steel pipe passes through a damp plastered wall. Such pipes should be wrapped and

pipes in chases in floors should be embedded in uniformly dense cement-sand mortar.

(5) Electrolytic corrosion can also be caused by *stray currents*, more particularly from a DC source.

Mechanically aided corrosion

a *Stress corrosion cracking* This is caused by the simultaneous action of a corrosive environment and a stress, whether induced in manufacture (eg by cold working) or applied in service. The critical environments for various metals are:

Metal	Environment
certain copper-based alloys eg manganese bronze	ammonia (eg arising from certain concrete foaming agents and adhesives)
certain aluminium alloys stainless steels	chlorides (above 80°C only)
lead	sulphates
high-strength steels	nitrates

b *Cavitation corrosion* A considerable drop in pressure in a liquid induced by a change in pipe diameter, partial blockages etc, produces cavities. These collapse violently and remove the protective coating from pipes thereby exposing an anodic area which being relatively small leads to active electrolytic corrosion.

c *Impingement attack* Entrained air bubbles or solid particles impinging on metal surfaces, eg at a sharp bend in a pipe, remove the protective film and lead to corrosion as above. The velocity of water in copper pipes should be less than 1·5 m/s particularly in salt water systems.

Practical precautions against corrosion

Arising from the foregoing discussion, some advice is offered to prevent corrosion. However, in cases which are not straightforward, expert advice should be sought at the design stage.

1 Select metals to suit the environment
2 Avoid damp conditions. In particular—
avoid crevices which could hold water or moist

dirt by filling them with weld or mastic or by providing drain holes

avoid contact with absorbent materials and protect metals from damp and corrosive agents, eg by paint or adequate concrete cover on steel reinforcement.

3 Avoid contact of dissimilar metals by interposing an electrical insulator, eg bituminous paint, synthetic rubber or resin-bonded laminates.

4 Avoid differential aeration of environments in contact with a metal.

5 In water (a) avoid excessive temperature and velocity, and stagnant conditions

(b) avoid obstructions and sharp changes in direction of pipes

(c) provide cathodic protection by fixing a sacrificial anode electrically connected to the relatively noble metal

(d) do not allow water to flow from a noble metal on to a base metal. If different metals must be used in the same water system cathodic metal must be placed downstream.

Specialized measures mainly restricted to industrial applications include treatments to reduce the electrical conductivity of water or its oxygen content, and the provision of an impressed current.

Some corrosive, and some protective electrolytic mechanisms are illustrated in figure 36.

The terms *anode* and *cathode* are used here in relation to corrosion processes occuring within cells which are delivering current—as distinct from *electrolysis* where current derives from an independent source. Electrons flow in the opposite direction to the 'conventional current' shown on the diagrams.

Other BRS Digests which deal with corrosion are:

59 and 120 steel reinforcement

70 iron and steel

71 non-ferrous metals

Forming metals

Complex components are often best made in more than one metal and employing many manufacturing processes. The choice of metals and processes requires highly specialized knowledge. Some of the more common methods of forming metals are outlined here:

Casting

The process of casting results in a coarse grain structure in which the regions of metal in contact with the mould can be particularly weak in tension. Ordinary castings are generally more brittle and weaker than their 'hot worked' counterparts in which the grain size is smaller, more uniform and

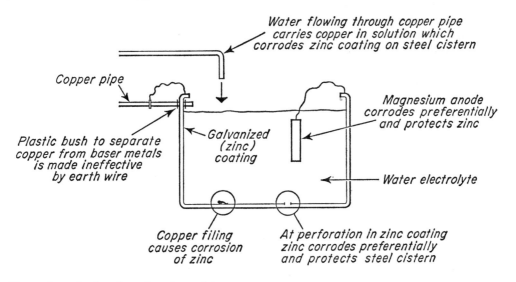

Water flowing through copper pipe carries copper in solution which corrodes zinc coating on steel cistern

Copper pipe

Magnesium anode corrodes preferentially and protects zinc

Plastic bush to separate copper from baser metals is made ineffective by earth wire

Galvanized (zinc) coating

Water electrolyte

Copper filing causes corrosion of zinc

At perforation in zinc coating zinc corrodes preferentially and protects steel cistern

36   Illustration of galvanic actions in a cistern

thus more suited to withstand impact loads and tensile stresses. However:

1 *Sand casting* is economical where a number of complex and identical objects such as rainwater goods and other components with internal passageways are required. If the cast metal is brittle, eg certain grades of cast iron, then walls of castings must be thick to prevent fracture. Other metals, eg cast steels, are more ductile and the reduced wall thickness leads to a weight reduction.

Most metals and alloys having melting points up to about 1500°C can be cast. Lead is easy to cast and suitable grades of iron, steel, bronzes and aluminium are available.

Although essentially simple in that molten metal is poured into moulds and allowed to cool, casting requires considerable knowledge and skill. Patterns to provide the shape of moulds and cores are usually made in wood in sizes which allow for shrinkage of metal in cooling. Moulds and cores are usually formed in special foundry sand, the cores often being held in their correct positions by *core nails* which are in due course included in the casting. Pouring of metal must be continuous to ensure even cooling, otherwise the casting may warp or crack. When the metal has solidified unwanted projections are removed by the *fettling* process. Patterns can be used many times but moulds and cores are broken up when the casting is removed. Sand castings are never completely smooth and may be distorted in cooling, so that surfaces which are required to have a precision fit to other surfaces must be cast oversize to allow for grinding or machining. Freedom from porosity in sand castings can never be guaranteed and continuously cast or wrought products should be used in preference for supporting members, eg in wall cladding.

2 *Continuous casting* is a process of casting small, usually rectangular shapes called *slabs or billets* in a continuous process. With steel, the heavy and costly plant used in the ingot making and heavy rolling processes conventionally used to form semi-finished products, is eliminated. Continuous cast billets are often used in tube making.

3 *Shell moulding* Very accurate mouldings are made in some metals by using thin resin-bonded sand shells supported in sand.

4 *Die casting* Accurate and permanent moulds of steel are used for mass producing small castings of low melting point metals, eg aluminium copper and zinc alloys. The practice of gravity die casting is similar to ordinary foundry practice but in pressure die casting, the molten metal is injected under high pressure to make complex shapes.

5 *Centrifugal casting* Metal is poured into a cylindrical steel mould rotating about its horizontal axis. When the metal has solidified rotation stops and the pipe or tube is withdrawn. The product is stronger and is less likely to contain defects than its sand-cast equivalent. Centrifugally cast products are often termed *spun* products and these should not be confused with spun sheet products. See page 187.

Rolling

Hot rolling is used to produce long lengths of sections, eg bars, strips, sheets and sections such as angles, channels and I-sections. Heavy rollers are used to reduce the section size and thus extend its length. With steel a billet or slab is heated to above 700°C prior to rolling so that rolling forces are reduced and the grain structure refined to improve the ductility of the finished product. Steel I-sections are produced up to 915 mm deep, and strip up to 1830 mm wide.

Cold rolling, again using heavy rollers, this process improves the surface finish, dimensional accuracy, hardness and strength of those hot rolled products it is applied to, eg steel sheet, which can be cold rolled up to 1830 mm wide.

Forging

Forging is a process of squeezing hot metal to shapes, the products being tougher than castings. Hammering by hand is rare today, most products being *drop forged* using mechanical hammers and suitable dies.

Extrusion

Heated metal is forced through a suitably shaped hole in a hardened steel die, to produce continuous solid or hollow sections including those which cannot be rolled such as finned sections. Metal can be disposed where it can be most effective and often sections can serve several functions.

Dimensional accuracy depends largely upon the thickness of the 'arms' of sections. Generally a large range of standard dies is available and the cost of new dies can be justified for large orders.

Drawing

Wire and tubes are pulled through tapered dies or a series of dies to reduce the thickness of the metal. Normally the metal is cold and the process improves its strength.

Pipe and tube making

Small diameter tubes are extruded as already described. Larger diameters are made by rotary forging the outside of a tube bloom while the inside is supported by a close fitting mandrel. Alternatively, flat strip is formed by a series of rolls and the edges of the heated metal are fused together under pressure or for higher quality work the edges of cold strip are welded electrically.

Forming from cold sheet

Suitable soft and ductile sheets can be shaped by cold forming. Prefinished products such as plastics coated steel sheets can be cold formed since most coatings withstand more deformation than the base metal.

Roll forming Corrugated and other profiled sheets, simple sections (beams and purlins) and complex sections are formed in any length by passing flat strip through a series of rollers. With steel the maximum strip thickness is normally 5 mm and the minimum economic run is about 3000 m, although for simple sections smaller quantities may compete with press-baked sections.

Pressing The *rubber press* can produce lightly dished or patterned products and building panels. The sheet is pressed over a wooden former by rubber pads which are placed on the sheet and pressurized by an oil filled rubber bag contained in the upper part of an hydraulic press. Tool costs (wooden former) being very low, it is possible to produce small quantities economically.

The *press brake* employs a V shaped die and punch which is able to form a bend with each stroke of the punch. It can be used to make limited quantities of troughed sheets and other open sections. Low tool costs and great versatility facilitate small quantity production (even *one-offs*). Length, unlike roll forming, is commonly

limited to 4 m although some presses produce sections above 9 m long.

Deep pressings are made in hydraulic presses using highly accurate matched steel dies which prevent the metal from buckling during the extensive deformation which takes place. It is important to realise that large dies are very costly and require mass production runs such as those provided by baths and car body panels.

Embossing and coining Thin sheet is embossed by a punch and die, or by passing between a pair of embossed rollers (*rigidized sheets*). In coining, a metal slug can be given different profiles on the two sides.

Stretch forming Sheet is held at the edges and stretched over a male former of simple shape.

Spinning Hemispheres, cones and similar regular shapes for lighting fittings and containers, up to about 1·2 m diameter, are shaped by forcing a rotating sheet against a rotating former. Copper, bronze aluminium alloys and stainless steels are the metals most commonly spun while cold. Domed ends for pressure vessels are spun from heated steel plate up to 4·3 m diameter.

Explosive forming is suitable for making 'one-off' components incorporating a high degree of complex curvature for which alternative processes, eg matched die pressing, would be totally uneconomic or technically difficult in the case of exotic metals used for example in aerospace work. The metal sheet is placed over a female mould which is often made of concrete suitably lined, the mould cavity is then evacuated and an explosive charge detonated in the water above the sheet forms it at high velocity into the mould.

Panel beating Irregular shapes are beaten from flat sheets, and damaged car bodies repaired, by this highly skilled hand work.

Bossing Sheet lead, soft temper copper, aluminium and stainless steel can be formed to complex shapes by bossing by hand using box-wood shapes and a mallet.

Joining metals

Mechanical, soldering, brazing and welding methods are considered here. Adhesives, dealt with in chapter 14, may be preferable where stress concentrations in thin sheet would be caused by mechanical fixings and where large areas are to be joined, without impairing the appearance of either part. However loss of strength in fires and creep may require to be taken into account in the selection and use of adhesives.

Mechanical joints

Nuts and bolts, and metal screws are useful where high strength joints may require to be separated later. Nuts and bolts require space on both sides to manipulate tools but single sided access is sufficient where a hole in one part receives a *self-tapping screw* which is hard enough to cut its own thread; where the hole is tapped to receive a *set screw*, where a *threaded stud* is cast or welded on one component, or where a *captive nut* is used. *Friction grip bolts* which indicate the correct degree of tightening are now commonly used in structural steelwork.

Ordinary *solid rivets* are inserted in prepared holes and a second head formed from the protruding shank with a pneumatic hammer. These require access from both sides and are of the type used in structural steelwork whereby the preheated rivet shrinks and compacts the joint upon cooling. Likewise, solution treated aluminium alloy rivets age-harden after the joint has been formed. *Hollow rivets* are available for single sided access. The hollow shank contains a mandrel which when pulled with a machine or lever tongs expands the shank and forms a head.

Soldering and brazing Most metals can be joined with an alloy which melts at a lower temperature than the melting point of the parent metals and which, although different in composition, alloys with them. Surfaces must be clean, fluxes being used to prevent oxidization.

a *Soldering* This term usually refers to *soft soldering* with tin-lead and sometimes lead-silver alloys which melt at temperatures below 300°C. The solder is added with a copper bit, which must first be cleaned and *tinned* with solder. Wide surfaces can be *sweated* by tinning both parts and holding them together while they are heated and then while the solder cools and hardens.

b *Brazing* Brazing, sometimes called *hard soldering*, gives stronger joints than soft soldering, but as it is done at a higher temperature (over 600°C) it is not suitable for joining metals such as lead which have low melting points. Steels containing chromium or aluminium are difficult to braze due to the oxide layer. The use of *silver solder*, an alloy of silver and brass, is increasing due to the strong joints (460 N/mm²) which can be made at low temperatures.

Welding Welding methods can be classified as:

(a) cold, (b) plastic and (c) fusion welding; carried out at normal, moderate and high temperatures, respectively. In all cases surfaces must be clean.

a *Cold welding* Soft metals such as lead and gold can be welded by hammering. Stainless steel and other alloys can be joined by ultrasonic vibrations when the parts are lightly clamped together.

b *Plastic welding* Metals such as wrought iron and, less readily mild steel, can be hammer welded at a temperature below their melting points, although the strength of the joint is somewhat less than that of the parent metals.

In *resistance welding* heat is provided locally by the resistance of metal to a heavy electric current at low voltage and the parts are pressed together. *Spot, stitch, seam, projection* and *butt* welds are of this type. *Spot welds* which can be used instead of rivets, are formed by small diameter electrodes which heat the metal locally and then press the parts together. *Stitch welds* are formed by an intermittently operated spot welding machine. *Projection welds* are formed by passing a current through multiple points of contact provided, for example, by small surface projections on metal plates or by overlapping wires as in wire mesh manufacture. *Seam welds* are formed either by two rollers or by one roller and a plate acting as electrodes. Wire and rods are *butt welded* by pressing their ends together and passing a current between them. Threaded studs and similar items are electrically *stud welded* with special guns onto surfaces. In *flash welding* heat is applied by striking an arc before applying pressure. *Friction welding* is a specialized process in which heat is generated by high speed rotation of one part relative to the other with an axially applied load.

c *Fusion welding* Fusion welding involves melting of the metals to be joined, either by a gas flame or an electric arc. In some cases a filler rod, often of similar composition to that of the parent metals, is used. Properly formed fusion welds are as strong as the parent metals. The main methods are:

(i) *Gas welding* Gas flames are of oxy-acetylene or propane for mild steel, atomic hydrogen for high temperatures up to about 4000°C, and oxy-hydrogen for low temperature lead welding, known as *lead burning*. Highly skilled operators are required but the equipment is cheap and portable, and the method is useful for joining thin steel sheet, plate and sections and for non-ferrous metals.

(ii) *Arc-welding* An arc is struck between two carbon electrodes or between a carbon electrode, or more commonly a welding rod, and the work, in each case with or without a filler rod. Arc welding is faster and gives deeper penetration than gas welding and is suitable for both thin and heavy sections and for both site work and automatic processes.

In both gas and arc welding, molten metal combining with oxygen and nitrogen from the air makes the joint brittle and less resistant to corrosion. To prevent this, joints must be protected by a suitable flux, by a blanket of inert gas provided from a cylinder, or by special coatings on electrodes.

In very heavy structures such as bridges it may be necessary to build up a weld in a number of separate passes. Alternatively, in vertical joints, joints can be formed in one pass by the electro-slag or electro-gas processes.

(iii) *Induction welding* Small metal parts are heated by being placed inside insulated coils through which an alternating current is passed. The method has the advantages that it is quick and little oxidization or discolouration occurs; but the high cost of equipment limits its use to high quantity production lines.

(iv) *Thermit welding* This method, which uses a metallurgical reduction process to produce molten iron, is useful where a large quantity of molten metal is required.

Costs

Owing to constant variations in the costs of metals the price factors given in table 70 can serve as a rough guide only.

Cost factors by weight			
Cast iron	6	Lead	23
Structural steel		Zinc	24
heavy sections	10	Aluminium	44
light sections	11	Stainless steel 18 : 10	90
Steel reinforcement		Copper	112
large diameter	12	Stainless steel 17 : 11 : 2½	124
small diameter	14	Tin	302

Table 70   Approximate cost factors of common metals

Ferrous metals

The tonnage of ferrous metals produced annually is more than 90 per cent of the total for metals as a whole. Cast iron and mild steel are cheap and form the bulk of production but, although relatively small, the output of special steels, eg stainless steel, is very important. Very little wrought iron is produced today. In general, ordinary ferrous metals can be worked easily and are less costly than the non-ferrous metals used in building. On the other hand except for *stainless steels* and *weathering steels*, eg *Cor-Ten,* ferrous metals, which are not properly and continuously protected, may corrode, and such sections may suffer serious loss of strength. Also corrosion products expand with considerable force, causing defects such as spalling of concrete cover which is of poor quality or inadequate thickness. Fire properties, see chapter 1.

Ferrous metals are discussed under the following headings:

Influence of carbon	Cast irons
Production of pig iron	Wrought iron
Types of metals	Steels

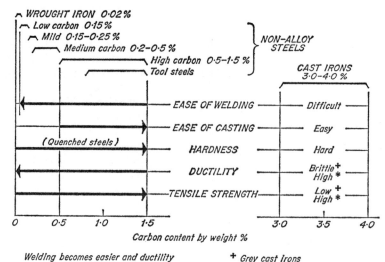

Welding becomes easier and ductility
becomes greater as carbon decreases

+ Grey cast irons
* Spheroidal graphite cast irons

37 *Influence of carbon on properties of the main ferrous metals*

Influence of carbon

All ferrous metals contain carbon. Small variations in carbon content of steels have important influence on their properties, see figure 37, eg tensile strength increases as the carbon content rises to about 1 per cent.

In cast irons the form in which carbon as graphite occurs, as well as its quantity, largely determines their properties. In grey cast irons – by far the most widely used of the cast irons – carbon in the flake form results in low ductility and both tensile strength and hardness generally decrease as the carbon content increases. On the other hand, the strength and hardness of nodular and malleable cast irons increases as the carbon content of the matrix increases. The high carbon steels and all cast irons have relatively low melting points and are suitable for casting.

Production of pig iron

All ferrous metals are made from *pig iron*. This is produced in a *blast furnace* typically 30 m high by 9 m diameter by heating a mixture of iron ore, coke, limestone and other materials designed to separate iron from the earthy material as heating proceeds. A blast of hot air injected at the base of the furnace reacts with the coke to melt the iron. Some of the carbonoke in the c combines with oxygen in the iron and is given off as gas and some of it combines with the molten pig iron, which is thereby deoxidized and acquires a high carbon content, some 3 to 4 per cent.

Blast furnace slag is an important by-product. It is used as concrete aggregate, see page 152; *road metal* and in cement manufacture, see page 143. By blowing water into the molten slag it is 'foamed' and *foamed slag* is used as aggregate for lightweight concrete, see page 171. *Slag wool* for thermal insulation is a further by-product. A new development *Slagceram* is made from molten blast furnace slag using a precisely controlled heat treatment process and can be cast in its final shape in solid or foamed form. It is likely to find use in building where strength, abrasion resistance or fire and chemical resistance are required.

Types of ferrous metals

We now consider cast irons, wrought iron and steels:

CAST IRONS

The British Cast Iron Research Association is at Alvechurch, Birmingham.

Cast iron is produced by re-melting pig iron together with steel scrap and cast iron scrap, and also by recarburizing steel charges. Its high carbon content makes it very suitable for casting but not for hot working. It can be machined and brazed. Cast irons do not possess the good inherent weldability of mild steels but weld adequate for many purposes can be obtained by using a suitable welding process and technique. This applies particularly to the most ductile grades of nodular and malleable irons which have matrix structures similar to those of a mild steel.

Cast iron supplemented the use of timber and masonry for members in compression in the eighteenth century, the first large iron structure being the bridge at Ironbridge, Shropshire, in 1799. Grey cast irons were used for the columns and arches of the Crystal Palace, 1851 (wrought iron was used for members in tension). Modern engineering cast irons have considerably higher tensile strengths and are used for structural components. Malleable cast irons are used extensively for small components and fittings while the more recently developed nodular cast irons are used for a wide range of castings varying from small fittings to relatively large structural components.

Ordinary grey cast irons break with dark grey crystalline fractures, while a wide variety of fractures occurs in nodular and malleable irons. Cast irons emit a 'dull note' when struck with a hard instrument. Resistance to corrosion is decidedly better than that of mild steel and superior to that of wrought iron and, because grey cast iron products are normally required to have thick sections, corrosion rarely affects their strength. As with other cast metals, as-cast surfaces are frequently not very smooth or true, and wall thicknesses may show some variation. Machining may be necessary where close contacting surfaces are required.

Cast irons may be classified as: *grey*, *nodular* (*or spheroidal*), and *highly alloyed* types. *Grey cast irons* are used for general purposes. Tensile strengths are from 155 to 400 N/mm² and typically about 300 N/mm² a realistic design stress being about 0.25 of the tensile strength. They have low ductility with elongations at failure of 0·5 to 1 per cent.

Nodular (*or spheroidal*) *and malleable cast irons* These irons have similar structures but the latter product is obtained by annealing a white cast iron. They have tensile strengths from 310 to 800 N/mm² and strengths over 950 N/mm² are achieved by special heat treatment. Unlike grey irons these irons are elastic with elongations of 2 per cent for the highest strength irons to 20 per cent for the lowest strength irons.

Highly alloyed cast irons are available for special resistance to corrosion, heat and abrasion, and for low temperature uses.

Grey iron products are economical where a number of identical, rigid, heat and corrosion resisting components are required and where weight due to their necessarily thick walls is not a disadvantage eg, bollards and gully gratings. Other uses include:

BS 416 : 1967, *Soil and waste pipes*
BS 460 : 1964, *Rainwater pipes*
BS 497 : 1967, *Manhole frames and covers*
BS 437 : 1970, *Drain pipes* and BS 1130 : 1943, *Fittings*
BS 2035 : 1966, *Water and gas mains*: 50·8– 1220 mm *diameter*
BS 779 : 1961, *Stoves, boilers* and *radiators*
BS 493 : 1970, *Air bricks*
BS 1189 : 1961, *Baths* (*vitreous enamelled*)[1]
Lavatory basins and sinks–vitreous enamelled– (less common).

Some components which were formerly made, almost exclusively, in cast iron are now often made in more recently developed materials. For example: plastics materials, which are lighter and do not require painting, are being used for drainage above and below ground and for baths which are lighter than cast iron baths and do not absorb heat (if less heat, scratch, and chemical resistant). Pitch-fibre pipes are flexible, and competitive in cost with cast iron for drains which do not carry solvents and which are buried sufficiently deep to require no protection against mechanical damage.

Centrifugal casting

Pipes and other cylindrical products are cast by pouring molten iron into permanent moulds which are spun at high speed. The liquid is flung against the lining producing a casting having uniform wall thickness. The resulting iron is denser and stronger than gravity cast iron, and pipes can be made in longer lengths. Products with nodular iron structures are called *ductile iron pipes*. Spun iron pipes for underground drainage are generally recognized as being superior to stoneware.

BS 1211 : 1958 describes *Centrifugally cast (spun) iron pressure pipes for water, gas and sewage.* Pipes with spigots and sockets are in three classes: *B, C* and *D* to resist 122, 183 and 244 m head of water, respectively. The Standard gives sizes and test procedures.

[1] Cast iron is an excellent base for a vitreous enamel finish – see *MBC: C and F, chapter 17.*

WROUGHT IRON

Wrought iron is a low carbon ferrous metal which is strong, extremely ductile, resistant to shock and which has relatively good resistance to corrosion. It is ideal for working at low temperatures, and although the best ferrous metal for hand wrought work, it is costly and skilled craftsmen are now few in number.

Historically, wrought iron was the chief metal for members in tension, thus the original chain encircling the dome of St Paul's Cathedral, London 1700 and the suspension chains for Telford's Menai road bridge 1819 were of wrought iron.

Wrought iron is made by melting pig iron together with millscale (iron oxide) in a small *puddling furnace* in which the impurities, including carbon, react with the millscale to produce a slag. Balls of more or less pure iron withdrawn from the furnace are hammered to expel slag, rolled, and rehammered to distribute more evenly the 1 per cent or so slag which remains elongated in the direction of rolling. The main properties are:

A very low carbon content: 0·02 to 0·03 per cent approximately.
Moderately high tensile strength: 355 N/mm² (it breaks with a fibrous fracture).

It is very ductile, elongation at failure is 25 to 40 per cent. Wrought iron is very tough and resistant to impact loads which together with ease of forging even when cold, account for its use for chains, crane hooks and anchors. Two pieces heated to white heat can be joined by hammering them together, but it cannot be cast, tempered, or gas or arc welded.

It is more resistant to corrosion than mild steel although protection is necessary in damp conditions.

BS 51:1939 (amended 1959) covers general engineering applications. Four grades A to D are described.

STEELS

Steels can be described as ferrous metals which are produced by removing impurities from pig iron and then accurately controlling the proportions of all the ingredients.

Means of producing steel on a large scale date

from 1856. In 1889 the Eiffel Tower was built in wrought iron, but in the same year the Forth railway bridge was erected in steel and from then onwards the use of steel for large structures was established.

Steels are now produced in a wide range of qualities and forms for specific applications including those with tensile strengths more than 1500 N/mm² and with high resistance to corrosion.

Organizations concerned with steel include:
The British Steel Corporation (BSC)
The Corporate Laboratories of the British Steel Corporation (BISRA) which includes the Steel User Service and the Corrosion Advice Bureau
The British Constructional Steelwork Association (BCSA)
The Steel Sheet Information Centre
The Stainless Steel Development Association (SSDA).

We now consider:

Primary manufacture of steels
Carbon contents of steels
Types of steels
  Structural steels
    slow rusting steels
  Sheet steels
  Alloy steels
    stainless steels
Heat treatments for steel.

Primary manufacture

In making steel, the carbon, silicon, phosphorus and other elements in pig iron are reduced in quantity by oxidation.

The main processes are:

1 *Converter processes* In 1856 Henry Bessemer devised a converter which provided the first method of making steel on a large scale, and steel then became more economical and more reliable for structural members than wrought iron.

Converters (not to be confused with furnaces), oxidize the high carbon, manganese silicon and phosphorus content of molten pig iron by blowing air, or more recently oxygen, into the melt. In about 20 minutes phosphorus, the last undesirable element, reaches an acceptable level. A controlled amount of carbon is added back to the melt and residual oxides and gases are removed by the addition of ferro-manganese.

Today most steel is made in LD converters which use low cost *tonnage oxygen.* They combine good scrap consuming capacity with a high production rate.

2 *The open hearth furnace* The open hearth process is responsible for a very small part of steel output. Gas and preheated air, now usually together with oxygen and oil, are used to heat a charge of pig iron and sometimes iron ore and lime with up to 50 per cent of steel scrap. Some carbon and most of the silicon are oxidized by the flame, and the remaining impurities are removed by the addition of iron ore, mill scale (the oxidized skin of a steel ingot) and lime.

3 *Electric furnaces* Electric arc and high frequency induction furnaces are used to produce alloy steels from molten steel and selected scrap. Shorter refining periods are possible by injecting oxygen. The high temperatures attainable allow both the melting of alloy additions and the removal of impurities.

4 *Spray steelmaking* This remarkable process, is simple, much more rapid than open hearth furnaces and might eventually permit the continuous production of steel sections. Molten pig iron is finely atomized by a blast of oxygen and converted to steel as it falls through a reaction chamber.

Carbon content of steels

All steels contain carbon but the description *plain carbon steels* is used to distinguish those steels which do not contain substantial proportions of alloying elements. These are subdivided into:

Low carbon steels (up to 0·15 per cent carbon) are soft and suitable for 'iron' wire and thin sheet for tin plate.

Mild steels (0·15 to 0·25 per cent carbon) are strong, ductile and suitable for rolling into sections, strip and sheet but not usually for casting. They are easily worked and welded. The group includes normal and high strength 'low alloy' weldable structural steels, see *Structural steels* next column.

Medium carbon steels (0·20 to 0·50 per cent carbon) are suitable for forgings and for general engineering purposes.

High carbon steels (0·50 to 1·50 per cent carbon).

Tensile strength increases to about 90 N/mm^2 as the carbon content increases to about 1 per cent and this strength can be further increased by heat treatment. Hardness increases up to about 1·5 per cent carbon content, but ductility decreases and high carbon steels are too brittle for structural work. They are also difficult to weld.

High carbon steels can be hardened for use as files and cutting tools, and they can be treated to the springy condition without loss of hardness. Like high carbon iron, high carbon steels are suitable for casting, eg heavy machine frames.

Types of steels

Having distinguished the types of steel by their carbon contents we look at steels for use in building under three headings:

1 Structural steels
2 Sheet steel
3 Alloy steels.

1 *Structural steels*

BS 4360:1969 describes *Weldable structural steels.* It includes dimensional tolerances for the sections described in BS 4 *Structural steel sections,* testing procedures and mechanical properties. Table 71 contains a few selected requirements, as a general guide only, for the four tensile strength ranges, each having subgrades with differing yield stress and notch ductility requirements. Rutile welding electrodes evolve hydrogen and if site conditions are not dry cracking of welds and adjacent metal can result. Figure 34 page 177 compares the tensile strength curves of the main structural steels with those of a typical non-ferrous metal.

BS 4 *Structural steel sections* comprises:
Part 1 Hot-rolled sections 1962 with amendments 1963 and 1964 describes: '*Universal*' beams, columns, bearing piles, etc. It gives dimensions of sections and weights per metre.
Part 2 Hot-rolled hollow sections 1965 Although more costly than 'open' sections such as I beams, resistance to bending and torsion is excellent and welded joints are neat in appearance.

Corrosion protection to inner surfaces of hollow

Grade	Maximum carbon per cent	Maximum sulphur and phosphorus – each – per cent	Minimum tensile strength N/mm²	Minimum yield stress N/mm² up to 16 mm thick[2]			Minimum elongation $5.65\sqrt{S_0}$	Previous related BS	Uses
				Plates	Flat bars Sections	Hollow sections			
40A	0·27	—		—	—	—		3706	general engineering
40B	0·25	—		230	240	—		—	
40C	0·22	0·060	400/480	230	240	—	25		notch-ductile[5]
40D	0·19	—		260	240	—		2762	
40E	0·19	0·050		260	255	—		—	
43A[1]	0·30[4]	—		—	—	—		3706	
43A[1]	0·30[4]	0·060		245	255	—		15	
43B[1]	0·26	—	430/510	245	255	—	22	—	notch-ductile[5]
43C	0·22	—	(430/540[3])	245	255	255		2762	
43D	0·19	0·050		280	255	255		2762	
43E	0·19	—		280	270	270			
50A[1]	0·27	—		—	—	—		968	high strength steels
50B	0·24	0·060		355	355	355		—	
50C[1]	0·24	—	500/620	355	355	355	20	—	notch-ductile[5]
50D	0·22	0·050		355	355	355		—	
55C[1]	0·26	0·050		450	450	450		—	
55E[1]	0·26	—	550/700	450	450	450	19	—	

[1] Including either 0·20/0·35 or 0·35/0·50 copper if specified in order.
[2] Yield stresses are lower for thicker plates and sections specified.
[3] Hollow sections.
[4] The average is lower.
[5] Have superior resistance to impact, eg for low temperature work.

Table 71   Extracts from BS 4360 : Part 2 1969 Weldable Structural Steels

sections is not needed if the section is fully sealed. The BS describes: dimensions, tolerances and properties of circular tubes from 27 mm × 3·2 mm to 1860 mm × 19 mm.

Rectangular (including squares) from 51 × 25 to 305 × 303 mm[1] and from 25 × 25 to 406 × 406 mm[1]. Hot rolled hollow sections are made in Grades 43C and 50C of BS 4360.

Other British Standards relating to structural steel include:

BS 4461 : 1969 *Cold worked steel bars for the reinforcement of concrete*

BS 4483 : 1969 *Steel fabric for the reinforcement of concrete*

BS 1449, describes steel plates from 3 mm thick upwards which can be welded to form a wide range of structures, eg heavy box columns and I beams larger than the standard beam sections.

[1] The range provided by manufacturers is up to 457 × 356 mm rectangles and 406 × 406 mm squares.

BS 2691 : 1969 *Steel wire for prestressed concrete*
BS 3617 : 1971 *Stress relieved 7-wire strand for prestressed concrete*

'*Weathering steel*' Plain carbon steels containing 0·2 per cent copper have better resistance to corrosion than mild steel but they must be protected from the weather. *Cor-Ten* (registered name), however, containing additions including 0·25 to 0·55 per cent copper, when exposed to alternate wetting and drying externally develop a tenacious oxide coating, russet-copper darkening to purplish brown in colour.

The small number of buildings and structures constructed in *Cor-Ten* steel in this country have developed the oxide coating in 18 months to 2 years as normally occurs in North America and Europe and over a period of ten years the loss of thickness expected is $\frac{1}{2}$ to $\frac{1}{6}$ that of ordinary mild steel. *Cor-Ten* is shot blasted at works to ensure uniform weathering. The usual painted identification marks are not possible.

It is important to drain away corrosion products formed during the first few years so they do not stain adjacent walling and paving.

Incidentally, although protective treatments are not necessary, weathering *steel* provides a better base for paint than ordinary steels. If a painted surface is damaged, oxide will not creep under adjacent painted areas.

In addition to possessing slow rusting properties *Cor-Ten* is a high-strength steel approximating in this respect to grades 50B and 50C.

Cor-Ten is used in the manufacture of sections, plates, sheet and coil. The current extra cost of *Cor-Ten* over that of ordinary mild steel of about 20 per cent can be set against savings in weight, protective treatments and maintenance.

2 Sheet steel

Steel sheet, described as not more than 3 mm thick, is used for wall and roof cladding, curtain wall panels, floor and roof trough decking, demountable partitions and furniture, ducting and rainwater goods. Sheet, and exceptionally mild steel sections up to 5 mm or even 6·3 mm thick, can be cold formed.

Sheet is available in mild steel, low alloy high strength steels including slow rusting *Cor-Ten* and in stainless steels in maximum widths of 1830, 1520 and 1320 mm respectively.

Sheet is available uncoated, and with factory applied corrosion resistant and decorative prefinishes which dispense with the need for costly and less effective shop and site treatments. Sheets prefinished with paint, PVC coatings and laminates are produced in a wide range of colours and textures in widths up to 1320 mm. With suitable precautions the usual forming methods can be used without damaging surfaces.

For a long maintenance-free life externally sheets must be galvanized before prefinishing.

The more important British Standards relating to steel sheet are:

BS 1449 (7 parts), *Requirements for hot and cold rolled steel plate, sheet and strip including stainless steel.*

BS 3083 : 1959 *Hot-dipped galvanized corrugated steel sheets for general purposes*

BS 2989 : 1967 *Hot-dip galvanized plain steel sheet and coil*, specifies 5 classes of steel up to 3 mm thick and 1520 mm wide.

BS2994 : 1958 *Cold rolled steel sections*, specifies dimensions and properties for angles, tees, channels and compound sections made from channels.

3 Alloy steels

Alloy steels contain substantial quantities of alloying elements to provide special properties such as ultra high strength, corrosion or heat resistance. In particular, alloy steels can be heat treated, see page 196, more effectively to provide required degrees of hardness and strength properties throughout their thickness rather than at the surface only. Discussion here is confined to stainless steels.

Stainless steels A stainless steel containing chromium was developed in 1913. Although stainless steel costs 8 to 12 times as much, per kg, as mild steel it is being used increasingly in building. It develops an invisible corrosion resistant film in air and has high resistance to organic and weak mineral acids. It is also resistant to high temperatures, is very hard and strong and has good appearance. See BRS Digest 121.

BS 1449 : Part 4 : 1967 *Stainless and heat resisting plate, sheet and strip* gives requirements for dimensions, chemical composition and mechanical properties. Stainless steels are available in rolled, extruded and drawn forms. They can be forged and cast and fabricated by normal methods including soldering, brazing and welding.

There are five standard *mill finishes* and four *polished finishes*. Welds may need to be polished. Polishes include a lustrous unidirectional dull polish obtained by grinding with fine abrasives and a mirror polish. Complex shapes which cannot be polished mechanically can be given bright to dull matt finishes by electro-chemical means. Strippable protective coatings should be used to prevent damage to surfaces during fabrication and erection.

In service the hard, smooth corrosion-free surface of stainless steel does not hold dirt readily, and light accumulations of non-greasy dirt may often be washed off with plain water. Stubborn deposits should be removed with soap impregnated non-scratching nylon or other plastic pot scourers. In each case the surface should be rinsed with clean water.

Stainless steels are classified as:

martensitic, about 13 per cent chromium
ferritic, usually about 17 per cent chromium and
austenitic, usually 16 to 19 per cent chromium together with 6 to 14 per cent nickel. Austenitic stainless steels which comprise about 70 per cent of production are non-magnetic, have high tensile strength and ductility, and welding and soldering properties are good. They cannot be hardened by heat treatment but working improves proof stress and ultimate strength, with some loss of ductility.

Some properties of the two principal stainless steels used in building, both of which are austenitic, are given in table 72.

Properties	18 per cent chromium 10 per cent nickel type 304	17 per cent chromium 11 per cent nickel 2½ per cent molybdenum type 316
Tensile strength N/mm^2	520–645	540–645
0·2 per cent proof stress N/mm^2	205–430	205–430
Elongation on 50·8 mm (average per cent)	30–25	30–25
Modulus of elasticity (E) N/mm^2	207 000	207 000

Table 72 Stainless steels BS 1449 minima for softened/work hardened conditions

Type 304 alloy is suitable for normal internal uses and externally in the country. In industrial atmospheres where good appearance is important *Type 316 alloy* is essential.

Uses

Tubes BS 4127 : 1972 describes *Light gauge stainless steel tubes 5 mm to 42 mm diameter.* These are more resistant to corrosion than copper tubes. Accelerated tests at the BRS and elsewhere have shown no adverse galvanic effects at copper/ stainless steel junctions and they are accepted by the British Waterworks Association and by virtually all water authorities in this country. Stainless steel tubes are cheaper, stronger and require less frequent support than copper tubes.

Hot water cylinders (under test)

Hospital and kitchen equipment

Sinks, lavatory basins and urinals

Windows a typical product comprises frames fabricated from 0·9 mm stainless steel and sashes in 0·7 mm sheet. Large sections are produced with stainless steel sheet used as a sheathing on wood or aluminium cores.

Sandwich panels Stainless steel sheet on light-weight cores of foamed plastics or honeycombed paper or foil.

Flashings of fully softened sheet. 0·46 mm is recommended externally and 0·38 mm for concealed flashings.

Load-bearing uses Cold worked stainless steel may have tensile strength approaching 1500 N/mm^2. Stainless steel was used for the 'new' chain encircling the dome of St Paul's Cathedral in 1926 and it is used as reinforcement for concrete where freedom from corrosion is critical. It is also very suitable for fixings for concrete and masonry claddings and less costly than copper alloys.

Heat treatments for steel

The mechanical properties of steels can be modified by subjecting them to one or more temperature cycles which alter the shape and size of the grains and the micro-constituents of the metal. As the carbon content of steels increases they become more amenable to heat treatment and a wider range of properties can be obtained. Common forms of heat treatment outlined in figure 38 are:

Hardening is obtained by heating steel above a critical temperature and then cooling it rapidly. Within limits the higher the temperature and the quicker the cooling, the harder but less ductile is the result.

Tempering gives hardened steel increased ductility with only a slight loss of strength, by reheating to a temperature below the hardening temperature followed by cooling at any rate. The higher the reheating temperature the greater is the ductility and also the loss in strength.

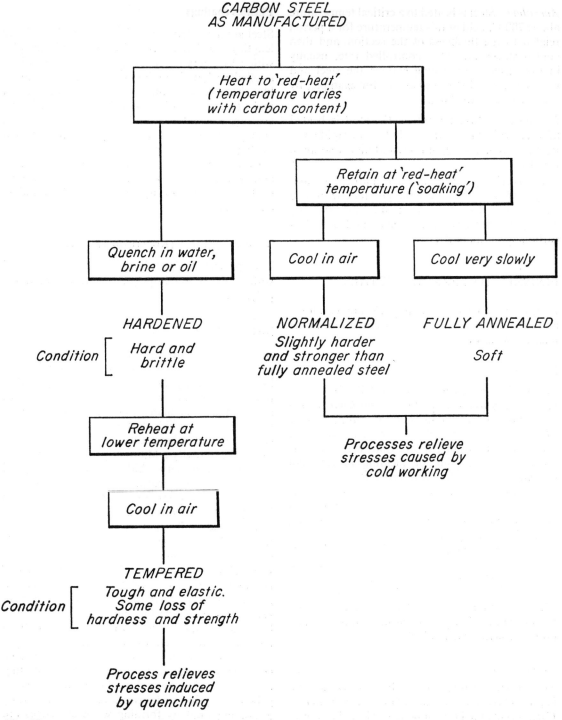

CARBON STEEL
AS MANUFACTURED

Heat to 'red-heat'
(temperature varies
with carbon content)

Retain at 'red-heat'
temperature ('soaking')

Quench in water,
brine or oil

Cool in air

Cool very slowly

HARDENED

Condition [*Hard and*
brittle

NORMALIZED
Slightly harder
and stronger than
fully annealed steel

FULLY ANNEALED

Soft

Reheat at
lower temperature

Cool in air

Processes relieve
stresses caused by
cold working

TEMPERED

Condition [*Tough and elastic.*
Some loss of
hardness and strength

Process relieves
stresses induced
by quenching

38   *Heat treatments for steels*

Annealing Steel is heated to a critical temperature above 700°C, held at this temperature for a period related to the thickness of the section, and then cooled slowly and at a controlled rate, usually in the furnace. Annealing softens the steel and removes internal stresses caused, for example, by welding or cold working.

Normalizing Like annealing, the steel is heated above a critical temperature, but more rapid cooling in air refines the grain size and higher strength results.

Case hardening The normal hardening and tempering processes become possible with low carbon steels if the surfaces are first carburized by heating the steel while it is surrounded with a carbonaceous material.

FINISHES TO FERROUS METALS

Finishes may be required for appearance alone, and often for protection against corrosion. Some finishes are now discussed.

Painting

The subject is treated fully in CP 2008 : 1966 *Protection of iron and steel structures from corrosion* and it is considered in *MBC: C and F*, chapter 17. Briefly, rust and mill scale must be removed. Protection is prolonged five-fold where this is done by shot-blasting or pickling rather than by weathering and wire-brushing. *Bonderizing* and *Parkerizing* are trade names for treatments in which the steel is treated in a solution of acid phosphates to produce a grey-black matt coating of insoluble phosphates which is a valuable rust-inhibiting pretreatment for paint and which is particularly effective in minimizing the lateral spread of rust under paint coatings.

Factory blast-cleaned and shop-primed and painted steel plates, sections and sheet prefinished plastics are likely to be much more durable than products having site-applied finishes.

Vitreous enamel

This provides a tough, colourfast, easily cleaned, highly corrosion resistant surface, see *MBC: C and F*, chapter 17. Components should not have sharp edges or corners if spalling is not to occur.

Plastics coatings

Steel sheet or strip up to 1320 mm wide and any length is available surfaced on one or both sides with PVC, acrylic, epoxide or phenolic coatings applied as liquids or laminates. These products, like those having paint coatings, can be pressed and otherwise fabricated without damage to the coating. For external and corrosive exposures a zinc pretreatment is necessary and lives up to thirty years can be expected.

Components such as handrails, gutter brackets and wire mesh can be given tough and durable coatings of PVC or nylon. See *MBC: C and F*, chapter 17.

'Colour Galbestos' (Robertson Thain Ltd)

This protected sheet is galvanized and coated with asbestos felt impregnated with a modified polyester resin.

Metal coatings

Many metals can be applied to ferrous metals but zinc affords cathodic protection at a relatively low cost and is by far the most commonly used in building. It is important to realise however that although zinc is many times more resistant to corrosion than mild steel it is not immune to corrosion and where zinc coated products are exposed externally additional protection by paint is usually necessary. Although factory applied paint or plastics coatings are superior to site finishes a zinc pretreatment is highly desirable if they are to be exposed externally.

The Building Regulations 1965 require that for the weather-resisting parts of walls and roofs sheet steel shall comply with either BS 2989 : 1967 *Class A Hot-dip galvanized plain steel sheet and coil* or with BS 3083 : 1959 *Type 200 Hot-dipped galvanized corrugated steel sheets for general purposes*. Both specifications require at least 0·61 and not more than 0·76 kg/m² zinc coatings including both sides of the flat sheet.

Wherever possible, to avoid damaging zinc coatings, they should be applied after all cutting and forming has been done but with steel sheet galvanized prior to fabrication, the zinc coating is not impaired by forming while cut edges are protected by the sacrificial zinc coating.

Methods of application of metal coatings

These include:

Electroplating
Cladding
Spraying
Hot-dipping (usually zinc coatings)
Sherardizing (with zinc).

These processes are carried out in the factory although metal spraying is also possible on the building site.

Electroplating A very accurate and uniform thickness of metal can be applied without distortion or loss of temper in the metal which is plated. The latter forms the cathode in a bath and metal is deposited on it either from a reactive anode or from the electrolyte. The process is not economical for thick coatings and coatings of zinc on steel are thinner than 'hot-dip coatings', from 0·01 to 0·03 mm. They can be applied also by a continuous process, and on one side only if required. BS 1706 : 1960 describes *Electroplated coatings of cadmium and zinc on iron and steel.*

Tin, zinc, aluminium and cadmium coatings on steel have the advantage that parts can be formed after having been plated, without cracking the coating. Chromium plating is very hard. It requires a surface free from blemishes and is applied on a thin *flash* coating of copper followed by a coating of nickel.

Cladding Metals are hot-rolled on a stronger, less durable or cheaper base so that a degree of alloying takes place at the interface. Thus steel can be clad with brass, nickel and aluminium.

Spraying Zinc or aluminium in wire or powder form is heated by an electric arc or gas flame, and the atomized metal is sprayed from a gun by compressed air. Adhesion is mainly mechanical and it is desirable to first roughen the surface by shot-blasting. A skilled operator can apply an even matt finish, of a thickness suitable for painting or a greater thickness for grinding and polishing. Applications include structural steelwork such as bridges.

Hot-dipping is the most commonly used process on steel products such as cisterns, corrugated and flat sheets, light structural sections and windows.

Essentially, after pickling in acid, drying and preheating, the object is dipped in molten zinc which forms an alloy layer with it. Baths exist in lengths up to 15 m long. Products sometimes have a characteristic spelter appearance, resembling frost on windows. Slight variations in thickness occur, particularly with shaped products due to the flow as the object is removed from the bath. Distortion resulting from the hot process can usually be avoided by correct design and galvanizing techniques, and it can be corrected mechanically.

Wherever practicable thick-walled components should be galvanized 'after manufacture' to avoid unprotected cut and drilled edges.

Two relevant British Standards are:

BS 2989 : 1967 *Hot-dipped galvanized plain steel sheet and coil*
BS 3083 : 1959 *Hot-dipped galvanized corrugated steel sheets for general purposes*

This Standard specifies four weights of zinc coatings from 0·38 to 0·61 kg/m^2, including both sides.

Sherardizing Relatively small objects such as nuts, bolts and door furniture are put into a cylinder containing zinc dust which is rotated and heated. An alloy of zinc and iron forms uniformly on the surfaces to a thickness which can be very accurately controlled. Screw threads and moving parts therefore do not have to be machined again after treatment. The grey, matt surface is a very suitable base for paint. It can be buffed and polished and if desired lacquered to prevent finger marks from showing.

Non-ferrous metals

The first cost of non-ferrous metals is usually much greater than that of ordinary ferrous metals, but the difference is often offset by their superior working properties and resistance to corrosion.

Tables 68a and 68b (pages 178–180) compare some of the more important properties of ferrous and non-ferrous metals with those of some non-metals.

The more common non-ferrous metals and their alloys are shown in figure 32 page 175 and are briefly described here, ie

Copper
Nickel, tin and cadmium
Zinc
Aluminium
Lead

Surface finishes on non-ferrous metals are described on page 211.

COPPER (Cu)

The Copper Development Association, Mutton Lane, Potters Bar, Hertfordshire, provides technical advice and many excellent publications dealing with all aspects of the properties and uses of copper and its alloys.

The three grades of copper used in building are:

Deoxidized copper This is used for domestic plumbing tubes, where welding is to be carried out and for general engineering purposes.

Fire refined tough pitch copper This contains oxygen and is stronger, and has higher thermal and electrical conductivity and higher resistance to atmospheric corrosion than deoxidized copper. It is used as sheet for fully supported roof coverings.

Electrolytic tough pitch high conductivity copper This metal is similar to fire refined tough pitch copper but contains less impurities. It is largely used for electrical conductors.

Properties

The salmon-red colour of clean copper is well known. Its alloys vary from red, gold and pale yellow to soft silver in colour. In ordinary atmospheres and waters copper develops a protective skin. In certain environments a green patina slowly develops, an effect which can be obtained more rapidly by chemical methods although in the case of copper roofing success depends very much on the climatic conditions prevailing at the time of treatment. Washings from copper may stain adjacent materials and inhibit the growth of lichen and they may give rise to the corrosion of other metals. See page 183.

Copper is, in general, very resistant to corrosive agents, particularly to sea water, but it is attacked by strong mineral acids and ammonia. Water containing a high proportion of free carbon dioxide is cuprosolvent. Up to 1·5 mg/l copper can be tolerated in drinking water, but low concentrations of copper greatly accelerate pitting corrosion of galvanized steel. Pitting corrosion of copper tubes has been caused by the cathodic scale deposited by soft moorland waters containing manganese salts and by the scale of carbon produced by the lubricant used in the process of extrusion, which is however normally removed at works. Films which lead to pitting corrosion of copper hot water cylinders have occasionally been deposited by certain hard or moderately hard well waters. However, the formation of a sound protective film in copper cylinders is assured by the installation of aluminium protector rods which control the electrochemical potential of the copper.

Copper in the annealed or hot worked condition is relatively strong and it is extremely ductile. Its strength characteristics and hardness can be increased by cold working, as shown below:

Condition	Tensile strength N/mm²	Hardness -diamond pyramid test	Elongation per cent 50 mm
As cast	155–170	45–55	25–30
After cold working	310–385	80–115	5–20
Annealed after cold working	215–245	40–50	50–60

Table 73

Copper is supplied in the fully annealed *dead soft, half hard* and *full hard* conditions.

Available forms

Wire, 0·025 to 5 mm diameter and *rod* made from cast bars by hot rolling followed by cold drawing. *Tube* from about 1·5 to 610 mm diameter drawn from cylindrical billets or cold drawn from hollow extrusions. *Plate,* ie flat material larger than 305 × 10 mm up to about 3·7 m long.

Sheet from 0·18 to 10 mm thick and wider than 460 mm.

Foil and strip from 0·025 to 15 mm thick from 150 mm to 915 mm wide.

Plate, sheet, strip and foil are either hot rolled from slabs or cakes or formed by electro-deposition.

Working copper

Unalloyed copper can be hot rolled, forged and extruded. In annealed condition it is eminently suitable for site working although work hardening may necessitate further annealing by heating to a dull red heat and quenching in water.

Copper and also its alloys can be joined by welding, brazing and soldering.

Uses

Copper is used for hot and cold water distribution, hot water cylinders, roof sheeting, flashings and electrical conductors and it is the main ingredient in brasses, bronzes and gunmetals. Small proportions of copper are added to other metals for various reasons: for example to improve the resistance to corrosion of structural steel, to facilitate the manufacture of cast iron and to increase the strength of aluminium alloys.

Thin films of copper or copper alloys can be electro-deposited on other metals and on non-metallic materials such as plastics the surfaces of which may have been made electrically conductive, and fascimiles in relief (electro-types) are made in this way. Bearings and bushes are made from powdered alloys impregnated with lubricants. Copper powder is used in some paints and copper oxide provides colours in glass and ceramic glazes. Copper salts are used in timber preservatives.

Copper-based alloys

These alloys have high resistance to corrosion, and high electrical and thermal conductivities. They have good mechanical properties and can be forged, pressed and easily machined. Certain alloys are suitable for casting in sand moulds, or for continuous casting which gives greater density and strength. They can be joined by welding, brazing and soldering.

Copper alloys darken with exposure, an appearance which can be preserved by washing, and coating with wax polish.

Approximate compositions of the common alloys are shown in figure 39.

We consider them here under the broad headings; A Brasses, B Brass-based alloys, C Bronzes, D Bronze-based alloys, E Copper-nickel alloys, F Copper-silicon alloys and G Copper-aluminium alloys.

A Brasses

Brasses are classified according to their zinc content, resulting metallographic structures and mechanical properties as *alpha*, *alpha-beta* and *beta brasses*. Figure 40 summarizes the properties of brasses having varying zinc contents.

Zinc content per cent	
less than 3	*Alpha brasses* are very suitable for cold working although they then usually require to be low-temperature annealed to prevent the possibility of stress corrosion (or 'season cracking').
10 to 20	*Gilding brass* can be heavily worked, and being rich golden in colour it is particularly suitable for decorative work.
30	*Cartridge brass* is very ductile and suitable for deep pressing, spinning and for drawing.
36 to 38	*Basis brass* is used for most ordinary cold pressings.
37 to 45	*Alpha-beta brasses* are best shaped while hot, cold working being reserved for finishing to size and to effect work hardening.
40	*Muntz metal* ('yellow metal') This is an important hot working brass, used for casting, extrusion, and as a brazing alloy for steels. Unfortunately, in acidic or alkaline waters of high chloride content it is subject to *dezincification* leaving porous copper and a bulky corrosion product. To prevent this, in some areas it is necessary either to increase the temporary hardness of the water or to use copper or gunmetal instead.
45 to 50	*Beta brasses* are too brittle for general use. However in *brazing brass* the melting point is low and the high zinc content is reduced by volatilization, and by diffusion into the metal being joined.

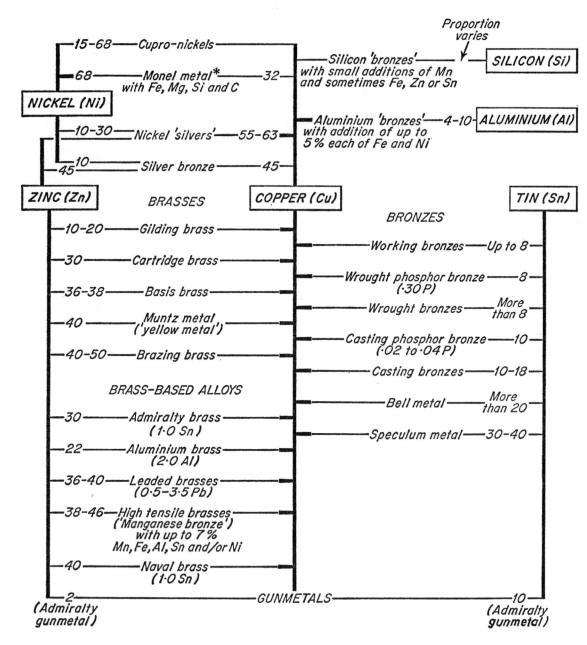

Proportion varies

15–68——Cupro-nickels

SILICON (Si)

Silicon 'bronzes' with small additions of Mn and sometimes Fe, Zn or Sn

68———Monel metal*——32—
with Fe, Mg, Si and C

NICKEL (Ni)

Aluminium 'bronzes'——4–10—ALUMINIUM (Al)
with addition of up to 5% each of Fe and Ni

10–30——Nickel 'silvers'——55–63—

45—10——Silver bronze——45—

ZINC (Zn)   BRASSES   COPPER (Cu)   TIN (Sn)

BRONZES

10–20——Gilding brass

Working bronzes——Up to 8—

30———Cartridge brass

Wrought phosphor bronze——8—
(·30 P)

36–38——Basis brass

Wrought bronzes——More than 8

40———Muntz metal ('yellow metal')

Casting phosphor bronze——10—
(·02 to ·04 P)

40–50——Brazing brass

Casting bronzes——10–18—

BRASS-BASED ALLOYS

Bell metal——More than 20

30———Admiralty brass
(1·0 Sn)

Speculum metal——30–40—

22———Aluminium brass
(2·0 Al)

36–40——Leaded brasses
(0·5–3·5 Pb)

38–46—High tensile brasses
('Manganese bronze')
with up to 7%
Mn, Fe, Al, Sn and/or Ni

40———Naval brass
(1·0 Sn)

2———————————GUNMETALS———————————10—
(Admiralty gunmetal)   (Admiralty gunmetal)

* Strictly a nickel alloy.

Note: Small amounts of lead are often added to brasses and gunmetals to improve their machinability and of nickel to improve casting and mechanical properties, resistance to wear and corrosion.

39   *Copper-based alloys – with approximate percentages of main constituents*

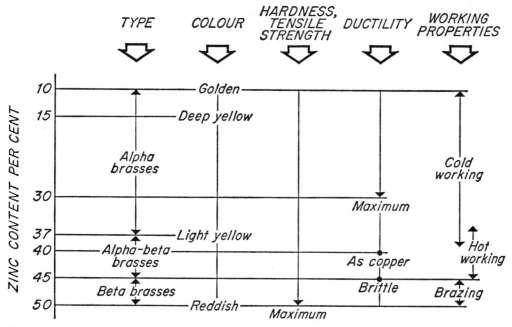

40 Brasses

B Brass-based alloys

Copper-zinc alloys with other additions include:
Admiralty brass Here the addition of tin to cartridge brass improves resistance to many forms of corrosion.

Aluminium brass This is more resistant to high velocity water than Admiralty brass.

Leaded brasses The lead addition increases ductility, but reduces strength, and provides superior machining properties and *engraving brasses*. These brasses are widely used for plumbing and electrical fittings in buildings.

High-tensile brasses, commonly called *manganese bronzes*, are based on 60 : 40 brasses with additions of Mn, Fe, Al, Sn and/or Ni up to about 7 per cent in all. Tensile strength in the chill cast or forged condition is as high as 695 N/mm². A proprietary high-tensile brass is *Delta bronze no. IV* which in the long term becomes dark bronze in colour, or can be artificially *toned*. The alloy has extremely high resistance to atmospheric corrosion, including salt and acid laden atmospheres, and does not stain adjacent materials. Although costly, Delta metal no. IV can be used as reinforcement in concrete to eliminate the risk of corrosion. However, in a moist atmosphere, galvanic corro-

sion can occur in contact with copper, phosphor bronze or aluminium bronze and its use is not recommended for load bearing fixings due to a possible risk of *stress corrosion*. The alloy is available in cast, and thick-walled tube form and as extrusions for windows, handrails and shop-fronts. It is very suitable for forgings including cramps for restraining (but not supporting) wall claddings.

Naval brass The addition of tin improves resistance to corrosion, and to some extent, strength. It is suitable for hot rolling, forging and for sand and die casting.

C True bronzes

True bronzes are alloys of copper with tin and are often called *tin bronzes*. Although costly, molten bronze is extremely fluid and ideal for large and intricate castings; the rich brown colour of which has been much favoured for sculpture. Bronze is still often employed for 'prestige' work in the form of nameplates often engraved and filled with enamel, door furniture, extrusions and sheet drawn on wood or metal cores for shop front and similar work.

Bronzes with up to 6 per cent tin content are

very similar to alpha brasses and like them they can be cold rolled or drawn, with consequent increase in the strength of the metal. *Wrought bronzes* with more than 8 per cent tin content can be cold worked after they have been annealed and have very high resistance to corrosion. *Casting bronzes* contain 10 to 18 per cent tin; ductility is reduced but in *bell metal* musical qualities result. *Speculum metal* with an even higher tin content takes a mirror polish and can be used for electroplating.

D   Bronze-based alloys

Phosphor bronze   An 8 per cent tin bronze which contains about 0·3 per cent phosphorus. Castings, usually continuously cast, are suitable for load bearing fixings. Heavy cold working makes the metal springy and suitable for purposes such as weather stripping.

Gunmetals   These tin bronze, zinc alloys, have excellent resistance to corrosion, and strength is moderately high. They are very suitable for casting, more so with the addition of lead which also improves machining and anti-friction properties.

E   Copper-nickel alloys

Tensile strength, ductility and hardness increase with nickel content.

Cupro-nickels are suitable for both hot and cold working. British 'silver' coins contain 75 per cent copper and 25 per cent nickel.

Nickel 'silvers' and *'silver bronzes'*, which are neither silvers or true bronzes, contain copper, nickel and zinc. Nickel silvers are hard and ductile but only the purer alloys can be hot worked. Silver bronzes have a rather higher zinc content and are suitable for hot working, including very complex extrusions, but not for cold working. They are very suitable for high class metalwork in buildings. Their excellent appearance can always be revived by cleaning and polishing.

F   Copper-silicon alloys

Silicon 'bronze' alloys have good corrosion resistance – particularly in sulphurous atmospheres and are used as access fittings for chimneys. Having high strength also, they are widely used as masonry fixings.

G   Copper-aluminium alloys

Aluminium 'bronzes' are bright golden-yellow in colour, very strong and resistant to corrosion. They can be annealed to make them soft and ductile.

Wrought alloys such as *Delta bronze no. VII* containing about 10 per cent aluminium, usually iron and sometimes also nickel and manganese, are available as rod and other extrusions including those suitable for load-bearing fixings for wall claddings.

Casting grades are available but the need for specialized foundry techniques restricts their use.

NICKEL (Ni)

Nickel is a white metal which is resistant to many acids, is hard and takes a high polish. It is used for electroplating food vessels, equipment for the chemical industry and on steel as a base for chromium plating.

Nickel is included in stainless steels and some copper alloys. *Monel metal* is a proprietary nickel containing 30 per cent copper and small proportions of iron, manganese and silicon. It has both high strength, about 510 N/mm², and elongation, about 45 per cent. Monel metal has extremely high resistance to corrosion and retains its properties at very high temperatures. It can be both cast and worked cold.

TIN (Sn)

Tin is a very costly, soft, weak metal with a low melting point, about 232°C. Extremely resistant to corrosion it is used as a coating on steel sheet (tinplate), and as a constituent in true bronzes and with lead in many alloys for bearings and in tinmen's and plumbers' solders.

CADMIUM (Cd)

Cadmium is malleable and ductile at room temperatures but brittle at 80°C. It is used for electroplating steel components such as screws and as an alloying element in metals for bearings.

CHROMIUM (Cr)

Chromium is well known for its high resistance to corrosion as a plating and in stainless steels and other corrosion resistant alloys. It is extremely hard and scratch resistant.

ZINC (Zn)

Information concerning the properties and uses of zinc can be obtained from the Zinc Development Association, 34 Berkeley Square, London, W1.

Metallic zinc is obtained either by electrolytic or thermal smelting of ores which contain the sulphide (zinc blende).

Properties

While the strength in tension of commercial rolled zinc (minimum 98·5 per cent zinc) is moderate, its ductility permits a moderate degree of bending and forming at ordinary temperatures but at very low temperatures the metal is brittle. Strength properties vary according to the direction of the grain.

The zinc/copper/titanium alloy although stronger is more ductile and has better creep strength than unalloyed zinc.

On exposure to ordinary atmospheres for some three to six months the initially bright surface of zinc tarnishes to a matt grey colour with the formation of an adherent protective layer consisting principally of basic zinc carbonate. The metal has good resistance to both inland and marine atmospheres, but is liable to slow and uniform attack by industrial atmospheres polluted with sulphur acids. Under average urban conditions, the maintenance-free life of zinc roofing conforming to CP 143 : Part 5 : 1964[1] is forty years for a roof laid to the minimum recommended fall of 1 in 80 approx 1° and in rural atmospheres or with steeper pitches the life will be longer. The metal is unaffected by most potable waters unless they are of an acid (eg peaty) nature or contain large amounts of carbon dioxide in solution.

Zinc is unaffected by Portland cement or lime in mortars once they have set. However, coating with a hard-drying bitumen paint is recommended where zinc is embedded in materials containing soluble salts, notably chlorides and sulphates, and

[1] For external work the thicknesses of zinc should not be less than 0·64 mm and for roofing the minimum thickness recommended is 0·78 mm (CP 143 Part 5).

gypsum plasters may attack unprotected zinc under damp conditions. Experience has shown that while contact corrosion by lead, tinman's solder, iron or aluminium is unlikely, contact with bare copper or copper rich alloys should be avoided. Thus drainage from copper should not discharge on to zinc surfaces and copper lightning conductors on zinc roofs should be suitably coated (see CP 143, Part 5).

In areas where water has a high temporary hardness, lime deposits often stifle electrochemical corrosion but copper tubes should preferably not be used in conjunction with galvanized cisterns and never with hot water cylinders.

Damp timbers may attack zinc and in particular contact with oak and Western red cedar must be avoided by interposing underlay felt. Water must not be allowed to drain from Western red cedar shingles on to zinc.

The coefficient of thermal expansion is relatively high (a 1 m length of unalloyed zinc expands nearly 26 mm with 56 deg C rise in temperature). This movement must be allowed for in roof coverings and particularly in components such as integral gutters.

Forms

Zinc is available mainly as sheet and strip but tubes, wire, rods and extrusions are also made. Traditionally, the standard sizes of zinc sheet have been 2400 × 920 mm and 2100 × 920 mm, but the material is now available as continuous strip in widths up to 1 m.

In the past the thickness of rolled zinc was specified by the English Zinc Gauge, but now all sheet metals with the exception of lead are measured in millimetres.

Uses

The main uses for zinc in building construction are: protective coatings on steel (ie galvanizing, Sherardizing, zinc spraying, see page 198); an alloying ingredient in copper/zinc alloys (see *Brass* page 201) and in the form of sheet or strip for roof coverings, wall cladding, gutters and flashings either in unalloyed metal (BS 849 : 1939), or in zinc/copper/titanium alloy which can be laid in continuous lengths up to 9 m.

Zinc alloy pressure castings to BS 1004 are used for door furniture as well as for window and bathroom fittings. They provide accurately formed components which can either be plated or stove enamelled. Die casting allows great freedom to the designer.

High purity zinc and special alloys are used for cathodic protection of steel structures and the hulls of ships in sea water.

Zinc oxide, zinc dust and lithopone are used as pigments in various types of paints (see *MBC: C and F*, chapter 17).

LEAD (Pb)

Information can be obtained from the Lead Development Association.

Lead, normally 99·9 per cent pure, is the densest, softest, weakest and one of the most durable metals commonly used in building.

Ductility is very high and lead can be cold worked into complex shapes without work hardening. Joining can be done by soldering or by *lead-burning*. See page 189. Creep of lead which is subject to continual stress within the elastic limit is not serious at normal temperatures if thicknesses of metal and the frequency of supports are adequate. BS 602 : 1971 for lead pipes stipulates minimum wall thicknesses which ensure that stresses will not exceed a safe level if horizontal pipes are supported at not more than 500 mm centres.

On the other hand the coefficient of linear thermal expansion is the highest of the common metals (see table 68, page 178) and fatigue resistance is relatively low so that if lead which is liable to thermal changes is not free to expand and contract cracking may occur.

Lead has a low melting point compared with other metals, thus:

	°C
Lead	327
Zinc	419
Aluminium	660
Copper	1083
Mild steel	1900

Lead in the form of soluble compounds is poisonous. Unless suitable precautions are taken lead paint should never be sprayed or rubbed down 'dry' and it should never be applied on objects which might be chewed by children or animals.

Resistance to corrosion

Freshly cut lead has a bright metallic lustre but when exposed to the atmosphere it forms an oxide film followed by a protective grey-blue coating of lead carbonate, which being insoluble does not stain other materials. Lead is not normally attacked electrolytically by other metals and it resists inorganic acids in varying degrees according to their concentration and the temperature. However, it can be attacked severely by certain organic acids, eg acetic acid and acids produced by timbers such as oak and Western red cedar and by lichens. Some waters which contain organic acids or free carbon dioxide are plumbosolvent. More than 0·1 mg/l of lead in drinking water is a danger to health but in this country the use of lead is not permitted where such concentrations occur.

Lead is not attacked by most soils but it is liable to corrosion by organic acids in wet peat soils and by incompletely burnt ashes in man-made ground. It is not appreciably affected by lime mortar but attack by Portland cement mortar or concrete can be serious if they remain wet.

Where necessary lead should be isolated from other materials by felt or building paper or by painting with bitumen; which should be on a hessian wrapping where pipes are below ground.

Uses

Lead is usually manufactured as pig lead, milled sheet, extruded tubes or as *lead wool*. Lead compounds are also used in paints and alloys.
Sheet
BS 1178 : 1969 *Milled lead sheet and strip for building purposes* includes requirements for quality.

Thicknesses are now measured in millimetres and designated by numbers which approximate to the old 'weight in pounds per square foot' descriptions. See table 67 page 176. Sheet is used for:

Weatherings and flashings Lead is suitable particularly for complex shapes, eg for flashings dressed over pantiles.

Roof coverings and wall cladding, see *MBC: C and F*, chapter 18. The cost of lead roof coverings has discouraged its use for that purpose on new buildings although there have been some interesting examples of lead wall cladding in recent years.

Damp-proof courses Lead becomes economical in lead-cored bituminous felt damp-proof courses (lead not less than 1·22 kg/m² to BS 743).

Pipes Lead pipes are extruded.
Most water undertakings in this country employ lead service pipes between their mains and premises and most connections to gas meters are carried out in lead because of its flexibility. However, being more costly than copper, stainless steel and plastics, lead is now little used for internal water services and wastes and very rarely for soil pipes.

Other uses of lead

In suitable thicknesses, lead, being dense and limp, is effective for sound insulation and for the absorption of vibration, eg beneath machines. An important use is for radiation shielding from X-rays, reactors and radioactive appliances; lead is included in X-ray protective glass.

Lead is occasionally cast, usually for sculpture on a bronze armature, and for ornamental rainwater pipes and heads.

Lead is still the most effective material for sealing joints in iron gas and water mains and around iron railing standards. The metal can either be 'run' in the molten condition or *lead wool* or *yarn* can be caulked.

Lead compounds are important pigments for paints, more particularly for external use.

Lead alloys

Solders are lead-tin alloys, sometimes with a proportion of antimony to BS 219 : 1959. *Soft solders.* Two copper bearing leads, BS 334 : 1934 *Chemical lead, type A silver-copper lead* and *type B tellurium lead* which are used in the chemical industry, have superior strength properties. In the form of *regulus metal* antimonial lead is used for cast fittings in laboratories and chemical plants. In engineering, lead alloy bearing metals permit deformation and require less lubrication.

ALUMINIUM (Al)

Information concerning aluminium can be obtained from the Aluminium Federation, 60 Calthorpe Road, Five Ways, Birmingham 15.

When the statue of Eros, Piccadilly Circus, London, was cast and erected in 1893 aluminium was a precious metal.

Aluminium is obtained from bauxite clay by electrolysis, approximately 17 000 kilowatt hours of electricity being required to produce 1 tonne of metal.

Aluminiums are either *pure*, ie containing 99 per cent or more aluminium, or they are *alloys*. Properties which are common to both types are discussed here.

Density is low, 2700 kg/m³, about the same as granite and about one third that of steel, 7850 kg/m³. Aluminium is second only to copper in thermal conductivity. Electrical conductivity is about sixty per cent that of copper. Aluminium has long been used for electrical conductors on the grid system and its use for building installations is being developed.

The coefficient of linear thermal expansion is 24×10^{-6}/deg. C at 20–100°C, about twice that for steel.

In ordinary atmospheres a thin, but dense, whitish film of oxide forms almost instantaneously and under damp conditions of external exposure roughening of the surface may follow if it is not kept clean. The products of corrosion do not stain adjacent materials and are not toxic to animals or plants. Aluminium may suffer electrolytic corrosion in damp or wet conditions and contact must be avoided with copper, copper alloys such as brass and to a less extent with bare mild steel. Contact with zinc is safe and under non-marine conditions, with lead and stainless steel.

Metallic salts such as those originating from water which has passed through copper pipes or over copper roof coverings must not be allowed to come into contact with aluminium.

Acids, such as those which may be used to clean building materials or which arise from decaying vegetable growths on tiled roofs, attack aluminium.

Free alkalis such as those in wet Portland cement also attack aluminium, and anodized aluminium surfaces must be protected from mortar splashes but attack ceases once a protective oxide layer has formed.

Aluminium is being considered for circulating water in certain closed circuits but it is not recommended for pipes conveying drinking water. Similarly it is not suitable for waste pipes and traps which would be attacked by bleach, strong detergents or soda.

British Standards have adopted the following symbols:

(a) *Form of material*

S   Plate, sheet and strip (BS 1470 : 1969)
C   Clad plate, sheet and strip (BS 1470 : 1969)
T   Drawn tube (BS 1471 : 1969)
F   Forging stock and forgings (BS 1472 : 1969)
R   Rivet stock (BS 1473 : 1969)
B   Bolt and screw stock (BS 1473 : 1969)
LM Castings (BS 1490 : 1970)
G   Wire (BS 1475 : 1969
E   Bar, extruded round tube and sections (BS 1474 : 1969)

(b) *Heat treatment*

Prefixes are:

H   Strain hardened (wrought material) designated *H1* to *H8* in ascending order tensile strength. Material subjected to cold work after annealing, to hot forming or to a combination of cold work and partial annealing/stabilizing
    Heat-treatable alloys, ie those which are strengthened by heat treatment.
N   Non-heat-treatable alloys
TB, TB7, TD, TE, alloys which have been
TF, TF7, TH, TS   subjected to various heat treatment processes

(c) *Condition* Suffix letters indicate the *temper* or condition of heat treatment:

M   As manufactured. Material which has been subjected to shaping processes in which there is no special control over thermal treatment or amount of strain hardening.
O   Annealed. (Wrought material). Material which is fully annealed.

'Pure' aluminium

In the annealed condition pure aluminium is weak, but work such as cold rolling or hammering increases its strength with some loss of ductility. It cannot be hardened by heat-treatment.

In normal atmospheres pure aluminiums have very good resistance to corrosion and are more resistant than the alloys. There are four grades:

		per cent	suitable uses
S 1	super-purity (softest grade)	99·99	roofing, flashing, ¼ H condition
S 1A	high-purity	99·80	
S 1B	medium-purity	99·50	
S 1C	commercial purity	99	most aluminium foils

Pure aluminiums are rarely suitable for casting. Owing to their high ductility they are particularly suitable in sheet form for weatherings and flashings which may require to be hand formed on site, and for fully supported roofing. Pure aluminium extrusions are suitable for non-load-bearing components such as edge trims, joint covers and mouldings.

Foil, defined as being less than 0·15 mm thick, can be used as thermal insulation (it has high reflectivity and low emissivity), eg adhered to *insulating plasterboards*. It is also an effective vapour barrier.

Aluminium alloys

For building purposes, the alloys most commonly used may contain magnesium, manganese, and silicon, together with a number of minor additions which increase the strength of pure aluminium. Strength is further improved by cold working or by heat treatments which are described later. Thus, aluminium alloys are used for corrugated and troughed roof sheeting, window sections, Venetian blind slats and for structural members.

Alloying reduces thermal and electrical conductivities but they remain high.

Some alloys, particularly those containing copper, are less resistant to corrosion than pure aluminium, but in 'breathable air' corrosion is unlikely to affect strength. Sheet and strip are sometimes clad with pure aluminium to improve their corrosion resistance.

Wrought alloys

These alloys which are suitable for rolling, pressing and extrusion are of two kinds:

(a) heat-treatable and (b) non-heat-treatable.

(a) *Heat-treatable alloys (prefix H)*

The tensile strength of these alloys is increased by heat treatment.

The heat-treatable alloys used in building include *H9* which contains magnesium and silicon which is largely used for extrusions for window frames, and the principal structural alloy *H30* which contains magnesium, silicon and manganese, but no copper.

There are three processes of heat treatment:

1 *Solution treatment (TB)* consists of heating in the range 500 to 530°C (the exact temperature will depend on the alloy) followed by rapid cooling and *natural ageing* which is accompanied by an increase in strength.

2 *Precipitation treatment (TE)* (or *artificial ageing*) consists of heating in the range 100 to 200°C for a suitable period according to the composition of the alloy.

3 *Full heat-treatment (TF)* combines solution and precipitation treatments. For example solution heat-treatment raises the tensile strength of the H30 structural alloy to a minimum of 190 N/mm², and full heat-treatment raises it to 310 N/mm² minimum with some loss of ductility.

(b) *Non-heat-treatable alloys* (prefix *N*)

Like pure aluminium these alloys gain strength by cold working, but not by heat treatment.

Examples of common alloys in the *H4* condition are:

Alloy	Alloying addition per cent	Tensile strength (guaranteed minimum) N/mm²	Properties and uses
N3	1·25 manganese	140	The simplest alloy. Corrugated and trough sheeting
N4	2·0 magnesium	225	
N5	3·5 magnesium	275	
N8	4·5 magnesium 0·75 manganese	345	High resistance to corrosion. Marine work.

All of the alloys listed can be welded with little loss of strength.

Casting alloys (*Suffix LM*)

These are used in building mainly for door and window furniture, rainwater goods, and statuary. The choice of alloy depends on whether the metal will be sand cast, gravity or pressure die cast, on the finish required and the strength that is necessary, some alloys being heat-treatable.

Structural alloys

Modulus of elasticity, coefficient of expansion, density and melting point are, for all practical purposes, the same for all alloys but tensile strength, ductility and durability vary with composition.

Alloys are available having a tensile strength equal to that of mild steel, but the modulus of elasticity of aluminium (68 900 N/mm²) is only about a third. Thus for the same sectional dimensions, spans and loadings, aluminium sections deflect nearly three times as much as steel sections. Where this is not acceptable an aluminium section of greater effective depth or second moment of inertia is required. Nevertheless in order to support the same load with the same deflection, an aluminium structure will rarely be more than half the weight of its steel equivalent.

Special consideration must be given to the resistance to torsional buckling, and local buckling of aluminium struts with thin-walls. These factors are discussed in CP 118 *Structural use of aluminium*.

Table 74 compares the mechanical properties of a typical aluminium structural alloy with those of structural mild steel.

Aluminium increases in strength at low temperatures, by as much as $33\frac{1}{3}$ per cent at −196°C, hence its use for the storage of liquid methane. However it loses strength at high temperatures more rapidly than steel. The *HE30-TF* alloy behaves as follows:

°C	Tensile strength N/mm²
0	367
20	352
100	301
150	261
200	212
250	113
400	30·9

Properties	Structural aluminium HE 30-TF	Mild steel BS 4390 grade 43
Density kg/m³	2700	7850
Ultimate tensile stress N/mm²	280–310	430–510
Modulus of elasticity (E) N/mm²	69 950	207 000
Elongation (min.) per cent	8 (on 50 mm)	22 (on 50 mm)
0·20 per cent proof stress (min.) N/mm²	239–270 N/mm²	—
Permissible bending stress (max.) N/mm²	162	162
Permissible stress/weight ratio (approx)	6	2

Table 74   Properties of aluminium structural alloy and mild steel

Jointing

Aluminium members can be joined with bolts or rivets, by soldering, welding or by adhesives.

Bolting and riveting

Bolting and cold riveting have the advantage of not requiring heat which in some circumstances upsets the properties of alloys, and the corners of window frames are often jointed in this way.

Soldering

Soldering is performed either with a flux (which may be corrosive and must be removed) or with a friction solder without flux. Care must be taken in the choice of materials and in design to avoid bi-metallic corrosion between the solder and aluminium. Generally, where moist conditions are expected joints should be wrapped or painted.

Solder joints are sometimes brittle and advice should always be obtained from the manufacturers.

Welding

Most aluminium alloys can be welded. Heat-treatable materials lose strength in the heat affected zone but non-heat treatable alloys give welds of up to 90 per cent efficiency. Difficulties arise in welding on the building site.

For example, the older oxy-acetylene process requires the use of an active flux which is corrosive and it is rarely possible to completely remove it on building sites.

Reliable welds can be produced without flux by the inert gas process using an electric arc with a protective envelope of argon gas. However, the equipment is heavy, the gas shield is disturbed by draughts and like oxy-acetylene welding its use is nearly always confined to the factory.

Adhesive bonding

Adhesive bonds, which are becoming increasingly reliable, are used, for example, for the corner joints of some windows.

Finishes to aluminium

Anodizing is an electro-chemical process which applies only to aluminium, forms a coating which is integral with, but harder than the parent metal. Anodizing enhances the appearance of aluminium, finger marks do not show, and so long as surfaces are kept clean it improves resistance to corrosion. Especially in damp conditions contaminants must not be allowed to build up on surfaces.

In anodizing, the natural oxide film is thickened by making the aluminium the anode in an electrical cell in which the electrolyte is usually sulphuric acid. Before being sealed the surface is porous and can be dyed. Some colours are very intense. Few colours are fade-resistant for use externally, gold, black, brown, dark blue and green are most suitable. Alloys with inherent colour, which do not require dyeing after anodizing, have been developed.

The appearance of anodized products is determined by the texture of the base, which may be chemically etched, mechanically polished or mirror-like. Although a few anodizing baths are up to $2.4 \times 1.2 \times 12.2$ m components are better anodized before assembly, because welds especially of heat-treatable alloys can cause local darkening, and process liquors trapped in mechanical joints may leak out later and cause stains.

Recommended minimum thicknesses are:

Externally	*mm*	
General architectural applications	0.025	(BS 3987 : 1966)
Where frequent cleaning is to be carried out, eg shop fronts	0.015	
Internally		
The thicker coatings are appropriate for the more arduous conditions	0.015 0.010 0.005	(BS 1615 : 1961)

Aluminium, either *mill finished* or *anodized*, is very liable to disfigurement by scratching or staining, eg by cement and lime which cohere very strongly, and leave marks when they are removed. Where appearance is important, components should be protected by removable wrappings. They must be carefully handled, and fixed only after all wet finishings are completed.

In industrial areas a monthly wash with water containing detergent, which may be done when the windows are cleaned may be required, but in rural areas an annual wash is usually sufficient.

Costs

Owing to the wide distribution throughout the world of the clays from which aluminium is made, its price is very stable.

The cost of *commercial purity* aluminium is about that of the simplest alloy and cost increases with greater purity and with greater complexity of alloys.

For economical utilization, advantage must be taken of its ease of forming, high strength/weight ratio and good resistance to corrosion, the cost of painting and re-painting can usually be saved. The suitability of certain grades of aluminium for extrusion leads to profiles in which material can be disposed so they fulfil several functions. Thus, glazing bars which support glass over a long span, keep out the weather and provide a channel on the inside for the collection of condensate are cheaper in aluminium than in other materials.

FINISHES ON NON-FERROUS METALS

Non-ferrous metals are often chosen because they do not require protection from destructive corrosion and because their appearance is often agreeable without special treatments. Surface finishes which preserve or enhance the natural appearance of non-ferrous metals are described below.

Mechanical treatments

Rough castings, forgings and welds may need *grinding*, or sometimes *hand filing*.

Shot blasting produces a rough texture.

Sand blasting gives a matt finish, the nature of which can be varied according to the sand, the air pressure used and the distance of the nozzle from the work.

Scratch brush working is usually done with rotating stainless steel brushes, the coarseness, size and speed of which determine the result. A 'satin' texture is very sensitive to finger marks and a lacquer should be applied (or in the case of aluminium the metal can be *anodized*).

Polishing, as an integral finish or as a base for applied finishes, is done with progressively softer mops and finer abrasives.

Electroplating

This process has received attention under *Ferrous metals*, page 199. A wide variety of metals can be used including gold, silver, tin and copper. Nickel-chromium plating, which gives a very hard finish, is commonly used on steel and on brass and zinc alloys. *Speculum metal*, a silver-like copper-tin alloy (see pages 202 and 204), has good resistance to corrosion and wear

Anodizing

This electro-chemical surface treatment for aluminium is described on page 210.

Applied finishes

With suitable preparation non-ferrous metals can be painted or lacquered for protection, or for decoration. See *MBC: C and F*, chapter 17.

Vitreous enamel, essentially glass, can be applied on copper and aluminium. See *MBC: C and F*, chapter 17.

Maintenance of finishes

Frequent cleaning may be needed to preserve a bright appearance. Finishes such as lacquers and anodizing should be kept clean with soapy water. When dry they can be polished with a light application of furniture cream. Metal polish and more drastic abrasives prevent the formation of a natural patina on metals and they should never be used on applied finishes.

10 Asbestos products

Asbestos, a silicate of magnesium, occurs as a dark green glassy rock which can be split into dull white extremely thin fibres from 2 to 900 mm long. These have good resistance to alkalis, neutral salts and organic solvents and the varieties used for building products have good resistance to acids. Asbestos is non-combustible and able to withstand high temperatures without change. Being strong in tension the fibres are used as reinforcement with Portland cement, lime, plastics and bitumen binders, eg in asbestos-cement and asbestos-silica-lime products, in vinyl floor tiles and in bitumen felts. Other uses are asbestos spray, fabrics and ropes.

The following products are dealt with here:

1 Asbestos-cement, asbestos-silica-cement and asbestos-silica-lime products
2 Resin-bonded asbestos sheets
3 Sprayed asbestos

1 ASBESTOS-CEMENT, ASBESTOS-SILICA CEMENT AND ASBESTOS-SILICA-LIME PRODUCTS

The materials used in these mixtures are usually asbestos fibres, Portland cement, fine silica and hydrated high calcium lime. Pigments are sometimes included.

Products are formed in open moulds by hand, more usually by the *Hatschek* process, and in some cases by extrusion. In the Hatschek process the slurry mixture is picked up by wire-mesh covered cylinders, transferred to a felt and then wound round a roller until the required thickness is obtained. The length of this *wet flat* corresponds to the circumference of the roller. Both moulded and cylinder-formed products are pressed to provide the required density and final shape, ie profiled sheeting, pipes, etc.

Asbestos-cement products are air cured for approximately four weeks. Asbestos-silica-lime and asbestos-silica-cement products are subjected to steam under pressure in an autoclave. Steam curing induces thorough hydration, reduces efflorescence and in asbestos-silica-lime products is essential to promote chemical bond between lime and silica. 2 to 2·5 per cent of Portland cement may be used in the latter case as a catalyst.

Products are unaffected by alkalis but the cement binder may be attacked by acids, depending upon their concentration and the density of the product. Products can be painted with alkali-resistant paint (see *MBC: C and F*). Some products are available with factory applied finishes and some with extremely durable PVF film surfaces in a range of fade-resistant colours.

While there is no evidence of the incorporation of asbestos in building materials having impaired the health of occupants, inhalation of substantial concentrations of dust over long periods of time causes asbestosis (a disease of the lungs). Asbestos Industry Regulations protect the health of factory workers. Cutting, grinding and similar operations are best avoided on the building site, but where they occur suitable respirators for operatives or dust extractors should be provided. Alternatively air-borne dust can be avoided by damping materials while they are being worked. Floors should be vacuum cleaned or sprinkled with damp sawdust before being swept.

Products are considered here in order of decreasing density as listed in Table 75 which shows that strength and thermal conductivity increase with density. The converse is true in respect of fire resistance.

a Fully compressed asbestos-cement products

BS 4036 : 1966 *Asbestos-cement fully compressed flat sheets* includes requirements for bending strength, appearance and finish together with tests for water absorption, frost cracking and density. The BS specifies sizes of 1·82, 2·44 and 3·04 × 1·21 m in thicknesses from 3·2 to 25·4 mm. The 3·2 mm sheet can be bent to form elliptical curves. *Glasal* (Cape Universal Building Products Limited), a

British Standard	Class	Dry density kg/m³	Thermal conductivity (k) W/m deg C	Bending strength (min) N/mm²
4036 : 1966	Fully-compressed asbestos-cement	1698 (min)	0·65[1] (approx)	22·06
—	Extruded asbestos-silica-cement	1602–1762 (average range)	0·58	18·75
690 : 1963	Semi-compressed asbestos-cement	1520[1] (approx)	0·43[1] (approx)	given as loads for thicknesses
3536 : 1962	Asbestos wallboards	881–1442	0·36 (max)	14·82 (1154–1442 kg/m³) 9·83 (881–1153 kg/m³)
	Asbestos insulating boards	881 (max)	0·144 (max) 0·115[1] (typical)	7·93 (722–881 kg/m³) 5·00 (513–721 kg/m³)

[1] Not BS requirements.

Table 75   Asbestos-cement and asbestos-silica-lime sheets

steam cured sheet with white and coloured mineral enamel semi-matt surface finishes is available approximately 3 and 6 mm thick. Typical applications for thicker sheets and boards of this density are wall cladding, pig pens, fascias and shelves. Turners Asbestos Cement Co, Limited make standard sills and window boards in natural grey and blue, with matt or polished surfaces.

Boards with an epoxide resin finish have good resistance to acids and alkalis and to temperatures up to 130°C and are suitable for laboratory bench tops and fume cupboards. Lengths are up to 2·4 m, widths up to 610 mm and thicknesses from 9·5 to 25·4 mm.

Other fully compressed asbestos-cement products include:

BS 3497 : 1967 Unimpregnated asbestos-cement boards (incombustible) for electrical purposes 3·2 to 38 mm thick.
BS 3503 : 1967 Bitumen impregnated asbestos-cement boards (self-extinguishing) for electrical purposes. Boards with matt and high gloss enamel finishes are suitable for electrical switchboards.
BS 486 : 1966 Asbestos-cement pressure pipes. These are used for water and sewage pumping mains and similar applications. Diameters are from 51 to 914 mm in lengths up to 5 m. Pipes are supplied with or without protective coatings.

b   Extruded asbestos-silica-cement products

Cape Universal Building Products Limited are developing standard extruded and autoclaved (Ace) products including a walling system, wall panels for agricultural use, claddings, sills and copings.

Extrusion avoids the stratification which can result from ordinary moulding techniques and gives high density and strength, and very smooth surfaces. As with metals and plastics extrusion lends itself to forming cellular and complex sections such as those incorporating fixing slots, and intricate joint profiles, which would otherwise require a considerable amount of fabrication. Purpose-made sections become economical in minimum quantities of about 100 tonnes (steel dies cost from £1000 to £2000). Profiles should be as nearly symmetrical as possible and have one essentially flat surface. The maximum width is 1·2 m, maximum height 190 mm and maximum cross sectional area 38 710 mm². Sections smaller than 19 355 mm² are produced by using a multiple die. The maximum cavity: solid ratio is 2:1. Cavities should not be smaller than 161 mm².

Recommended paint treatments are chlorinated rubber-based paint or two coats of acrylic/silicone emulsion paint.

c Semi-compressed asbestos-cement products

These products contain about 70 to 80 per cent Portland cement by weight, with a density of about 1520 kg/m³. They are moderately strong and resistance to continuously applied loads increases with age. Resistance to impact, however, decreases in a short period of years, and in roofing adequately supported corrugated, trough and other inherently strong profiles should be employed, and cat walks must be provided for maintenance personnel.

The slightly rough and open texture of some products increases with weathering and the sheets tend to darken with age. Products can be cut with a hand saw or more readily with a high speed carborundum disc, and they can be shaped with a coarse file.

Although *non-combustible* and classified 'Ext S.AA' (BS 476 : Part 3 : 1958), if restrained the material often cracks in building fires, and does not merit any fire resistance grading when tested in accordance with BS 476 : Part 1 : 1953.

In industrial atmospheres the expected life of forty years can be extended by protective finishes.

Products are described by the following British Standards:

BS 690 : 1963 *Asbestos-cement slates, corrugated sheets and semi-compressed flat sheets* includes tests for resistance to acidified water, breaking loads and water absorption.

Slates which are used for roofing and wall cladding are discussed in *MBC: C and F*, chapter 18.

Corrugated sheets are specified in fourteen profiles 25 to 178 mm deep in lengths of 1·219 to 3·048 m in 152 mm increments. Widths vary from 0·762 to 1·283 m and thicknesses from 5·6 to 9·5 mm.

Most profiles can be obtained curved to a minimum radius of 1·372 m. A range of fittings is available including those such as roof ventilators with soaker flanges which when used in conjunction with asbestos-cement roofing dispense with the need for separate flashings.

Flat sheets are used as wall claddings, eaves soffits, bath panels and for similar purposes. Surfaces are available with a natural finish or works applied paint.

BS dimensions are:

$$0{\cdot}914 \times \quad 1{\cdot}829 \qquad \times \quad 4{\cdot}8 \text{ and } 6{\cdot}4 \text{ mm}$$
$$1{\cdot}219 \times \begin{cases} 1{\cdot}829 \text{ and} \\ 2{\cdot}439 \end{cases} \times \begin{cases} 4{\cdot}8, 6{\cdot}4, \\ 9{\cdot}5 \text{ and } 12{\cdot}7 \text{ mm} \end{cases}$$

Other products in this density include:

BS 567: 1968 *Asbestos-cement flue pipes and fittings* (*light quality*). These are intended primarily for gas appliances.

BS 569 : 1967 *Asbestos-cement rainwater goods*

BS 582 : 1965 *Asbestos-cement soil, waste and ventilating-pipes and fittings.*

BS 835 : 1967 *Asbestos-cement flue pipes and fittings, heavy quality.* These have thicker walls than the BS 567 pipes.

BS 2777 : 1963 *Asbestos-cement cisterns* are described in sizes from 17·27 to 700·07 litres with close fitting lids. The material is 1522 kg/m³ and walls and bottoms are generally 12·7 mm thick so the 381 litre cistern weighs about 65 kg. A life well in excess of forty years can be expected.

BS 3656 : 1963 *Asbestos-cement pipes and fittings for sewerage and drainage.* These are manufactured in three classes with differing crushing loads in diameters from 102 to 914 mm in lengths up to 5 m. The pipes are suitable for gravity flow at atmospheric pressure.

BS 3717 : 1964 *Asbestos-cement decking* for roofs

BS 3954 : 1965 *Asbestos-cement ducting* for flues and ventilation

BS 3973 : 1966 *Asbestos-cement cable conduits and troughs*

Other semi-compressed asbestos-cement standard products include tiles for covering mastic asphalt and built-up felt roofings, and weatherboarding. Specially moulded products have included large window louvres, fish breeding tanks and corrugated profiles to support and protect river banks, such as Cape Universal's *Unibank* sheet.

d Wallboards and insulating boards

BS 3536: 1962 *Asbestos insulating boards and asbestos wallboards* states that the boards have a 'substantially greater proportion of asbestos fibres than is used in asbestos-cement sheets to BS 690 and should not be confused with them as they are intended for quite different uses'.

Reduced density and strength are accompanied by increased thermal insulation and fire resistance and these boards are particularly suitable for wall, ceiling and roof linings.

1 Asbestos wallboards

These are intermediate in density between semi-compressed asbestos-cement and insulating boards. Such a product is *Asbestos wood* (Turners Asbestos Cement Company Limited) which contains almost equal proportions of asbestos and cement (but no wood, although its working properties bear some resemblance to that material). Sizes are 3·048 and 2·438 × 1·219 m × 3·2, 4·8, 6·3, 9·5 and 12·7 mm. The 4·8 mm sheet can be bent to a radius of 2·440 m.

2 Asbestos insulating boards

These, the least dense asbestos boards, are suitable for use where thermal insulation and fire resistance are the main requirements. Moisture absorption is high, they absorb temporary condensation with some loss of thermal insulation, but water causes no deterioration, and the boards regain their original properties on drying out. They are stable in extreme conditions of temperature and moisture.

Boards can be nailed without pre-boring, sawn, *Surform* planed or sanded. The 9·5 mm board can be bent to a radius of 2·150 m. Tolerances on sizes, but not sizes themselves are given in BS 3536.

Asbestos insulating boards take two forms:

(a) *Asbestos-cement insulating boards* An example is the *Turnabestos* board by Turners Asbestos Cement Company Limited. Sheet sizes are 1·219 to 3·048 m in 305 mm increments × 0·610 and 1·219 m × 6·4, 9·5 and 12·7 mm 2·438, 2·743 and 3·048 m lengths are available in 19 and 25·4 mm thicknesses. Ceiling panels with bevelled edges, including perforated panels intended primarily for use in suspended ceilings with sound absorbent material above them, are made in sizes up to 1·219 m square, in thicknesses of 9·5 and 12·7 mm.

(b) *Asbestos-silica-lime insulating boards* are made from asbestos fibres, silica, and hydrated lime which are pressed and autoclaved. *Asbestolux* products made by Cape Universal Building Products Limited have either natural or sanded surfaces. Alkalinity being low they can be painted with oil paint without pretreatment. Moisture movement of normal boards is 0·17 mm per 1000 mm from normal moisture content to saturation, and 0·2 mm per 1000 mm for the *Special purpose board*.
Sizes are:

Normal boards (density 721 kg/m^3) 1·220, 1·830, 2·440, 2·740 and 3·050 m × 0·610 and 1·220 m × 6·4, 9·5 and 12·7 mm
Door facings (sanded) 2·134 × 0·914 m × 6·4 mm
Special purpose boards (density 577 kg/m^3) (sanded both sides, primarily for factory applied veneers) 2·445 and 3·054 × 1·222 m × 9·5, 12·7, 19·0 and 25·4 mm
Ceiling panels with square or bevelled edges, including various perforated or linear patterns, are available with natural, and two factory applied paint finishes. They are made in various sizes in thicknesses of 6·4, 9·5 and 12·7 mm.

Turners Asbestos Cement Co Ltd manufacture *LDR panels*, also 577 kg/m^3, in sizes:

2·438, 2·743 and 3·048 m × 0·610 and 1·219 m in a range of thicknesses from 9·5 to 30·2 mm. Uses include ventilation ducting, flues for gas appliances and insulation of industrial ovens. Panels veneered with plastics, aluminium and stainless steel sheets can be used for wc cubicles, partitioning and infill panels in curtain walling.

2 RESIN BONDED ASBESTOS SHEETS

These consist of synthetic resin impregnated asbestos paper, fabric or felt, bonded under heat and pressure. Dependent upon the resin employed laminates resist temperatures up to 220°C and absorb 0·2 to 1·0 per cent water after twenty four hours immersion.

The laminates can be machined by normal engineering methods. Sizes are up to:

2·438 × 1·219 m in thicknesses of 2·0, 3·2, 4·8 and 6·4 mm.

3 SPRAYED ASBESTOS

Asbestos fibres with Portland cement sprayed onto surfaces and pressed to the thickness required is left with a rough texture or floated with a fine slurry. Adhesion is good on brickwork, concrete and steel.

BS 3590:1970 *Sprayed asbestos insulation* states that the dry coating must contain at least 55 per cent asbestos fibres and the results of specified tests must be:

Bulk Density kg/m^3	Maximum thermal conductivity (k) W/m deg C
80	0·04
over 80–160	0·05
over 160–240	0·06

Minimum sound absorption of 25·4 mm thickness:

Frequency Hz	125	250	500	1000	2000	4000
Coefficient of sound absorption	0·20	0·30	0·55	0·75	0·70	0·70

The *Building Regulations 1972* Schedule 8, gives fire resistance periods for densities of 140 to 240 kg/m^3 applied on structural steel stanchions weighing not less than 45 kg/m and on beams weighing not less than 30 kg/m as follows:

Thickness mm	Time hours
10	1
15	$1\frac{1}{2}$
19	2
44	4

11 Bituminous products

The bituminous products comprise; bitumen, natural or derivative, coal tar and pitch. Their general properties are discussed first followed by descriptions of each material.

Properties

(a) Bituminous products are usually dark brown or black and composite products rely for any colour upon aggregate or pigments.
By the addition of pigments to 'albino' bitumens, which are light grey, colours, usually confined to reds and brown, are possible.

(b) They resist the passage of water and water vapour. Materials applied hot or constituted with a solvent are more likely to be impervious than bituminous emulsions. Bituminous material must be supported by structural walls or floors in positions such as basements where water is under pressure.

(c) Although bituminous materials are combustible composite products such as mastic asphalt and pitch mastic are not readily ignited and do not support combustion.

(d) In general, bituminous products are durable materials resistant to acids, alkalis, sugar, milk and brewing liquids and natural bitumens are more durable than derivative ones. Although pitch is more resistant than bitumen to fats and oils contact with these should be avoided. Oil in floor polishes can be damaging and oil in ordinary paints causes crazing. Conversely, bituminous paints 'bleed through' ordinary paints.

(e) Bituminous products are softened by heat and by sunlight. Over long periods these effects are particularly damaging to pitch. Thermal insulation below roof coverings prevents heat being absorbed by the structure and the covering becomes hotter and is liable to deteriorate in consequence. To reduce this risk, exposed surfaces should be finished with a light-reflecting material such as lime wash and tallow, mineral particles or stone chippings.

(f) Bituminous products flow under mechanical stress, particularly at high temperatures. The appropriate grade must be used for industrial floors, damp-proof courses and wherever resistance to flow, spreading and indentation is required.

(g) Bituminous products are damaged by overheating before use but to avoid premature cooling they should be heated as near the work as possible.

(h) Natural bitumen and coal tar products may be poisonous and only specialized products are suitable for contact with drinking water. Coal tar contains phenol which is toxic to plants and moulds. This is of value in coal tar creosote (BS 144 : 1954) see page 86, and some phenol is replaced in pitches which are required to inhibit plant growth.

(i) Pitch mastic evolves fumes when it is hot and in confined spaces care must be taken to avoid inhaling them.

(j) Although the bituminous materials are a 'family' it is important that they should not be intermixed or applied over one another.

Bituminous products comprise:

BITUMEN

Bitumen is a non-crystalline solid or viscous material comprising complex hydrocarbons which is soluble in carbon disulphide, softens when it is heated, is waterproof and has good powers of adhesion. It was used in building work in 3000 BC. Bitumen lacks 'body' and stability and is rarely used by itself but as an ingredient in mastic asphalt, adhesives and paints and as a saturant. *Bitumastic* is a registered trade name and should be used only for the proprietary product to which it refers. Confusingly, in the USA bitumen is called asphalt and because the cheapest thermoplastic tile contains bitumen, it is known as an *asphalt tile*, whereas in this country an asphalt tile is a compressed mastic asphalt product containing aggregate.

Natural bitumen occurs in Lake Trinidad, West Indies, where it is associated with finely divided mineral matter as *Lake asphalt* and from which it can be extracted and refined. It also occurs in limestones known as rock asphalts in France, Sicily, Switzerland and Germany.

Derivative bitumens are distilled from mineral oils.

Uses of bitumen

Mastic asphalt

The ingredients in mastic asphalts are:

Suitably graded aggregate:

Crushed limestone (or silica rock for acid resistance) and/or
Natural asphaltic rock, a limestone which contains bitumen
Asphaltic cement, natural or derivative bitumen
Fillers, to reduce temperature movement
Fluxing oils are sometimes added to adjust hardness.

Natural rock mastic asphalt as it is called, carries more bitumen without loss of stability and is more durable than a mastic based on ordinary limestone and it is also more costly.

Mastic asphalts are used for:

d.p.c.s., see *MBC: S and F*, Part 2
tanking of basements, see *MBC: S and F*, Part 2
floorings, see *MBC: C and F*, chapter 12
roof coverings, see *MBC: C and F*, chapter 18

Other uses of bitumen

1 'rolled asphalts' for roads (known in many parts of the USA as bituminous concrete)
2 macadam, for external paving
   BS 1621 : 1961 describes *Bitumen macadam with crushed rock or slag aggregate*
3 paints, see *MBC: C and F*, chapter 17
4 damp-proof membranes
5 adhesives for wood-block flooring, cork slabs, insulating linings and felts
6 a saturant for roofing, damp-proof course sheathing and sarking felts
7 waterproof building papers (BS 1521 : 1965)
8 bonded glass-fibre products, see page 237
9 impregnated foamed polyurethane joint fillers
10 impregnated cork joint fillers, see page 269.

COAL TAR

Coal tar runs at a lower temperature than bitumen and oxidizes much more easily. Ordinary coal tar is suitable for many of the applications of bitumen other than the very heavy duties.

Tar-latex compositions, eg *Synthapruf*, have very good adhesion and slight permeability.

Uses include:

BS 802 : 1967 *Tarmacadam with crushed rock or slag aggregate*
BS 1241 : 1959 *Tarmacadam and tar carpets (gravel aggregate)*
BS 1242 : 1960 *Tarmacadam 'Tarpaving' for footpaths, playgrounds and similar works.*

PITCH

Pitch is the residue after distilling tar from coal *fluxed back* with some of the by-products. Coal tar and pitch soften at lower temperature, are less plastic, less able to resist temperature variations and are less costly than bitumen. Pitch is not suitable for damp-proof courses and as roofing it should be used only for temporary work.

BS 1310 : 1965 describes *Coal tar pitches for Building purposes*

Uses include:

An ingredient in pitch mastic used for flooring, see *MBC: C and F*, chapter 12
In paints, see *MBC: C and F*, chapter 17
Fluxed eg, for damp-proof membranes
A saturant for felts
An impregnant in pitch-fibre drain pipes.

12 Glass

Glass is used in building mainly as flat glass, products such as lenses, and as glass fibres. In this country little glass for windows was used in secular buildings before the Elizabethan period. Up to the middle of the nineteenth century the spun crown glass process which was most commonly used, severely limited clarity and the size of panes but in 1851 the production of sheet glass by blowing cylinders and then flattening them, made possible the glazing of the Crystal Palace with panes as large as 1245×254 mm. The first continuous process of drawing glass was developed in 1913 and most flat glass used today is drawn sheet. In 1923 Pilkington Brothers Ltd developed a continuous process of grinding and polishing rough cast glass and in 1959 they developed the float glass process by which most clear plate glass is produced today.

Glass and its use in modern building is dealt with in:

Glass in architecture and decoration R. McGrath and A. C. Frost, Architectural Press Ltd
BS 952 : 1964 (amended April 1965) *Classification of glass for glazing and terminology for work on glass*
CP 152 : 1966 *Glazing and fixing of glass for buildings*
CP 145 : 1951 *Patent glazing*
Publications of Pilkingtons and glass merchants.

This chapter deals with:

Manufacture
Properties of glass
Types of glass, page 226
Glass products, page 232
Work on glass, page 237
Costs, pages 227 and 237
Glass fibre products, page 237.

Manufacture

Today molten glass is produced in continuous furnaces. An ordinary glass *batch* consists mainly of sand, soda ash, limestone and dolomite, a small amount of alumina, a few residual materials and broken glass (*cullet*). Iron oxide in ordinary glass made in this country gives it a slight green tint – although this can be removed by the inclusion of manganese with arsenic or selenium. Other additions impart special properties such as tints, opacity, sparkle, chemical resistance, low thermal movement, heat absorption or rejection and improved working properties.

Products are produced by several basic processes:

Blowing by mouth, for *antique* glasses and for special shapes, by machine for bottles, etc.
Drawing for ordinary sheet glass for windows.
Rolling for *rough cast* and patterned glasses (wire can be incorporated in the glass during rolling).
Grinding and polishing of rough cast glass.
Floating to give parallel and flat surfaces so that vision is not distorted.
Pressing for lenses, hollow glass blocks, etc.
Extrusion and blowing of fibres for insulation and staple tissues, see page 237.
Extrusion and drawing of fibres for reinforcements and textiles, see page 237.

After forming to the shape required glass must be cooled slowly (*annealed*) to relieve the strains which would otherwise result. The description *annealed glass* is used to distinguish ordinary glass from the toughened product (see page 228).

Properties

Headings are:

Appearance	Durability
Density	Strength properties
Melting point	Thermal movement
Visible light transmission	Thermal insulation
Solar heat transmission	Sound insulation
Ultra-violet transmission	Behaviour in fire.

Appearance

Ordinary glass is transparent and more or less

colourless. Transparent, translucent and opaque glasses can be coloured in four ways:

1 *Pot* colour is uniform throughout its thickness
2 *Flashed* glass has an extremely thin layer of transparent coloured glass applied to one surface during manufacture
3 Coloured ceramic pigment fused on one side
4 *Painting*, see page 237.

Surfaces of glass which are formed directly from the kiln are bright and lustrous, ie *fire-finished*. This applies to *antique* blown glass, drawn sheet and float glass.

Density

2560 kg/m³ (for comparison: *Perspex* (ICI) 807, Aluminium 2771, Steel 7850 kg/m³.

Melting point

1500°C approx. (Aluminium 660, Steel 1900°C.)

Visible light transmission

Table 76 gives average values for some glasses and for *Perspex* (ICI).
   Light diffusion and obscuration, see page 227.
   Refractive index 1·52 (approx).

Solar heat transmission

Ordinary glass is relatively transparent but solar heat rejecting glasses are available, see page 230.

Ultra-violet transmission

Ordinary glass transmits a very small proportion of the sun's ultra-violet rays, and virtually none in the so-called *health band.*

Durability

Glass is extremely durable in normal conditions. BS 952:1964 *Classification of glass for glazing and terminology for work on glass* states:
'All window glass should be of such quality that surface deterioration will not develop after glazing under normal conditions of use, provided the glass is cleaned at reasonable intervals.' It is, however, attacked by hydrofluoric and phosphoric acids and by strong alkalis, eg caustic soda. Alkaline paint removers which are not properly cleaned

	Directed light	Diffuse light
6 mm clear plate	90	
6 mm clear sheet	90	
Flemish – small and large		
Hammered no. 2		85
Pacific		
Plain cathedral		
Reeded – broad and narrow		
Spotlyte		
5–10 mm rough cast		80–85
Deep Flemish		84
12 mm clear plate	88	83
Glasgow hammered	—	
Cross reeded		82
Pinstripe		
Arctic – small		81
Arctic – large		
Rattan		80
6 mm wired clear plate		
6 mm wired rough cast		
Atlantic		75
Sparkel		
Stippolyte		74
Cotswold		
Borealis		70
Prismatic	70–75	65
Glass blocks		50
Perspex (ICI) (for comparison)	92	85

Table 76   Average light transmissions of glasses (per cent)

off, and even water running onto glass from new concrete, may cause trouble.
CP 152 *Glazing and fixing of glass for buildings* states that because all glasses are subject to deterioration by the action of water they should not be allowed to remain wet when stacked face to face.

221

Strength properties

Although glass is elastic right up to its breaking point it is completely brittle so there is no *permanent set* which in ductile materials gives warning of impending failure. It is weak in tension and glass of uniform manufacture varies very widely in strength so that safe stresses have to be computed from the results of tests on a very large number of samples. Another characteristic is that resistance to shock loads is about twice that to static loads which can be withstood indefinitely.

Allowable working stresses are usually calculated for a risk of not more than 1 per cent if glass

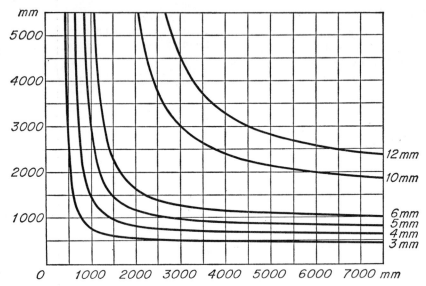

41 Recommended thicknesses for float glass (glazed on four edges where wind loading is 1000 N/m²) CP3: 1952, chapter V.

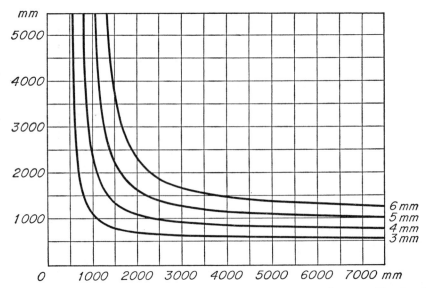

42 Recommended thicknesses for clear sheet glass (glazed on four edges where wind loading is 1000 N/m²)

is subjected to the most severe combination of loadings which could ever foreseeably occur, the likelihood of such a combination happening simultaneously being so remote that risk is virtually eliminated. Examples of maximum working stresses usually allowed in flat glasses are:

	Sustained load N/mm²	Momentary load (3 seconds) N/mm²
Sheet glass up to 6 mm	14·0–17·0	35·0–41·0
Clear plate (float or polished) 6 mm	8·5–11·0	24·0–29·0
Rolled pattern glasses	7·0–9·0	21·0–24·0
Wired glasses, 6 mm	7·0–8·5	19·0–22·0
Toughened, 6 mm	41·4–44·8	not applicable

It will be seen that clear plate glass is weaker than sheet glass and that wire in glass reduces its strength. Opaque glasses are appreciably weaker than clear glass.

Lower working stresses must be employed where: special risks of breakage exist, eg in schools, where panes are not square in shape, perforated or not fixed on all edges.

Minimum glazing thicknesses and maximum sizes

It is important to realize that maximum manufacturing sizes are not necessarily safe glazing sizes, which depend upon the type and thickness of glass, the length and breadth of panes, the method of fixing and the stresses to which the glass will be subjected in service.

Procedures for determining safe minimum thicknesses of glass for various purposes are detailed in CP 152 : 1966 *Glazing and fixing of glass for buildings*. In this country Pilkington Brothers Ltd provide an advisory service.

External glazing For external glazing the wind loading is based on the probable maximum three second wind velocity acting simultaneously as pressure on one side and as suction on the other. A wind loading is arrived at by applying a factor to the predicted wind speed to take into account the height of the building and the environment. The recommended minimum thickness of a given type of glass in vertical windows glazed on four edges can then be read off from graphs for the particular wind velocity.

For ready reference, figures 41 and 42 show the recommended maximum glazing sizes for various thicknesses of float and sheet glasses glazed on four edges in vertical windows where the wind loading is 1000 N/m², which may be considered to be typically average. To use the graphs, find the point on the grid where the two dimensions of the glass intersect, and then move across the graph to the right. The first curve reached indicates the recommended minimum thickness. Thus, where it is intended to glaze a window with 3000 × 2000 mm float glass the recommended thickness is 10 mm. The graphs may also be used to ascertain the largest size for a given thickness of glass. Thus 850 × 850 mm is the largest square pane which it is recommended should be glazed with 3 mm glass, and a rectangle 2500 × 500 mm is also acceptable.

Safety from injury Where the risk of breakage cannot be sufficiently reduced, eg by protective rails or by indicating its presence by visible motifs, suitably thick glass should be used or glass which is unlikely to cause serious injury if it is broken, ie toughened glass, laminated safety glass, or where it is required to be fire-resisting, glass such as copper-light or wired glass which do not cause injury so readily if they are broken. Alternatively, strong and durable scrim can be fixed with a durable adhesive to the back of ordinary glass.

The following sizes are generally considered to be reasonably safe for internal glazing except where otherwise recommended:

Thickness mm	Maximum area m²	
	Annealed glass	Toughened glass
3	0·186	not
4	0·279	recommended
5	0·372	0·929
6	0·743	2·973
10	1·486	5·946
12	2·973	7·432

CP 152 : 1966 gives recommendations in respect of four categories of risk for glass glazed in frames in accordance with good practice: For example in respect of glass which is fixed on all four edges: glass which protects differences in levels, eg balustrades, which does not exceed 0·7 m² should be 6 mm toughened glass or annealed glass at least 12 mm thick. Also in buildings used mainly by juveniles glass up to sill height and all glass in doors should be toughened except where fire regulations require the use of wired glass or copper light glazing. Areas exceeding 0·2 m² should be not less than 6 mm thick. In domestic buildings glass which would be potentially dangerous to children, particularly near floor level, should be toughened. Upper panels in 3 mm annealed glass which is liable to damage by slamming doors should be limited to 0·5 m². All glass at high level in gymnasia should be toughened. Generally roof glazing should be toughened, wired or laminated.

Thermal movement

Because the coefficient of thermal expansion for glass, of 76 to 80×10^{-7} per deg C, is lower than that of the materials in which it is normally fixed, allowance should be made for movement. Also thermal stresses arising where one part of a glass pane is at a different temperature from other parts can lead to breakage. This is particularly likely where dark coloured glass, or clear glass with a dark background are exposed to the sun while the edges being shaded by beads are at a much lower temperature and are put into tension. To reduce the centre-edge differential beads should not be wider than 10 mm and dark heat-absorbing frames are to be preferred to white or polished aluminium frames. A ventilated cavity behind glass helps in cooling it, and incidentally in removing condensation especially if it 'breathes' to the outside. If insulation material must be in contact with the back of glass a toughened glass should be used. It is also important that the edges of such glass should be cut cleanly, nipped or shelled edges, particularly of heat-rejecting glass, create points of weakness in the critical shaded zone.

Thermal insulation

Although glass is dense and is a good conductor of heat (k = 1·05 W/m deg C), its surface resistances are high and typical double glazing provides thermal insulation approximating that of a 105 mm brick wall. Double glazing almost halves the heat lost through a single pane, the optimum gap being about 19 mm. Table 77 gives some typical values for thermal transmittance through glazing and walls.

	'U' – W/m^2 deg C[1]
Single glazing	3·98–7·38
Double glazing with gaps:	
5 mm	2·78–4·09
6 mm	2·67–3·81
12 mm	2·39–3·36
19 mm	2·33–3·18
80 mm glass blocks	2·5
105 mm Solid brick wall with 16 mm dense plaster	3·0
105 mm brick outer leaf, 50 mm unventilated cavity, 100 mm lightweight concrete block inner leaf 16 mm dense plaster	0·96

[1] Thermal transmission ranges are for differences in orientation and exposure to wind.

Table 77   Thermal insulation of glazing compared with walls

Because double glazing provides better thermal insulation from conducted heat than single glazing, condensation is less likely to form on the room side glass surface of the assembly. However, if the inner and outer panes are not hermetically sealed at their edges water vapour can condense on the inside of the outer pane as it does on single glazing. This tendency is reduced if the cavity is ventilated to the outside and the inner pane is sealed from the room atmosphere.

Factory sealed units contain dry air so that condensation cannot form inside the cavity and dust cannot enter. Variations in the external air pressure and temperature subject the glass to stresses which tend to break down the less effective edge seals.

Double glazing units are discussed under *Glastoglas* and *Mark IV units*, page 232. Hollow blocks, page 233, and *Profilit* units in double

Glass thickness mm	Single glazing		Double glazing with gaps less than 50, 100 and 200 mm									
	Opening lights closed	Fixed lights and opening lights with seals[1]	Opening lights – closed				Fixed lights and opening lights with seals[1]					
			No absorbent material to sides of gap		With absorbent material to sides of gap		No absorbent material to sides of gap			With absorbent material to sides of gap		
			100 mm	200 mm	100 mm	200 mm	less than 50 mm	100 mm	200 mm	less than 50 mm	100 mm	200 mm
3	18	23	22[2]	24[2]	28[2]	31	26[2]	34	38	28[2]	37	41
4	18	25	22[2]	24[2]	28[2]	31	28	36	40	30[2]	39	43
6	18	27	22[2]	24[2]	30[2]	33	30	38	42	32[2]	41	45
10	20	30	25	27	33	36	33[2]	41	45[2]	35[2]	44	48[2]
12	22[2]	31	—	—	—	—	—	—	46	—	—	49
25	—	34	—	—	—	—	—	—	—	—	—	—

[1] Air-tight weatherstrip or special cushion seals. [2] Estimated values.

Table 78   Approximate ($\pm$ 3 dB) average sound reduction in decibels (dB 100–3150 Hz)

thickness, page 234, are other forms of double glazing.

Sound insulation

Thicker glasses are more effective particularly at the low frequencies characteristic of traffic noise. For superior insulation, double glazing is necessary. Cavities less than 100 mm wide are comparatively less effective than for thermal insulation, a cavity of 200 to 300 mm should be used.

Table 78 gives sound reduction values for various weights of glass and types of windows. It will be seen that the normal air leakages which occur around closed opening lights are very important.

Hollow glass blocks (see page 233), give 35 to 40 dB reduction.

Behaviour in fire

Although non-combustible, ordinary glass breaks and later melts in fires and double glazing shows no significant advantage over single glazing. Glass is a good conductor of heat and radiation from glass can render narrow escape routes ineffective.

Nevertheless, certain types of glass in sufficient thicknesses, and suitably fixed, provide a useful degree of *fire resistance* (see page 36), eg

$\frac{1}{2}$ *hour rating*

(a) 6 mm wired glass or 6 mm copperlight glazing not more than 0·4 m² in area in timber frames, at least 19 mm thick (measured in critical directions so as to protect the glass) (to prevent ignition of the timber on the side remote from the fire)

(b) 6 mm wired glass or 6 mm copperlight glazing not exceeding 1 m² in area in reinforced concrete or metal frames the latter to have a melting point not less than 900°C, which precludes the use of lead and aluminium

(c) glass blocks bedded in mortar in panels up to 6 m².

1 hour rating

Wired glass or copperlight glazing as above but in metal frames having a melting point not less than 980°C.

Types of glass

We consider the types of glass under the following headings:

1 *Translucent glasses*
  rough cast

wired rough cast
patterned glasses

2 *Transparent glasses*, page 227
  clear sheet
  clear plate

3 *Special glasses*, page 228
  Products formed from the above glasses are considered later under *Glass products*, see page 232).

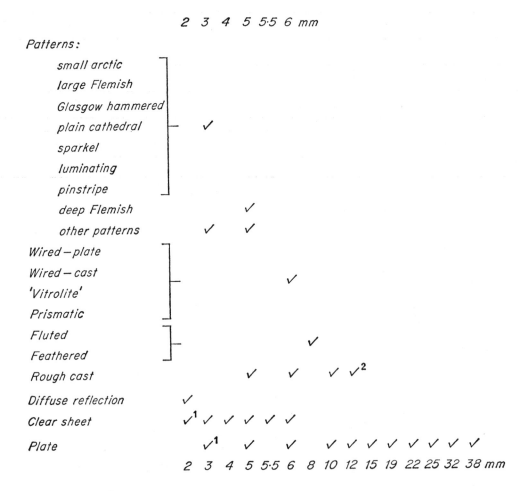

2   3   4   5   5·5   6   mm

Patterns:

	2	3	4	5	5·5	6	8	10	12	15	19	22	25	32	38 mm
small arctic		✓													
large Flemish		✓													
Glasgow hammered		✓													
plain cathedral		✓													
sparkel		✓													
luminating		✓													
pinstripe		✓													
deep Flemish			✓												
other patterns		✓	✓												
Wired – plate				✓											
Wired – cast				✓											
'Vitrolite'				✓											
Prismatic				✓											
Fluted						✓									
Feathered						✓									
Rough cast			✓	✓		✓	✓[2]								
Diffuse reflection	✓														
Clear sheet	✓[1]	✓	✓	✓	✓	✓									
Plate	✓[1]	✓		✓		✓	✓	✓	✓	✓	✓	✓	✓	✓	✓

[1] Not recommended for general glazing

[2] Greater thicknesses can be obtained to order

Table 79   Thicknesses of glasses   *Note.* Vitrolite is no longer manufactured

1 Translucent glasses

Rough cast Rough cast glass, so called because it was formerly cast on sand beds, is now made by passing molten glass between rollers which impart a characteristic pattern on one side. The other side is smooth, but the method does not permit optically true surfaces to be obtained. It is made in only one quality.

Table 79 shows the available thicknesses of which 6 mm is the most common and this thickness is available with wire incorporated during rolling.

Maximum available sizes are related to minimum stresses which are likely to occur in service.

Wired rough cast glass Wire mesh is embedded centrally in the thickness of rough-cast glass during rolling. The wire does not reinforce glass but holds the pieces together in the event of breakage so that wired glass can be described as a *'safety glass'*. It cannot be toughened. To prevent injury from flying fragments wired glass can be used in doors in schools, in balustrades and similar situations. Wired glass is essential for roof lights, except small domes. Broken wired glass should be promptly replaced to avoid sudden collapse when the wires rust.

Wired glass is scheduled as *fire resisting* as detailed in Table 'F', London Building (Construction) By-laws 1952 and is designated EXT AA (BS 476 Part 3 *External fire exposure roof tests*). Fire resistance of wired glass is discussed on page 225.

Wired glass is made in two patterns of wire mesh electrically welded at the intersections:

Georgian: 13 mm sided square-vertical/horizontal mesh.
Diamond: 20 mm sided square-diagonal mesh.

Both wire patterns are provided in 6 mm rough cast in sizes up to 3710 × 1830 mm.

Patterned glasses In selecting patterns ease of cleaning must be considered together with obscuration and diffusion properties.

Obscuration depends on the depth and complexity of patterns and upon the relative light intensities on the two sides of the glass and the distance of the object from the glass. Where practicable Pilkington Bros Ltd classify their patterned glasses A to E for low to high diffusion and a to e for low to high obscuration. Table 80 shows patterns classified by diffusion, obscuration and price and notes the patterns available in tints.

	Price group		Price group
A—a		**C—a**	
Flemish, small[1]	1	Hammered no. 2[1]	1
Plain cathedral	1		
Broad reeded	2	**C—b**	
Narrow reeded	2	Arctic large[1]	1
Reedrop	2	Glasgow	
		hammered	1
		Luminating	2
B—a		Pinstripe	2
Flemish, large	1		
Rattan	2	**C—c**	
		Stippolyte	1
B—b		Cotswold	2
Broad reedlyte	2		
Narrow reedlyte	2	**D—c**	
Deep Flemish		Arctic, small	1
Frostlyte	2	Atlantic	1
Siesta	3	Cross reeded	2
Shiplyte	3		
		D—d	
B—c		Sparkel	1
Festival	2		
Pacific	1	**E—e**	
Spotlyte[1]	2	Borealis	2

[1] Available in certain tints.
A—E low to high diffusion
a—e low to high obscuration

Table 80 Patterned glasses – diffusion, obscuration and cost groups

Where an obscured glass is required in sizes larger than those available in rolled patterned glasses, float or thick drawn sheet with an acid etched or sandblasted treatment can be used.

2 Transparent glasses

Clear sheet glass (drawn sheet) Sheet glass is usually drawn up vertically from a tank of molten glass into an annealing tower by wheels which grip the edges of the sheet, the rate of drawing determining the thickness of the glass. At the top of the tower the glass is cut into suitable lengths.

BS 952 states that: 'Sheet glass has natural fire-finished surfaces but because the two surfaces are never perfectly flat and parallel, there is always some distortion of vision and reflection'. This can be minimized by glazing the glass with the line of draw parallel to the ground. There are three main BS qualities:

OQ   *Ordinary glazing quality*
       suitable for general glazing work. It is examined but minor defects are permitted.

SQ   *Selected glazing quality*
       used where a superior type glass is required.

SSQ   *Special selected quality*
       used for very high grade work, eg pictures and cabinets.

(*Horticultural quality* is inferior to *OQ*.)

Even *SSQ* glass is never completely free from distortion but it is substantially less costly than clear float plate glass of equal thickness and is otherwise satisfactory where very high quality glass is not required.

Table 79 shows that the choice of patterns is restricted where thicknesses greater than 3 mm are required. A limited range of tints is available in *OQ* glass only.

Clear plate glass   BS 952 describes this glass as having: 'Flat and parallel surfaces providing clear undistorted vision and reflection, produced either by grinding and polishing or by the float process'.

Polished plate glass is produced by passing a ribbon of rough cast glass through machines which in turn, grind and smooth the two sides simultaneously. The glass is then cut and each side polished in turn.

6 mm *polished wire clear plate* in both *Georgian* and *Diamond* patterns is normally available in sizes up to 3300 × 1830 mm.

There is only one quality of wired glass, but glass can be selected, if so ordered, so that the lines of the wire are true and square. In glazing Georgian wired glass, it may well be desirable to align the wires, either vertically or horizontally, in adjoining squares.

Float glass is produced by the recently developed method of floating a continuous ribbon of molten glass across the surface of molten tin, in a controlled atmosphere, whereby the upper surface is fire-polished and the other surface is polished by contact with the metal. Both sides are flat and parallel.

BS 952 Qualities of clear plate glass

GG   *Glazing quality for glazing*
       suitable for general work

SG   *Selected glazing quality*
       suitable for superior work and for mirrors and bevelling

SQ   *Silvering quality*
       suitable for high-class mirrors and wherever a superfine glass is required.

6 mm is the most common thickness and is supplied unless one of the other thicknesses shown in table 79 is specified. 6 mm and certain other thicknesses are available in a number of tints. Mirrors are dealt with on page 236.

3   Special glasses

a *Toughened glass*   When suitable glass is heated and then suddenly cooled by jets of cold air the surfaces are put into compression and the interior into tension. There may be some distortion but the glass becomes much stronger, tougher and more flexible than it was in its original annealed condition. When fixed normally, the resistance to impact of toughened glass is about seven times, and resistance to loads applied without shock about four times that of annealed glass.

Normally the allowable working stress for sustained loads is from 41 to 45 N/mm^2 compared with 14·0 to 17·0 for annealed sheet glass. The modulus of elasticity is not altered by toughening, so that like safe strength in tension, deflection is increased about four times.

Uses which exploit the strength properties of toughened glass include suspended all-glass assemblies without frames, mullions or glazing bars; frameless panels for balustrades and machinery guards.

Toughened glass is 'de-toughened' if it is exposed to temperatures above 295°C for too long or too frequently, it is not fire-resisting, but it has very superior resistance to thermal shock. For example, it can be heated above 200°C and have cold water poured over it, it withstands splashing with molten metal or one side, can be heated evenly to 250°C while the other side is at ordinary atmospheric temperature without suffering damage.

The remarkable properties of toughened glass depend upon the balance of stresses being maintained, if the outer skin is disturbed the energy locked up in the glass is expended in shattering the whole piece into small fragments. Unfortunately the surfaces of toughened glass are no more resistant to scratching than those of ordinary glass and the edges are equally vulnerable to damage. All cutting to size, grinding, drilling and any other work on the glass must therefore be done before toughening is carried out.

Loss of vision is a serious disadvantage in broken car windscreens, but unlike annealed glass, fragments of fully toughened glass are unlikely to cause serious injury to individuals. Thus fully toughened glass is one type of *safety glass*, and is useful in building work where ordinary glass would be liable to breakage and injury (see *Safety from Injury*, page 223).

Toughened glass may be recognized by a brand mark, a pattern of slight discolouration when it is viewed in certain lighting conditions or by polarized light, and sometimes by small indentations along one edge left by the tongs used for suspending the glass during toughening.

Toughened glasses manufactured by Messrs Pilkington Brothers Ltd are:

Armourplate polished or float, clear or tinted plate glass, heat-rejecting *Anti-sun* and *Spectrafloat* glasses. Doors, usually 12 mm thickness

Armourcast rough cast glass
Doors usually 12 mm for external and 10 mm for internal uses

Armourclad clear plate and cast glasses with:
coloured ceramic fused on one side in 10 standard colours. Other colours can be ordered. When used as cladding the coloured surface is placed inwards. *Armourclad* insulating panels made in certain sizes with a 25 mm backing of glass fibre have a U value of $1 \cdot 1$ W/m^2 deg C.

Armourglass narrow reeded, broad reedlyte and Cotswold patterns.

Opal glasses can be toughened but not always as effectively as plate glass. Subject to certain limitations bent glass can be toughened.

Limitations upon the size of holes and their proximity to edges and to each other are given in figure 43. Many configurations of notches are practicable but the radii of re-entrant corners must not be less than the thickness of the glass.

There are further restrictions on the diameter of holes in glass which is from 50 to 150 mm wide.

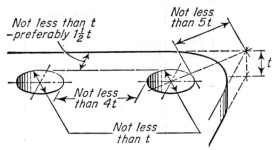

43   *Minimum dimensions appertaining to holes in toughened glass*

Inquiries should be submitted regarding holes more than 25 mm diameter.

In fixing toughened glass, edge clearance must avoid contact with hard materials.

b *One-way glasses* No glass gives one-way vision under all lighting conditions. One-way glasses depend upon the lighting on the 'viewing' side being less intense than on the reverse.

They include:

Venetian Mirror Broad strips of mirror which face the room alternating with narrow lines of clear glass. The usual proportions lie between 6 and 12 : 1.

Transparent mirror In this product a thin metallic film applied to float/plate glass reflects the major proportion of light which falls upon it. The metal film must be protected from abrasion.

Tinted glasses Glass with integral colour, and laminated glass with a coloured interlayer.

c *Diffuse reflection glass* Diffuse glass is useful for glazing pictures and instrument dials. Both surfaces are very lightly textured so that when fixed within 20 mm of the object to be viewed it is completely transparent and there is no reflection.

d *Prismatic glass* This is a translucent rolled glass having parallel prisms on the 'inside' face, which deflect light. It is made in one quality only in a nominal overall thickness of 6 mm. There are three types, for different angles of incidence:

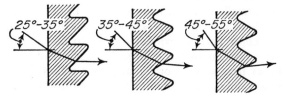

	Thick-ness	Designations		Colour	Solar radiant heat			
		Visible light transmission	Total solar radiant heat transmission		Reflection	Absorption	Direct trans-mission	Total rejection
	mm	percentages			percentages			
Float	6	85/84		normal	8	12	80	16
Spectrafloat surface modified	6, 10, 12	50/67		bronze	10	34	56	33
	10, 12	50/62		bronze	9	43	48	38
Solarshield metal coated & laminated	6, 10	12/24		bronze	45	47	8	76
		15/23		gold	48	43	9	77
		38/35		gold	42	35	23	65
Calorex cast body-tinted glasses	3	65/53		green	5	63	32	47
	5	55/48				70	25	52
	6	48/45				75	20	55
Antisun Atlantic and Pacific Patterns Roughcast	3	80/72		green	6	33	61	28
	5	76/66				42	52	34
	6	72/61				49	45	39
Float[2]	5	78/66				42	52	34
	6	74/61				49	45	39
Glass blocks	80	approx.50/60[1]		white				40

[1] Reducing to negligible transmission where the angle between the sun's rays and the surface of glass block panel is less than 30°. [2] Also available 10 mm and in grey and bronze 6, 10 and 12 mm.

Table 81 Visible light and solar radiant heat transmissions of glasses manufactured by Pilkingtons

Where the angle of incidence is more than 60° reflection from the smooth surface is so great that prismatic glass ceases to serve a useful purpose.

Prismatic glass can be used with the prisms horizontally to throw light to the backs of rooms and to reduce glare on working surfaces by glazing the upper parts of windows so as to direct the sun's rays on to the ceiling. Although here the upper faces of the horizontal prisms collect dirt, it does not detract from its ability to redirect light, and the straight line pattern is easy to clean. Alternatively, prismatic glass can be glazed with the prisms placed vertically so as to direct light sideways.

e *Solar heat rejecting glasses* Ordinary glass transmits a high proportion of the short-wave solar radiation. Objects in buildings, which are heated by short-waves, re-radiate heat of a much longer wave-length to which glass is opaque. Thereby, heat is 'trapped' producing the well known 'hot house' effect. Solar heat-rejecting glasses often reduce costs in air conditioning and reduce sky glare and/or reflected glare. See table 81.

Spectrafloat is produced on the float glass production line. While the ribbon of glass is still at a high temperature it is electrically conductive and metallic ions are driven into one surface to a controlled depth and concentration. At present normal production is limited to a bronze tint in 6, 10 and 12 mm thickness which can be toughened if required.

In glazing Spectrafloat glass the modified surface must be placed inside.

Solarshield is a transparent glass which rejects heat mainly by the reflection provided by a thin metallic film on the inner face of one of two panes of glass which are laminated together.

Calorex is a fairly dark blue-green body tinted rough cast glass with the highest degree of infra-red radiation rejection while transmitting about half of the visible light.

Antisun is a softly tinted blue-green glass which combines a measure of relief from solar radiant heat with a higher light transmission. It is manufactured in rough cast, *Atlantic* and *Pacific* patterns and in clear plate. The latter glass has been used for airport control buildings.

To obtain full value from heat absorbing glass, heat which is absorbed by the glass must be prevented from being radiated into or conveyed by convection into rooms. Ventilators immediately above windows help to cool the glass, but ideally, heat absorbing glass is fixed outside the normal glazing, with gaps above and below.

Breakage can result from differential heating caused by shading parts of the glass and special care is necessary in fixing to accommodate increased thermal movement. Edge cover must therefore be kept to a minimum and not exceed 10 mm (or 16 mm for *patent* [puttyless] glazing). It is essential that the edges of heat rejecting glasses are clean cut to avoid weak spots and glazing clearances all round must be at least 3 mm for panes up to 760 mm major dimension and 4·5 mm for panes with a greater major dimension.

f *Heat resisting glass* has a low coefficient of expansion and, in consequence is more resistant to changes in temperature than ordinary glass.

(Toughened glass is also resistant to thermal shock, see page 228.)

Heat resisting glass is transparent but its thickness varies and it may contain air-bubbles and other defects.

BS 952 gives the following thicknesses and maximum sizes:

	Thickness mm	Normal maximum size mm
Blown	2·0–7·0	609·6 × 609·6
Pressed	5·0–10·0	508 mm diameter approx.
	12·0–15·0	254 mm diameter approx.

g *X-ray resistant glass* Usually a polished plate glass containing a large proportion of lead oxide, which has a high degree of opacity to X-rays.

h *Opal glasses* Opal and opalescent glasses, which may be white or coloured, vary from a faint milkiness in the case of flashed opal to virtual opacity (BS 952 : 1964). Types are:

Rolled opal glass made in one quality in thicknesses of 6, 8 to 9 and 11 mm.

Polished opal glass is made either by the float process or one or both surfaces are ground and polished. It is made in one quality in white, black and a range of colours, in thicknesses of 6, 8, 10, 12 and 16 mm.

Pot opal and flashed opal sheet glass Pot opal glass (uniform in colour throughout its thickness), tinted opal flashed on clear sheet and white opal flashed on tinted sheet are available in one quality in certain thicknesses.

i *Coloured opaque glass* Coloured opaque glass provides a durable and easily cleaned finish for shop fronts, table tops, shelves, kitchen and bathroom walls, and infilling panels in curtain walls.

Fixing Glazing and fixing should conform to CP 152 : 1966. Fixing should be firm but not rigid. There should always be a clearance joint filled with mastic between the edge of an installation and surrounding structures, including pavements where glass is taken below pavement level.

Methods of fixing are: mechanical by edge framing, clips or screws, with mastic or 'solid'.

Mechanical fixing Where used externally it must be treated as a heat-absorbing glass, see *Thermal movement*, page 224. Clearances should be allowed all round glass as follows:

3 mm for major dimensions up to 750 mm
5 mm for greater major dimensions

All cladding glasses should be raised off the bottom frame member by two setting blocks, adjusted in thickness to equalise as far as possible the clearances round the glass.

In large panes or where high wind pressures are expected PVC, neoprene or similar distance pieces are required at the back and front of the glass to prevent the glazing compound from being squeezed out. The latter must be able to withstand repeated stretching and compression and often high temperatures without cracking or losing adhesion to the adjacent surfaces. See *Mastics*, chapter 16.

Clips must be insulated from direct contact with the glass and screws must be sleeved to prevent them touching the edges of the holes through which they pass.

Mastic fixing After sealing porous backgrounds mastic can be applied in daubs of about 40 mm diameter and at 80 mm centres so that when the glass has been pushed back to 5 to 6 mm from the background the bed is nearly continuous. Skirtings should be fixed as nearly solid as possible.

Vertical glass must be supported at the base by anchors to the wall. Packing pieces may be dislodged later and should not be used at the base. Where glass ashlars are used in more than five courses or more than 2·4 m above the base additional supporting anchors should be introduced at every four or five courses. Externally, installations over 2·4 m high must be secured by clips fixed to the background and projected over the face of the glass and insulated therefrom. Alternatively cover strips may be used to hold the glass in position.

Solid fixing Where high hygienic standards or high impact resistance are required bedding must be 'solid'. With this method of fixing glass sizes should not exceed 600 × 450 mm. The methods advised are:

Latex cement Only temporary supports are required whilst curing takes place.

Cement-lime mortar and elastic interlayer, Here supports and clips or cover strips are required as for mastic fixing.

j *'Antique' glasses*

A wide range of clear and coloured glasses are hand made by traditional means and are therefore costly. Varying thicknesses cause variations in depth of colour, characteristic 'defects' contribute visual interest, and the surfaces are fire-finished and consequently lustrous. *Antique* glasses are used for decorative work, to diffuse vision and for restoration of old buildings in which modern glass would be out of place.

Glass products

a *Laminated glass*

Laminated glass consists of two sheets of glass cemented together with an interlayer of polyvinyl butyral. It is more resistant to breakage than wired glass. Breakage usually occurs without complete loss of vision and the fragments are held in position by the interlayer, hence the name *safety glass*. However, where fire resistance is required, wired glass or copper-light glazing is necessary.

With a tinted interlayer, laminated glass provides one-way vision in ambulances and taxis.

b *Double glazing units*

The advantages of double glazing in reducing thermal loss and condensation and the advantages in sound insulation have been discussed on pages 224 and 225.

Pilkington Brothers Ltd make two factory-sealed units:

1 *Glastoglas* This is an all-glass unit in which the edges of the panes are fused together, made in

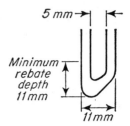

44   *Standard 'Glastoglas' all glass unit*

about 170 stock rectangular sizes from 255 × 380 mm up to 1270 × 1778 mm × 11 mm wide with 5 mm air space. Certain sizes can be supplied with 7 mm air spaces and with 3 or 4 mm glass, and units can be supplied in obscured glasses. Owing to pressure differences between the inner and outer air the units must not be taken above 800 m without reference to the manufacturer.

2 *Mark VI metal edge unit* Two panes of glass are bonded to a metal spacer with additional caulking compound and a metal sheath. Units are made to order with 5, 6 and 12 mm air spaces. Unlike *Glastoglas*, units can be made in non-rectangular shapes, larger sizes and with most kinds of glass. Mark VI units can be made to order with more than two panes for conditions of severe cold or high humidity, and also for use at altitudes above 800 m.

In new work rebates with sufficient depth and upstand should be provided so that standard units can be used but for glazing narrow rebates in existing sashes stepped *Mark VI units* which reduce the sight size slightly, see figure 45, are available.

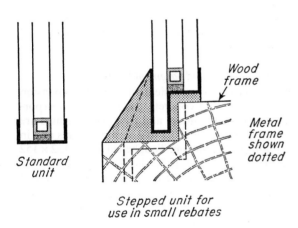

Wood frame

Metal frame shown dotted

Standard unit

Stepped unit for use in small rebates

45 *'Insulight' Mark IV units*

Mark VI units with a minor dimension greater than 1930 mm require a rebate depth of at least 25 mm. Glazing should be performed in strict accordance with the manufacturer's instructions. For example all units must be glazed with a non-setting compound, but some, such as *Glastoglas* units, may be fronted with metal casement putty or polysulphide sealant. Beads with a minimum of 3 mm non-setting compound at front and back

are advisable for larger windows, and resilient, non-absorbent distance pieces must be used opposite each other on both faces of the units.

Edge clearances between unit and frame must be at least 3 mm all round for units up to 2·8 m and not less than 5 mm for larger units.

Units should be set on two non-absorbent resilient blocks each about 40 mm to 150 mm long and 3 mm wider than the thickness of the unit.

c *Glass blocks*
Glass blocks comprising two 'trays' of glass fused together are used to construct non-loadbearing walls or screens. These are described by BS 1207 : 1961. Blocks are made in white, red, amber, blue and green glass, and in various patterns.

Panels provide:

Thermal transmittance $U = 2·5$ W/m² deg C average for a north wall which is approximately equal to the value for a 215 mm solid plastered brick wall.

Solar heat transmission Hollow glass blocks provide a form of solar heat rejecting glazing – see page 230. Transmission is negligible where the angle of incidence of the sun's rays is less than 30° and increases to approximately 60 per cent maximum where the sun's rays are normal to the panel and where there are no shading devices.

Visible light transmission of panels of white blocks is about 50 per cent.

Light diffusion Various patterns provide a degree of privacy with much greater depth of light penetration into rooms and more evenly distributed illumination than normal transparent glazing.

Fire resistance ½ hour (BS 476 : Part 1 : 1953 *Fire tests on building materials and structures*) in panels built in mortar up to 2·4 × 2·4 m (test ref: FROSI 4899).

Sound insulation 35–40 decibels over the frequency range 100 to 3150 Hz.

Ventilation can be provided by special blocks of all glass construction.

Appearance Blocks are made in white, red, amber, green and blue glass in various patterns:

Sizes

240 × 240 × 80 mm
240 × 115 × 80 mm

115 × 115 × 80 mm
190 × 190 × 80 mm
146 × 146 × 98 mm
190 × 190 × 100 mm (for glass/concrete roofs)

Installation Glass blocks are non-load-bearing and must be built independent of the main structure. The manufacturers' instructions should be closely followed. There are four methods:

1 In situ traditional – using dry 'fatty' mortar

2 In situ supported – using 'stiff' mortar and steel reinforcement

3 Precast panels

4 Dry – for internal use only – using plastics spacer strips.

d 'Profilit'

This product of Pilkingtons Brothers Ltd consists of rectangular troughs 262 mm wide × 41 mm deep in lengths up to 6 m in 6 mm rough cast

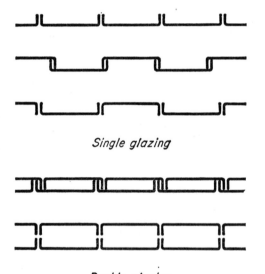

Single glazing

Double glazing

glass with or without eight embedded longitudinal wires. Uses include translucent walls, screens, lay lights and roofing. Large unsupported areas of glazing are possible, their size depending upon prevailing wind pressures and whether units are used either in single thickness or in double thickness so as to form thermal insulating cavities.

Panels must be firmly held at all edges but have clearances at top and ends to avoid any load being transferred from the structure. Internally, self-adhesive PVC extrusions can be used to seal the joints between units. Externally, in sheltered conditions special compressible *Neoprene* gaskets can be used to give a 4 mm joint. In severe exposures and in greater lengths preformed mastic strips with an external capping of butyl or polysulphide sealant are recommended. Where mastics or sealants are used spring clips are needed to control the width of the joints.

e *Corrugated glass*

Corrugated glass produced in 6 mm rough cast glass, with and without wire in its thickness can be used for glazed walls and screens and for roof glazing. Profiles match 76 and 152 mm corrugations in metal and asbestos-cement sheets.

f *Glass domes*

Glass domes are made for use as roof lights in rough cast glass in sizes from 457 mm to 1829 mm diameter in 50·8 mm increments, and in rectangles up to 2·438 × 1·219 m. Certain sizes are available in wired glass.

g *Glass lenses and pavement lights*

Glass having a coefficient of thermal expansion similar to that of concrete, *lenses* can be incorporated in concrete floors and roof slabs. Lenses are pressed in moulds in 95 to 229 mm squares and in a diameter of 206 mm. Toughened lenses 152 × 152 × 51 mm are suitable for heavy duty. Resistance to impact loads is five times greater than that of annealed lenses and should they be broken they expand and the fragments remain in position, as they do also in fire thereby preventing the passage of flame and burning material. Toughened lenses withstand a thermal change of 180 deg C.

Pavement lights are made in white glass 101·6 × 101·6 × 22·2 mm for incorporation in precast or in situ reinforced concrete frames at the following centres to carry loads up to 1953 kg/m³.

Centres of glass	Depth of construction
mm	mm
127·0	63·5
152·4	101·6
165·1	121·0

h *Glass slates and tiles*
These match ordinary slates and tiles and provide an economical means of lighting roof spaces, farm buildings etc.

i *Copper lights* (electro-copper glazing)
Copper light units consist of glass held in very narrow electrically welded or specially interlocking copper cames. A copper strip is laid between the glass squares and metal is deposited electrolytically to retain the glass. They combine very neat appearance with good vision (wire is not required in the glass), and fire resistance. The LCC Bylaws 1965 allow a period of $\frac{1}{2}$ hour fire resistance for 6 mm glass 'in direct combination with metal the melting point of which is not lower than 982·2°C in squares not exceeding 15486/mm² in area'.

j *Leaded lights*
Lead cames soldered at their intersections have been used for many centuries to support small pieces of glass, often irregular shaped and of varying thickness. Today, large units of glass are sometimes used and without recourse to painting or firing. A range of cames of varying weights is available, in *round, rounded, beaded* and *flat* sections, including those with steel cores. Cames are wired to saddle bars which should be hot-dip galvanized steel, or preferably bronze.

Work on glass

Toughening has been considered on page 228. Glass can be modified in many other ways for utilitarian or decorative reasons involving some highly skilled techniques. These are often costly but the product has the inherent durability of glass. Processes include the following:

a *Glass appliqué*
Rich decorative effects are obtained inexpensively by sticking together with transparent adhesive one or more coloured pieces of glass. The spaces between the pieces of applied glass may be filled with pigment.

b *Fused glass*
A wide range of interesting and rich visual effects are obtained by melting pieces of coloured glass together.

c *Bending*
After being heated most glass can be bent around formers. Opals, tinted glass and wired glass may present difficulties. Uses for bent glass include non-reflecting windows, showcases and domes.

d *Edge work*
Cut edges may be ground and smoothed and if required polished. Examples of commonly used standard edge shapes include:

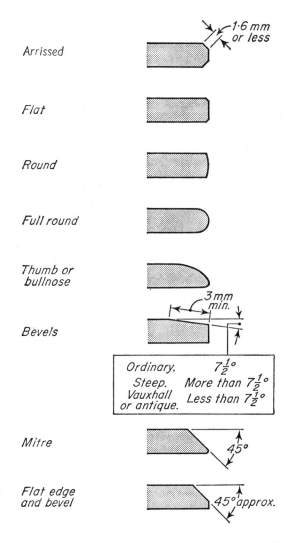

Arrissed — 1·6 mm or less

Flat

Round

Full round

Thumb or bullnose

Bevels — 3 mm min.

Ordinary. $7\frac{1}{2}°$
Steep. More than $7\frac{1}{2}°$
Vauxhall or antique. Less than $7\frac{1}{2}°$

Mitre — 45°

Flat edge and bevel — 45° approx.

e *Surface work*

1 *Brilliant cutting* Very precise incisions of various shapes, necessarily tapering at their ends, are made with a stone wheel, smoothed by a willow wheel with powdered pumice and polished with a felt buffing wheel. Edge lighting emphasizes the brilliance of cut glass.

2 *Engraving* Very fine incisions made with a small copper wheel, fed with oil and emery powder may be polished as for brilliant cutting.

3 *Chipping* Hand chipping of glass slabs gives a jewel-like quality. Typically 25 mm thick coloured translucent slabs are set flush in concrete reinforced with non-ferrous metal armatures or they are set in epoxide resin composition recessed 6·5 mm from the face of the glass. Variations in the width of the opaque concrete or composition provide their own visual interest. Concrete units made by White-friars Ltd with tongued and grooved edges are generally less costly than leaded glass units.

4 *Grinding* Surfaces ground with abrasives give a fine texture and varying degrees of coarseness.

5 *Sand-blasting* is performed by directing a jet of sand on glass. The process can be used to provide privacy or decoration. On polished pot opaque glasses, especially black, the textured sand-blasted surface is lighter and contrasts with the polished surface. The process can also be used to remove thin layers of opal or coloured flashed glass. Hard edges and various depths, including graded effects, can be obtained by skilful manipulation of stencils. Shaped holes such as keyholes can only be cut by sandblasting. There are five main finishes:

   (i) *Surface or matt* A flat obscured finish.

  (ii) *Peppering* A very light sandblast which does not entirely remove the polished surface, giving a mottled effect.

 (iii) *Deep or gravé* A more deeply bitten surface, parts of which can be filled with colour.

 (iv) *Modelled* Deeply bitten, but in varying depths giving a mottled appearance.

  (v) *Shaded* Graded from clear to full obscuration.

6 *Acid etching* A mixture of hydrofluoric acid and an alkali (usually sodium bifluoride) etches glass leaving a white frosted surface, smoother than a sand-blasted one. There are four main finishes:

   (i) *White acid* from one application of acid only.

  (ii) *Satin or velvet* from one application of acid followed by a neutralizing alkali

 (iii) *Embossing* Designs in relief are referred to as 'embossed' because they appear so when viewed from the reverse side of clear glass. Embossing may be *single*, *double*, or *triple* according to the number of applications of acid.

 (iv) *Stippling* results by strewing grains of mica over glass before it is flooded with acid.

7 *Silvering* Silver or other metals can be deposited on any glass, flat or textured, for decoration, to create the illusion of greater width, height or length in rooms, or to reflect light into interiors, to provide vision around blind corners or to create one-way vision. See *One-way glasses*, page 229.

SG or *SQ* qualities of plate glass are suitable depending on the optical standard which is required. High quality mirrors have a coating of copper deposited on the silver, followed by undercoat paint and a layer of enamel which is then stoved. In damp atmospheres or where there is danger of attack by sulphur, eg in the atmosphere, in clinker blocks or fixing media the back must be further protected by at least 0·075 mm lead foil. If attack by alkalis could arise an alkali-resistant coating is necessary. In special atmospheres such as hairdressing salons aluminium foil may be preferable to lead foil.

8 *Gilding* Both gold and glass are extremely durable and many ancient gilded glass mosaics survive. Nevertheless the back of gilded glass should be kept dry to prevent deterioration. Gold leaf, available in various qualities and thicknesses and in colours from pale lemon to deep gold, is applied on isinglass (a transparent fish glue). For ordinary work, the first layer of gold is *faulted* by applying leaf to any blemishes but for the best work two layers are applied.

Edges of the gold are trimmed and sealed with clear gold size, the back is polished, to give added lustre the gold may be scalded, and it is then protected with paint.

Other metals which can be applied in the leaf form include silver, platinum, copper, aluminium and tin.

Costs

Cost factors by unit area

Clear sheet

mm	OQ	SQ
2	100	119
3	114	134
4	195	224
5	315–420	356–485[1]

Cast glass

mm	
5 rough cast	192
6 rough cast	200
10 rough cast	294
6 toughened rough cast	510
10 toughened rough cast	646
6 hexagonal wired	227
6 Georgian wired	230
6 *Armourclad* (standard colours)	561
10 *Armourclad* (standard colours)	790
3 *Calorex*	179
5 *Calorex*	268
6 *Calorex*	330

Clear plate

mm	GG	SQ
3	621–961	
6	478–765	561–910
10	655–1245	
6 wired	820	
6 toughened	790–1280[1]	
6 *Spectrafloat*	990	
6 *Solarshield*	2970	
10	3620–4140	
6 *Armourclad* (standard colours)	946	
10 *Armourclad* (standard colours)	1150	
6 silvered (GG)	1051–1600[1]	

Patterned

	Group 1	2	3
3 mm	173	224	244
5·5 mm	336	436	480
Standard tints	306		
Prismatic	257		

Work on glass

Sandblasting all over:

coarse finish	212
medium finish	238
fine finish	289

[1] According to size.

Table 81a Approximate cost factors for glasses by unit area

9 *Painting* Coloured ceramic enamels, metal oxides and stains painted and fused on glass are equally durable as the glass. Examples of stained glass by John Piper are to be seen in Coventry Cathedral and the Liverpool Metropolitan Cathedral.

Glass-fibre products

Glass fibres were made in ancient Egypt. The modern products can be classified as glass 'wools', glass-fibre reinforcements and glass and staple tissues. (The name *Fibreglass* is a trade name relating to the products of Fibreglass Ltd.) They are used for thermal, sound and electrical insulation, as a reinforcement in plastics products (GRP), see chapter 13, in plaster (GRG) see *MBC: C and F*, chapter 13. Alkali-resistant fibres are used in cement (GRC).

Glass wool

Glass wool is produced from fibres about 0·0061 mm diameter thrown out from apertures in a rotating dish, or by dropping molten glass through apertures and breaking them into lengths by a blast of super-heated steam. The wool, sprayed with a binder and formed into random masses is supplied: loose; in rolls interleaved with paper; in quilts covered with bituminous paper and stitched with thread; in wired and asbestos cloth covered mattresses and in rigid and flexible sections and strips for lagging pipes. Bitumen-bonded glass fibres are provided as mats. Resin-bonded glass fibres are provided as *mats* and *boards*.

Glass-fibre reinforcements

Glass-fibre reinforcements are formed as continuous filament fibre which is used in the form of rovings or chopped strand mat made from 51 mm lengths of filament.

Continuous glass textiles

102, 204, 408 or 816 filaments are formed into continuous strands. These are processed to produce yarns for weaving into tapes for electrical insulation and into fabrics, including curtains.

Staple tissue

Staple tissue is made from glass strands drawn to 762 mm lengths by steam. It is used for filters, reinforcing bitumen bonded roofing felt and for battery separators.

13 Plastics and rubbers

Both plastics and rubbers are polymers consisting of large chain-like molecules. Plastics are dealt with here and rubbers are dealt with on page 256.

Plastics

Forms and uses of plastics in buildings include:
    sections, including tubes
    mouldings
    sheets and films
    cellular forms, see page 253
    adhesives, see chapter 14, page 258
    paints, see *MBC: C and F*
    plastics coatings, see page 198 and *MBC: C and F*, chapter 17.

Plastics[1] are by common consent taken to be mainly organic materials derived from petroleum and, to a small extent, from coal which at some stage in processing are plastic when heated.

Like paints, rubbers and mastics, plastics consist of molecules joined together to form chain molecules, or polymers which are normally randomly coiled. Identical molecules or monomers, when polymerized, produce homopolymers. Two or more different monomers produce copolymers (eg ethylene/vinyl acetate copolymers)

| Monomer molecules | Homopolymer chains | A copolymer chain |

Two distinct types of plastics can be distinguished: thermoplastics and thermosetting plastics. The *thermoplastics* always soften when heated and harden again on cooling, provided they are not overheated. Thermoplastics are described on page 243.

Thermosetting plastics undergo an irreversible chemical change in which the molecular chains cross-link so they cannot subsequently be apprec-

[1] In this context, 'plastics' is a singular noun, not to be confused with the adjective 'plastic'.

iably softened by heat. Excessive heating causes charring. Thermosetting plastics are described on page 249.

The range of properties in plastics materials is so great that generalizations are of limited value. Generally, however, plastics are light in weight, have good strength : weight ratios, are durable and they resist a wide range of chemicals. They have low thermal conductivity and are *combustible* as defined by BS 476. Properties vary widely depending upon the basic formulation and the presence of additives such as stabilizers, ultra-violet absorbers, fire retardants, reinforcements, fillers and pigments. Table 82 gives typical properties of plastics used in building.

Plastics lend themselves to a wide range of manufacturing techniques, and products are available in a wide range of forms, solid and cellular, from soft and flexible to rigid, from transparent to opaque, and in all colours and textures.

Plastics for building are dealt with in the following publications:

Plastics and You, R. Lushington, Pan 1967
Plastics, Rubbers and Fibres, L. Chubb, Pan 1967 (good descriptions of methods of manufacture)
Plastics in the Modern World, E. G. Couzens and V. E. Yarsley, Penguin Books Ltd 1968
Plastics in the Building Industry, P. Reboul and R. G. Bruce Mitchell, George Newnes 1968
Plastics, E. G. Couzens and V. E. Yarsley, Pelican 1968 (August) New Building Group
Publications of the British Plastics Federation, 47–48 Piccadilly, London, W1, eg *Insulation Products* and *Corrugated Plastics Sheeting*

(Information about Plastics can be obtained from the Information Department of the Federation.)

Material	Density kg/m^3	Coefficient of linear expansion per deg C × 10^{-3} and mm/m/deg C	Max. temperature recommended for continuous operation °C	Tensile strength N/mm^2	Behaviour in fire
Thermoplastics Polythene:[1]					
Low density	913	0·198	72	6·89–15·9	Melts and burns like
High density	945	0·144	94	20·7–37·9	paraffin wax
Polypropylene	897	0·108	110	34·5	
Polystyrene	1041	0·072	70	41·4	Melts and burns readily
Polymethyl methacrylate (acrylic)	1185	0·072	70	68·9	
Rigid PVC[2] (UPVC)[3]	1394	0·054	56	55·1	Melts but burns only with great difficulty
Plasticized PVC[2]	1281	0·072	38–66	10·3–24·1	Melts, may burn – depending on plasticizer used
Nylon	1121	0·081	80–121	48·3–82·8	Melts, burns only with difficulty
Thermosetting Phenolic laminates	1410	0·027	121	82·8	Highly resistant to ignition
Melamine laminates	1442	0·027	121	96·5	
GRP[4] laminates	1602	0·018	93	138	Usually inflammable, but relatively flame-retardant grades are available

[1] High density and low density polythene differ in their basic physical properties, the former being harder and more rigid than the latter. The values shown are for typical materials but may vary considerably, depending on composition and method of manufacture.
[2] PVC = Polyvinyl chloride.
[3] UPVC = Unplasticized polyvinyl chloride
[4] GRP = Glass-reinforced polyester

Table 82 Typical properties of plastics used in building information based on BRS Digest 69

PROPERTIES OF PLASTICS

The present lack of interrelation between test methods and of a co-ordinated and agreed system for comparing the properties of different plastics materials is being rectified by the BSI. However, it cannot be overemphasized that test results rarely relate directly to the conditions in which materials will be used and, in the absence of expert advice, they should be taken only as a general guide.

Specific gravity

This is similar to that of wood, about 0·9 to 2·2.

Strength

Plastics have tensile strength: weight ratios which are much more favourable than those of most metals but the modulus of elasticity (E) is low, even compared to aluminium and glass, and rules them out for load-bearing beams. Thermoplastics are also precluded from such use by their tendency to creep under sustained loading coupled with a serious loss of strength at elevated temperatures.

However, the low modulus of elasticity ceases to be a disadvantage in continuous surface structures in which the load is uniformly distributed over the whole surface and these structures are also better adapted to accommodate the characteristically high thermal movement of plastics materials. They would also accommodate creep although most surface structures are likely to be formed in a thermosetting material in which creep is very small.

Behaviour at elevated temperatures

Creep and degradation are more rapid at high temperatures and strength properties are reduced. Thermoplastics soften at points which are not well defined, in most cases between 60 and 110°C.

Behaviour in fire

All plastics are combustible and *spread of flame*[1] over the surfaces of some plastics is high. However, by reason of the inherent molecular characteristics of plastics such as PVC, or by the inclusion of fire retardant additives, many plastics are very difficult to ignite, and some are self-extinguishing.

For example, an element comprising two skins of glass fibre reinforced polyester with a 19 mm cellular phenolic core, had a 'fire resistance'[1] of 15 minutes when tested by the Fire Research Station.

Thermal conductivity

For 'solid' plastics this property is also similar to that of wood. Expanded plastics have considerably lower values. See page 254.

[1] As defined by BS 476: 1953. See chapter 1, page 36.

Electrical properties

Plastics are excellent insulators but electrostatic charges attract dust and the sparking can be a hazard where inflammable vapours are present.

Thermal movement

Thermal expansion of plastics materials is generally several times, and in some cases as much as ten times, that of steel. For example, a 3·7 m long rigid PVC gutter expands about 6 mm in response to normal temperature variations in this country.

Moisture movement

Most plastics absorb very little water; the chief exceptions, cellulose acetate and certain types of nylon, swell with moisture absorption.

Durability

Plastics do not rot or corrode and in general they have extremely good resistance to the chemicals normally encountered in building work.

The performances of plastics products vary widely with the type and grade of polymer and with any compounding ingredients used, the control exercised in manufacture and the dirt deposits, temperature and weather peculiar to the situation in which they are exposed.

BRS Digest 69 *Applications and durability of plastics* points out that few plastics have been available long enough to assess their durability in use. For the time being, predictions must rely largely upon knowledge of composition and manufacture, and upon accelerated laboratory ageing tests.

The Digest states: 'Sunlight, particularly its ultraviolet component, is the most significant single factor responsible for the breakdown of plastics and for producing changes of colour. Ultra-violet radiation initiates many of the chemical reactions by which plastics are oxidized and degraded. These are often chain reactions which are accelerated by favourable conditions of warmth, oxygen and moisture.' An increase in temperature of about 10 deg C doubles the rate of chemical reactions which lead to breakdown. Moisture is needed for many reactions initiated by ultra-violet light to continue and often contributes to loss of bond between resins and fillers or reinforcement.

Moist salt-laden air combined with a high

ultra-violet light intensity in coastal exposures present severe conditions, while the combined effects of warmth, moisture and sunlight in the tropics are much more drastic. However pigments, and also dirt deposits, filter ultra-violet light and reduce the rate of breakdown and some plastic materials, in particular acrylics and polyvinyl chloride, have retained their physical properties well externally for a number of years. Colour retention, as in paints, depends upon the correct choice of pigments.

COSTS

Compared with other building materials the cost per pound of unformed plastics materials is in some cases high and machines and moulds often involve high capital investment. However manufacture is economical in labour, and complex products which in other materials would have to be assembled from separate parts can often be formed in one operation. Thus the cost per unit volume of products is generally favourable, and further savings may accrue from ease in handling, fixing and in maintenance.

	Cost factors by weight
PVC resin	100
Phenolic	110
Polythene (Low density)	112–140
Plasticized PVC	118–178
Urea formaldehyde	104–163
Polystyrene (unmodified)	140
Polystyrene (toughened)	170
Polythene (high density)	170–185
Polypropylene	170–192
Melamine formaldehyde	222–244
Cellulose acetate	252
Glass fibre reinforced polyester (GRP)	266–369
Acrylic resin	284
Acrylonitrile butadiene styrene (ABS)	318
Acetate	458
Nylon	556

Cost factors for common plastics (approx)

FORMING METHODS

Plastics articles can be formed by many diverse techniques, some of which are not applicable to other materials.

Table 83 lists the main processes for forming building products of which hand lay-up spraying and some foaming techniques are feasible on the building site.

Continuous processes

Extrusion

Tubes and complex sections can be extruded in thermoplastics by forcing the *melt* through a suitably shaped die and cooling it as it emerges.

Film blowing

Air is blown into an extruded tube to form a cylindrical balloon of film in thicknesses from 0·01 to 0·25 mm.

Film and sheet casting

Hot melt or solution is fed over a chilled roll or on to a chilled moving band.

Calendering

This is the forming of sheet by passing a plastics *melt* between hot rolls followed by cooled rolls. By this means two or more sheets can be laminated together or bonded to a hessian or felt backing as in some flooring materials.

Other continuous processes are:

Paste spreading } see *MBC: C and F,*
Spraying } chapter 17

Discontinuous processes

Moulding methods

1 *Compression moulding* Powder or preformed pellets of thermosetting resins are placed in a mould which is then closed, heated and subjected to pressure. The charge is plastic for sufficient time to fill the mould before the molecules irreversibly cross-link and the charge sets.

Apart from practical limitations such as shapes which present difficulties in filling moulds or which cannot be extracted from moulds very intricate mouldings are possible. Metal and other inserts can be incorporated in injection and compression mouldings.

2 *Transfer moulding* This is a form of compression moulding in which plastic material in a *shot cavity* is preheated before being forced through channels into a mould. The process can be used for thermosetting as well as thermo-

Process	Suitable[1] Material	Products	
		Precision[2]	Economical volume of production[3]
CONTINUOUS			
Extrusion	TP (TS)	1–2	A
Film blowing	TP	2	A
Film and sheet casting	TP (TS)	2	A
Calendering	TP	1–2	A
Paste spreading	TP	2	B
Spraying	(TP) TS	2	C
(with or without fibre reinforcement)			
DISCONTINUOUS			
Moulding:			
compression	(TP) TS	1	A
transfer	TP TS	1	A
injection	TP (TS)	1	A
blow moulding	TP	2–3	A
slush	TP	3	C
rotational	TP	2	C
Thermo-forming from sheet			
simple pressing	TP	3	C
blow forming	TP	2	B
deep drawing	TP	2	B
punching die process	TP TS	2	B
vacuum forming	TP	2–3	B–C
drape forming	TP	2–3	B–C
Laminating			
fibre reinforced products			
hand lay-up (GRP)	TS	3	C
mechanical lay-up (RP)	TS	3	C
sheet forming	TS	3	A
Coatings			
dip coating	TP	2	C
sinter coating	TP TS	2	C
Casting	TP TS	2	B–C
Foaming	TP TS	2	A–C

[1] TP thermoplastics; TS thermosetting plastics (less commonly employed materials are in parentheses).
[2] 1 high; 2 medium; 3 low.   [3] A large; B medium; C small.

Table 83   Methods of forming plastics products

plastic materials and is suitable for delicate or complicated articles.

3 *Injection moulding* Thermoplastic granules or powder are made plastic by heat and injected into a mould in which they cool and harden. The process is rapid, several small products are made together in a single mould and mouldings as large as a 273 litre cistern can be formed. Thermosetting plastics can now be formed by injection moulding.

4 *Blow moulding* A soft pliant tube is extruded and the halves of a mould close round it nipping

it together at the top and bottom. At the same time a probe punctures the tube, air is blown in and the plastics material takes the shape of the mould.

Cold water cisterns are being made by blow moulding an enclosed 'tank' and cutting it to form two units each of which has 227 litre (actual) capacity.

5 *Slush moulding* A simple method whereby PVC paste is poured into a heated mould, the excess is removed and the moulding is gelled in an oven.

6 *Rotational moulding* This is used to form large hollow articles such as cold water cisterns. A measured quantity of thermoplastics powder, usually low density polythene, is placed in a female mould which is rotated about two axes and heated so that the plastic sinters over the internal surface of the mould forming a wall of uniform thickness.

Thermo-forming from sheet

In these processes thermoplastics sheets are heated and made to conform with a single sided mould.

1 *Simple pressing* Heated sheet is clamped on a die plate and pressed into shape by a former. The process may be assisted in the early stages by a vacuum on the reverse side of the sheet.
2 *Blow forming* Heated sheet is formed by clamping it at the edges and blowing a bubble with or without a female mould.
3 *Deep drawing* A sheet is lightly clamped at the edges so it can slip and pull out in order to conform to the shape of a plunger which is pressed onto it.
4 *Punching die process* This is similar to deep drawing but both a die and a roughly matched punch are used.
5 *Vacuum forming* of preheated thermoplastic sheets is done over a mould which is perforated with small holes through which air is extracted sucking the sheet in so it assumes the shape of the mould. To form local deep draws the process is *plug assisted*. The size of mouldings is limited by the width of available sheets which is at present 1·52 m.

Vacuum formed articles display the interesting phenomenon known as *plastic memory*, whereby when they are heated, because heating of the flat sheet before forming was insufficient to re-orientate the molecules, the product tends to revert to its original flat condition.

Casting Casting in open moulds is possible in the case of polymethyl methacrylate (eg *Perspex*), epoxides, polyesters and even PVC.

Discontinuous processes described elsewhere are:

> Laminating: GRP lay up, see page 252
> Sheet laminates, see page 253
> Coatings, see *MBC: C and F*, chapter 17
> Foaming, see page 253.

JOINING

Plastics components generally can be joined by screws, bolts, snap action and by adhesives, and thermoplastics can be joined by:

Heat welding

The materials to be joined are pressed together and momentarily heated by: *high frequency heating*, *hot-knife*, ultra-sonic or by *friction* methods. Welding by hot gas and filler rod can be done on the site by skilled operators.

Solvent cementing

A very easy and convenient method of jointing materials such as PVC, *Perspex* and polystyrene, but not polythene or polypropylene.

THERMOPLASTICS

When thermoplastics are heated the molecular chains are able to move relative to one another. In most cases softening points, which are not generally well defined, occur between 60 and 110°C and up to about 171°C for some nylons and polyacetals.

On cooling, thermoplastics regain their original degree of stiffness, a process which can be reversed repeatedly, provided the material is not heated so much as to cause degradation. Clearly, thermoplastic products cannot be used near to sources of heat (table 82 recommends maximum temperatures for continuous operation), but thermoplasticity makes for versatility in forming methods. With a few exceptions, thermoplastics unlike thermosetting plastics, are softened and swell in various organic solvents and may be dissolved by them.

Thermoplastics vary from hard and rigid to soft and pliable and have wide ranges of other properties when they are modified by additives. Under prolonged and constant stress they exhibit increasing deformation with time (ie *creep* or *cold flow*) and permissible working stresses must take this phenomenon into account.

Apart from the natural polymer cellulose, nearly all thermoplastics are prefixed 'poly'.

The properties relevant to the main building uses of the following thermoplastics are now considered.

Polythene (PE)
Polyvinyl chloride (PVC)
Polyvinyl fluoride (PVF)
Polyvinyl acetate (PVAC)
Polypropylene (PP)
Polymethyl methacrylate (PMMA)
    (eg *Perspex* (ICI))
Polystyrene (PS)
Polytetrafluorethylene (PTFE)
Acrylonitrile butadiene styrene (ABS)
Cellulose nitrate (CN)
Cellulose acetate (CA)
Cellulose acetate butyrate (CAB)
Coumarone indene resin
Nylon (PA – polyamides)
Polyacetals (POM)
Polycarbonates (PC)

Polythene (PE)

Polythene (more correctly described as polyethylene), is one of the polyolefin group. It is made in high density (*HD*) and low density (*LD*) forms. Both forms have high thermal movement, are extremely resistant to many chemicals at room temperature and are good electrical insulators. They burn without external aid. They have high impermeability to water and to water vapour. A degree of permeability to gas does not preclude the safe use of polythene tubes for conveying drinking water near to gas pipes below ground (see *Model Water Byelaws* 1966 edition, HMSO).

Low density polythene (specific gravity 0·91 to 0·93) is resilient and very tough, particularly at low temperatures. It softens at about 80 to 105°C.

High density polythene (specific gravity 0·94 to 0·97) is less resilient and tough and softens at a higher temperature. Natural polythene which is colourless and translucent, embrittles and loses strength in sunlight within about three years. However, carbon black pigmentation increases the serviceable life considerably. Even items such as cisterns are often exposed to sunlight before they are installed and are required to include carbon black in their composition.

Uses include:

Cold water cisterns and floats Polythene cisterns which are designed so they will not be overstressed, are 'expected to last for the life of a building' and polythene floats 'appear to be very suitable'. (BRS Digest No. 69).

Water pipes Water is less liable to freeze but if it does so less damage will result in polythene pipes than in metal pipes. In other respects it is expected that polythene pipes of the correct gauge and density to suit the service pressure properly supported and fixed with slight *snaking* to take up thermal movement in long runs should carry cold water for at least fifty years. The high thermal movement of polythene precludes its use for conveying hot water in buildings.

The narrow temperature range suitable for fusion welding necessitates close control of the operation in a factory or a workshop on the building site. If this is not possible, compression joints must be used in spite of their clumsy appearance.

Bath, basin and sink wastes Polythene is not normally attacked by ordinary effluents including strong detergents and fats, and waste pipes are expected to remain serviceable for thirty years at least. However paint strippers, cleaning fluids and similar solvents can cause deterioration and polypropylene pipes are more suitable in such circumstances, particularly where very hot water is discharged.

Damp-proof courses and membranes In gauges suitable to resist building loads, polythene damp-proof courses can be expected to last indefinitely. BS 743 : 1970 *Materials for damp-proof courses* requires the materials to be 95 per cent by weight pure polythene with at least 2 per cent by weight carbon black the sheet to be not less than 0·46 mm thick and to weigh about 475 g/m². Again, the black rather than the translucent form prevents degradation by sunshine before installation. The minimum recommended thickness for d.p.m.s. is 0·127 mm.

Separating membranes Polythene film can be used as a separating membrane between screeds or floor tiles and concrete slabs. Tests have shown that a '250 gauge' film 0·064 mm thick separating a lean concrete base from a thick concrete slab offered only about one tenth of the resistance to relative movement of that offered by a bitumen emulsion membrane.

Chemical resisting membranes Polythene sheeting is permeable to mineral oils and petrol causes swelling but a *1000 gauge*, 0·254 mm film, can be used to prevent certain chemicals penetrating downwards into a reinforced concrete floor, or as an isolating membrane where it is desired to lay a screed on certain contaminated bases.

Temporary glazing and protection 'Natural' polythene film and sheet last for a year or two in direct sunlight or for three or four years in shaded positions if they are not unduly stressed by wind and of the appropriate gauge. Temporary glazing should be not less than *250 gauge*, 0·064 mm, and preferably *500 gauge*, 0·127 mm, while temporary roofing in exposed positions may require to be *1000 gauge*, 0·254 mm, gauge. Film containing carbon black, however, is expected to last for at least ten years even in direct sunlight.

Concrete curing Polythene film coverings reduce evaporation from concrete surfaces and where it is laid on hardcore it prevents loss of moisture downwards.

Polyvinyl chloride (PVC)

Polyvinyl chloride in either the 'natural' rigid form or made flexible by the addition of plasticizers, is versatile and low in cost.

PVC can be recognized by a greenish tinge to the flame when it burns and an acrid odour when the flame is extinguished. It has very good weathering properties and is unaffected by dilute or concentrated acids and alkalis. It is attacked by aromatics and is soluble in ketones and esters. It begins to soften at about 70°C. Creep is rather high and at very low temperatures it has reduced impact strength.

Ordinary PVC is not suitable for hot water pipes. Recently developed *chlorinated PVC* (CPVC) shows promise here, but the problem of accommodating thermal movement, although less than that of polythene and polypropylene, remains.

As in all plastics and paints, colour stability depends mainly on the pigment system. Generally colours, in particular reds and yellows, fade when they are exposed externally.

Unplasticized ('rigid') PVC (UPVC)

In this form PVC is suitable for soil and rainwater pipes. It burns only with great difficulty and is self-extinguishing.

Uses include:

Ventilation ducts These should perform well indefinitely if allowance is made for thermal movement and if they are not heated by very hot air or an external source of heat.

Soil and waste systems Pending the publication of a specialized BS the requirements for composition and performance of pipes for domestic purposes are those contained in BS 3506:1969 *Specification for unplasticized PVC pipe for industrial uses*. Joints can be formed by solvent cementing but long lengths must have joints which will provide for thermal movement throughout the life of the pipe.

The low softening point of rigid PVC makes it necessary to protect stacks against fire where they pass through separating floors. Distortion of ordinary rigid PVC waste pipes can occur with continuous full-bore flows at 70°C and discharges from some washing machines which are at 80°C or above may cause distortion after about two minutes. However, certain waste systems in recently developed chlorinated PVC (CPVC), are claimed to be capable of taking boiling water.

Rainwater goods Unplasticized PVC gutters and downpipes are cheaper than cast iron goods and the BRS state that although there is some loss of resistance to impact good service may be expected for twenty years or more. Owing to the difficulty in obtaining light-fast pigments, they are made in black, grey and white material.

Water mains Unplasticized PVC is stronger in tension and more rigid than polythenes. Pipes are made in diameters of 50·8 to 152·4 mm and much

245

larger to order. Pipes to BS 3505 : 1968 properly laid in trenches, or by mole plough, should have a life of fifty years.

Transparent and translucent sheets The natural material is virtually colourless but darkens with prolonged exposure to light and coloured sheets are available. Corrugated sheets, usually 1·6 mm thick, are cheaper than polyester resin glass-fibre reinforced sheets, but less fire resistant.

The Building Regulations 1972 permit the use of rigid PVC sheeting which is self-extinguishing when tested in accordance with method 508A of Part 5 of BS 2782 : 1970, for roofs more than 6 m from any boundary. Nearer to boundaries it can be used for roofs to garages, conservatories and outbuildings not exceeding 40 m² in floor area, and for roofs or canopies over balconies, open car ports, covered ways and detached swimming pools. PVC sheeting is also available with wire-mesh reinforcement. Flat sheet has been used for safety glazing in doors and windows.

Corrugated opaque sheets These should remain mechanically sound for at least twenty years. However, colour is likely to change within a few years and they may become rather liable to impact damage. If backed with thermal insulation and exposed to the sun, degradation will be accelerated and dark sheets may distort.

Electrical conduits and accessories Rigid PVC conduits are available in *light* and *standard* gauges (flexible PVC conduits are also available). Compared to steel conduits they are light and easy to bend and fix. Mechanical joints, which avoid weakening the tube by threading, and the saddles accommodate the relatively high thermal movement. Where necessary joints can be cemented to exclude air, dust and water. Although a separate earth wire is required it is claimed that the fixed cost of PVC systems is lower than that of steel systems. A British Standard is being prepared.

Window frames and sashes Lack of rigidity and high thermal movement has discouraged the use of plastics by themselves and at present they tend to be used mainly as a protection on wood and metal frames and sashes. Nevertheless, one manufacturer is producing windows having sashes formed with unplasticized PVC hollow extrusions.

Other uses of unplasticized ('rigid') PVC include expanded rigid PVC, see page 256.

Plasticized (flexible) PVC

This is very suitable for extrusion, injection moulding, calendering and blowing into film. The ease of ignition and rate of burning depend upon the type of plasticizer which is used.

Uses include:

Floor coverings The most important use of flexible PVC in building is in vinyl sheet and tile floor coverings, see *MBC: C and F,* chapter 12.

Sarking This must resist high temperature and wind pressure without draping excessively between the rafters.

Water stops The BRS state that 'provided they are of sufficiently heavy section to permit site handling and that differential movements between the concrete sections are not excessive, there is every indication that they will perform satisfactorily indefinitely'.

Preformed joint seals PVC extrusions have been used as loose baffles and as tubular or cruciform gaskets to be held in compression. See chapter 16.

'Clip-on' extrusions Sections of PVC are available to fit over standard handrail cores with a minimum radius of 76 mm. After heating, preferably with a hot air blower, the extrusion is fixed from the top downwards, care being taken to avoid stretching and to allow an overlap for shrinkage. Joints are butt welded by pressing the contacting surfaces together after softening them with a hot plate or knife.

Bright colours are available but where rails are exposed to sunlight, black PVC is recommended. Reinforcing bridges underneath the core are advisable at bends.

Electrical cable insulation PVC has good electrical insulation and it is water resisting, flexible and self-extinguishing.

BS 6004 : 1969 deals with *PVC insulated cables,* BS 6500 : 1969 *Insulated flexible cords* and BS 6746 : 1966 *PVC insulation and sheathing of electric cables.*

Flat roof coverings A proprietary sheet consisting of PVC laminated to impregnated asbestos is intended as a single layer flat roof covering, the laid cost of which is stated to be comparable with that of three layer built up felt. The manufacturer suggests that the covering will remain serviceable for over 20 years.

Wall tiles

Coatings are described in *MBC: C and F*. They include: dipped and sprayed melt coatings, *organosol* and *plastisol* paste coatings, film and sheet.

Expanded PVC. See page 256.

Cast plasticized PVC may be used as moulds for concrete.

Polyvinyl fluoride (PVF)

Polyvinyl fluoride has recently been used as a surface film bonded to asbestos cement, metal and plywood sheets. If it is not damaged, the BRS expect a decorative and protective life of at least 20 years.

Polyvinyl acetate (PVAC)

The uses of PVAC are limited by its low softening point to:

Adhesives for joinery, see chapter 14
Emulsion paints
Plaster bonding agents
Screed bonding agents } See *MBC: C and F.*
In-situ floor coverings

Polypropylene (PP)

This relatively new polyolefin material softens at a higher temperature than most common thermoplastics and like nylon and polytetrafluoroethylene (PTFE), a very costly material, it can be sterilized. However, polypropylene pipe systems for conveying hot liquids must be very carefully designed to accommodate its high thermal movement. Polypropylene homopolymers have low impact strength in cold conditions but copolymers are suitable in this respect for all normal conditions found in building in this country. Polypropylene is attacked by chlorinated solvents. Sheet is not so easily vacuum formed as PVC or ABS. Specific gravity is low, about 0·90.

Uses include:

Fittings for pitch fibre pipes
Traps to waste fittings

Waste pipes
Road gullies
Expansion tanks
WC cisterns, siphons, etc
WC seats
Chair shells.

Polymethyl methacrylate (PMMA)

This clear acrylic resin is best known in the sheet form as *Perspex* (ICI) and is also available as a powder for injection moulding (*Diakon*, ICI). A related form of resin is used in acrylic paints.

Polymethyl methacrylate begins to soften at about 90°C and can be moulded at about 140°C. It burns with a yellow flame, like paraffin wax, and has a sweet odour when the flame is extinguished.

It is not attacked by strong solutions of alkalis and it resists most dilute and many concentrated acids, fats and mineral oils. It is dissolved by many organic solvents and can be cemented by solvents. The BS for domestic baths requires them to be labelled with a warning to the effect that some dry cleaning agents and paint strippers, and burning cigarettes, cause damage.

Sheet material

Sheet material is cast in transparent, translucent and opaque forms in a range of bright colours and textured surfaces are available. Resistance to impact is very much better than that of glass although inferior to that of glass-fibre polyester resin products.

Unlike ceramics, glass and vitreous enamel, polymethyl methacrylate surfaces may soon lose their initial gloss and although easily scratched, they can be restored with metal polish.

Light transmission of clear sheet is about 92 per cent (glass about 90 per cent). Its ability to *pipe* light can be exploited in internally illuminated signs.

Crazing has occasionally resulted from poor annealing during manufacture, but when exposed to the weather sheet has good resistance to ultra-violet radiation and a life of at least 40 years may be expected.

Uses for transparent and translucent sheet include:

Corrugated sheeting
Roof lights including domes

Lighting fittings
Illuminated signs.

Uses for opaque coloured sheets include:

Sinks and drainers
Baths (BS 4305 : 1968 *Baths for domestic purposes made from acrylic sheet*)
Basins
Shower cabinets
Urinals.

Polystyrene (PS)

A low-cost thermoplastic, in its unmodified form (BS 1493 : 1958) is crystal clear but inclined to be brittle and can be recognized by a metallic ring. It is also available in *high-impact, medium impact* and other grades and in the expanded form. It is attacked by certain organic solvents such as white spirit, softens in boiling water and burns readily with a sooty flame. Transparent polystyrene yellows and weakens on exposure to ultra-violet light.

BS 2552 : 1955 *Polystyrene tiles for walls and ceilings* specifies materials, dimensions, opacity, colour fastness and finish of injection moulded tiles. Fronts are glossy or matt and backs are recessed to facilitate fixing with adhesive.

Sizes are:

101·6 and 152·4 mm square
101·6 × 50·8 and 25·4 mm
152·4 × 76·2, 38·1 and 25·4 mm
2·54 mm overall
1·575 mm minimum
} thickness

Other uses include:

Water-waste preventers
Lighting fittings
Concrete formwork
Paint (mainly of copolymer form), see *MBC: C and F*
Expanded polystyrene. See *Cellular plastics*, page 253.

Polytetrafluorethylene (PTFE)

This thermoplastic is highly resistant to heat and many chemicals and solvents and has a very low coefficient of friction. It is, however, very costly indeed and is used only for special applications such as sliding expansion joints in heavy structures and for wrapping as a film around pipe threads to lubricate them so that joints can be tightened by hand. The resistance of PTFE to heat is demonstrated by non-stick cooling utensils.

Acrylonitrile butadiene styrene (ABS)

ABS distorts at about 85°C, a higher temperature than PVC, but it deforms more than is desirable in an ordinary domestic hot water system and the cost is higher.

ABS is extremely tough and strong and retains good impact strength at low temperatures. It supports combustion, evolving black smoke in burning, and is recognizable by a bitter smell as well as those of styrene and rubber.

Specific gravity is low, ie 1·02.

Uses include

ABS is very suitable for vacuum forming and small boats and taxi-cab roofs are made in this way. ABS waste pipes and fittings and drain inspection chambers are available.

Cellulose nitrate (CN)

Cellulose nitrate, first developed in the form of celluloid in 1862, is water-white, easy to shape and has good water resistance. However, it is highly inflammable and in buildings it is used only for certain paint finishes, see *MBC: C and F*.

Cellulose acetate (CA)

This is similar to celluloid and is very tough but burns much less readily. In burning it can be recognized by a yellow flame followed by a smell of burning paper and vinegar.

It has high moisture movement, poor water resistance and embrittles at high temperatures and is used only to a limited extent for:

binder in emulsion paints, see *MBC: C and F*
lighting fittings
door furniture
coverings for handrails.

CA is also extruded as a tape with interlocking edges for wrapping spirally around circular cores to provide non-slip hand-grip.

248

Cellulose acetate butyrate (CAB)

This transparent material is tough and has lower moisture absorption than cellulose acetate.

It has been used for conveying natural gas and for illuminated signs and is also used for coatings, see *MBC: C and F*, chapter 17.

Casein (CS)

Casein is made from milk whey reacted with formaldehyde. It has a high moisture movement. It is used to a very limited extent for small items such as drawer pulls and as an adhesive, see chapter 14, page 260.

Coumarone indene

These resins are used as a medium in paints; as an alkali-resisting finish, as an electrical insulating varnish and as a binder in *thermoplastic tiles*, see *MBC: C and F*.

Nylons

There are many forms of nylon (polyamide resins) the most important in building being *Nylon 6*, *Nylon 66* and *Nylon 11*. Nylons are off-white. They are outstanding among thermoplastics for their resistance to organic solvents, oils and fuels and resistance to caustic alkalis up to 20 per cent concentration is good at room temperature. Among the few chemicals which attack nylons are mineral acids, phenols and cresols, although dilute aqueous solutions of these chemicals have little effect.

Nylons are tough, have high strength, excellent wear resistance, a low coefficient of friction and ability to absorb any particles which would score shafts making it a very suitable material for gears. Nylons damp vibrations and noise, and bearings can be run with water or even without lubrication. They can be machined by normal methods. They are good electrical insulators at normal temperature and humidity and have better resistance to high temperatures than many other thermoplastics. Unlike other plastics, nylons absorb up to 2 per cent moisture with some swelling and loss of strength. If a cold metal point is pressed onto a heated surface and drawn away, threads form fairly easily. Nylons burn with difficulty with a yellow flame and when extinguished a smell similar to that of burning hair remains.

Apart from its use as fibre it is used for nuts and bolts, castors, curtain rail and sliding door fittings and ball valve assemblies. The BRS states that: 'Nylon has been used in door and window furniture and cold water fittings and seems durable enough for these applications. It has also been used with encouraging success as coatings for railings and outdoor furniture', see *MBC: C and F*, chapter 17. It is not, however, suitable for hinges to fire-resisting doors.

Polyacetals (POM)

These have a dense crystalline structure and resemble metals in many respects. They are heavy (SG = 1·42), strong and rigid but they are resilient while having very little creep under continuous stress. They have high resistance to heat, abrasion and organic chemicals and dimensional stability is good. However, polyacetals are costly and their use is mainly confined to plumbing components such as taps, gear wheels etc.

Polycarbonates (PC)

These also have remarkable properties which may justify their high cost in uses such as vandal-proof glazing. Polycarbonates are dense, hard, tough, and have high tensile strength and ductility rather like a metal. They are transparent with a slight amber tint but 86 per cent light transmission. Polycarbonates are dimensionally stable, the softening point is high, about 130°C, and they are virtually self extinguishing.

THERMOSETTING PLASTICS

Cross-linking, which produces a characteristically rigid structure, is brought about by a chemical curing agent (*catalyst* or *hardener*). In resins such as epoxides and polyesters the reaction occurs at room temperature while in resins such as phenol formaldehyde (*Bakelite*) the catalyst becomes active only when subjected to heat and pressure. Generally, the higher the temperature the more rapid is the cure.

Subsequently, thermosetting plastics cannot be appreciably softened under the influence of heat, which is in many cases an advantage, and essential for structural adhesives.

The properties and costs of *thermoset* products are influenced very much by fillers such as wood flour, asbestos fibre, cotton flock, silica and metallic powders and reinforcement such as glass or asbestos fibres.

Thermosetting plastics are generally rigid and hard and resist scratching to varying degrees. Compared with thermoplastics creep is very small, although greater than that of most metals.

The main uses of thermosetting plastics in building are as impregnants for paper and fabrics, adhesives, binders for glass-fibre reinforced plastics and binders in paints and clear finishes.

The main thermosetting plastics are:

Phenol formaldehyde (PF)
Urea formaldehyde (UF)
Melamine formaldehyde (MF)
Resorcinol formaldehyde
Polyesters (UP)
Polyurethanes (PU)
Epoxide resins (EP)
Silicones (SI).

The main properties and uses of these plastics are as follows:

Phenol formaldehyde (PF)

Phenol formaldehyde or *Bakelite*[1], first produced commercially in 1910, is the cheapest thermosetting resin.

Various properties result from differing resin formulations and wood flour, cotton flock or macerated fabric and asbestos give brittle, tough and heat resistant mouldings respectively. Products are usually black or brown in colour. When a lighted match is held to the corner of a moulding the vapour has a characteristic odour of phenol.

Uses include

Mouldings, eg electrical accessories, door furniture, WC seats (dark colours)
Impregnants for paper and fabric laminates, see page 253
Paints, see *MBC: C and F*, chapter 17
Adhesives, see page 261
Cellular or foamed products. See *Cellular Plastics*, page 253.

---

[1] *Bakelite* is the trade name for phenolic materials manufactured by Bakelite Xylonite Ltd.

Urea-formaldehyde (UF)

A clear thermosetting resin; products are usually white or brightly coloured. It is self-extinguishing and has a fishy smell when it burns.

Uses include

Mouldings, eg electrical accessories, WC seats
Paints, including stoving enamels. See *MBC: C and F*, chapter 17
Adhesives, see page 261, eg for particle board manufacture
Cellular or foamed products. See *Cellular Plastics*, page 253
Paper and textile treatments.

Melamine formaldehyde (MF)

Melamine resins are clear but can be made in a wide range of bright and lightfast colours. They resist hot and cold water better than urea formaldehydes and modern resins are claimed to give good durability when they are exposed externally. Being hard and very resistant to cigarette burns they are used to surface *decorative paper laminates*, see page 261.

Like urea formaldehyde, melamine formaldehyde has a fishy smell when it burns and is self-extinguishing.

Uses

Mouldings, eg door handles
Clear finishes, see *MBC: C and F*, chapter 17
Surfaces to *decorative paper laminates*, see page 253
Surfaces to hardboards and plywood
Adhesives, see chapter 14.

Resorcinol formaldehyde

The chief use for this type of resin which is dark red in colour is as a water and boil-proof adhesive for wood, see page 261.

Polyester resins (UP) (unsaturated)

The available resins have a wide range of properties. Some can withstand temperatures over 230°C for short periods without degradation.

Polyester resins harden without heat or pressure and are used mainly with glass fibre reinforcement (see page 252). A different type of polyester is used as a film with aluminium deposited on it, stretched over a frame to provide a mirror. It is extremely lightweight and does not show condensation or cause injury when it is broken. Polyester resins are also used in:

Paints
Clear finishes } *MBC: C and F*, chapter 17
In-situ floor coverings with aggregate, *MBC: C and F*, chapter 12.

Polyurethanes (PU)

This group has an even wider range of properties than polyesters.

Uses include

Paints
Clear finishes } *MBC: C and F*, chapter 17
Sealants, see chapter 16
Foams, see *Cellular Plastics*, page 253.

Epoxide resins (EP)

For most uses, epoxide systems are provided in two parts, as resin and curing agent or hardener and the properties of the latter have considerable effect on the physical properties of the hardened product as also have inclusions such as glass fibres, mineral fillers and aggregates, fabrics and metallic powders.

Epoxide resins are extremely tough and stable, have excellent electrical properties and very good resistance to chemicals, especially to acid and alkaline solutions. They adhere well to most materials, including impervious ones, partly because no volatiles are released during hardening. For the same reason hardening shrinkage is very small. Adhesion to timber in wet conditions, however, is not good.

Uses include

In-situ flooring, see *MBC: C and F*
Concrete repair compositions
Paints, see *MBC: C and F*, chapter 17
Clear finishes, see *MBC: C and F*, chapter 17
Glass-fibre reinforced plastics, see page 252
Adhesives, see chapter 14.

Silicone resins (SI)

The family of silicone resins have several valuable properties including that of water repellency and of acting as a lubricant, eg in polishes.

Uses include

Paints, see *MBC: C and F*, chapter 17
Transparent water proofers and water repellents for masonry and brickwork, see *MBC: C and F*, chapter 17
Mastics, see chapter 16
An ingredient in floor and furniture polishes.

PRODUCTS

Various plastics mouldings and extrusions have already received mention under *Forming*, page 241, and under the respective materials, eg clip-on handrail coverings, page 246. Other products described in other chapters are:

Plastics coatings, *MBC: C and F*, chapter 17
Mastics, chapter 16
Particle boards, chapter 3
Adhesives, chapter 14
Floorings, *MBC: C and F*, chapter 12.

Products considered here are:

Hot water pipes
Transparent and translucent plastics
Fibre-reinforced plastics
Sheet laminates
'Improved wood'.

Hot water pipes

Tests carried out at the BRS on plastics pipes for hot water services[1] show that ordinary PVC and high density polythene are unsuitable, and ABS and polypropylene are likely to be suitable only in closely controlled and relatively low temperature systems. Recently developed chlorinated PVC (CPVC) has relatively good high temperature characteristics and 'shows promise'. It is interesting to note that even here, although thermal movement is reduced, success must await the development of an expansion joint which will accommodate movement which is three times greater than that of copper pipes.

Transparent and translucent plastics products

Transparent plastics are lighter and tougher than glass, do not break into dangerous fragments and

[1] BRS Current paper CP7/68 *Trial of plastics pipes for hot water services* by J. R. Crowder and A. Rixon.

some of them, eg *Perspex*, transmit more light than glass. On the other hand, they are more costly. They are more easily scratched and like all plastics tend to acquire an electrostatic charge which attracts dust. Also, their weathering properties vary but in all cases are inferior to those of the equivalent pigmented plastics, and glass.

The softening point of the thermoplastics is much below that of glass and all plastics burn, although flame retardant grades are available.

Transparent forms of the following plastics are used in building:

polythene (films only) polyvinyl chloride polymethyl methacrylate (*Perspex*) cellulose acetate cellulose acetate butyrate polystyrene polycarbonate	thermoplastic

melamine formaldehyde
   surfaces on decorative
   laminates
polyurethane (clear finishes)
epoxides
	thermosetting

Glass-fibre reinforced polyester resin products, which are translucent, are described below.

Fibre-reinforced plastics

These products are formed from fibres arranged in uni-directional, multi-directional or random patterns and impregnated with synthetic resin. Some complex shapes can be formed and very large mouldings are possible. The fibres are usually glass, in mat, roving or fabric form (hence *glass fibre reinforced plastics* (GRP)), but cellulose, asbestos and other fibres are sometimes used.

The resin is usually polyester, but here again, epoxide, phenolic and others are used.

Hand *lay-up* of the resin and fibres has a high *labour content* but the process is simple requiring only a rigid mould. Surfaces can be improved by withdrawing air from the underside of the *lay-up* or by pressing it against the mould by means of an inflated bag.

For mass production, mechanized spray lay-up is employed and hollow articles can be formed by winding resin-coated fibres around a former (filament winding). Articles such as water cisterns

and tanks are pressed between metal dies, giving water resistance superior to that obtained by cold contact moulding, greater accuracy and a good finish on both sides. Dies are often heated to give more complete curing.

Glass-fibre reinforced polyester resin products, especially those with unidirectional reinforcement, have high strength and resistance to impact, and a strength : weight ratio superior to that of mild steel. Stiffness is greater than many plastics although much less than that of mild steel. The best products are likely to remain structurally sound for considerably more than 30 years.

Externally, exposure of the fibres in poor products can slowly lead to the breakdown of their bond with the resin, and surfaces weather better if they are protected with a *gel-coat* of resin. Difficulty in repairing scratched surfaces makes GRP unsuitable for urinals and less suitable for baths and basins than PMMA. Some GRP sheet is now protected with a PVF film.

Typical unpigmented products have initial light transmissions up to 70 per cent, but inferior ones expecially in self-extinguishing grades, may suffer serious loss of transparency in 10 years. Colours exposed to the weather may fade in about 5 years.

Ordinary glass fibre reinforced polyester plastics have *Class 3 medium spread of flame* (BS 476 : Part 7 1971) but with flame retardant additives they can be raised to *Class 2* or even to *Class 1.*

Uses include

Translucent sheets (flat and profiled, clear or pigmented)
Rooflights (50·8 mm thick with honeycomb core)
Cold water cisterns and hot water cylinders
Cladding panels
Architectural features, eg church spires
Formwork for concrete
Moulded chairs
Shower cubicles
Roof edge trim – for mastic asphalt and felts

Window mullions 101·6 × 50·8 mm
Channels, up to 305 × 102 × 8 mm
Circular tubes, up to 152·4 mm dia. × 4·8 mm
Square tubes, up to 50·8 × 50·8 × 3·175 mm.

These sections can be used for a variety of purposes such as: guard rails, fencing, cable troughing and conduits and for light structural work.

One manufacturer produces windows with hollow GRP frames jointed with aluminium spigots.

Sheet laminates

Laminates of paper, wood, asbestos, glass fibres and fabrics can be impregnated with plastics and hot pressed into sheets.

Some products which are extremely tough have strengths approaching that of some metals and are suitable for mechanical parts such as gear wheels. Their appearance is however dark and unattractive and in time they lose gloss and fade.

Decorative paper laminates have a pattern printed on the top sheet of paper and this is surfaced with clear melamine formaldehyde with a matt, satin or gloss finish. In addition to a very wide range of standard patterns, artists' originals can be incorporated to order. The surface is impervious and highly resistant to organic and dilute mineral acids, alcohols, oils and in some cases to alkalis. It is easy to keep clean, does not taint foodstuffs and is resistant to burns by cigarettes so that the cigarette resistant grade incorporating an aluminium foil lamina is not usually required. However, the surface is scratched by coins passed over counters, and is not suitable as a cutting board in kitchens.

Special grades are now deemed sufficiently durable for use externally.

BS 3794 : 1964 describes *Decorative Laminated Plastics sheet* as follows:

Class 1 1·6 mm nominal thickness, with one decorative surface and the reverse roughened or treated to aid adhesion to a base

Class 2 3·2 mm nominal thickness, with a decorative surface both sides

Classes 1A and 2A include a metal foil lamina.

A typical product consists of ten sheets of kraft paper, impregnated and bonded with phenol formaldehyde. The laminate is 1·6 mm thick in sizes up to 2743 × 1219 mm and the back is usually sanded to give a key for adhesive.

Sheets can be sprung to a radius of 150 mm below which a *post-forming grade* is required. They must be adhered overall to a rigid background (they are available ready-mounted on plywood).

The edges of laminates are inclined to delaminate if they are knocked and should be protected.

'Improved' wood

This comprises resin-impregnated thin wood veneers superimposed on each other and subjected to heat and pressure.

Whereas the specific gravity of plywood is about 0·5, improved wood, by reason of the high resin content and the pressure to which it is subjected, has a specific gravity up to 1·35.

Particle boards

These consist of wood or other cellulosic particles bonded under pressure usually with urea formaldehyde, see chapter 3, page 93.

CELLULAR PLASTICS (FOAMED AND EXPANDED PLASTICS)

Some plastics can be formed into rigid or flexible cellular materials either by a chemical change which causes an additive to evolve gas or by aeration of the soft plastic.

BRS Digest 93 *Cellular plastics for building* and BPF Building Group Booklet *Insulation Products* are very useful sources of information. Table 84 gives properties of various cellular plastics and table 85 gives suitable uses.

Densities commonly vary from between 16 and 72 kg/m^3 so that although they are combustible, contribution to the *fire load* is negligible. 'k' values as low as 0·020 W/m deg C are obtainable.

Cellular plastics have either *closed* or *open* cells. Expanded plastics have a substantially closed-cell structure and foamed plastics can have either closed cells or cells which are mostly interconnected. Closed cells provide the best thermal insulation and products float on water but absorb very little. Those having a water vapour diffusance of 0·067 g/MNs are considered to be suitable as vapour barriers in building applications, although joints must be sealed, and an additional vapour sealing skin may be desirable. *Open* cell materials provide flexible material for upholstery and air filters.

Polystyrene

Expanded polystyrene is resistant to fresh and sea water, acids other than concentrated nitric acid, alkalis, alcohols and to animal and vegetable oils.

Material	Density	Compressive stress at yield point	Coefficient of linear expansion	Thermal conductivity at 10° C	Thermal resistivity (Reciprocal of thermal conductivity value) 1/k	Maximum temperature recommended for continuous operation	7 days' water absorption	Water vapour diffusance[2] 25 mm thick board at 18° C	Behaviour in fire
	kg/m^3	$N/m^2 \times 10^4$	per deg C $\times 10^{-5}$	W/m deg C	m deg C/W	°C	Volume per cent	g/m^2s bar	
Expanded polystyrene bead boards extruded extruded, with surface skin	16 24 32 40 (mean)	7 12 27 27	5–7 7 7	0·035 0·033 0·035 0·032	29 30 29 31	80[1] 80[1] 75[1] 75[1]	3·0 2·5 1·5 1·0	0·015 0·0095 0·003 0·003	Softens and collapses Flame-retardant grades available
Expanded polyvinyl chloride (PVC)	40 72	27 90	3·5 5	0·035 0·043	29 23	65 65	3·0 3·8	0·005 0·003	Collapses but burns with difficulty
Foamed urea-formaldehyde (UF)	8	Negligible	9	0·038	26	100	Fairly high	0·18	Resistant to ignition
Foamed phenol-formaldehyde (PF)	32	14	2–4	0·036	28	130	High	0·19	Highly resistant to ignition
Foamed rigid polyurethane (fluorinated hydrocarbon blown)	32	17	2–7	0·020–0·025	50–40	100	2·5	0·011	Generally inflammable. Flame-retardant grades available
Expanded ebonite	64	27	5	0·029	34	50	1·0	0·0003	Flame retardant

[1] These temperatures may be slightly lower for flame-retardant grades. Manufacturers' advice should be sought in cases of doubt.

[2] 0·0067 g/m²s bar is considered a suitable value for a vapour barrier in building applications but because of the risk of interstitial condensation within a cellular material, an additional vapour-sealing skin may be required.

Table 84 Typical properties of cellular plastics used in building (f.p.s. and SI equivalents are rounded off). From BRS Digest 93 Cellular plastics for building.

Cellular plastic	Form	Blocks	Boards	Sheets	Mouldings	Loose fill	Liquid(s) for in-situ foaming[1]
Expanded polystyrene bead board extruded	rigid	✓	✓	✓	✓	✓	
	semi-rigid		✓	✓			
	rigid		✓				
Expanded PVC	rigid	✓	✓	✓			
	flexible	✓	✓		✓		
Foamed urea-formaldehyde	rigid and friable	✓					✓
Foamed phenol formaldehyde	rigid and friable	✓					✓
Foamed polyurethane	rigid	✓	✓	✓	✓		✓
	semi-rigid			✓	✓		✓
	flexible	✓		✓	✓		✓
Expanded polythene	semi-rigid			✓			
Expanded ebonite	rigid		✓				

[1] For filling cavities or coating surfaces.

Table 85   Types, forms and uses of Cellular Plastics

It is very readily attacked by ketones, esters, chlorinated hydrocarbons, benzene, fuels, turpentine and ether. Adhesives and paints must not contain solvents. Ultra-violet light gradually embrittles surfaces but they can be decorated with water based and emulsion paints, with wallpaper or they can be plastered.

Expanded polystyrene boards are manufactured either: (a) from beads or (b) by extrusion.

(a) Beads of expandable polystyrene are heated to form closed cell products as light as 16 kg/m³ with a low k value of 0·035 W/m deg C and very low compression strength, 7×10^4 N/m². *Bead-boards* cut from blocks by an electrically heated wire have a smoother surface than those cut by a band saw.

(b) Extruded boards have a simpler and more regular structure. They are slightly denser but absorb less water and have lower water-vapour diffusance.

The Expanded Polystyrene Product Manufacturers' Association grades boards and blocks as:

EHD   extra high duty
HD   high duty
SD   standard duty
RD   restricted duty
ISD   impact sound duty
SE   self-extinguishing.

British standards for boards are:

BS 3837 : 1965 *Expanded polystyrene boards for thermal insulation purposes.* These are *bead-boards* not less than 12·7 mm thick for use in temperatures up to 75°C.

They are made in two densities 16 and 24 kg/m³. Each density is in two grades: *Grade N*, normal, and *Grade SE* which is *self extinguishing* when tested in the manner prescribed, with *spread of flame* equivalent in hazard to *Class 1* BS 476. (As a wall and ceiling lining the boards absorb little sound even in the form of perforated *acoustic tiles*.) BS 3932 : 1965 *Expanded polystyrene tiles and profiles for the building industry* deals with products which are usually made by the bead-fusion process. Pre-compressed boards sandwiched between a floating screed and a structural base in suitable constructed floors are effective in reducing the transmission of impact and air-borne sound, see *MBC: E and S*.

Boards are used as preformed roof screeds, wall and ceiling linings, as insulation to ground floors and below floor warming installations and as cores for sandwich panels. Boards are used for lagging cold water cisterns, but they are not suitable for insulating hot water systems, except those with closely regulated temperatures.

Expanded polystyrene can be formed, or cut from blocks, in special shapes including preformed lagging for cold water pipes. It can be carved and used as formwork to produce relief on concrete surfaces. It is useful for forming holes and channels in concrete where crushing will not occur and subsequent removal is easy by burning, solvent action or by mechanical means. Unfused expanded beads have been used as a loose fill for cavities and as an aggregate for lightweight concrete.

Polyvinyl chloride

Plasticized PVC is available in the cellular form as *flexible* sheets and as rigid cellular PVC. The cells are closed and very small and permeability to water vapour is low.

Expanded rigid PVC is more expensive than expanded polystyrene but much less flammable and it is relatively strong. In a density of 72 kg/m^3 the crushing strength is 90×10^4 N/m^2 and it is a useful core for thermal insulating stressed-skin constructions. The surface gives a good key for plaster with uniform suction. BS 3869 : 1965 deals with *Rigid expanded PVC for thermal insulation purposes and building applications*. It specifies two densities:

(a) 1·5 and up to (but not including) 24·03–32·04 kg/m^3 and
(b) 48·06 kg/m^3 and above

in blocks, boards and sheets not less than 12·7 mm thick for use in temperatures up to 50°C. It describes a self-extinguishing grade (*SE*) and method of testing.

Urea formaldehyde

The cellular product has poor strength properties but is comparatively inexpensive and can be injected into cavities in walls with considerable improvement in thermal insulation. However, foamed urea formaldehyde tends to shrink and fissure so that good control is required to completely fill cavities.

In exposed areas where walls may be subject to severe driving rain, walls should be rendered and the BRS states that: 'the technique should not be used in buildings where rain penetration problems have previously occurred'.

Wall cavities must not be filled before construction is complete in case mortar droppings collect on the set foam and convey moisture from the outer to the inner leaf.

Phenol formaldehyde

Phenolic foams from 16·02 to 320·37 kg/m^3 can be formed in-situ with special equipment by stirring a rapid-acting acid hardener into liquid phenolic resin to which a foaming agent has been added.

The material is self-extinguishing and can be used at a continuing temperature of 130°C or for shorter periods up to 200°C.

Polyurethane

The material is available in flexible grades with an open or closed cell structure and rigid grades with closed cells.

Density can be controlled down to about 24 kg/m^3 with a high strength : weight ratio. Foamed polyurethane provides excellent thermal insulation (k is 0·025 W/m deg C for a density of 32 kg/m^3). Although more expensive than foamed polystyrene, it is suitable for use at higher temperatures. There is no odour, transmission of water vapour is low, and dimensional stability and resistance to many chemicals and solvents is high. It adheres strongly to surfaces and is used as a structural core in stressed skin sandwich construction.

RUBBERS

Rubbers are similar to thermosetting plastics but differ in the ease with which the molecular chains are able to uncoil.

In 1844 Charles Goodyear (USA) patented a process for heating natural milky white rubber latex, a natural polymer, with sulphur to make a non-tacky product. In manufacture, acids are added to the latex. The spongy coagulum is first 'masticated', fillers, are added to modify the properties and price, and carbon black to increase strength in tension and improve wearing properties. After forming, the product is vulcanized by heating under pressure, usually with sulphur. The process is analagous to the hardening of thermosetting plastics, in which the individual macro molecules cross-link (or bridge) forming a three dimensional network, although in rubbers cross linking is sufficient only to provide the required degree of resilience. In vulcanization strength and elasticity are increased and sensitivity to changes in temperature is reduced. *Ebonite* is a fully vulcanized hard rubber.

Today, modified-natural and synthetic rubbers, often called *elastomers*, have a very wide range of properties and are used in many building products. Unlike natural rubbers, materials such as *Neoprene*[1] and butadiene-acrylonitrile have good resistance to oils and solvents. Butyl is extremely tough, has excellent resistance to acids, good weather resistance and is unique in its low permeability to air. Nitrile rubber has excellent resistance to oil and aromatic hydrocarbons and is used in adhesives.

Polysulphides have excellent resistance to oils and solvents and low permeability to gas. Silicones are resistant to many oils and chemicals. They have outstanding heat resistance and good electrical properties. Mechanical properties, however, are generally not so good as those of other synthetic rubbers.

Recently developed ethylene-propylene rubbers have extremely good resistance to ozone and to ageing, and look promising for use as roof coverings.

Uses include:

Adhesives, see chapter 14.

Adhesive tape.

Paints, see *MBC: C and F.*

Anti-vibration and sound absorption. Rubber is useful as anti-vibration mountings for machinery and as a floor covering or underlay to absorb impact noise. Rubber can also be used as resilient mountings for floorings.

Roof coverings. In butyl or composite *Neoprene*, *Hypalon*[1] sheets are a recent development. It remains to be seen whether cost is competitive with bituminous felts. See *MBC: C and F.*

Mastics. Butyl, polysulphide and silicone synthetic rubber mastics are used for sealing joints, see chapter 16, and natural rubber is often included in bitumen-based mastics.

Gaskets. *Neoprene* is particularly able to maintain tight contact with surfaces, but natural rubber, butyl and PVC are also used. See chapter 16.

Preformed seals for wall cladding joints. *Neoprene* extrusions are suitable as loose baffles and for tubular or cruciform sections to be held in compression.

Electrical insulation.

Thermal insulation. This is provided by *Onazote*,[1] an expanded ebonite, manufactured by the Expanded Rubber and Plastics Co. Ltd. Density is about 64 kg/m³. It has a closed cell structure and water absorption is very low, ie 1·5 per cent after 7 days. The 'k' value is low, 0·029 W/m deg C. It can be used continuously at temperatures up to 50°C.

[1] Trade names.

14 Adhesives

Natural adhesives, glues or 'cements' have been in use for thousands of years but recently the development of products which give rapid bonds, extremely high strengths and which are durable in damp conditions or where exposed to the weather has brought adhesives into the structural and mass production fields. Most combinations of surfaces can be successfully bonded, a large range of products is available, but some of them are highly specialized. In the absence of standards for quality and for methods of testing, the advice of manufacturers should be sought in the selection of adhesives for particular uses.

Good references are:

Adhesives, by Eric W. Allen contained in *Specification 1972*, Architectural Press Ltd.
Adhesives guide, Joyce Hord B.Sc., British Scientific Instrument Research Association.

Adhesion may be due to *specific adhesion*, *mechanical adhesion*, or both. Specific adhesion is due to molecular attraction between surfaces which are in very intimate contact, as happens where smooth sheets of glass stick together without any intervening glue, and where liquid adhesives with good wetting properties make similarly close contact with surfaces. Mechanical adhesion occurs where bonding agents key into porous surfaces.

For maximum bond strength surfaces should be brought into close contact to give a thin glue line. With wood/wood bonds a gap of 0·076–0·15 mm gives the greatest strength. The term *gap-filling* can be misleading. Although for many glues it is used in its literal sense, BS 1204 : Part 1 : 1964 *Synthetic resin adhesives (phenolic and aminoplastic) for wood – Gap-filling adhesives* describes them as those which do not craze due to initial shrinkage when they are used in films up to 1·3 mm thick.

Contact glues give *instant tack*, but generally surfaces must be clamped together until a bond is achieved while avoiding excessive pressure which would cause 'glue starvation'. Some modern adhesives give very good bonds even between smooth metal and glass, but roughening or etching of such surfaces is usually desirable.

Surfaces to be joined must be firm, clean, usually dry, and free from grease, so that the glue is not adversely affected either mechanically or chemically.

Glued joints are mechanically efficient. By distributing loads evenly over wide areas they avoid the concentrated local stresses which are the weakness of nails, screws, bolts and rivets. Almost all *wood adhesives* are stronger than most timbers, ie those having shear strengths less than about 21–28 N/mm². Consequently durability and convenience in use are usually the criteria in choice of glues for woodwork, rather than strength. Table 86 compares the durabilities of adhesives for wood. Wood preservatives and water repellents are not compatible with many glues: in some cases only resorcinol formaldehyde is suitable. Specialist advice should be obtained in this respect. At present no glue gives a permanent structural bond with timber that has been treated with fire retardants. Where there is an existing coating such as paint on a surface, the effective bond strength can be no greater than that of the coating to the base.

Joints which are subject to shear stress are stronger than those subject to tension, and peel stress should be avoided. It is important to note that although with overlaps up to about 25 mm the increase in strength is approximately linear, with greater overlaps it does not increase proportionately.

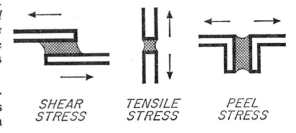

SHEAR STRESS   TENSILE STRESS   PEEL STRESS

Type of adhesive	Full exterior conditions	Semi-exterior and damp interior conditions	Dry interior conditions	Class (BS 1204)
PF RF and combinations	25 years expected	indefinitely long		WBP
MF MF : UF Fortified UF	5–10 years	10–20 years estimated		BR
UF	2–5 years	5–10 years	indefinitely long	MR
Casein	1–2 years	2–5 years		—
PVA	comparable with casein[1]			—
Animal	fail in a few months	1 year		—

[1] FPRL Bulletin no. 20.

Table 86   Durability of adhesives for wood

Adhesives set in one of the following ways by:

1 Gelling on cooling and subsequent loss of moisture, a process which is reversed by re-heating, eg animal glues.
2 Loss of moisture or solvent by evaporation and absorption into the materials being joined, eg starch pastes, PVA and rubber-based adhesives.
3 Loss of moisture and some chemical change, eg casein and thermosetting resins such as urea-, phenol-, melamine and resorcinol formaldehyde.
4 Raising glue which is water soluble to a critical temperature at which solvents evaporate and it becomes an insoluble solid, eg protein glues and some synthetic resin adhesives, although here a catalyst is usually required to accelerate the reaction.
5 An irreversible chemical reaction accelerated by a hardener or catalyst, eg epoxides or polyesters.

Shelf life is the time during which an adhesive can be stored without deterioration.

Pot life is the time available for using an adhesive after it has been prepared.

Closed assembly time is the period during which the parts can be moved to obtain the exact position desired.

The durability of adhesives varies widely. Forest Products Research Bulletin 38 : 1968 edition *The efficiency of adhesives for wood* describes the behaviour of many types. BS 1204 gives classifications for phenolic and amino plastics, summarized here as follows:

WBP (*Weather and boil-proof*) Highly resistant to weather, micro organisms, cold and boiling water, steam and dry heat

BR (*Boil resistant*) Good resistance to boiling water, but fail under prolonged exposure to weather. Withstand cold water for many years. Have good resistance to micro-organisms

MR (*Moisture resistant*) Moderately weather resistant and will survive full exposure for a few years. Withstand prolonged exposure to cold water, but only limited exposure to hot water. Resistant to micro-organisms.

INT (*Interior*) Withstand cold water for a limited time only and only suitable for occasional damp conditions. Not necessarily resistant to micro-organisms.

These definitions are also applicable to plywood adhesives and to plywood as described in BS 1455 : 1963.

Broadly, adhesives can be classified:

1 by properties:
   close contact or *gap-filling*
   contact or *requiring sustained pressure*
   internal only or *external*
   rigid or *flexible*

2 by materials to be joined:

eg ceramic tile adhesives, and flooring adhesives, *MBC: C and F.*

3 by composition of adhesive.

Adhesives are considered here under the latter heading with particular regard to their use for wood/wood, concrete/concrete bonds and for general purposes.

TYPES OF ADHESIVES

Natural adhesives

These include starch and blood glues which are used for cheap plywood, animal, casein and bituminous glues.

Animal glues

Animal glues made from hides, skins, bones and sinews are now rarely used except for hand work. See BS 745 : 1969 *Animal glue for wood.* They are supplied in the solid form or as a jelly for hot application, and as a prepared liquid for cold application. In dry conditions animal glue gives strong wood/wood bonds but above about 80 per cent RH it is attacked by micro-organisms, and even where fungicides are added animal glue and other natural glues are suitable only for interior uses.

Casein glues

Casein glue, described by BS 1444 : 1970 *Cold-setting casein adhesive powders for wood* is made from soured milk curds dried and ground to a fine powder and mixed with an alkali and fillers. The *pot life* of powder dissolved in cold water is 5 to 24 hours and hot-setting caseins have a *pot life* of 12 to 24 hours after liquid stabilizers or hardeners are added.

Casein is easy to use at ordinary temperatures. It sets by a chemical action which is not unduly sensitive to temperature, and by evaporation of water. In dry conditions the hardened glue has good resistance to heat and develops high strength. However, when wet it loses strength and is not durable externally. Casein is suitable for bonding wood to linoleum, plasterboard, asbestos-cement and to decorative laminated plastics sheets and

for general joinery – although the alkaline constituent causes dark red or purple stains with timbers such as oak which have a high tannin content.

Bituminous adhesives

BS 3940 : 1965 *Adhesives based on bitumen or coal tar* describes types for: (i) laying wood flooring blocks and mosaic, linoleum sheets and tiles, thermoplastic and vinyl-asbestos tiles, ceramic floor tiles and quarries; (ii) bonding roofing felt; (iii) bonding paper/paper and paper/fabric laminates.

Bituminous adhesives are available for use hot and as emulsions and solvent solutions for use cold. They have good resistance to water and many chemicals, but tend to flow at higher temperatures and staining can result from migration of the bitumen. Coal tar emulsion adhesives have less tendency to flow at higher temperatures, and the inclusion of rubber enables them to accept small movements.

Thermoplastic adhesives

Polyvinyl acetate (PVA)

These adhesives described by BS 4071 : 1966 *Polyvinyl acetate (PVA) emulsion adhesives for wood* are white liquids, transparent when set, which generally do not discolour other materials although some grades stain in contact with ferrous metals. They are easy to use and do not blunt cutting tools.

The water resistance of PVA is superior to that of ordinary animal glues although slightly inferior to that of specially formulated types. PVA is suitable for joints which will not be required to resist high continuous stresses, in particular for bonding joinery, paper, leather, cloth and similar materials to be used in dry conditions. It is used as a bonding agent to provide adhesion for plaster or mortar on smooth surfaces such as glazed ceramic tiles and in cement : sand floor screeds and levelling compounds.

PVA adhesives are provided in one part with a shelf life of at least six months, usually as a liquid but one product is in a gelled form with a resulting shorter setting time. Setting is by loss of water which can be accelerated by artificial heat.

Synthetic resin thermosetting adhesives

These adhesives are capable of extremely high strength, in some cases even when joining metals and although they are combustible their performance at high temperature is superior to the natural and thermoplastic types. They are in some cases extremely resistant to moisture and micro-organisms, but they tend to blunt cutting tools. Hardening is essentially by heat action which is usually accelerated by either a catalyst or hardener enabling practicable curing times to be achieved at room temperatures, or very fast times at elevated temperatures. The resin and hardener may be mixed together immediately before use or alternatively dry powdered resin and hardener supplied ready mixed are activated by water. Where fast setting is required the resin is applied to one surface and the hardener to the other, and hardening begins when the surfaces are brought together. In each case special techniques and close control of gluing operations are necessary and BS 4169 states that bonds of the requisite standard for laminated timber structures are rarely possible on the building site.

British Standards are:

BS 1203 : 1963 *Synthetic resin adhesives (phenolic and aminoplastic) for plywood*
BS 1204 *Synthetic resin adhesives (phenolic and aminoplastic) for wood*
    Part 1 : 1964 *Gap filling adhesives*
    Part 2 : 1965 *Close contact adhesives*
BS 4169 : 1970 *Glue laminated timber structural members*

Urea formaldehyde

These colourless adhesives are inexpensive and are widely useful in building where they are not exposed to the weather. *Uses include*: laminated timber construction, joinery (UF adhesives are available with exceptionally long closed assembly times) and in the manufacture of plywood and particle boards.

Urea formaldehyde is available as a one-part adhesive which includes an acid hardener, requiring dissolution in water, or with a separate hardener as a *two-part* adhesive.

Normal UF glues are classified as *MR* but inclusion of resorcinol or melamine in the hardener (*fortified UF glues*) brings the durability classification up to *BR*.

Phenol formaldehyde

Phenol formaldehyde adhesives are classed as *WBP* (not affected by weather or boiling). They are provided in an alkaline solution, or film suitable only for weather-proof or *marine* plywood manufacture, which set at temperatures from about 115°C.

A cold setting glue for timber assembly and constructional work is provided in an acid-hardened non water soluble form. Durability classification is *WBP*.

Melamine formaldehyde

Although comparatively expensive, these adhesives, like UF adhesives, are colourless and can be used for similar purposes and particularly for veneering where increased durability or heat-resistance are required.

They are provided as a film for setting at 100°C or as a powder to be mixed with water and hot pressed at 95°–130°C.

The durability classification of melamine-formaldehyde adhesives is *BR*.

Resorcinol formaldehyde

This reddish-purple adhesive is more costly than phenol formaldehyde but easier to use at low curing temperatures. It is available for curing at room temperatures, and more rapidly up to about 70°C. It has a long *shelf life* and the *pot life* after adding a hardener, usually in powder form, is from 1 to 5 hours at 20°C.

Although water soluble until cured, when hardened the durability classification is *WBP*.

Resorcinol formaldehyde is used to form extremely strong and durable joints in timber structures with a moisture content not exceeding 15 per cent at the time of bonding. For less exacting applications even higher levels can be tolerated. It is also suitable for bonding plastics, rubber and alkaline materials such as asbestos-cement sheets.

Epoxide resins

These two-part resin adhesives, eg *Araldite* (CIBA [A.R.L.] Ltd) are costly but possess remarkable properties, adhesion being excellent to almost all surfaces, in most cases both internally and externally. Epoxide adhesives can be resilient, electrical resistance is high and they are water and water vapour proof. They are highly resistant to water, most acids, alkalis and solvents.

Epoxide resins are transparent and ideal for glass showcases and for appliqué glass techniques (chapter 12, page 235), but colour can be introduced in manufacture. Most grades cure in 24 hours at room temperature, in 1 hour at 80°C or in $\frac{1}{2}$ hour at 100°C. Since they harden without giving off any volatile matter, shrinkage is negligible and they can be used for joining non-porous materials such as metals and glass. Metal/metal bonds can have a shear strength of 14 N/mm² for cold cured systems and 21 N/mm² or more for hot cured systems. Concrete/concrete bonds which can be stronger than concrete are being used increasingly, eg for bonding the precast segments which form the shell roof of the Sydney opera house.

Epoxide resins are used, with sand or powdered stone, for repairing concrete and masonry. Mortars with a 2 : 1 filler : binder ratio have a crushing strength of about 103·5 N/mm².

Dry bonds with timber are excellent but long term weathering or prolonged soaking in water can produce breakdown of the joint more rapidly than with conventional *WBP*, *BR* or *MR* adhesives. Also, because epoxide adhesives soften at temperatures ranging from 60°C to well over 120°C according to formulation, they do not qualify for the WBP classification of BS 1204.

Rubber adhesives

These natural or synthetic rubber-based adhesives are provided in a volatile solvent or as emulsions ready for use, either for application to one surface only, or as *contact* adhesives to be applied to both surfaces for a *two-way dry stick*. After allowing 10 to 30 minutes for the solvent to evaporate the surfaces are brought together and an immediate contact bond is obtained. There is little or no opportunity for adjustment, but contact adhesives are very suitable for bonding plastics laminates, fabrics, aluminium, and sheet floor coverings. Wood joints are not of great strength, and the tendency to flow under constant load renders them unsuitable for structural work. In general, these types of rubber adhesives are not durable in external exposures.

For fixing boards to walls, gap-filling conditions are obtained by bonding onto walls horizontal strips of adhesive-impregnated foam pads (*Bostik pads*)[1] and bonding the boards to them. This system has the advantage of accommodating any movements of the board and of the background.

[1] Bostik Ltd., Leicester.

15 Mortars for jointing

BRS Digest 58 *Mortars for Jointing* is a very useful reference on the subject of mortar for laying bricks, blocks and masonry.

Mortar should have good properties, develop early strength, bond well to the units, provide sufficient *final* strength without cracking or other deterioration, and be durable. Mortar must cohere so that it does not slip off the trowel too readily, but it should spread easily and remain plastic so that the units can be adjusted for line and level. It should also retain water so that it does not stiffen in contact with absorptive bricks. All this makes for a good brick to mortar bond, which is an important factor in preventing rain penetrating a wall.

Once the units have been laid mortar should develop strength quickly to avoid squeezing out by the superimposed load and in order to resist frost during its early life.

Final strength must be adequate but it is important to note that the strength of mortar is not directly related to the strength of brickwork, and for any brick strength there is an optimum mortar strength, above which further increases in mortar strength do not increase that of the brickwork.[1]

Where medium strength bricks are used 1:2:9 mortar gives brickwork 10 per cent weaker, and 1:3:12 mortar gives brickwork 20 per cent weaker than 1:3 mortar. Excessively strong mortar tends to concentrate the effects of any movement into fewer but relatively wider cracks, which may extend through both bricks and mortar, are unsightly and may admit water. With relatively weak mortar any cracking occurs as hair cracks distributed throughout the joints. Flexibility is particularly necessary in mortars used with calcium silicate and concrete bricks and lightweight concrete units which have high drying shrinkage. A relatively weak mortar is also better able to absorb expansion of new clay bricks.

TYPES OF MORTAR

Portland cement is usually the principal binding

[1] See *MBC: Structure and Fabric Part 2.*

agent, often with the addition of *fat* (high calcium) lime, semi-hydraulic lime to retain water and improve adhesion to absorptive units (see page 137) or of an air-entraining agent.

High calcium limes stiffen only as they dry out, and strength development by absorption of carbon-dioxide is too slow for modern mortars. Magnesian limes which develop more strength are used to some extent in the Midlands and North of England. Eminently hydraulic limes develop strength reasonably quickly and can be used where the limes, and operatives skilled in slaking and handling them, are available. To avoid expansion of mature mortar, slaking of lime must be complete before it sets and loses its plasticity. Because hydraulic limes do not possess the same degree of workability (*fatness*) and ability to retain water of non-hydraulic limes, they are less suitable for use with Portland cement. There is no British Standard for hydraulic limes: information on the subject is contained in CP 121 : 101 : 1951 *Brickwork.*

Portland cement mortars

Portland cement contributes high early and final strength, and rapid hardening Portland cement gives even greater early strength. See page 139. Both types are described by BS 12 : 1958.

Sulphate resisting Portland cement can be used to provide superior resistance to attack by sulphates, eg in sulphate-bearing soils, or in bricks or blocks which contain sulphate salts, although the added sulphate resistance of lean mortars may be negligible.

Portland cement, lime ('compo') mortars

The leanest workable Portland cement mix is 1 volume Portland cement and about 3 volumes of clean sand but such a mix is stronger than required for most purposes. By substituting non-hydraulic or semi-hydraulic lime to BS 890 : 1966 for part of the cement in a 1 : 3 mix, strength and the tendency to crack can be reduced, while improving workability, water retention and bonding properties.

Type of construction	Weather Exposure	Type of bricks or blocks[2,3]	Mortar group	
			No risk of frost during construction	Frost may occur during construction
Load bearing, engineering	any	Clay (class A or B, calcium silicate (class 5) or concrete	1	
Retaining walls	any	Clay class (A or B), Calcium silicate (class 4) or concrete	1 2	
Sills and copings	any	Clay (generally class A or B) Calcium silicate (class 4) or concrete	1 or 2 2	
Parapet walls (rendered)	any	Clay (with low sulphate content) Calcium silicate (class 3) or concrete	3	5 or 3
Parapets (not rendered) external free standing walls, work below d.p.c.	any	Clay (with low sulphate content) Calcium silicate (class 3) or concrete	1, 2 or 3 3	
External walls between eaves and d.p.c.	severe[1]	Clay, Calcium silicate (class 2) or concrete	3	
External walls between eaves and d.p.c.	sheltered or moderate	Clay Calcium silicate (class 2) or concrete	3 4	5 or 3
Backing to external solid walls	—	Clay Calcium silicate (class 1) or concrete	3 4	5 or 3
Inner leaf of cavity walls	—	Clay Calcium silicate (class 1) or concrete	3 4 or 6	4
Internal walls	—	Clay Calcium silicate (class 1) or concrete	4 or 6 4 or 6	3 5 or 3

[1] Severe exposure applies to external walls in districts with a driving rain index of 7 m²/sec or more, and to high walls in districts with an index of 6 m²/sec or more. For more detailed information see BRS Digest 23.
[2] Clay bricks BS 3921. (Classes are given only where strength is particularly important.)
[3] Calcium silicate bricks BS 187. Concrete bricks BS 1180.

Table 87   Mortars for uses   Based on information from MPBW Advisory Leaflet 16

Mortar group	Hydraulic lime: sand	Cement[1]: lime[2]: sand[3]	Masonry cement: sand	Cement[1]: sand[3] with plasticizer	
1	—	$1:0-\frac{1}{4}:3$	—	—	Increasing strength but decreasing ability to accommodate movement
2	—	$1:\frac{1}{2}:4-4\frac{1}{2}$	—	—	
3	—	$1:1:5-6$	$1:4\frac{1}{2}$	$1:5-6$	
4	$1:2-3$	$1:2:8-9$	$1:6$	$1:7-8$	
5	—	$1:2:8-9$ with plasticizer to entrain 8 to 12 per cent air	—	$1:7-8$	
6	$1:3$	$1:3:10-12$	$1:7$	$1:8$	

←————————————Approximately equal strength————————————→

————————————Increasing resistance to damage by freezing————————————→

←————Improving bond and consequent resistance to rain penetration————

[1] Normal Portland cement, or sulphate-resisting Portland cement where sulphates are present in soil, (see Cements page 138) or where clay brickwork is likely to remain wet.

[2] Non-hydraulic or semi-hydraulic lime putty. It should preferably be soaked at least overnight before use. If lime is measured as dry hydrate the amount can be increased up to 1·5 vols for each vol. of lime putty.

[3] Where a range of sand contents is given the larger quantity should be used for sand that is well graded and the smaller quantity for coarse or uniformly fine sand.

Table 88   Mortar mixes (Information from MPBW Advisory Leaflet 16)

Portland cement, plasticizer mortars

An alternative, and very common means of improving the workability of cement-sand mixes and thereby reducing their cement content, is by the use of plasticizers which entrain air into the mortar. The pores allow for expansion so that plasticized mortars have greater resistance to frost both before and after hardening, than cement-lime-sand mixes.

Aerated cement-sand mortars are also more resistant to sulphate attack than cement-lime-sand mortars of the same strength. On the other hand, plasticized mortars have poor water retention and achieve weaker bond with absorptive bricks than cement-lime-sand mortars.

It will be seen from tables 87 and 88 that aerated cement-sand mixes leaner than 1 : 8 or richer than 1 : 5 are not recommended.

Masonry cement mortars

Mortars based on these cements have properties intermediate between cement-lime-sand and cement-plasticizer mortars. They are based on Portland cement, together with a very fine mineral filler and an air-entraining agent which provide workability. The manufacturers' instructions should be carefully followed.

High alumina cement mortar

High alumina cement to BS 915 : 1947 (amended), see page 145, provides high early strength (but not quick setting), and superior resistance to high temperatures and to attack by chemicals including sulphates, but not alkalis.

It should not, however, be used where it will be both moist and above 29°C for long periods. Air-entraining agents increase workability. Alternatively, ground chalk or limestone may be added – but not lime.

SAND

Sand should comply with BS 1200 : 1955 (amended 1963) *Building sands from natural sources*. It should be free from clay, salts and other contaminants and correct grading is important. Both coarse and fine gradings require more water to achieve equal workability, with consequent reduction in the mortar strength. Very fine sand is not suitable for mortars for engineering brickwork with hydraulic lime. (Grading is defined on page 152.)

BATCHING

Measurement of materials should be done in gauge boxes, and *bulking of sand* (up to 40 per cent for damp sand, see page 158), should be allowed for. In the case of cement - lime - sand mixes the effect of bulking is reduced if cement is added to lime and sand *coarse stuff* just before use. Dry hydrate should preferably be soaked at least overnight to improve its plasticity, but if this is not done the proportion of lime should be increased.

MIXING

Mixing can be done by hand, or by machine. Prolonged mixing of cement-lime mortars improves their plasticity and water retention, particularly in high speed mixers or activators. Prolonged mixing of aerated mortars however may cause excessive air-entrainment and loss of strength. Aerated mortars cannot be mixed effectively in mortar mills. Portland cement mixes should be discarded if they have not been used within two hours after adding the cement – since their strength cannot be recovered by *knocking up*.

BRICKLAYING IN COLD WEATHER

Bricks should be kept dry before laying, and mortar should not be weaker than:

(i) 1 cement : 1 lime : 5–6 sand, (ii) 1 cement : 5–6 sand with an air-entraining plasticizer, or (iii) 1 masonry cement : 4½ sand.

Calcium chloride cannot be relied upon to prevent frost damage and, being a hygroscopic salt, it may cause dampness in walls.

POINTING

Integral jointing is preferable but if a separate pointing mix is desired, perhaps containing coloured cement or a special sand, it should not be appreciably stronger than the bedding mortar. Repointing of weak bricks or stones should be done with a mortar containing only sufficient cement to resist weathering.

SELECTION OF MORTAR MIXES

Tables 87 and 88 recommend mortars for various conditions. They take into account:

type of unit and its strength, moisture movement and density
conditions of exposure – internal, sheltered external or severe external exposures
frost hazard during construction
likelihood of attack by sulphates in bricks or soils.

Table 88 shows that the proportion of cementitious binder (cement or cement with lime) required to fill the voids in a well graded sand is about ⅓ by volume. Coarse and uniformly fine sands require a higher proportion of binder to fill the voids.

16 Mastics and gaskets

Mastics and gaskets are used to seal joints against rain, air, dust, odours and sound and may be required to stretch through the full range of combined moisture and thermal movements three or four hundred times a year.

References include:

BRS Digests 36 and 37 *Jointing with mastics and gaskets 1 and 2.*

BRS Digest 137 *Principles of joint design.*

A guide to the use of sealants and mastics, Architects' Journal Information Sheet 1603, 5 June 1968 by R. G. Groeger. The guide includes a list of standards and a list of products with their properties and recommended uses.

Flexible Sealing Materials, MPB and W Advisory Leaflet no. 70 (HMSO).

BS 3712 Parts 1 and 2: 1964 *Methods of Test for Building Mastics (other than mastic asphalt)*, standardizes terminology and test procedures only.

A BS Code of Practice entitled: *Cladding of natural stone and pre-cast concrete (non-loadbearing)* is in course of preparation.

Joint Sealants and Joint Design (1969): Bostik Ltd, Leicester, is an extremely useful reference.

Mastics

Materials which can accommodate a limited amount of movement, such as linseed oil putty for glazing (BS 544), and some materials for fixing tiles, glass and sheets are sometimes called *mastics*, but in this chapter the term is applied to *plastic mastics* and *elastic mastics* or *sealants* which adhere to surfaces.

Movements are usually small and fairly slow, but where they are restrained by friction, as happens in spigot and socket joints in aluminium curtain walling, a *slip-stick* action occurs and the rapid movement can cause mastics to fail.

Joints must be sufficiently wide to accommodate the expected movement but excessive width wastes mastic, which is costly, and the mastic may slump. Consequently the width of mastic filled joints must be related to the properties of the mastic to be used, the expected movement and also inaccuracies in dimensions of units and in construction. See BRS Digest 84 *Accuracy in building – where, when, how much?* and BRS Digest 85 (second series) *Joints between concrete wall panels; the design of open drained joints.*

If movement at a joint is greater than can be accepted by a mastic it may be necessary either to increase the frequency of joints or to adopt open drained joints.

FORMS AND TYPES OF MASTICS

The forms and types of mastics available are described in table 89.

FORMS

Mastics are made in consistencies suitable for application by hand, gun, by pouring or as a pre-formed strip or tape.

Knife or trowel application requires a mastic which is soft but not too tacky.

Gun application requires a soft mastic which can be extruded through a nozzle by hand or air pressure.

Mastics for *pouring* into joints are based on either bitumen which requires heating before use, or for cold pouring on polysulphide rubber or polyurethane.

Tapes or strips are available in a variety of shapes, sizes and hardnesses. They are generally only suitable where they will be held in compression without being squeezed out, or where movement is small and here it may be necessary to prime the surfaces to be joined.

Hard mastics are available for flooring joints and to take light loads, but usually 'spacers' or mortar must be provided to relieve mastics of all loads. See CP 202.

TYPES OF MASTICS

Mastics are based on viscous media with inert fillers and in some cases with solvents which facilitate application and then evaporate. The properties of the main types are given in table 89.

It is important to differentiate between *plastic non-setting mastics* and *elastic mastics* or *sealants*.

Plastic mastics

Most oil, bitumen, polyisobutylene and some butyl rubber based materials have *plastic flow*. (They are not plastics materials as defined in chapter 13, page 238.) They are squeezed out by constant pressure, or by pulsating movement such as those caused by the action of high winds on large panels and tend to slump in vertical joints more than about 13 mm wide.

The maximum recommended elongation for plastic mastics in butt joints is only 5 to 15 per cent although the rate, rather than the extent of movement, determines their ability to retain adhesion and cohesion. Where movement is small and slow good quality oil-based (oleo-resinous) mastics are likely to be satisfactory in the more sheltered positions.

Butyl mastics are suitable for bedding window and door frames and the better grades with low slump characteristics are usually satisfactory for glazing with beads. Acrylic mastics are sold for sealing gaps between baths, lavatory basins and wall surfaces.

Elastic mastics

Elastomeric mastics or *sealants* include polysulphide rubber, silicone, polyurethane and some of the butyl rubber mastics. Polyurethane and polysulphide rubber mastics are supplied in two parts, the base and a curing or vulcanizing agent, which must be very thoroughly mixed together immediately before use. The resulting product is sticky and is best applied by a gun. It is important to realise that it remains plastic for a few days, during which it may be unable to accept loads such as the weight of glass in sashes, however, when thoroughly cured, the mastic is able to accept compression without extruding, and to withstand elongation in some cases up to 75 per cent in shear. Polysulphide and silicone mastics may have some plastic flow but polyurethane is truly elastic.

Greater stresses are imposed on adhesion to joint surfaces by elastic sealants than by plastic materials and to avoid adhesion failure, soft elastic sealants are preferred.

Elastic mastics are durable but costly, and in order to take full advantage of their superior flexibility joints must be, as far as possible, of uniformly optimum width and depth. These conditions of accuracy are possible in metal assemblies such as curtain walling and here elastic mastics may be essential to accommodate *stick-slip* movements with only short periods spent at full elongation. High grade sealants such as polysulphide or silicone are also very suitable for capping two-stage joints; sealed inside with mastic strips or with preformed synthetic rubber gaskets, and are advisable for pointing around windows and doors in the more exposed weather conditions.

Two-part polysulphide sealants are probably best for glazing with beads, and for narrow joints in external tiling and mosaics (see *MBC: C and F*), where movement is often considerable. Joints in flooring should be filled with a hard grade of sealant to minimize dirtying and treading in of grit.

Silicone products, which are obtainable in a translucent form, a very durable white and a wide range of colours, are very suitable for sealing around baths, sinks and basins and for joints in wall tiling.

SELECTION OF MASTICS

Manufacturers should be consulted at an early stage in the design of joints and their written assurance should be obtained as to the suitability of the materials they recommend.

Not all of the very wide range of types and formulations with widely varying properties are provided by all manufacturers.

Mastics, especially those which satisfy the more exacting requirements, are costly both to buy and to apply, so that a long life is very desirable. However, although the effects of fourteen days' storage at 70°C, usually approximate to those of a year's natural weathering, laboratory ageing tests on new materials require years of correlation with field experience.

Factors which must be taken into account in the selection of mastics include:

Function of joint
Weather seal in cladding; flooring movement joints; glazing.
Exposure of joint
Maximum total extension of joint and toleration of movement of mastic
Compatibility with other materials
Other surfaces, alkalis in concrete; primers; back-up materials; setting blocks; other mastics.
Durability
Freedom from: adhesion failure; cracking; crazing; cohesive tearing; slump in open joints; hardening.
Resistance to: weather; traffic.

Position of joint and ease of application of mastic
Vertical; horizontal; upward or downward facing; accessibility.
Appearance
Tendency to stain adjacent materials; colour; suitability for paintings.
Cost
Mastic, fillers; primers, etc; labour; 'cost-in-use'.

DESIGN OF JOINTS

This subject is dealt with in *Mitchell's Building Construction: Structure and Fabric* Part 2 but some considerations relevant to the use of mastics are discussed here.

Because the life of mastics is much shorter where they are exposed to the action of light and air, and where they are subject to the movements which are greater on exposed faces 'where possible, complete reliance against rain and wind penetration should not be placed on the mastic seal'. (BRS Digest 36) Thus, provided they are accessible should renewal ever be necessary, mastics are best protected from the weather and used mainly as air and dust seals, see figure 46 and the lap joints in figures 47 and 48.

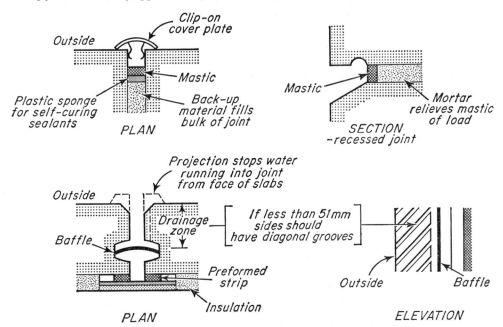

46   *Mastics in protected positions*

Medium	Nature	Available forms	Skinning setting or tack-free time hours	Maximum width of joints[1] mm	Maximum total extension in service Butt joints per cent	Shear joints per cent	Minimum depth of ... in join mm
Oleo-resinous one part	Plastic form skin	strip knife grades gun grades	24 24 24	51 25 13 25–31 special grades	2 5–15 15	5 20 30 (better grades 40)	6 9·5 13 up to 25; for very joints
Bitumen-rubber one part (BS 2499 : 1966 *Hot applied joint sealing compounds for concrete pavements*)	Mainly plastic some form a skin	strip knife grades gun grades (solvent type) pourable grades (for hot application in horizontal joints in paving)	— — — when cool	51 25 or more 13 up to 51·0 (horizontal joints)	10 10 10 10–15	20 20 20 20–30	6 13 19 19
Butyl (and related polymers) one part	Plastic some form a skin and Elastic types	strip knife grades gun grades	— 24 24	51 25 13 25 (special grades and techniques)	2–10 2–10 5–15	5–25 5–25 10–40	6 6[4] 6[4]
Acrylic one part	Plastic with slight elastic 'memory'	gun grades	12	13 (or wider by use of special techniques)	15 25 (terpolymer type)	30	6[4]
Polysulphide one part (US Federal specification TT-S-00230)		gun grade	24	19	15[2]	30[3]	6[4]
two part (BS 4254 : 1967 *Two-part polysulphide-based sealing compounds for the building industry*)	Elastomeric may have some plastic flow	gun grades pourable grades	48 24	13 25 or wider by use of special techniques	15–33[2] 15–33	40–75[3] 40–75[3]	6[4] 6[4]
Silicone one-part	Elastomeric may have some plastic flow	gun grades	2 (full cure takes 7–14 days)	25 (or wider by use of special techniques)	probably similar to polysulphide sealants		6[4]
Polyurethane two-part	Elastomeric	knife grades gun grades pourable grades	24	51	probably 20	probably 50	6[4]

[1] The minimum width should be preferably 6 mm and never less than 3 mm.

Table 89   Mastics for movement joints (the information is intended as a guide only and the advice of m facturers should be obtained in the design of joints and selection of mastics, primers and back-up materi

Comments		Colour	Life expectancy in external movement joints (years)
ace oxidizes rapidly, but in particular, gun grade mastic remains soft below tection, if only by paint, prolongs life iesion: fair-good. Strip mastics may require primers. y slow movements can cause cohesive failure.		Grey and wide range of colours	2–10
rable grades generally more flexible than the solvent type but overheating destroys r properties. Very suitable for joints in mastic asphalt and tarmacadam paving ace tends to oxidize, craze and discolour icult to paint iesion: fair		Black	2–3 (solvent type)
			5–10 (hot applied)
e range of properties y to place and recent formulations retain softness well ability is affected by nature of movement. Some butyl mastics split through the re when subjected to repeated slow movements. Dark colours have superior ability iesion: fair. Some strip mastics require primers d resistance to alkalis		Grey and black (standard)	2–15
ave similarly to many butyl mastics st be applied 'hot' 50°C ht dirt pick-up ole to breakdown if subjected to prolonged wetting		White and wide range of colours	15–25
ners are required to provide adhesion to ous or friable surfaces and on the inside lass to prevent loss of adhesion caused unlight passing through aline surfaces may require to be sealed revent staining during the curing od istance to acids, alkalis, petroleum and ents is generally good, but not to rinated hydrocarbons, eg trichloroethy-	Cure by absorption of moisture. A skin forms rapidly but cure of interior may be very slow, particularly in large joints and in cold dry weather. Not suitable where appreciable movement is likely before curing is complete. It is recommended that the two-part type should be used where the calculated movement exceeds 10 per cent	Aluminium black also available in dark greys and colours (not all colours are light fast)	15–20
icult to replace	Cure by chemical reaction rapidly at normal temperatures. Less risk of failure due to movement during cure than with one-part type. Extremely flexible		20–25
e by absorption of moisture from air, slowly especially in cold or dry conditions in thick sections although some types cure faster than one-part polysulphide seal- . able under water. Good adhesion, but elasticity places adhesion under stress and aration of surfaces is extremely important. Primers are required on most porous aces and on some non-porous surfaces		Translucent, white and wide range of colours but pick up dust which is difficult to remove	possibly 20 little British experience
ly elastic, therefore adhesion under stress is only fair-poor aration of surfaces is extremely important ners may be required		Cream grey, black	possibly 15 limited experience

maximum tolerance for movement is obtained where the width of sealant is twice the depth.
maximum tolerance for movement is obtained where the depth is not less than the width.
ater depths may be necessary to allow for inaccuracies in joints in masonry, brickwork and concrete.
th of mastic is measured perpendicular to the weather surface for shear (lap) or butt joints.

Butt and lap joints compared

Butt joints are easier to form, but for equal movement in joints the extension of mastic in a lap joint is only about half that in a butt joint. Also, in lap joints the mastic is usually better protected from the weather and should it fail in adhesion to one surface, serious leakage is less likely than with similar failures in a butt joint, as shown below:

Width of mastic

For given overall movement in a butt joint, the movement per unit width of mastic increases as the width of the joint decreases and the joint must be sufficiently wide to avoid overstressing the mastic. Joints should never be narrower than 3 mm and preferably at least 6 mm wide. Also mastic must be free to move over the full width of a joint, unlike the examples shown in figure 48

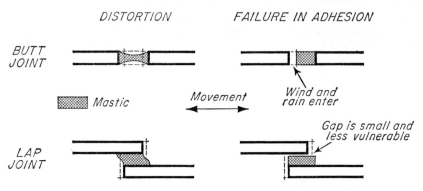

47   *Butt and lap joints compared*

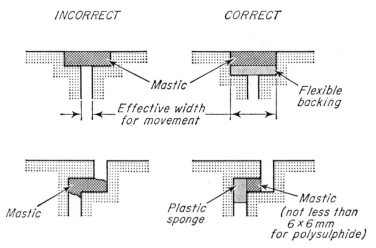

48   *Effective widths of joints*

Size of joint

The width and depth of mastic in a joint must be carefully considered. Table 89 shows maximum widths and minimum depths. The width/depth ratio is also important. See footnotes to the table.

where adhesion to panels limits the effective width of the mastic. Particularly where elastic mastics are used, a flexible backing such as polythene or polyurethane sponge is required to ensure that they are effective over their full width, and there-

272

fore subject to a much lower percentage movement.

The maximum extensions which various mastics will tolerate in service are given as percentages in table 89 and, if the expected movement in a joint is known, the minimum widths in butt and shear joints can be calculated.

Summarized, the design steps are:

(a) estimate movement due to moisture and thermal changes

(b) determine minimum width for the mastic intended to be used

(c) allow for manufacturing and assembly tolerances

(d) determine design width of joint.

Depth of mastic

Where necessary, *back-up materials* such as fibreboard, rope or expanded plastics, should be provided to limit the depth of mastic, and to give a stop against which the mastic can be forced to ensure good adhesion with the surfaces to be joined. In closed joints back-up materials must compress easily.

Oleoresinous mastics can be allowed to adhere to back-up materials, but with rubbery mastics adhesion to inflexible back-up materials can seriously affect their performance. With these it is essential either to use a suitable parting agent or to interpose a flexible back-up material such as polyurethane or polythene sponges, as may be recommended by the supplier of the mastic. See figure 48.

APPLICATION OF MASTICS

Good workmanship is essential for forming satisfactory joints with mastics and specially trained operatives should be employed.

As far as possible, application of mastics is best delayed until irreversible drying shrinkage of concrete, and settlements have taken place. Surfaces to be joined must be free from loose matter and clean. Aluminium, especially extrusions, must be cleaned with solvents, using frequently changed rags to remove grease. Surfaces must be dry; a gas torch or hot air blower may be required.

A primer supplied by the maker of the mastic should be applied to surfaces:

1 To reduce absorption of the medium from the mastic by porous surfaces, or staining of the surrounding material.
2 To prevent attack on oleoresinous mastics by alkaline surfaces.
3 To improve adhesion.
4 To prevent loss of adhesion by action of water, eg in new concrete.

Joints in ceramic tiling, and particularly in ceramic floor tiling, should be finished concave rather than flush, to avoid bulging of the mastic later due to expansion of the tiles.

Gaskets *see overleaf*

273

Gaskets

Gaskets of rubber or plastics depend upon being held in compression rather than upon adhesion to surfaces and unlike sealants they can be stressed immediately an assembly is completed. Cellular materials and tubular sections are more readily compressed than solid materials and sections and can in some cases accommodate twenty five per cent movement in butt joints.

Gaskets can be compressed by direct loading at the time of assembly, or by readmitting air to tubes which were evacuated before the parts were brought together. See figure 49 below. In either case, if a continuous seal is to be obtained even when a joint is fully extended, joints must be of reasonably uniform width and the sides must be regular and smooth. Alternatively, gaskets grip and seal the edges of panels which are snapped into slightly undersized grooves; or compression may be provided by keyed zip insert strips. See figure 50.

Intersections between horizontal and vertical gaskets can be weak spots and they are best welded.

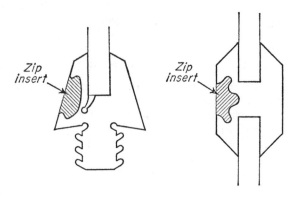

50   Gaskets for glass and sheets

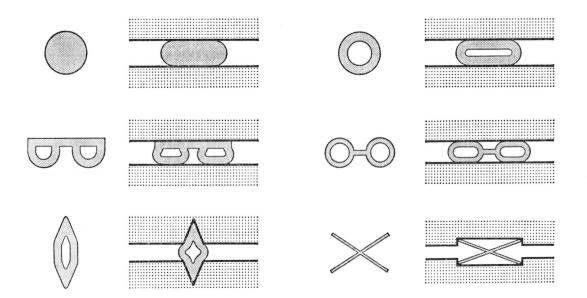

49   Gaskets for use in compression: shown before and after being compressed

Cl/SfB

The following tables are based on the *Construction Indexing Manual* published by the RIBA (1968). References are given to the volumes and chapters in *Mitchell's Building Construction* in which aspects of each classification are dealt with.

The following abbreviations are used:
- *E & S: Environment and Services*
- *M: Materials*
- *S & F (1): Structure and Fabric*
- *S & F (2): Structure and Fabric*
- *C & F: Components and Finishes*

Table 1 Elements

(1) Substructure

(10) *Site**
(11) Excavations, land drainage *S & F (1)* 4, 8, 11; *S & F (2)* 3, 11
(12)
(13) Floor beds *S & F (1)* 4, 8; *S & F (2)* 3
(14)
(15)
(16) Foundations, retaining structures *S & F (1)* 4; *S & F (2)* 3, 4
(17) Pile foundations *S & F (1)* 4; *S & F (2)* 3, 11
(18)
(19) *Building**

(2) Primary elements

(20) *Site**
(21) External walls, walls in general, and chimneys *S & F (1)* 1, 5, 9; *S & F (2)* 4, 5, 7, 10
(22) Internal walls, partitions *S & F (1)* 5; *S & F (2)* 4, 10; *C & F* 9
(23) Floors, galleries *S & F (1)* 8; *S & F (2)* 6, 10
(24) Stairs, ramps *S & F (1)* 10; *S & F (2)* 8, 10
(25)
(26)
(27) Roofs *S & F (1)* 1, 7; *S & F (2)* 9, 10
(28) Frames *S & F (1)* 1, 6; *S & F (2)* 5, 10
(29) *Building**

(3) Secondary elements if described separately from primary elements

(30) *Site**
(31) Secondary elements in external walls, external doors, windows *S & F (1)* 5; *S & F (2)* 10; *C & F* 3, 4, 5, 7
(32) Secondary elements in internal walls, doors in general *S & F (2)* 10; *C & F* 3, 7
(33) Secondary elements in or on floors *S & F (2)* 10

(34) Balustrades *C & F* 8
(35) Ceilings, suspended *C & F* 10
(36)
(37) Secondary elements in or on roof, roof lights, etc *S & F (2)* 10; *C & F* 6
(28)
(39) *Building**

(4) Finishes if described separately

(40) *Site**
(41) External wall finishes *S & F (2)* 4, 10; *C & F* 14, 15, 16
(42) Internal wall finishes *C & F* 13, 15
(43) Floor finishes *C & F* 12
(44) Stair finishes *C & F* 12
(45) Ceiling finishes *C & F* 13
(46)
(47) Roof finishes *S & F (2)*; *C & F* 18
(48)
(49) *Building**

(5) Services (mainly piped, ducted)

(50) *Site**
(51) Refuse disposal *E & S* 13
(52) Drainage *E & S* 11, 12
(53) Hot and cold water *E & S* 9, 10; *S & F (1)* 9; *S & F (2)* 6, 10
(54) Gas, compressed air
(55) Refrigeration
(56) Space heating *E & S* 7; *S & F (1)* 9; *S & F (2)* 6, 10
(57) Ventilation and air-conditioning *E & S* 7; *S & F (2)* 10
(58)
(59) *Building**

(6) Installations (mainly electrical, mechanical)

(60) *Site**
(61)
(62) Power *E & S* 14
(63) Lighting *E & S* 8
(64) Communications *E & S* 14

* *These classes are not used in general documentation but have special application in project documentation.*

(65)
(66) Transport   *E & S* 15
(67)
(68) Security
(69) *Building**

(7) Fixtures
(70) *Site**

(71) Circulation fixtures
(72) General room fixtures
(73) Culinary fixtures   *C & F* 2
(74) Sanitary fixtures   *E & S* 10
(75) Cleaning fixtures
(76) Storage fixtures   *C & F* 2
(77)
(78)
(79) *Building**

* *These classes are not used in general documentation but have special application in project documentation.*

Tables 2/3 Construction Form/Materials

Table 2 is never used without Table 3

Table 2 Construction form

E Cast in situ *M* 8; *S & F (1)* 4, 7, 8;
S & F (2) 3, 4, 5, 6, 8, 9

F Bricks, blocks *M* 6, 12; *S & F (1)*
5, 9; *S & F (2)* 4, 6, 7

G Structural units *S & F (1)* 6, 7, 8, 10;
S & F (2) 4, 5, 6, 8, 9

H Section bars *M* 9; *S & F (1)* 5, 6, 7, 8;
S & F (2) 5, 6

I Tubes, pipes *S & F (1)* 9; *S & F (2)* 7

J Wires, mesh

K Quilts

L Foils, papers (except finishing papers)
M 9, 13

M Foldable sheets *M* 9

N Overlap sheets, tiles *S & F (2)* 4; *C & F* 18

P Thick coatings *M* 10, 11; *S & F (2)* 4;
C & F 12, 13, 18

R Rigid sheets, sheets in general *M* 3, 12, 13;
S & F (2) 4

S Rigid tiles, tiles in general *M* 4, 12, 13;
C & F 12, 15

T Flexible sheets, tiles *M* 3, 9; *C & F* 17

U Finishing papers, fabrics *C & F* 17

V Thin coatings *C & F* 17

X Components *S & F (1)* 5, 6, 7, 8, 10;
S & F (2) 4; *C & F* 2, 3, 4, 5, 6, 7, 8

Y Products

Table 3 Materials
In formed products

e Natural stone *M* 4, *S & F (1)* 5, 10;
S & F (2) 4

f Formed (precast) concrete, asbestos based
materials, gypsum, magnesium based
materials *M* 8; *S & F (1)* 5, 7, 8, 9, 10;
S & F (2) 4, 5, 6, 7, 8, 9; *C & F* 13

g Clay *M* 5; *S & F (1)* 5, 9, 10; *S & F (2)*
4, 6, 7

h Metal *M* 9; *S & F (1)* 6, 7; *S & F (2)*
4, 5, 7

i Wood *M* 2, 3; *S & F (1)* 5, 6, 7, 8, 10;
S & F (2) 4, 9; *C & F* 2

j Natural fibres and chips, cork, leather *M* 3

m Mineral fibres *M* 10; *S & F (2)* 4, 7

n Rubbers, plastics, asphalt (preformed),
linoleum *M* 11, 12, 13; *S & F (2)* 4, 9;
C & F 12

o Glass *M* 12, *S & F (1)* 5; *C & F* 5

In formless products

p Loose fill, aggregates *M* 8, 10, 15

q Cement, mortar, concrete, asbestos based
materials *M* 7, 8, 10, 15; *S & F (1)* 4, 7, 8;
S & F (2) 3, 4, 5, 6, 8, 9

r Gypsum, special mortars, magnesium based
materials *M* 15; *S & F (2)* 4; *C & F* 13

s Bituminous materials *M* 11; *S & F (2)* 4

Agents, chemicals, etc.

t Fixing, jointing agents, fastenings, iron-
mongery *M* 14; *C & F* 7

u Protective materials, admixtures *M* 1, 2, 8,
9; *C & F* 17

v Paint materials *C & F* 17

w Other chemicals

x **Plants**

y **Materials in general** *M* 1

Table 4 **Activities Requirements**

Activities

(Af) Administration, management in general
(Ag) Communications in general
(Ah) Preparation of documentation in general
    C & F 11
(Ai) Public relations in general
(Aj) Controls in general
(Ak) Organizations in general *M* Introduction
(Am) Personnel, roles in general
(An) Education in general
(Ao) Research, development in general
(Ap) Standardization, rationalization in
    general *C & F* 1, 11
(Aq) Testing, evaluating in general
    C & F 1

(A1) **Management** (offices, projects)
(A2) Financing, accounting
(A3) Design, physical planning *S & F (1)* 4;
    S & F (2) 3
(A4) Cost planning, cost control, tenders,
    contracts *M* Introduction
(A5) Production planning, progress control
    S & F (2) 1, 2; *C & F* 1
(A6) Buying, delivery
(A7) Inspection, quality control *C & F* 1; *M* 155
(A8) Handing over, feedback, appraisal
(A9) Arbitration, insurance

(B) **Construction plant** *S & F* 11; *S & F (2)*
    2, 11

(C) **Labour***

(D) **Construction operations** *S & F (1)* 11;
    S & F (2) 2, 11

Requirements, properties

(E1) **Construction requirements** *S & F (1)*
    1, 2; *S & F (2)* 1; *C & F* 1
(E2) **User requirements** *E & S* 1, 2, 3, 4, 5,
    6; *C & F* 1
(E3) Types of user
(E4) **Physical features** *C & F* 1
(E6) **Environment in general, amenities**
    E & S 1, 2, 3, 4, 5, 6
(E7) External environment *E & S* 1, 2, 3, 4,
    5, 6
(E8) Internal environment *E & S* 1, 2, 3, 4,
    5, 6
(F) Layout, shape, dimensions, tolerances,
    metric *S & F (1)* 2; *C & F* 1
(G) Appearance, aesthetics, art
(H) **Physical, chemical, biological factors,**
    technology *C & F* 1
(I) Air, water *E & S* 2, 3; *S & F (1)* 5
(J) Heat, cold *E & S* 5
(K) Strength, statics, stability *S & F (1)* 3
(L) Mechanics, dynamics *S & F (1)* 4;
    S & F (2) 3
(M) Sound, quiet *E & S* 6
(N) Light, dark *E & S* 4, 8
(Q) Radiation, electrical
(R) Fire *M* 1; *S & F (2)* 10
(S) Durability, weathering defects, failures,
    damage *M* 1, *S & F (1)* 4; *S & F (2)* 3
    4, 5
(U) Special requirements, efficiency, working
    characteristics
(V) **Effect on surroundings**
(W) **Maintenance, alterations**
(Y) **Economic, time requirements** *S & F*
    (1) 2; *S & F (2)* 3, 4, 5, 6, 9

* These classes are not used in general documentation but have special application in project documentation.

Index